R&D and Productivity

A National Bureau
of Economic Research
Monograph

R&D and Productivity

The Econometric Evidence

Zvi Griliches

The University of Chicago Press

Chicago and London

ZVI GRILICHES is the Paul M. Warburg Professor of Economics at Harvard University and director of the Productivity and Technical Change program at the National Bureau of Economic Research. He is past president of the Econometric Society and of the American Economic Association and a member of the National Academy of Sciences.

The University of Chicago Press, Chicago 60637
The University of Chicago Press, Ltd., London
© 1998 by The University of Chicago
All rights reserved. Published 1998
Printed in the United States of America
07 06 05 04 03 02 01 00 99 98   1 2 3 4 5
ISBN: 0-226-30886-3 (cloth)

Library of Congress Cataloging-in-Publication Data

Griliches, Zvi, 1930–
    R&D and productivity : the econometric evidence / Zvi Griliches.
        p.   cm. — (A National Bureau of Economic Research mono-
    graph)
        Includes bibliographical references and index.
        ISBN 0-226-30886-3 (cloth : alk. paper)
        1. Research, Industrial—Economic aspects.   2. Industrial produc-
    tivity.   I. Title.   II. Title: R & D and productivity.   III. Title:
    R and D and productivity.   IV. Series.
    HC79.R4G74 1998
    338'.06—DC21   97-33587
                                                                        CIP

♾ The paper used in this publication meets the minimum requirements of the American National Standard for Information Sciences—Permanence of Paper for Printed Library Materials, ANSI Z39.48-1992.

Relation of the Directors to the
Work and Publications of the
National Bureau of Economic Research

1. The object of the National Bureau of Economic Research is to ascertain and to present to the public important economic facts and their interpretation in a scientific and impartial manner. The Board of Directors is charged with the responsibility of ensuring that the work of the National Bureau is carried on in strict conformity with this object.

2. The President of the National Bureau shall submit to the Board of Directors, or to its Executive Committee, for their formal adoption all specific proposals for research to be instituted.

3. No research report shall be published by the National Bureau until the President has sent each member of the Board a notice that a manuscript is recommended for publication and that in the President's opinion it is suitable for publication in accordance with the principles of the National Bureau. Such notification will include an abstract or summary of the manuscript's content and a response form for use by those Directors who desire a copy of the manuscript for review. Each manuscript shall contain a summary drawing attention to the nature and treatment of the problem studied, the character of the data and their utilization in the report, and the main conclusions reached.

4. For each manuscript so submitted, a special committee of the Directors (including Directors Emeriti) shall be appointed by majority agreement of the President and Vice Presidents (or by the Executive Committee in case of inability to decide on the part of the President and Vice Presidents), consisting of three Directors selected as nearly as may be one from each general division of the Board. The names of the special manuscript committee shall be stated to each Director when notice of the proposed publication is submitted to him. It shall be the duty of each member of the special manuscript committee to read the manuscript. If each member of the manuscript committee signifies his approval within thirty days of the transmittal of the manuscript, the report may be published. If at the end of that period any member of the manuscript committee withholds his approval, the President shall then notify each member of the Board, requesting approval or disapproval of publication, and thirty days additional shall be granted for this purpose. The manuscript shall then not be published unless at least a majority of the entire Board who shall have voted on the proposal within the time fixed for the receipt of votes shall have approved.

5. No manuscript may be published, though approved by each member of the special manuscript committee, until forty-five days have elapsed from the transmittal of the report in manuscript form. The interval is allowed for the receipt of any memorandum of dissent or reservation, together with a brief statement of his reasons, that any member may wish to express; and such memorandum of dissent or reservation shall be published with the manuscript if he so desires. Publication does not, however, imply that each member of the Board has read the manuscript, or that either members of the Board in general or the special committee have passed on its validity in every detail.

6. Publications of the National Bureau issued for informational purposes concerning the work of the Bureau and its staff, or issued to inform the public of activities of Bureau staff, and volumes issued as a result of various conferences involving the National Bureau shall contain a specific disclaimer noting that such publication has not passed through the normal review procedures required in this resolution. The Executive Committee of the Board is charged with review of all such publications from time to time to ensure that they do not take on the character of formal research reports of the National Bureau, requiring formal Board approval.

7. Unless otherwise determined by the Board or exempted by the terms of paragraph 6, a copy of this resolution shall be printed in each National Bureau publication.

(Resolution adopted October 25, 1926, as revised through September 30, 1974)

To Ted, in memoriam,
who got me started,
and to my students and associates,
who kept me going.

Contents

Acknowledgments

Except for the first two essays, all the papers reproduced in this volume were written during my association with the NBER Productivity Studies program. The bulk of the support for this work came from the National Science Foundation, which has supported my work more or less consistently since 1956. Additional support was provided by the Ford Foundation, the Sloan Foundation, the Bradley Foundation, and the Mellon Foundation. I am indebted to my collaborators and former students for help with this work and for much more. They are thanked individually in the various essays. I am also very grateful to the late Jeanette DeHaan and to Jane Trahan for editing, typing, and sustaining me through the process of getting this book together. I also thank the American Economic Review, the Scandinavian Journal of Economics, the RAND Journal of Economics, and the University of Chicago Press for permission to reprint these essays. Last but not least, Diane Asséo Griliches for providing the environment that made it all possible.

1   Introduction

The essays collected in this volume cover most of my work on the relationship of productivity growth to R&D expenditures in industry. That technical change was a major source of measured productivity growth was already clear to me while I was a graduate student at the University of Chicago in the mid-1950s. This was the message emerging from the agricultural data developed by the U.S. Department of Agriculture (USDA) and the national data constructed by the NBER (see, e.g., Barton and Cooper 1948; Schmookler 1952; Fabricant 1954; Abramovitz 1956). It was also clear that such technological changes were not purely "exogenous." They were the result of economic activity, especially where its main purpose was to generate such changes, as in organized public and private research. My teacher, Theodore Schultz, actually attributed *all* the productivity growth in agriculture to public investments in agricultural research (Schultz 1953). While the idea that the rate and direction of technical change were both influenced by economic incentives was neither surprising nor new, there was almost no quantitative evidence for this view then. It was my belief (and presumption) that one could use the newly available econometric techniques to establish such facts and to provide measures of their magnitude. This belief provided much of the inspiration for my work that was to follow.

Technical change is usually measured by changes in some index of total factor or, more precisely, multifactor, productivity (TFP, or MFP) at the firm, industry, or economy-wide level. Besides pervasive measurement errors, there are three circumstances that govern these changes that may be wholly or partially "endogenous" to the economic system: (1) New knowledge spreads through training and the adoption of new equipment that embodies the current "state of the art." Whether one thinks of the diffusion of new technology (and organizations and institutions) as a disequilibrium and learning phenomenon, or as an equilibrium process that is affected by adjustment costs and asymmetric information, is largely a semantic issue. What is important is that this process of diffusion is influenced by economic forces and incentives. (2) New techniques, inputs, and products can all be thought of as outward shifts in the "production possibilities frontier." They result from conscious efforts by scientists, engineers, entrepreneurs, and various other tinkerers, both formal and informal, to improve the existing state of technology. (3) The production of such economically valuable new knowledge depends, at least in part, on the generation of new scientific knowledge in universities and other institutions, both at home and abroad, which is itself subject to economic constraints and influences.

My earliest research concentrated on the first two topics: an econometric analysis of the diffusion of a new technology, hybrid corn (Griliches 1956, 1957b), and the measurement of the returns to public and private research investments in this and related technologies (Griliches 1958b). Central to the first paper was the concept of a diffusion curve or path. For the purposes of this analysis, I used the logistic curve in which "time" is essentially exogenous (as it was also to be in the concurrent and subsequent theories of technological change). I was not entirely happy with such a formulation and had explored in an appendix to my thesis an alternative model that made the rate of adoption a direct function of profitability, with improvements in the "quality" of the technology (rising relative yields of hybrid versus open pollinated corn) and the fall in its price as its major driving forces. The arrival of partial-adjustment distributed-lag models led me to try them as an alternative framework for the analysis of technical change in my work on the demand for fertilizer in agriculture (Griliches 1958a). That work interpreted the growth in fertilizer use as a lagged response to the continued decline in its real price.

At about the same time, I started working on the direct measurement of technological change using output over input indexes. This was based on the earlier work in agriculture summarized for me by Schultz (1953; see also Ruttan 1954, 1956) before the topic was transformed by Solow's (1957) elegant reformulation. The stylized facts that had emerged were quite troublesome: the lion's share of the observed growth in output was attributed to "technical change" or, more correctly, to the "residual."

Having come to this problem with a background in econometrics, I found the spectacle of economic models yielding large residuals rather uncomfortable, even when the issue was fudged by renaming them technical change and then claiming credit for their "measurement." My interest in specification analysis (Griliches 1957a) led me to a series of questions about the model used to compute such residuals and also, especially, about the ingredients—the data—used in the model's implementation. This led me to a research program that focused on the various components of such computations and alternatives to them: the measurement of the services of capital equipment; issues of deflation, quality change, and appropriate depreciation concepts; the measurement of labor input and the contribution of education to its changing quality; and most relevantly for this volume, the role of left-out variables (inputs) such as public and private investments in R&D. I also worried about formula misspecification issues, especially economies of scale and other sources of disequilibria, which led me to a continued involvement with production function estimation. This program of research, which was announced, implicitly, in "Measuring Inputs in Agriculture" (Griliches 1960) and found its fullest expression in my two papers on agricultural productivity (Griliches 1963, 1964), has served me well. It was similar, in certain aspects, to the line pursued by Denison (1962) at about the same time, except that I put more emphasis on its econometric aspects, that is, on the explicit testing of the various proposed adjustments and attributions to sources of growth.

It was in this context that I turned to an analysis of the contribution of public expenditures on agricultural research to overall productivity in agriculture, using U.S. state data. By the mid-1960s I was moving to more general analyses of the productivity growth puzzle in manufacturing and in the economy at large (Griliches 1967; Jorgenson and Griliches 1967) and beginning my search for microdata with the hope that such processes could be better studied at lower levels of aggregation (see, e.g., Griliches and Ringstad 1971). More recently, I have started looking at the third aspect of this puzzle: the role of science and the productivity of the social resources invested there (Adams and Griliches 1996). The essays collected in this volume are, however, limited largely to the second range of topics, chronicling and describing the quest to understand and measure the contribution of R&D to the growth of productivity, both at the firm and industry levels.

I should note that by the time I shifted my attention to the contribution of industrial R&D a few others were already studying some of its aspects. The pioneers were Minasian (1962), who analyzed the relationship of productivity growth to R&D expenditures in eighteen chemical firms; Mansfield (1965), who analyzed the growth of productivity for ten chemical and petroleum-refining firms and ten two-digit-level manufacturing industries; and Terleckyj (1958), who used two-digit SIC-level industry data to attack the same question (see the summary of his work in Kendrick 1961, 181–84). Related work was also being done by Conrad (Brown and Conrad 1967), Nelson (1959, 1962), Scherer (1965), and Schmookler (1962).[1] I viewed my own contribution as pushing this line of research forward using much larger and more representative databases and employing more advanced econometric techniques.

This volume starts with my 1979 essay, "Issues in Assessing the Contribution of Research and Development to Productivity Growth," which provides a framework for much of the research that was to come and also identifies and

---

1. At one point, Conrad, Mansfield, Scherer, Schmookler, and I all belonged to the same study group at Princeton, which was organized by Jesse Markham with the support of the Ford Foundation. Nelson and I also served on the planning committee for the 1960 Minnesota conference, cosponsored by the NBER and the Social Science Research Council, on the rate and direction of inventive activity, under the chairmanship of Simon Kuznets.

describes many of the difficulties that haunt this line of research to this day.[2] It exposits the R&D capital model which has become a standard tool in this field and outlines the spillovers problem and suggests several approaches to its solution, some of which were taken up later by my students (e.g., Jaffe 1986) and/or reinvented (Romer 1990). Chapters 3 and 4 report the results of a major, two-decades-long effort to gain access to the detailed individual firm–level data on R&D collected by the Bureau of the Census for the National Science Foundation (NSF) and to match them to parallel company data in the censuses of manufactures and enterprise statistics. Chapter 3 was started in the mid-sixties, presented at the NBER Conference on Research in Income and Wealth in 1975, but not published until 1980. It analyzed the 1957–65 growth rates and the 1963 levels of productivity for 883 U.S. manufacturing firms and related them to their past R&D expenditures (among other variables). It concluded that the various estimates "indicate an overall elasticity of output with respect to R&D investments of about .07, which can be thought of as an average of .1 for the more R&D-intensive industries such as chemicals and .05 for the less intensive rest of the universe. . . . [It implies] .27 as the overall estimate of the average gross excess rate of return to R&D in 1963. . . . It is 'gross' because . . . our measures [do not] allow for any depreciation of past R&D investments, and it is 'excess' because the conventional labor and fixed capital measures already include the bulk of the current R&D expenditures once" (71).

I started discussing the updating of this study with the NSF and the Bureau of the Census in 1976. What looked at first like a reasonably simple job became a major effort when it turned out that the old project tapes had been inadvertently blanked by the Census and that the data for the 1958 and 1963 census of manufactures could not be retrieved in machine-readable form. Luckily, most of the original R&D schedules could still be found, though they had to be repunched from scratch. After much work a new data set was created, covering 652 U.S. manufacturing firms for which growth rates could be computed for the 1967–77 period and which could also be matched to 1972 Census schedules. This took much effort and time, as did the analysis stage, so that the final results were published only in 1986. The major advance in this study was the ability to distinguish between basic and other R&D expenditures, and between privately and federally financed R&D expenditures. The interesting findings were (1) R&D contributed positively to productivity growth and seemed to have earned a relatively high rate of return. Moreover, there was no evidence of a decline in returns between the two studies, the first covering 1957–65 and the second 1966–77. (2) Basic research appeared to be more important as a productivity determinant than other types of R&D. (3) Privately financed R&D expenditures were more effective, at the firm level, than federally financed ones. The analysis of these data was updated in the 1980s by

2. Most of my relevant earlier work has been reprinted in Griliches (1988a).

Lichtenberg and Siegel (1991) and the earlier results have stood the test of time. Additional work using this database has been done recently by Adams and Jaffe (1996).

The difficulties and long delays involved in working with confidential Census data led us to look at other, more "open" data sources. In the 1970s detailed firm income and balance sheet data became available in machine-readable form as part of the Compustat tapes. At the same time the U.S. Patent Office had begun to computerize and make available its records. In the early 1960s I had become friends with Jacob Schmookler (see Griliches and Schmookler 1963) and after his untimely death in 1967 thought that it would make sense to extend some of his research program using the newly available and more easily accessible data and more advanced econometric techniques. All of these considerations led to the initiation of a large, NSF-sponsored research project at the NBER in 1978. The primary task of this project was to match data for U.S. manufacturing firms in the various Compustat tapes (including those on the over-the-counter market) with the records of their patenting activity. That also turned out to be a project of larger size and greater difficulty than we had anticipated, both because of the large amount of merger activity among U.S. firms and because the patent office records did not contain comparable firm identifiers. The latter problem led us to write a complicated lexicographic matching program, which worked, but not perfectly, and required much additional manual checking and correction. Ultimately we constructed a large panel data set, based on the Compustat population in 1976 and covering (to varying degrees) about 900 firms for the years 1958–78. This panel was later extended to 1984 and then again to 1989, and it may be extended again in the near future (see Hall et al. 1988). The effort to analyze these data brought together a number of first-rate students and collaborators. Many of the first round results of this work were summarized in a series of papers presented at the 1981 NBER conference at Lenox, Massachusetts, and published subsequently in Griliches (1984). Three papers from that volume, focusing primarily on the productivity-R&D relationship, are reproduced here.

Some of the results of that project are not covered in this volume, though most of the patent work is discussed in chapter 13, "Patent Statistics as Economic Indicators." Also missing here is work that focused on market value as an alternative measure of success for a firm's innovative endeavors, such as Griliches (1981) and Cockburn and Griliches (1988), and papers whose primary purpose was the development of appropriate econometric methodology (Hausman, Hall, and Griliches 1984; Hall, Griliches, and Hausman 1986).

Chapter 5 was the result of the beginning of my collaboration with Jacques Mairesse of the Institut National de la Statistique et des Études Économiques (INSEE), Paris, which has now continued for close to twenty years. Besides a keen mind and strong econometrics and statistics training, Mairesse brought to the collaboration an interest in microdata and access to parallel data sets collected by French statistical organizations. We also went on, with the help of Fumio Hayashi, to extend our research to parallel data sets on Japanese firms, and to worry about many methodological problems connected with the analyses we were pursuing (see Mairesse and Griliches 1990; Griliches and Mairesse 1998). The major contribution of chapter 5 was to break out of the straitjacket of the confidential Census-NSF data and show that, without imposing reasonable values on other coefficients, the "within" time dimension of the data is not rich enough to deliver a clear estimate of the R&D effect on productivity. We also tried to deal with the simultaneity problem by developing a "semi-reduced-form" system of equations which yielded rather high estimates of the contribution of R&D capital to productivity growth relative to that of physical capital. And it was the first paper to raise the possibility, in this context, that the non–fully competitive environment in which some of our R&D-intensive firms operate may affect the interpretation of such results. This issue would reappear in the literature spawned by R. E. Hall's 1988 paper and was reanalyzed by Klette and Griliches (1996). I shall come back to this topic under the rubric of "unfinished business" in chapter 12.

One of the problems with firm-level data is that firms, especially large U.S. firms traded on national stock markets, are often not homogeneous entities but rather conglomerates of various types of activity. In this sense, our data were still not "micro" enough. Chapter 6, written with Kim Clark, tried to get around this problem by using proprietary data at the "business unit" level, a more homogeneous subdivision of the firm. The analysis was based on 1970–80 data for 924 such business units in manufacturing. It found a significant relationship between TFP growth and R&D expenditures, implying a rate of return on the order of 18 percent, and no evidence of any deterioration in the productivity of R&D during the 1970s. It did find some evidence of spillover effects in the sense that returns to R&D were higher in those businesses where major technical changes had occurred within the recent past.

Chapters 7 and 8, written jointly with Jacques Mairesse, represent our effort to extend such analyses beyond the United States and to provide them with a comparative perspective. Chapter 7 focuses on the French-U.S. comparison; chapter 8 extends it to parallel Japanese data. In doing that we encountered many measurement and comparability issues, but the basic message kept coming through: R&D is important, but the differences in the productivity growth experience across countries do not seem to be connected to the R&D process—the estimated coefficients are largely the same. Nor can R&D account for the worldwide slowdown in productivity growth that occurred in the late 1970s and early 1980s. The estimated effects are just too small for that.[3]

Chapters 9 and 10, written with Frank Lichtenberg, take us back from the

---

3. The issue of the worldwide slowdown in the growth of productivity has preoccupied me and other researchers through much of the past two decades. For a further discussion of the role of R&D in this see Griliches (1988b).

micro level to the more aggregate industry level. The problem with such analyses is the difficulty of matching industry definitions across data sources. As part of this effort, I was instrumental in bringing the Penn-SRI-Census four-digit SIC-level database to the NBER where it has been continually updated (see Bartelsman and Gray 1996 for the latest revision). Industry-level R&D series have been available only at the two-digit SIC level for total R&D and at the more relevant product-field level, for a mixture of two- and three-digit-level industries, for applied R&D expenditures only. The focus in chapter 9, which uses time series on 28 two-and-a-half-digit manufacturing industries, is again on whether there was a decline in the "fecundity" of R&D expenditures over time and on the role of federally financed R&D expenditures in this story. It finds a strong relationship between TFP growth and private (but not federally financed) R&D expenditure intensity, and no observable decline in this relationship through the period of observation (which ended in 1976). A more detailed industrial look is taken in chapter 10, using the three-digit SIC business-line level R&D data collected by the Federal Trade Commission (FTC) in 1974 under Scherer's leadership. Using the NBER four-digit-level productivity database, we constructed TFP measures for 193 manufacturing industries for the years 1959–78 and used alternative measures of product and process R&D and own (used in the same industry) and imported R&D (based on the 1974 "technology flows" matrix constructed by Scherer [1984]) to reexamine some of Scherer's (1982) conclusions. We found that own R&D has a relatively large and "significant" estimated rate of return, on the order of 0.30, and that it does not decline significantly between 1959–68 and 1974–78, while the contribution of imported R&D, which appears to be sizable, cannot be estimated with much precision. This may be due, in part, to our use of manufacturing industries only, while imported R&D may have its largest effects in some of the nonmanufacturing sectors such as agriculture, transportation, and finance.

Most of the work discussed up to now, except for the papers with Lichtenberg, is based on firm- or business-unit-level microdata, measuring largely *private* returns to R&D, rather than the possibly more interesting *social* returns. I was well aware of the importance of knowledge spillovers in the generation of technological change (see the lengthy discussion in chap. 2), but had no access to data which would allow an entry into this topic. I did, however, send a number of my students on the search for such spillovers and some of them were able to produce evidence for their existence (Evenson 1968; Evenson and Kislev 1973; Schankerman 1979; Jaffe 1986). Chapter 11 was written partly in response to the appearance of the "new growth theory" and the rather limited acquaintance of its practitioners with the previous empirical literature on this topic. It recycled parts of the 1979 "Issues" paper, to remind them of its existence, and surveyed the accumulated literature on spillovers and the conceptual and econometric problems associated with their estimation. The evidence that had accumulated in the meantime was actually quite impressive and, if taken at face value, would assign a greater role to R&D in the generation of productivity growth and possibly also in its slowdown.

There were several components to the new growth theories relevant to our story: the emphasis on endogenous technical change, the emphasis on R&D spillovers, and the importance of imperfect competition in the R&D context. That technical change was endogenous was not "news" to me. That is what we had been studying all along in our work on diffusion (Griliches 1957b), on the role of purposive R&D expenditures as generators of such change (Griliches 1964), and on the impact of the economy on inventive output (Griliches and Schmookler 1963). And the theory was not particularly new either (see the citations in chap. 11).

The other main component of this literature was the emphasis on the importance of R&D spillovers and their incorporation into aggregate growth models.[4] While this was not great news to us, the increased interest in this area generated by the literature revitalized both the theoretical and the empirical research on such spillovers, especially at the aggregate level (Coe and Helpman 1995 is a leading example of such work). But estimating such spillovers is very hard and the empirical results to date do not justify, in my mind, the original claims made for such theories. The estimated magnitudes are just not large enough to explain major differences in growth rates over time and over countries. Knowledge and knowledge generation is indeed the major source of productivity growth in the long run. But our ability to describe and quantify its flows is still quite rudimentary (see chap. 14 for further reflections on this topic).

A major advance brought about by these new theories was the explicit integration of the R&D process with market equilibrium in imperfectly competitive markets. While the older literature was well aware of the "appropriability" problem due to the "nonrivalrous" nature of R&D output, this had not been fully integrated into the earlier growth models or reflected adequately in empirical work (though there is already some discussion of it in chap. 5; see also Klette and Griliches 1996 for a more detailed exposition of the implications for empirical estimation of such models). The new theories also revived interest in "creative destruction" (see, e.g., Aghion and Howitt 1992) of knowledge-based quasi-rent positions, a topic discussed earlier under the label of "depreciation" of knowledge or R&D stocks (see Pakes and Schankerman 1984), and they gave impetus to a whole new range of studies (such as Caballero and Jaffe 1993 and Putnam 1997).

It is beyond the scope of this introduction to survey all the parallel and subsequent work by others on this range of topics. Chapters 2 and 11 already do

---

4. See Romer (1986, 1990) for the original statement and also chap. 2 in this volume for the simple spillover equation, then Barro and Sala-i-Martin (1995) and Grossman and Helpman (1991) for excellent expositions of this literature.

some of that. Moreover, a number of high-quality, comprehensive surveys have appeared recently: Australian Industry Commission (1995, vol. 3, app. QA); Mairesse and Sassenou (1991); Mairesse and Mohnen (1995); Nadiri (1993); and Hall (1996) (see also Griliches 1995). The first reference alone lists 27 studies estimating the returns to R&D at the firm level, 28 at the industry level, 10 at the country level, and 20 studies for agriculture alone. By and large they confirm the results of our earlier studies and I feel comfortable reproducing that work in this volume. There are, however, a number of methodological problems afflicting most of these studies. Some of them have already been outlined in chapter 2 and the output measurement problem will be reemphasized in chapter 14. Chapter 12 describes some problems that arise in defining and measuring R&D "capital" and its depreciation and the econometric problems involved in getting credible estimates of the returns to it. The chapter also presents new estimates of the contribution of R&D to production at the firm level, using some of the latest econometric techniques. The basic results are not changed much by updating either the data or the estimation technology, but their credibility remains shaky, since the causal interpretation of R&D affecting subsequent productivity levels is based almost entirely on the assumed lag structure. Ideally we should have some "natural" experiments which would produce exogenous changes in R&D expenditures. An analysis of the consequences of unanticipated R&D tax credits which impinge differentially on different firms depending on their tax situation might prove useful in this context. Another source of identifying assumptions could be the various governmental R&D subsidy programs pursued at different times and with different intensities in France, Israel, Japan, Norway, and other countries. Changes in such programs could serve as a source of exogenous shifts that would help us to identify the productivity effects of R&D more credibly. In the meantime we have to be careful and modest in interpreting such results. They are the best we have, but much remains to be done to pin them down more securely.

All of the work discussed above focuses primarily on the role of R&D as an *input* into the productivity-growth-generating processes. But by the time R&D effects are measured in the subsequent data on productivity growth, they are rather difficult to trace, both because of long and variable lags and because productivity measures are subject to many other influences and measurement difficulties, such as business-cycle-induced fluctuations in capacity utilization. It would be nice if one had a direct measure of the *outputs* of inventive activity to use in evaluating the effectiveness of various incentives for investing in R&D. Such considerations and hopes led us to invest heavily in the study of patent data and what they could teach us about the process of invention. A number of good students and research associates were involved in several projects arising out of that data collection effort and we published much on this topic. Chapter 13 does several things: (1) It summarizes much of our own work on this range of issues. (2) It sets it in the historical context of the field and also provides brief summaries and references to the rest of the relevant literature, not just to our own. (3) It discusses a major substantive issue, namely, whether one can take the declining ratio of patents received per R&D dollar as an indicator of diminishing returns and a decline in the fecundity of R&D. I will not summarize here what is already a long survey summarizing many other studies except to note that the answer to the implicit question in (3) is "not proven."

When I wrote chapter 13, I was under the illusion that we had mined out this topic and that I was closing the subject. Luckily, I was wrong. A number of very interesting studies of patents, their role in innovation, and what they can teach us about it have followed, many of them done by my students and their students. A short list of these studies, beyond those already mentioned above, would include Cockburn and Henderson (1997); Henderson and Cockburn (1996); Jaffe, Trajtenberg, and Henderson (1993); Kortum (1993); Kortum and Lerner (1997); Lach (1994); Lanjouw, Pakes, and Putnam (1996); and Schankerman (1997). (See also Scherer 1996 and Van Reenen 1996.)

The final essay in this volume, my presidential address to the American Economic Association, returns to a major theme of chapter 2: the difficulty of estimating the productivity returns to R&D in a world of imperfect output measurement. Many of the current technological changes are occurring in sectors where we have almost no decent measures of output, such as health and finance, or where these measures are flawed, such as the increasingly complicated high-tech computer and communication sectors. Moreover, these sectors have been growing in importance, accounting currently for close to two-thirds of the overall U.S. economy. This essay is a call for a review and expansion of the national income accounts to include more and broader measures of economic welfare, especially those that would bring the value and quality of human time into this framework. It is also a meditation on why we are not getting better data and a plea for a lowering of expectations of what economics can deliver in this area. Inventive activity is a truly creative and highly uncertain act. We can study it, try to comprehend it better, and support it, but we are unlikely to be able to control it finely, nor should we try.

References

Abramovitz, M. 1956. Resource and output trends in the U.S. since 1870. *American Economic Review* 46 (2): 5–23.

Adams, J. D., and Z. Griliches. 1996. Measuring science: An exploration. *Proceedings of the National Academy of Sciences* 93 (November): 12664–70.

Adams, J. D., and A. B. Jaffe. 1996. Bounding the effects of R&D: An investigation using matched establishment-firm data. NBER Working Paper no. 5544. Cambridge, Mass.: National Bureau of Economic Research, April.

Aghion, P., and P. Howitt. 1992. A model of growth through creative destruction. *Econometrica* 60 (2): 323–51.

Australian Industry Commission. 1995. *Research and development*. Report no. 44. Canberra: Australian Government Publishing Service, 15 May.

Barro, R. J., and X. Sala-i-Martin. 1995. *Economic growth.* New York: McGraw-Hill.

Bartelsman, E. J., and W. B. Gray. 1996. The NBER manufacturing productivity database. NBER Technical Working Paper no. 205. Cambridge, Mass.: National Bureau of Economic Research.

Barton, G. T., and M. R. Cooper. 1948. Relation of agricultural production to inputs. *Review of Economics and Statistics* 30 (2): 117–26.

Brown, M., and A. Conrad. 1967. The influence of research on CES production relations. In *The theory and empirical analysis of production,* ed. M. Brown, 341–72. Studies in Income and Wealth, vol. 31. New York: National Bureau of Economic Research.

Caballero, R. J., and A. B. Jaffe. 1993. How high are the giants' shoulders? In *NBER macroeconomics annual 1993,* ed. Olivier Blanchard and Stanley Fischer, 15–74. Cambridge, Mass.: MIT Press.

Cockburn, I., and Z. Griliches. 1988. Industry effects and appropriability measures in the stock market's valuation of R&D and patents. *American Economic Review* 78 (2): 419–23.

Cockburn, I., and R. Henderson. 1997. Public-private interaction and the productivity of pharmaceutical research. NBER Working Paper no. 6018. Cambridge, Mass.: National Bureau of Economic Research, April.

Coe, D., and E. Helpman. 1995. International R&D spillovers. *European Economic Review* 39, no. 5 (May): 859–87.

Denison, E. F. 1962. *The sources of economic growth in the United States and the alternatives before us.* Supplementary Paper no. 13. New York: Committee for Economic Development.

Evenson, R. E. 1968. The contribution of agricultural research and extension to agricultural productivity. Ph.D. diss., University of Chicago.

Evenson, R. E., and Y. Kislev. 1973. Research and productivity in wheat and maize. *Journal of Political Economy* 81 (6): 1309–29.

Fabricant, S. 1954. *Economic progress and economic change.* New York: National Bureau of Economic Research.

Griliches, Z. 1956. Hybrid corn: An exploration in the economics of technological change. Ph.D. diss., University of Chicago.

———. 1957a. Specification bias in estimates of production functions. *Journal of Farm Economics* 39 (1): 8–20.

———. 1957b. Hybrid corn: An exploration in the economics of technological change. *Econometrica* 25 (4): 501–22.

———. 1958a. The demand for farm fertilizer: An econometric interpretation of a technical change. *Journal of Farm Economics* 40 (3): 591–606.

———. 1958b. Research cost and social returns: Hybrid corn and related innovations. *Journal of Political Economy* 66 (5): 419–31.

———. 1960. Measuring inputs in agriculture: A critical survey. *Journal of Farm Economics* 42 (5): 1411–27.

———. 1963. The sources of measured productivity growth: U.S. agriculture, 1940–1960. *Journal of Political Economy* 71 (4): 331–46.

———. 1964. Research expenditures, education and the aggregate agricultural production function. *American Economic Review* 54 (6): 961–74.

———. 1967. Production functions in manufacturing: Some preliminary results. In *The theory and empirical analysis of production,* ed. M. Brown, 275–340. Studies in Income and Wealth, vol. 31. New York: National Bureau of Economic Research.

———. 1981. Market value, R&D and patents. *Economics Letters* 7: 183–87.

———, ed. 1984. *R&D, patents, and productivity.* Chicago: University of Chicago Press.

———. 1988a. *Technology, education, and productivity: Early papers with notes to subsequent literature.* New York: Basil Blackwell.

————. 1988b. Productivity puzzles and R&D: Another nonexplanation. *Journal of Economic Perspectives* 2 (4): 9–21.

————. 1995. R&D and productivity: Econometric results and measurement issues. In *Handbook of the economics of innovation and technological change*, ed. P. Stoneman, 52–89. Oxford, U.K., and Cambridge, Mass.: Basil Blackwell.

Griliches, Z., and J. Mairesse. 1998. Production functions: The search for identification. In *The Ragnar Frisch centennial symposium*, ed. S. Ström. Economic Society Monograph Series. Cambridge: Cambridge University Press, forthcoming.

Griliches, Z., and V. Ringstad. 1971. *Economies of scale and the form of the production function*. Amsterdam: North-Holland.

Griliches, Z., and J. Schmookler. 1963. Inventing and maximizing. *American Economic Review* 53, no. 4 (September): 725–29.

Grossman, G. M., and E. Helpman. 1991. *Innovation and growth in the global economy*. Cambridge, Mass.: MIT Press.

Hall, B. H. 1996. The private and social returns to research and development. In *Technology, R&D, and the economy*, ed. B. Smith and C. Barfield, 140–62. Washington, D.C.: Brookings Institution and American Enterprise Institute.

Hall, B. H., C. Cummins, E. S. Laderman, and J. Mundy. 1988. The R&D master file: Documentation. NBER Technical Working Paper no. 72. Cambridge, Mass.: National Bureau of Economic Research.

Hall, B. H., Z. Griliches, and J. A. Hausman. 1986. Patents and R&D: Is there a lag? *International Economic Review* 27 (2): 265–83.

Hall, R. E. 1988. The relation between price and marginal cost in U.S. industry. *Journal of Political Economy* 96 (5): 921–47.

Hausman, J. A., B. H. Hall, and Z. Griliches. 1984. Econometric models for count data with an application to the patents-R&D relationship. *Econometrica* 52 (4): 909–38.

Henderson, R., and I. Cockburn. 1996. Scale, scope, and spillovers: Determinants of research productivity in the pharmaceutical industry. *RAND Journal of Economics* 27 (1): 32–59.

Jaffe, A. 1986. Technological opportunity and spillovers of R&D: Evidence from firms' patents, profits and market value. *American Economic Review* 75 (6): 984–1002.

Jaffe, A., M. Trajtenberg, and R. Henderson. 1993. Geographic localization of knowledge spillovers as evidenced by patent citations. *Quarterly Journal of Economics* 108 (3): 577–98.

Jorgenson, D. W., and Z. Griliches. 1967. The explanation of productivity change. *Review of Economic Studies* 34 (3): 249–83.

Kendrick, J. W. 1961. *Productivity trends in the United States*. NBER General Series, no. 71. Princeton, N.J.: Princeton University Press.

Klette, T. J., and Z. Griliches. 1996. The inconsistency of common scale estimators when output prices are unobserved and endogenous. *Journal of Applied Econometrics* 11: 343–61.

Kortum, S. 1993. Equilibrium R&D and the patent R&D ratio: U.S. evidence. *American Economic Review* 83 (2): 450–57.

Kortum, S., and J. Lerner. 1997. Stronger protection or technological revolution: What is behind the recent surge in patenting? Boston University and Harvard Graduate School of Business. Mimeo.

Lach, S. 1994. Non-rivalry of knowledge and R&D's contribution to productivity. Working Paper no. 289, Hebrew University, Jerusalem, June.

Lanjouw, J., A. Pakes, and J. Putnam. 1996. How to count patents and value intellectual property: Uses of patent renewal and application data. NBER Working Paper no. 5741. Cambridge, Mass.: National Bureau of Economic Research.

Lichtenberg, F., and D. Siegel. 1991. The impact of R&D investment on productivity: New evidence using linked R&D-LRD data. *Economic Inquiry* 29 (2): 203–29.

Mairesse, J., and Z. Griliches. 1990. Heterogeneity in panel data: Are there stable production functions? In *Essays in honor of Edmond Malinvaud,* ed. P. Champsaur et al., 3: 193–231. Cambridge, Mass.: MIT Press.

Mairesse, J., and P. Mohnen. 1995. Research & development and productivity: A survey of the econometric literature. Université du Québec à Montréal and CIRANO, December. Mimeo.

Mairesse, J., and M. Sassenou. 1991. R&D and productivity: A survey of econometric studies at the firm level. *STI Review* (Paris: OECD) 8: 9–43.

Mansfield, E. 1965. Rates of return from industrial R&D. *American Economic Review* 55: 863–73.

Minasian, J. 1962. The economics of research and development. In *The rate and direction of inventive activity,* ed. R. R. Nelson. NBER Special Conference Series, vol. 13. Princeton, N.J.: Princeton University Press.

Nadiri, M. I. 1993. Innovations and technological spillovers. NBER Working Paper no. 4423. Cambridge, Mass.: National Bureau of Economic Research.

Nelson, R. R. 1959. The simple economics of basic scientific research. *Journal of Political Economy* 67 (June): 297–306.

———, ed. 1962. *The rate and direction of economic activity.* NBER Special Conference Series, vol. 13. Princeton, N.J.: Princeton University Press.

Pakes, A., and M. Schankerman. 1984. The rate of obsolescence of knowledge, research gestation lags, and the private rate of return to research resources. In *R&D, patents, and productivity,* ed. Zvi Griliches, 73–88. Chicago: University of Chicago Press.

Putnam, J. 1997. The value of international patent rights. Boston: Charles River Associates.

Romer, P. M. 1986. Increasing returns and long-run growth. *Journal of Political Economy* 94 (5): 1002–37.

———. 1990. Endogenous technological change. *Journal of Political Economy* 98 (5): S71–S102.

Ruttan, V. W. 1954. *Technological progress in the meatpacking industry, 1919–1947.* Marketing Research Report no. 59. Washington, D.C.: Department of Agriculture.

———. 1956. The contribution of technological progress to farm output, 1950–75. *Review of Economics and Statistics* 38 (1): 61–69.

Schankerman, M. 1979. Essays on the economics of technical change: The determinants, rate of return and productivity impact of research and development. Ph.D. diss. Harvard University.

———. 1997. How valuable is patent protection: Estimates by technology field. London School of Economics. Mimeo.

Scherer, F. M. 1965. Corporate inventive output, profits, and growth. *Journal of Political Economy* 73: 290–97.

———. 1982. Interindustry technology flows and productivity growth. *Review of Economics and Statistics* 64 (4): 627–34.

———. 1984. Using linked patent and R&D data to measure interindustry technology flows. In *R&D, patents, and productivity,* ed. Z. Griliches, 417–64. Chicago: University of Chicago Press.

———. 1996. The size distribution of profits from innovation. Discussion Paper no. 96–13. Zentrum für Europäische Wirtschaftsforschung, Mannheim, Germany.

Schmookler, J. 1952. The changing efficiency of the American economy, 1869–1938. *Review of Economics and Statistics* 34 (3): 214–31.

———. 1962. Economic sources of inventive activity. *Journal of Economic History* 22 (March): 1–20.

Schultz, T. W. 1953. *The economic organization of agriculture.* New York: McGraw-Hill.

Solow, R. M. 1957. Technical change and the aggregate production function. *Review of Economics and Statistics* 39 (3): 312–20.

Terleckyj, N. 1958. Factors underlying productivity: Some empirical observations. *Journal of the American Statistical Association,* 53 (June): 593.

Van Reenen, J. 1996. The creation and capture of rents: Wages and innovation in a panel of U.K. companies. *Quarterly Journal of Economics* 111 (1): 195–226.

I The Conceptual Framework

2 Issues in Assessing the Contribution of Research and Development to Productivity Growth

2.1 Introduction

Economists have used two rather different styles of research in their attempts to assess the contribution of research and development (R&D) expenditures to economic growth: historical case studies and econometric estimates of production functions containing an R&D variable. There have been a number of detailed case studies of particular innovations tracing out their subsequent consequences (see Griliches (1958) and Mansfield et al. (1977) for examples and Griliches (1973) for a survey). Much can be and has been learned through such studies. They are, however, very data- and time-expensive and are always subject to attack as not being representative, since they tend to concentrate on prominent and successful innovations and fields. Thus, it is never quite clear what general conclusions one can draw on the basis of such studies.

The econometric production function approach tries to meet these objections by abandoning the interesting detail of specific events and concentrating instead on total output or total factor productivity as a function of past R&D investments (and other variables). Here *all* productivity growth (to the extent that it is measured correctly) is related to *all* expenditures on R&D and an attempt is made to estimate statistically the part of productivity growth that can be attributed to R&D (and sometimes, also, to its components). While the production function approach is more general than the case study approach, it is also coarser and suffers from all the problems that beset attempts to infer causality from behavioral data on the basis of correlational techniques. Never-

Reprinted from the *Bell Journal of Economics* 10, no. 1 (Spring 1979): 92–116. Copyright © 1979 American Telephone and Telegraph Company.

This paper was written during my stay at the Institute for Advanced Studies, The Hebrew University, Mount Scopus, Jerusalem. The work on this paper was supported by NASA and NSF. I am indebted to Henry Herzfeld, Carol Kitti, Ariel Pakes, and Mark Schankerman for helpful comments.

theless, currently it is the only available general way of trying to answer questions about the contribution of R&D to growth. It is the purpose of this paper then to explore both the promise and the problems raised by this approach. Some of these problems are conceptual and semantic: What do we want to measure? Others are substantive: What do we measure? And others are statistical-methodological: How can we tell from the data what happened?

Productivity and its growth are best discussed in the context of a "production function," $Y = F(X, \ldots)$, which describes the relationship between various inputs X and final output Y. Productivity ($A = Y/X$) is then defined as the ratio of output (Y) to some index of the total input X and its determinants are then discussable in terms of the list of variables included in X, the mathematical form assumed for the production function $F(\ )$, the particular empirical observations chosen to represent Y and X and the statistical methods used to infer the properties of $F(\ )$ from the data.

A major conceptual issue in any such study is the definition and scope of Y. Are we talking about GNP, the change in some measure of national wealth, or an even broader concept of economic welfare? In the health sector, for example, a major product of research and development is the reduced morbidity of the population. To the extent that R&D affects the workforce and increases hours of work, it will affect X and Y in a parallel fashion and have no effect on A as it is conventionally measured. Moreover, to the extent that it affects the morbidity of children and nonworking wives, it may not show up in our measures at all or show up perversely (e.g., an improvement in the health of children would be associated with less hospitalization, a smaller demand for drugs, and a resultant decline in GNP as it is conventionally measured).[1]

A semantic issue is what do we mean by the "contribution of research and development to growth"? Is it the partial derivative of Y with respect to some measure of research and development flow (R) or stock (K) or is it the total derivative, including the indirect effects of a change in research and development on Y through the induced changes in X? That is, are we asking about the marginal effect of an additional dollar spent on R&D holding all other investments constant, or are we asking for the total effect of a particular R&D investment, including the contribution of all the other investments (in equipment and training) induced by it? To some extent this is a distinction between economic-accounting approaches and causal-historical ones. Most of the economic literature has interpreted the question in the first, partial sense, though occasionally one can find some dissenting voices (Gordon, 1968 and Rymes, 1971). It is a semantic issue, since a complete model of this process can answer both questions and derive the answer to one of them from the other. But it does

---

1. Of course, some of the freed resources will be spent on something else. The point of the illustration is, however, the fact that the "productivity" in the health sector as conventionally measured may in fact decline as the result of R&D.

reflect differences in emphasis and should be kept in mind in interpreting and framing statements intended to affect research and development policy.

Measurement issues arise both in the case of output and in the case of inputs. Difficult problems exist in the measurement of output in the government and service sectors. Problems arise also in the measurement of output in the private goods sector for complex and changing goods. They are essentially the dual of the familiar "quality change" problem in the construction of price indices. Unfortunately, the more research and development intensive is an industry, the more likely is its output to be subject to such measurement problems. Problems arise also in defining the "stock" of research and development and in developing appropriate deflators for it.

Serious difficulties in econometric inference result from the fact that most of the variables of interest tend to move together over time and space, making it hard to untangle their separate effects. Moreover, it is not easy to establish causality. Research and development investments are themselves affected by the level of output and by past profits and productivity, forcing one to formulate simultaneous equations models and to turn towards much more complex estimation techniques.

Clearly the issues alluded to above exceed by far the scope of one modest survey paper. In what follows I shall, by and large, accept the existing national income accounting framework and interpret the question of the contribution of research and development to productivity as referring to aggregate or industrial productivity measures as they emerge from these accounts.[2] Also, I shall join the majority of the writers on this subject by trying to estimate the *partial* contribution of R&D to growth, holding the contribution of other inputs (labor and capital) constant. Since I have discussed the conceptual and measurement issues at some lengths earlier (Griliches, 1973, 1977), here I shall only briefly recapitulate some of the major points.

The paper proper starts with a brief outline of the production function model used in analyzing returns to R&D and then proceeds to discuss in turn two very difficult problems: the measurement of output in R&D intensive industries and the definition and measurement of the stock of R&D "capital." The latter concept leads us to a discussion and modeling of the spillover effects of R&D (Section 2.2) and to suggestions for possible measurement of such effects via the concept of technological distance between firms and industries (Sections 2.3 and 2.4). Somewhat more familiar econometric problems (multicollinearity and simultaneity) are taken up in Section 2.5, and Section 2.6 is devoted to problems arising more specifically in the R&D context. Conclusions and

---

2. There is a whole literature criticizing the aggregate production function approach. Within its own frame of reference there are serious problems of aggregation (Fisher, 1969) and one can also raise questions about the profit maximizing or cost minimizing framework that underlies much of this work (Nelson and Winter, 1974 and elsewhere).

recommendations for additional data collection and new research are to be found in the last section of the paper.

2.2 A Model

Let $Y = F(X, K, u)$ be the "production" function connecting some measure of output, Y, at the micro or macro level, to the "inputs" X, K, and u, where X stands for an index of conventional inputs such as labor and capital, K is a measure of the current state of technical knowledge, determined in part by current and past research and development expenditures, and u stands for all other unmeasured determinants of output and productivity. Define also $A = Y/X$ as the level of (total factor) productivity, and $\tau = y - x = (dY/dt)/Y - (dX/dt)/X$ as its rate of growth. Let us also assume that there exists a relationship between K, the current level of technological knowledge, and $W(B)R$, an index of current and past levels of research and development expenditures, where $W(B)$ is a lag polynomial, describing the relative contribution of past and current research and development levels to K, and B is the lag (backward shift) operator. Thus,

$$K = G[W(B)R, v],$$

where v is another set of unmeasured influences on the accumulated level of knowledge and

$$W(B)R_t = (w_0 + w_1 B + w_2 B^2 + \ldots)R_t = w_0 R_t + w_1 R_{t-1} + w_2 R_{t-2} + \ldots$$

Now the various issues mentioned above can be restated in terms of what we would like conceptually Y, X, K, and R to measure, what the problems with actual measures available to us are, what we need to assume about the world for the relationships $F(\ )$, $G(\ )$, and $W(B)$ to exist and be of interest to us, what we want to know about them, and how we are going to find it out in the face of imperfect data and with the presence of unmeasured forces u and v.

For example, just to write the function $F(X, K, u)$ implies the assumption of separability of the conventional inputs X (labor and capital) from the series of past and current research and development investments R. Similarly, writing $W(B)R_t$ as a linear function of all past R&D investments implies that there are no diminishing returns or rising costs at the annual R&D level.[3] One can look at such assumptions either as a statement about the properties of the real world or as a statement about the conditions for the approximations implied in the construction of aggregate indices of total input (X) or the stock of knowledge capital (K), not to mislead us too much. Given the limited quantity and quality of the data available to us, such assumptions are not really testable (for attempts at such tests cf. Berndt and Christensen (1974)). In what follows I shall

---

3. An alternative approach would complicate this model further by adding an annual knowledge production function of the form $\dot{K} = H(R,K)$ and defining K accordingly.

ignore these "garden variety" index number problems and concentrate instead on the problems peculiar to research and development.[4]

Nor will I worry much here about the functional form of $F(\ )$. For expositional simplicity I shall assume it to be Cobb-Douglas and assume that the unmeasured factors u can be considered as random after the introduction of a time trend into the equation to represent the systematic component of the unmeasured factors. Then we can rewrite F as:

$$Y = DC^{\alpha}L^{\beta}K^{\gamma}e^{\lambda t + u},$$

where D is a constant, t is a time index, e is the base of natural logarithms, and α, β, γ, and λ are some of the parameters we are interested in estimating. If we had more and better data, we could try for a more complex description of the production process, using more general functional forms such as the CES or the translog, and introducing more parameters to be estimated.[5] But for the purposes of this paper, this simple characterization will suffice.

Let us define a conventional total input index X as:

$$X = C^{s}L^{1-s},$$

where s is the observed factor share of physical capital. Let us assume, for a while, that s is observed correctly and that it is proportional to the true coefficient of capital, i.e., $s = \alpha/(\alpha + \beta)$, and there is no error in computing the true *relative* shares of labor and capital. Then measured total factor productivity,

$$A = Y/X = DX^{\alpha+\beta-1}K^{\gamma}e^{\lambda t + u},$$

depends not only on the contribution of research capital K, the contribution of the trend t in the other unmeasured factors, and the random factor u, but also on the level of other inputs X, as long as there are nonconstant returns to scale $(\alpha + \beta \neq 1)$. Moreover, any error of measurement in one of the inputs will transmit itself directly to the productivity measure. For example, let the "true" relevant measure of L be given by $L = Q_L N$, where Q_L is the average "quality" per worker and N is the total number of workers. Now if N rather than L is used in the construction of X, then measured productivity will be given by:

$$\tilde{A} = Y/\tilde{X} = D\tilde{X}^{\alpha+\beta-1}Q_L^{\beta}K^{\gamma}e^{\lambda t + u},$$

where $\tilde{X} = C^{s}N^{1-s}$, and similarly for errors in the measurement of C. Since the issue of errors of measurement in C and L has been discussed at length else-

---

4. See Diewert (1977) for a recent discussion of the necessary assumptions for the existence of such composite commodities as "labor," "capital," and "research capital."

5. To estimate a more general functional form we would need to observe firms utilizing very different combinations of factors of production. But since most firms face rather similar factor prices, why should they have very dissimilar factor ratios? In our context, the issue of the functional form $F(\ )$ is not very interesting or crucial unless we are interested in the specific interaction of K with a particular input (e.g., if we suspect a particular complementarity between physical and research capital). As far as the role of K itself is concerned, the functional form issue can be investigated by adding the square or other nonlinear functions of K to the equation.

where (Griliches, 1963; Jorgenson and Griliches, 1967), I only want to remind the reader about their potential importance in any practical context.

The issues we want to concentrate on here are the definition of Y, the measurement of K, and the estimation of γ.

2.3 The Measurement of Output in Research and Development Intensive Industries

One of the major difficulties in measuring the contribution of research and development to economic growth is the fact that much of it is performed in industries whose product is itself badly measured. In three major areas of public research and development investments, defense, space, and health, the output measures are based on inputs and hence cannot and do not reflect the improvements in productivity which have been achieved with the help of research and development investments. In space exploration output is measured by man-days and expenditures on equipment and does not rise or fall with the success of the venture. In defense, companies sell equipment to and build battleships for the government. Again, there are no price indices of military aircraft that take into account their improved performance in terms of speed or maneuverability nor are there price indices that reflect the improved resolution and range of radar equipment. Defense purchases are almost always deflated by cost indices and, except for the fact that such indices are often not exactly consistent with the industry data, the resulting productivity measures should show no growth, even though large research and development expenditures have been made successfully to improve the performance of such items.

A similar problem arises in the measurement of output in the service sector, especially in health. The output of physicians is measured basically by the number of patient visits and the output of hospitals is measured by patient days. Any improvement in the performance of these activities in the sense of a higher frequency of cure of specific ailments not only will not show up as an increase in the product of this sector, but might actually lead it to register a decline.

The problem is more complex with new or improved products which are sold directly to consumers, such as pocket calculators or drugs. Here the measurement of output will depend on the market structure of the industry and the procedures used by the statistical agencies (e.g., the Bureau of Labor Statistics in the United States) in constructing the relevant price indices. If the producer of the new item were a perfectly discriminating monopolist, he would capture all the social returns to the innovation. Since most monopolists cannot discriminate perfectly and since their market position is far from secure, the actual revenue received by them will fall short of what could have been realized by a discriminating and secure monopolist. What happens to price indices will depend on whether they allow for the "quality" improvements embedded in the new item or not. By and large they do not make such quality adjustments.[6] Instead, the new product is "linked in" at its introductory (or subsequent) price with the price indices left unchanged. Hence measured output goes up by the revenue received, costs go up by the increased utilization of inputs in production, and productivity goes up by the amount of the total return to the innovation that the innovator succeeds in appropriating for himself. Subsequently, the entry of other competitors with similar products may force him to lower the price, but that will not increase measured output, since his revenues will decrease proportionately except as the reduction in price results in growth of the overall market for this product. The social return from this erosion of the original innovator's monopoly position will be recorded in the conventional measures. More generally, the amount of social returns reflected in the productivity measures will depend, in part, on how early the price of a new item is included in the official price index. The tendency of statistical agencies is to include it rather late, after the new product has "matured" a bit, and after its price has declined to "normal" levels, thereby missing much of the social contribution of such an invention. Actual scenarios are, of course, even more complicated than outlined above, but the long and the short of it is that official productivity measures in consumer goods industries such as drugs, where no "quality" adjustments are made, reflect only the original private returns appropriated by the inventors and the consumer surplus arising from the subsequent research of competitors which erodes their original market positions.

A simplified example may be of some help here. Imagine an invention of a more sensitive (faster) photographic color film. Let the demand curve for this film be as follows: at $100 per roll only 100 rolls would be sold, at $1 per roll 10,000 rolls will be sold, with all other prices and quantities given by the straight line passing through these points ($q = 10,100 - 100p$). Let the average and marginal cost of producing a roll of this film (after the invention) equal $1, including normal markup for overhead. This is also the price of the old film on the market of which 8,000 units were being sold originally. We are assuming then that the new film substitutes for the old film, that at $2 everyone will switch over to the new film, and that at the $1 price the market will expand by an additional 2,000 units.

Now there are several possibilities:

(1) Imagine that this new film was developed by NASA and is licensed freely to everybody. Then the price will be $1, and 10,000 units of the new film (and none of the old) will be sold. Total cost in the film industry will go up from 8,000 to 10,000, as will total revenue. If, as is likely, the statistical

---

6. Methods for incorporating more extensive "quality" adjustments into the official indices are available but require a much more detailed data base. See Griliches (1971) for a review of the "hedonic" indices literature.

agencies do not interpret this as a fall in the real price of color film, both input and output will have been measured as having increased proportionately and *no increase* in productivity will be recorded.

(2) If this film instead has been produced by a private inventor with a foolproof patent on it, then it would pay him as a monopolist to produce 5,000 units at a price of $5.01 per unit and leave 3,000 units of the old film to be produced at $1 per unit. Now industry revenue will increase to 25,050 + 3,000 = 28,050, while the total cost remains at 8,000, implying an increase in measured productivity of 250 percent (as against zero in the previous competitive, freely licensed case).

(3) Now imagine the possibility that this monopolist could discriminate in the sales of this film individually and get each individual to pay him the maximum price he would be willing to pay for the privilege of using this film. Such a monopolist could collect $510,000 from his sales of 10,000 units at an average price of $51 per unit. In this case revenue will have increased by 511/8 = 64-fold, while costs will have gone up by only 25 percent, which implies a 52-fold increase in productivity. This is exactly the "true" increase in productivity which occurred in case 1 but could not be measured there, since the whole benefit was passed on to the consumer without its being measured anywhere.

(4) It is possible that in situation 1 or 3 the statistical agency notices that all of the previous users of the old film (at the $1 price) are willing to pay at least $2 per roll for the new film and declares that the "quality" of the new film is at least double that of the old one or, in other words, that the real price of film has declined by 50 percent. Then real output will have been measured to increase from 8,000 to 20,000 (in old film units) or by 150 percent while costs (inputs) will have gone up only by 25 percent, which implies a (approximately) 100 percent growth in measured productivity. This is clearly not the right number (case 3 has the correct computation), but it is better than nothing. Unfortunately, such computations are made only in a few industries. Among the major CPI components only automobiles and, recently, housing prices are subject to quality adjustments. Lack of such adjustments can lead to very serious biases in some industries. In computers, for example, the national income accounting convention has been to show no price change whatsoever. There is independent evidence, however, that the "real" price of computers has been falling by about 20 to 30 percent per year in the last decade, leading to a very serious downward bias in the estimate of output and productivity growth in this industry. (See Chow (1967) and Sharpe (1967), among others.)

(5) If the innovation is not a consumer product but is used instead as an input in another industry, then the missing productivity is only misplaced (provided the output of the using industry is correctly measured). If the film discussed above is used only commercially to replace elaborate lighting arrangements, then its contribution would show up in an increase in the

productivity of the photographic services industry (rather than the film industry). Similarly, computer-using industries have really bought more input than has been measured and will therefore show a rise in their productivity, even though the true productivity increase occurred in the computer-producing industry. Thus, to the extent that the output of the invention-using industries is well measured, the returns to such research and development can be found in the aggregate data (though not correctly attributed). But as we have already noted, in many important invention-using sectors such as government, health, and education, output is not well measured, and hence the productivity of the purchased and mismeasured inputs will also not be reflected there.

Up to this point we have been discussing primarily product innovations. Cost-reducing innovations will, of course, be reflected in the productivity measures as long as they occur in industries where output is measured independently of input. Conventional productivity measures reflect, therefore, the cost-reducing inventions made in the industry itself, the privately appropriated part of product innovations within the industry, and the social product of inventions in the input-producing industries which have not already been reflected in the price of purchased inputs.

A word also should be said here about simple cross sectional comparisons. The revenues of a firm reflect its current and past research and development activities. These private returns, however, can exceed the social ones if they occur at the expense of another firm. If, for example, the research and development of a particular firm doubled its revenue by taking it away from a preexisting rival, then, this is not a social return. It is just a transfer. It is more likely, however, that social returns exceed private ones, since only a fraction of them is appropriated by the original inventors.

To summarize, much of reported research and development is expended in areas where its direct contribution cannot be measured. In an earlier paper (Griliches, 1973), I estimated these areas to account for about half of all reported research and development. An additional large component of research and development is aimed at final consumer product rather than process innovations and is reflected in productivity measures only to the extent that producers succeed in appropriating its fruits. Since much of the product of research and development is entirely unmeasured and much of the rest is mismeasured, it is not surprising that it has been rather difficult to find its traces in the data.

2.4   The Measurement of Research and Development Capital

In Section 2.2 we talked about knowledge capital (K). Empirically it is too broad a concept; it aspires to and contains too much. We can, however, focus on the contribution of identified investments in advancing the state of knowledge in a particular (or related) area(s). The contribution of "science" in general to a particular industry is probably not measurable, since there is no way of knowing how much "science" is actually used in one industry versus another.

Focusing on the contribution of industrial R&D, we can rewrite the definition of K as:

$$K_t = a_0[W(B)R_t]^\eta e^{\mu t + v},$$

where $W(B)R$ is some lag function of past R&D investments, μt is the trend component of all other influences on the state of knowledge, and v is the random transitory component of it. Substituting this into our production function formula, one can absorb η into the γ parameter of the production function, the trend component μt into the general efficiency trend term λt, and the v term into the overall disturbance term u. This leaves us with $W(B)R$, a measure of R&D "capital," as the topic to be discussed in this section.

There are three major issues in the measurement of such "capital":

(1) The fact that the research and development process takes time and that current research and development may not have an effect on measured productivity until several years have elapsed forces one to make assumptions about the relevant lag structure $W(B)$.
(2) Past research and development investments depreciate and become obsolete. Thus the growth in the net "stock" of research and development capital is not equal to the gross level of current or recent resources invested in expanding it.
(3) The level of knowledge in any one sector or industry not only is derived from "own" research and development investments but also is affected by the knowledge borrowed or stolen from other sectors or industries. Thus, the productivity of industry i will depend also on the research and development investments of industries j and h, among others.

Before we proceed to discuss these issues in turn, two other remarks are in order. First, we are obviously aware that there are very different levels and types of knowledge and that research and development results are embodied in people, blueprints, patents, books, and oral tradition. To try to aggregate such diverse items into one notion (index) of research and development "capital" is quite presumptuous. The "sin" of aggregation, however, is not so different here from that committed when constructing measures of national output where bushels of wheat, haircuts, and striptease hours are aggregated into one GNP figure, or "physical" capital which aggregates buildings, planes, computers, and shovels. The difference is, and this is the import of the second remark, that in most of the conventional cases the components to be aggregated have an observable market counterpart to which a value can be attached. A piece of equipment is sold and can be resold at a market price. The results of research and development investments are by and large not directly observable. Research and development capital is fundamentally an "input" rather than an "output" measure. In this, however, it is not so different from, say, the plant construction component of physical capital measures, which are also largely based on cost cumulations rather than on a market valuation of the final results.[7] Nevertheless, the lack of direct measures of research and development output introduces an inescapable layer of inexactitude and randomness into our formulation.[8]

There are several lags involved in the research and development–productivity nexus. First, a particular research and development project may take more than a year to complete. Second, when complete and if successful, it may still take some time before a decision is made to use it or produce it. Once an innovation decision is made, it may show up in the firm's revenue stream only with another lag. If a process innovation, it may be introduced gradually, affecting only parts of the firm's cost structure in the beginning. If a product innovation, it may take time for consumers to find out about it and to accept it. At the aggregate firm level there are many such projects that have started at different dates and are in different stages of fruition. More generally, the convolution and aggregation of many such lag structures should lead to a rather flat but somewhat bell-shaped lag structure connecting total firm research and development to its subsequent productivity (Griliches, 1967).

There is also the issue of depreciation or obsolescence of this capital. If one distinguishes between the firm-specific knowledge capital and the general state of knowledge in the industry as a whole, then at least as far as the first is concerned, it is quite clear that its earning capacity erodes over time, both because better products and processes become available and because its own knowledge begins to lose its specificity (it leaks to other firms in the industry). Thus, from the private point of view there is depreciation of this capital, probably at a rather high rate (see Pakes and Schankerman (1978) for some scattered evidence on this point). This fact, together with the rather short-term nature of much commercial research and development (see the discussion by Mansfield and others in Williams (1973, pp. 87–90)), would imply a research and development lag structure that peaks somewhere between three to five years earlier and then declines rather rapidly, with little of the original research and development product remaining "private" past ten years or so.

The question of depreciation is much more complicated for social research and development capital measures at the industry or national level. The fact that private knowledge loses its privacy and hence its value is a private loss, not a social one. Nevertheless, there is likely also to be some depreciation in

---

7. Note that nothing tangible corresponds to this notion of R&D "capital." It is just an alternative to expensing R&D as a current input. Ideally it would equal the value of the firm's "know how" and should be related to the excess of market value over appropriately depreciated and deflated book value. See Ben-Zion (1977) for an attempt at measurement in this vein.

8. I shall ignore here the possibility of using patents or publication counts as indices of research and development output. They are only available for a limited range of sectors and industries.

social knowledge. Some of the new products may make the knowledge about older products and processes redundant. Alternatively, much of what is measured as investment in research and development is not "net" investment from a social point of view, since it replaces already existing knowledge. If 50 percent more investment is needed to produce an alternative product that is 10 percent superior to the older version, it may be pursued from the private point of view, since with about half the investment one can appropriate most of the rent collected by the inventors of the earlier version. But from the social point of view, if research and development capital were measured by "output," it would only go up by 10 percent rather than 50. We can say then, equivalently, that either only a fraction of current research and development flow is to be thought of as a net addition to the social stock of knowledge capital or that some fraction of the preexisting stock of this capital is replaced (depreciated) annually. The real problem here is our lack of information about the possible rates of such depreciation. The only thing one might be willing to say is that one would expect such social rates of depreciation to be lower than the private ones.

The problem is even more difficult as far as the measurement of public R&D "capital" (such as is generated by NASA, the Department of Agriculture, universities, and other similar organizations) is concerned. Components of this type of R&D capital that contribute to productivity growth in the industrial sector are likely to be subject to both lengthier lags and lower depreciation rates. It is hard to see, however, where one could get relevant evidence on this topic.[9]

The last major issue is that of "spillovers," the effect of "outside" knowledge capital—outside the firm or industry in question—on the within-industry productivity. The level of productivity achieved by one firm or industry depends not only on its own research efforts but also on the level of the pool of general knowledge accessible to it. Looking at a cross section of firms within a particular industry, one will not be able to distinguish such effects. If the pools of knowledge differ for different industries or areas, some of it could be deduced from interindustry comparisons over time and space. Moreover, the productivity of own research may be affected by the size of the pool or pools it can draw upon. This would lead to the formulation of models allowing for an interaction between the size of individual and aggregate research and development effort.[10]

A simple model of such within-industry spillover effects is given by

$$Y_i = BX_i^{1-\gamma}K_i^\gamma K_a^\mu$$

9. Some work has been done on the contribution of publicly supported research in agriculture to productivity. See Griliches (1973) for a review of this literature.

10. See Evenson and Kislev (1975, Chapter 4) for an example of such a "borrowing" function involving scientific publications.

where Y_i is the output of the ith firm which depends on its index of conventional inputs X_i, its specific knowledge capital K_i, and on the state of aggregate knowledge in this industry K_a. Note that I have assumed constant returns in the firm's own inputs, X_i and K_i. This simplifies the example greatly. Now let us assume that: (1) the aggregate level of knowledge capital $K_a = \sum_i K_i$ is simply the sum of all specific firm research and development capital levels; and (2) own resources are allocated optimally and all firms in the industry face the same relative factor prices. Then we know that the individual K_i to X_i ratios will be given by

$$\frac{K_i}{X_i} = \frac{\gamma}{1 - \gamma}\frac{P_x}{P_k} = r,$$

where P_x and P_k are the prices of X and K, respectively, and r, the K/X ratio, does not depend on i. We can aggregate our individual production functions:

$$\sum_i Y_i = \sum_i BX_i(K_i/X_i)^\gamma K_a^\mu = \sum_i BX_i r^\gamma K_a^\mu = Br^\gamma K_a^\mu \sum_i X.$$

Now since the K_i/X_i ratios are equal to r, so also is $\sum K_i/\sum X_i$, which we can substitute back into this equation, yielding:

$$\sum_i Y_i = B\left(\sum_i K_i/\sum_i X_i\right)^\gamma K_a^\mu \sum_i X_i = B\left(\sum_i X\right)^{1-\gamma} K_a^{\mu+\gamma},$$

where, by assumption, $\sum_i K_i = K_a$. Thus, we get an aggregate production function with the coefficient of aggregate knowledge capital being higher ($\gamma + \mu$) than at the micro level (γ only), since at the aggregate level it reflects not only the private but also the social returns to research and development.[11] The above formula provides a framework for reconciling micro and macro results in this area.[12]

Of course, this formula is rather simplistic and is based on a whole string of untenable assumptions, the major ones being: the assumption of constant returns to scale with respect to X_i and K_i and the assumption of common factor prices for all firms within an industry. These assumptions could be relaxed. This would add a number of "mix" terms to the equation, indicating how aggregate productivity would shift if the share of, say, the larger firms, were to increase (as in the case of economies of scale). If the mix of firms stays stable, such refinements do not add much. In any case, the above formula was presented to suggest the nature of a class of results that one could get from such assumptions, rather than to set out a final model of such phenomena.

---

11. The effect of aggregated private "knowledge" is K^γ. The total spillover effect of this knowledge is K^μ. Since we have assumed that all private knowledge spills over to some extent and have measured it as $K_a = \sum K_i$, the total effect of all private knowledge at the aggregate level is given by $\gamma + \mu$, rather than just by γ.

12. The first time I saw this type of formulation was in an unpublished note by Grunfeld and Levhari (1962).

The problem is much more complicated when we realize that we do not deal with one closed industry, but with a whole array of firms and industries which "borrow" different amounts of knowledge from different sources according to their economic and technological distance from them. The concept of such a "distance" is very hard to define empirically. If we return to our previous example and now interpret the index i as referring to industries rather than firms, it makes little sense to define K_a as $\sum_i K_i$. Rather

$$K_{a_i} = \sum_j w_{ij} K_j$$

is the amount of aggregate knowledge borrowed by the ith industry from all available sources. K_j measures the levels available in these sources, while w_{ij}, the "weighting" function, can be interpreted as the effective fraction of knowledge in j borrowed by industry i. Presumably w_{ij} becomes smaller as the "distance," in some sense, between i and j increases. Thus we need an additional distributed (lag) over space function to construct a measure of the stock of borrowed knowledge.

On what should such a weighting function be based? There have been earlier suggestions based on "vertical borrowing" concepts: Brown and Conrad (1967) used the input-output table to measure the "closeness" of industries proportional to their purchases from each other, while Terleckyj (1974) used the capital and intermediate inputs purchases matrix weights, assuming that "borrowed" research and development is embodied in purchased inputs. Raines (1968) used the "horizontal" product field classification of NSF to include inputs to an industry's research and development and also the research and development expenditures of other industries which were reported as belonging to its product field.

Actually, there are two distinct notions of research and development "spillovers" here which are often confused in the literature. The first one, research and development intensive inputs purchased from other industries at less than their full "quality" price, is related to issues in the measurement of capital equipment and materials and their prices and is not really a case of pure knowledge spillover. If capital equipment purchase price indices reflected fully the improvements in their quality, i.e., were based on hedonic calculations (Griliches, 1971), there would be no need to deal with this problem. As currently measured, however, total factor productivity in industry i is affected not only by its own research and development but also by productivity improvements in industry j to the extent of its purchases from that industry and to the extent that the improvements in j have not been appropriated by its producers and/or have not been incorporated in the official price indices of that (i) industry by the relevant statistical agencies. The use of purchase flow weighted research and development measures assumes that social returns in industry j are proportional to its research and development investment levels and that the amount of such returns transferred to industry i is proportional to its purchases (or stocks) from industry j.

A good example of such productivity transfers would be the computer industry. It has had a tremendous real productivity growth, most of it unmeasured in its official indices, and most of it unappropriated within the industry itself (because of rather intensive competitive pressures). Different industries have benefited differentially from it, depending on their rate of computer purchases. One way of accounting for it would be to adjust upward the relevant capital equipment figures by their computer content. The alternative is to "import" the computer industry's research and development in proportion to the purchases from it.

But these are not real knowledge spillovers. They are just consequences of conventional measurement problems. True spillovers are the ideas borrowed by the research teams of industry i from the research results of industry j. It is not clear that this kind of borrowing is particularly related to input purchase flows. The photographic equipment industry and the scientific instruments industry may not buy much from each other but may be, in a sense, working on similar things and hence benefiting much from each other's research. One could argue that this is what the SIC classification is for. Presumably, the usefulness of somebody else's research to you is highest if he is in the same four-digit SIC classification as you are; it is still high if he is in the same three-digit industry group as you are; and, while lower than before, the results of the research by a firm in your own two-digit classification (but not three-digit) is likely to be more valuable to you than the average results of research outside of it.[13] The problem arises when we want to extend this scale across the other two-digit industries. Here there is no natural order of closeness (e.g., is "leather" closer to "food" or to "textiles"?).

The following alternatives appear reasonable and worth trying: (1) grouping three-digit SIC categories into clusters based on a priori notions about the extent of commonality in their technological and scientific base; (2) using the NSF's applied research and development product field by industry table to induce a distance metric, on the assumption that if an industry is doing research and development on some other industry's products, it is in some sense closer to it technologically than if it does not; (3) using company industrial diversification data from the Census of Enterprises to compute an alternative technological closeness metric; and (4) using information on rates of cross referencing of patents across product fields to infer the technological distance between them.[14] In each of these cases one will have to assume some simple weighting

13. The situation is further complicated by the fact that the major R&D performers are conglomerates, spanning several SIC four-, three-, and even two-digit classifications. The NSF's applied R&D product field data help here a little but not enough. Complete within-firm product line breakdowns along the lines suggested by the FTC would be very useful in this context.
14. Work along lines (2) and (4) is being pursued by Schankerman (1979) and myself.

functions (e.g., the influence declining exponentially with the particular concept of distance) or group the data into a few categories: immediate neighborhood, related fields, and the rest. The available data will not support very refined approaches. There just are not enough degrees of freedom or independent variations in such productivity and research and development series to allow us to estimate very fancy distributed lag schemes over both time and all other industries.

The alternative to the search for such a concept of technological closeness or distance is to use the research investments of different industries as separate variables. But that is not really feasible. At best we would have about 20 years of data for each of about 20 industries. We cannot include 20 separate R&D variables in each of the industry equations; there simply will not be enough degrees of freedom there. We therefore have to aggregate somehow and that is what the idea of technological distance is for: to tell us how to weight the different research series and collapse them into one or a few variables so that we can estimate and assess the empirical importance of R&D spillovers. With such estimates we would compute not only the return to particular R&D in its "own" industry but also the total returns to R&D including the spillovers beyond its borders.

In trying to construct a research and development capital stock measure at the firm or industry level we face, thus, two major tasks: deciding on the appropriate lag structure and finding the right weights for "outside" research and development to represent borrowed knowledge and spillovers. Unfortunately, we have not enough theoretical or factual knowledge to guide us in these tasks. They will have to be solved empirically. The available data base, however, does not inspire much confidence in our ability to do so.

Before we conclude this section, we have to mention one other garden variety measurement problem: the lack of a research and development deflator. There is no official research and development deflator index available currently. NSF is using the implicit GNP deflator which is not so high-skill labor intensive as would be appropriate for a research and development input price index. Battelle publishes a research and development "cost" index, based on Milton (1972), but that appears to be an index of total cost (including other inputs) per scientist. It does not hold either the composition of the research and development labor force or the quantity of other inputs purchased constant. In short, it is not a price index. S. Jaffe reviewed the problem in NSF (1972) and suggested the use of a weighted index of labor compensation and the implicit price index in the nonfinancial corporate sector. That seems the best that one can do at the moment from secondary sources, but there is no reason why a better research and development input price index could not be constructed on the basis of primary sources. The NSF surveys ask for quite a bit of detail on the composition of research and development expenditures while the Battelle (previously Los Alamos) research and development scientists' compensation surveys have a great deal of data on the composition and compensation of the research and development labor force. This detail could be used to construct a whole set of separate research and development deflators for each of the major research and development performing industries.

2.5   Econometric Problems

Besides the measurement problems discussed above, there are two other serious econometric problems facing the analyst in this area: multicollinearity and simultaneity. Although both are common, "garden variety" econometric problems, each has serious consequences. The problem of multicollinearity arises from the fact that many of the series we are interested in moved very much together over the period of observation. That being the case, it is then difficult (often impossible) to infer their separate contributions with any precision. There are no cheap solutions to this problem. It requires either less-collinear data, more prior information, or a reduction in the aspiration level of the questions to be asked of the data.

Micro-time-series data at the individual firm or establishment level are probably the best way to reduce the multicollinearity that plagues such series at the industry- or economy-wide level. There is much more variability in the R&D histories of particular firms than in the R&D histories of the corresponding industries. This variability can be used to answer questions about the R&D lag structure, the relative effects of government- versus privately financed R&D, or of basic versus applied research, and so on. Such "gains," however, come only at a serious cost. As noted above, at the micro level one can ask only questions about private returns to R&D. Very little of their social returns is detectable at this level.[15]

The analysis of industry-level data can be facilitated somewhat by the imposition of reasonable a priori restrictions. Thus, the use of total factor productivity measures as dependent variables already imposes on the data a set of implicit assumptions about the functional form of the production function and about specific values of its parameters; for example, it sets the output elasticities equal to their observed factor shares.

A similar problem will arise in trying to determine the exact shape of the R&D lag structure. To do that one has to have many years of R&D data and treat each of these years as a separate variable. But, in fact, R&D expenditures are highly correlated from year to year. Thus, it is unlikely that one can estimate their separate contribution with any precision (see Griliches (1967) for a more detailed discussion of such problems). Here it is probably best *to assume*

---

15. This does not mean that one cannot study the social returns to R&D at the micro level, but that would require a much more detailed data base with information on the magnitude of the actual technological breakthroughs and estimates of the relevant demand elasticities. See Mansfield et al. (1977) for details of such an approach. It goes far beyond the production function framework considered here. It is based, however, largely on confidential private information and is thus difficult to reproduce, extend, and evaluate.

a functional form for the lag distribution on the basis of prior knowledge and general considerations and not to expect the data to answer such fine questions. That is, a "solution" to the multicollinearity problem is a moderation of our demands on the data—our desires have to be kept within the bounds of our means.

The simultaneity problem refers to the possible confusion in causality: future output and its profitability depend on past R&D, while R&D, in turn, depends on both past output and the expectation about its future. With long time series and detailed lag assumptions one may be able to analyze a recursive equations system with current output depending on past R&D, and past R&D depending on past rather than current output. In cross sectional data with only a few observations per firm, it is much harder to make such distinctions, particularly since current expectations about the future are based on current and past data.

It may be useful to outline the problem in somewhat more detail. In the context of simple static profit maximization a complete production and input choice model would consist of the production function,

$$y = \alpha c + \beta l + \gamma k + u,$$

assuming a Cobb-Douglas functional form and denoting the logarithms of corresponding variables by lower case letters, and marginal revenue product equals marginal cost conditions of the form,

$$y - c = a_1 + \pi_1 + v_1,$$

$$y - l = a_2 + \pi_2 + v_2,$$

$$y - k = a_3 + \pi_3 + v_3,$$

where the π's are the respective real factor prices of the various inputs, the v's are random errors in factor demand conditions, and a's are constants which depend on the coefficients of the production function and the product demand and factor supply elasticities (in the case of imperfect competition). (See Nerlove (1965) for more detail on this type of model.) We can solve this system of equations for k in terms of the π's, v's, and u, and write the resulting "reduced form" equation as

$$k = D\{-\alpha(\pi_1 + v_1) - \beta(\pi_2 + v_2) - (1 - \alpha - \beta)(\pi_3 + v_3) + u\},$$

where

$$D = 1/(1 - \alpha - \beta - \gamma).$$

Under these assumptions, it is clear that k is a function of u and that a simple OLS estimate of the production function would result in a biased estimate of γ, since the "independent" variable of interest (k) is in fact correlated with the disturbance in the same equation.

There are several "solutions" to the simultaneity problem. First, if one has good series on the π's, the real factor costs of the various inputs, one could use them as instrumental variables for the estimation of the production function. Unfortunately, in the R&D context one is unlikely to have good factor price series.[16] Even if one had the prices, they are likely to be highly collinear over time. Second, if one is willing to assume that disturbances in the input choice equations, the v's, are independent of the production function disturbance u, one could use input-output ratios, say $k - y = \pi_3 + v_3$, as instruments, since by hypothesis they are independent of u. This is known in the literature as the "indirect least squares" method. The implicit assumption of certainty about the future underlying such a static model makes little sense, however, in the R&D context. What is maximized here is the present value of all future profits, and the relevant output concept is an expected one and not the current one, especially if current output (and demand) is subject to special and transitory circumstances. In such a context not all of the "u" is transmitted to the factor demand equations (see Mundlak and Hoch (1965) and Mundlak (1963) for a more detailed exposition of such "partial transmission" models) and the indirect least squares method alluded to above is not consistent anymore. One needs a way of estimating the ratio of the permanent (transmitted) variance in u before one can use such methods again. Third, if both time series and cross sectional data are available and one is willing to assume a simple permanent-transitory transmission model: $u = \mu + t$, where μ is the permanent component which affects input demand choice while t, the transitory component, does not, then consistent estimates can be had from the within-firm covariance estimates of the parameter. This is equivalent to allowing a separate constant term (dummy variable) for each firm, which would absorb the μ term in it. Unfortunately, such data sets are rare. Moreover, the covariance approach may exacerbate other problems, such as errors in the variables, which may also afflict these kinds of data. Fourth, one may be able to find other "indicator" variables which may be related to the permanent components of the variables of interest and hence may help to solve the identification problem in such models.

For example, data may be available on the stock market value of the firm S. If this measure is proportional to the permanent output of the firm, then taking logarithms and ignoring constants, we can write

$$ s = y - t + \varepsilon, $$

where ε is a random term uncorrelated with either μ or t. Now one can use input to value of the firm ratios ($k - s$, etc.) as components of the indirect

---

16. First, there are no published R&D deflators at the two-digit SIC level; second, if they were available, they would still be very highly correlated with the cost of labor and cost of capital indices, which are likely to be major ingredients of such indices. What we will not have are changes in "real" R&D costs in a field caused by various technological breakthroughs.

least squares procedure alluded to above.[17] More generally, a more explicit formulation of the expectation formation mechanism, together with the use of additional indicator variables such as the value of the firm, its physical capital investment policy, and the number of patents it has received, may allow us to formulate and estimate a more general "unobservables" type model (Griliches, 1974).

To recapitulate, the possible mutual dependency of R&D investments on past and future expected output requires careful attention to model formulation and specification and better and more detailed data to support the application of more sophisticated estimation techniques. Without a careful consideration of such issues, one may wind up reporting something as an estimate of the effect of R&D on output which may be mostly a reflection of the effect of output on R&D rather than vice versa.

2.6   Special Problems

There are several special questions that one would like to have answered in this context:

What are the relative returns to basic versus applied research?

Are the returns to government-financed R&D similar to those of company-financed R&D?

What are the "spillover" effects of government-financed R&D in sectors where the direct effects are almost unmeasurable (e.g., NASA R&D spending)?

How can one distinguish between economies of scale and R&D-induced productivity growth?

It would be interesting to distinguish between returns to basic and applied research, especially at the aggregate level. At the micro level, if firms allocate their resources rationally, the *private* ex post rates of return on different types of research should be about the same (except, possibly for some differences due to their differential riskiness) and we should not be able to distinguish among them. At the industry level one could conceivably find significant differences if, say, the appropriability of the results of basic research is more difficult than the appropriability of applied research. Also, the definition of "basic" implies a potentially wider range of applicability and an a priori higher externality component in its results. Thus, one might expect that the discrepancy between social and private returns would be higher, other things equal, in industries with a higher basic to total R&D ratio. Unfortunately, it may prove very difficult to isolate such effects. Basic research accounts for only about 3

17. The actual model will have to be more complicated, since the value of the firm depends not on expected output but on expected profits, hence also indirectly on planned input expenditures. See Ben-Zion (1977) for an attempt to use the market value of the firm to infer the depreciation rate of R&D expenditures.

percent of the total R&D expenditures in industry. Also, the lag structure of its effects is likely to be flatter and more variable, and hence more difficult to estimate. Therefore, one should not be too surprised if attempts to estimate the separate contribution of basic research fail. Nor should this be interpreted as implying the unimportance of basic research. It may only reflect the inability of our data to reveal such effects.[18]

There is much more basic research done in universities and government institutes than in industry, but it is almost impossible to assess its independent effect on productivity. At the industry level all industries are to some extent beneficiaries of the same research effort. There are no data, however, (except for agriculture) which could connect different expenditures on basic research to specific industries. At best there is a breakdown by fields of science but there is little quantitative information on the differential importance of "scientific fields" for different industries. One could try to construct differentially weighted "relevant" basic research series for different industries, but the results are likely to be quite collinear, and this approach does not appear to be too promising. At the aggregate level one has only one time series to explain and the basic research time series is likely to be no different from many other trending aggregate series. Without much more detail on the structure of basic research and on how it is used (if at all) in industry, it is unrealistic to expect to uncover its effects by econometric methods.[19]

Similar issues arise in the attempt to distinguish between the effects of publicly and privately financed R&D. Within any firm one would not expect to find much of a difference. A dollar is a dollar irrespective of source (unless there are explicit expenditure and accounting rules connected with the use of federal R&D money which lead to inefficiencies). But a concentration of federally supported R&D expenditures in one area may lead to an overall decline in the rate of return to all R&D there. This may explain the difference between the results of Griliches (1975a), who found no differential effect of federal versus private company R&D dollars on the levels and rates of growth of total factor productivity at the *firm* level, and Terleckyj (1975), who found a significant discount of federal R&D dollars as far as their effect on productivity at the two-digit aggregated industry level is concerned.[20] Within an industry, at the firm level there should not be much of a difference between the effectiveness of different dollars, while at the aggregate level different rates of federal

18. In a recent still unpublished paper Mansfield (1980) does find a significant separate impact of basic R&D expenditures on industry productivity growth rates. This indicates that the paragraph above may be too pessimistic.

19. There is always the route of detailed historical case studies but they are subject to problems of selection bias and incomplete coverage.

20. Both studies are based on cross sections of growth rates. Terleckyj covers the years 1948–1966 while Griliches uses only 1957–1965. Terleckyj uses 1958 R&D intensity data while Griliches uses 1957–1965 R&D levels and growth rates. Griliches also finds that the estimated rate of return is lower in industries with high levels of federal R&D support (e.g., electrical equipment, aircraft, and missiles).

R&D investment must imply differences in ex post private and social returns, unless these expenditures are directed primarily at areas where there is private underinvestment in R&D (a large ex ante gap between social and private returns) and concentrated on the less appropriable portions of it.

It might be interesting to look at this more from the "R&D investment function" side. Does federal R&D substitute for or complement private R&D investments? This would depend, in part, on the specific conditions and rules which accompany such federally financed expenditures. Holding federal funds constant, a firm that invests more of its own money than another presumably faces better investment opportunities or is more certain of appropriating a larger fraction of the total return.

Both in this case and in the previously discussed basic versus applied research context, questions are raised as to whether the different types of research are "substitutes" or "complements." Technically, this is a question about the functional form of the production function. In the Cobb-Douglas case all inputs are "complements." This is true of inputs that are considered separately (e.g., labor and capital, and basic and applied research if they have been entered separately with different exponents). When inputs are just added together into one aggregate total R&D measure, the implicit assumption is made that they are infinitely substitutable at the dollar-per-dollar rate. It is rather difficult to investigate questions of functional form with the usual kinds of data (see Griliches and Ringstad (1971) for a more detailed discussion of such difficulties). If one knew more about the differential price (real capital costs) of federal versus company R&D investments, one could investigate this problem through an analysis of input demand equations. Functional form differences are difficult to detect at the production function level, since the different curvature parameters are of second-order importance there. But at the input demand structure level these same parameters (such as the elasticity of substitution) have a first-order effect and thus may be easier to estimate. This, unfortunately, requires us to have the "right" prices for the different types of input—a feasible but very difficult task.

The third question, the detection of the "spillovers" from governmental R&D, was discussed earlier in the context of defining a notion of "borrowed" R&D. A model was outlined which "weighed" the contribution of the jth industry's R&D to the stock of borrowed knowledge in industry i in proportion to some notion of the relevant technological distance between them. Besides the "borrowability" of a particular piece of knowledge of industry i from industry j, there is also the question of differential social productivity of R&D in different industries. There may be effectively more to borrow from some industries than others, per dollar of their R&D expenditures. We would like to be able to test hypotheses of the form "NASA R&D was more productive in the sense of having higher spillovers into the civilian economy than, say, DOD-financed R&D." Statistically this would consist of separating our measures of the total stock of borrowed R&D into components (NASA R&D, DOD R&D,

other federal R&D, industry R&D, etc.) and asking whether they have consistently different effects on the productivity growth of other industries. It is feasible to try such an approach. Whether the available data can sustain such an effort is unclear, however.

The last question, the role of economies of scale in all of this, refers really to two somewhat distinct phenomena. The usual measures of total factor productivity are very much affected by short-term fluctuations in capacity utilization. To get a correct measure of the shift in technological opportunities of an economy (or industry), some adjustments or allowances have to be made for it. Also, there are industries where the longer-run trends in productivity are affected by changes in the scale of consumption. For example, part of the productivity growth in the telephone communications industry is attributable to the rise in calls per subscriber. Similarly, in the electric utility industry, spreading the peak load may lead to significant gains in measured productivity. Some of these changes may be related to earlier R&D expenditures but most are not. The data should be adjusted, if possible, so as not to confuse the issues.

A second type of interaction of R&D with scale occurs in industries where the technological results have been biased towards larger-scale enterprises. Here the payoff to R&D may be delayed if the market does not grow so quickly as anticipated. Moreover, the growth in the market and the growth in the number of "large" customers may, in turn, affect the direction of the R&D effort itself.

There is no satisfactory theoretical framework yet for discussing both the R&D decision process and the returns to it in a world of increasing returns to scale. These few cryptic remarks can at best serve as a placemark for future research. To pursue this topic further here would take us, however, too far afield.

2.7   Previous Work

In this section I shall review briefly several recent studies of R&D returns which fall within the framework of this paper in the sense that they use both the production function framework and econometric methodology to derive their results.

The study which deals with the most aggregate level is the Chase Econometrics Associates' (1975) report, "The Economic Impact of NASA R&D Spending." It is a time-series study (14 to 18 years) of aggregate total factor productivity growth as it relates to distributed lag terms of past NASA R&D expenditures and "other" R&D expenditures. It finds extremely high returns to NASA R&D (on the order of 40 percent per year in perpetuity and more than double the returns to all other R&D). There are several difficulties with this study (see Griliches (1975b) for detailed comments) and it is difficult to accept its results at face value. First, it looks for returns to NASA R&D at the total GNP level, rather than in the sectors where one could have hoped to measure the effect of the spillover of such R&D nontautologically. Second, there is a relatively short time series available to the authors for this purpose. Finally, the results are brittle with respect to the various assumptions and data adjustments made. Minor changes in procedure and variable definitions lead to substantial changes in the results. The study is interesting in that it disaggregates total R&D into two components (NASA vs. other), uses a distributed lag formulation to capture the delays in the effects of R&D over time and makes various adjustments for changes in capacity utilization over time. Unfortunately, the shortness of the time series and the use of a problematic dependent variable make their results both imprecise and difficult to interpret.[21] In addition, they impose the same lag structure on both NASA R&D and all other R&D. But as I have argued above, only the spillovers of NASA R&D should show up in such aggregate productivity figures, and surely they must have a different lag structure from most of the other R&D which is short term and has relatively quick direct returns.

At the aggregate two-digit industry level, there is a series of studies by Terleckyj (1974, 1975, and 1977) which relate a cross section of estimated rates of total factor productivity growth (1948–1966) for 20 to 33 two-digit industries to a number of R&D intensity ratios and other variables. Two findings stand out in these studies: (1) variables that "work" (at this level) are functions of private R&D investments and not of federally financed ones (as contrasted with the CEA study of the effects of NASA R&D); and (2) an average of R&D in "other" industries, weighted in proportion to the industry's purchases from them, has a significant influence on productivity growth. The significance of the "own" R&D intensity ratio in such studies is not surprising, and was observed in earlier studies by others (e.g., see Griliches (1973)). The major new finding is the large and statistically significant coefficient of his "borrowed" R&D measure. Terleckyj does not distinguish, however, between whether this variable works because of the mismeasurement of the inputs bought by the respective industries and whether the variable works because of the use of the input-output matrix weights as measures of technological "distance" between industries. If the first reason is true, the results are less interesting than they appear at first sight. For example, it is quite likely that his productivity measures (taken from Kendrick (1973)) underestimate the contribution of equipment capital and hence overestimate productivity growth in industries which had a relatively high investment in equipment. This occurs because the Kendrick measures weight capital by stock rather than flow weights and overdeflate them (cf. Jorgenson and Griliches (1972) for additional discussion of these and related issues). Since equipment industries are relatively R&D intensive, the resultant variable may be nothing more than a correction to the originally er-

---

21. They use total GNP instead of the more relevant private civilian economy concept. Also their use of the Council of Economic Advisers' "potential" output series is debatable. The results do not survive the switch to Denison's potential output or Jorgenson's real output series.

roneously constructed productivity series. If the measure is supposed to represent technological distance and capture the pure spillover effects of R&D elsewhere, its logic would require the use not of the direct input-output matrix weights but of the corresponding "total" weights, which would take into account the flows of information both directly from i to j and indirectly from i through h and g to j, and so forth. Here, too, the sample is small and the evidence is brittle.[22]

At the micro (firm) level Griliches (1975a) related total factor productivity growth measures for 883 large U.S. companies during the 1957–1965 period to various measures of the growth in R&D capital and found a sizeable and significant effect of R&D on productivity growth. This study is also subject to serious limitations. First and most importantly, because of the nature of the data base (individual company reports), only questions about *private* returns to R&D could be asked. Second, because of the shortness of the available time series, no effort was made to investigate the lag structure of R&D effects. And third, only rudimentary attention was paid to the simultaneity problem.

2.8 Some Conclusions and Recommendations

One of the major points of this paper is the plea for realism as to what the production function approach can and cannot accomplish. Given good data, it can tell us something about average returns to R&D investments in the past and whether they appear to be changing over time. It may be able to indicate industries where returns have been especially high or low, but it will not be able to tell us whether a particular proposed R&D project is a good bet or not.

Given the kind of data we have and are likely to have in the near future, there are questions that one is unlikely to be able to answer from such data: e.g., questions about the exact time structure of the effects of R&D on productivity or the role of "science" and "basic" research in all of this. The level of "science" in the aggregate changes only very slowly, and we have no good way of assessing its differential impact on different industries. Unless a cause (stimulus) has varied much in its intensity over time or in its effects over industries, one is unlikely to be able to isolate it reliably by standard econometric techniques. In studying the contribution of NASA's R&D to the growth of the U.S. economy, we are faced with the fact that at the aggregate level we have only one cycle to work with: a rapid and continuous rise in NASA's R&D expenditures to the mid-1960s and then a more or less continuous decline to the mid-1970s. Given reasonably long and variable lags in the effects of such investments, we have, at best, only two observations, one up and one down. Given all else that is happening at the aggregate level at the same time, we are unlikely to

---

22. A recent study by Mathtech (Agnew and Wise, 1978) using similar data but annual observations (instead of growth rates) is unable to detect a significant effect of such input-output table weighted borrowed R&D measures.

be able to estimate reliably the contribution of a cyclical factor whose one cycle roughly corresponds to the time range of the available data.

This does not mean that the topic cannot be studied at all, only that the production function framework is not the suitable avenue for it. One could presumably identify a list of specific *products* of NASA research and trace out their subsequent impact on productivity in other industries. This, however, would require a much more micro-oriented approach.

At the moment, the lack of relevant data and the conceptual poverty of our models are the major impediments to progress in this area. As far as data are concerned, we have needs at both the macro (industry) and micro levels. At the macro (industry) level a consistent set of total factor productivity measures corresponding to the 24 two- and three-digit industry detail given in the NSF's R&D publications (or the 32 industries corresponding to the applied R&D detail) is needed. These productivity measures should use consistent output and capital deflation methods, be clear about the treatment of sales to government, if possible exclude the R&D expenses and labor force from its measures of current inputs, and be up to date (i.e., go through 1976 or 1977 rather than end in the late 1960s as most of the studies have done). This will require a review and construction of industry price indices which should be consistent, as much as possible, in their treatment of quality change.

A price deflator is needed for the conversion of the R&D expenditures to "real" magnitudes. The earlier work of Jaffe (NSF, 1972) can and should be updated and extended.

The data on R&D collected by the NSF could also be improved. Industry codes use 1967 definitions which lack detail in some high technology areas and may be also out of date by now. Conversion to 1972 codes will have to be made. Coverage of subcontractors of R&D is almost nonexistent. Also, the basic unit surveyed is a firm, not an establishment. Many of the large R&D performing companies are conglomerates. An effort should be initiated to collect R&D data either at the establishment level (which has a more clearly defined industrial identity) or at the "product line" level, as has been recently suggested by the FTC. More effort should also be invested in improving the "Applied R&D by Product Field" estimates.[23]

At the micro (company) level the Census-Griliches-NSF Large-Company panel (1957–1965) should be reconstructed and updated to 1975. Efforts in this direction are now in progress.

Because of confidentiality problems and difficulties in access to census-based data, another "open" firm panel should be created from the published (mainly SEC) record. See, for example, the recent compilations in *Business Week* on this topic. This data set could be matched to other data for the same

---

23. NSF-Census should also write up and publish the results of their "Response Analysis" efforts of the Industrial R&D Survey rather than just allude to them (see p. 20 of NSF 1977).

firms available in such sources as the Compustat tape, and the Patent Office records on patents applied for and granted by product field.

At the conceptual level we need more research on two very difficult topics: (1) how to measure the public product (and hence also the returns to R&D) in such important sectors as space, defense, and health; and (2) how to conceptualize and estimate technological distance between firms and industries and the associated notions of externalities and spillovers in research.

The first really corresponds to efforts to improve and expand the national income accounts towards more welfare-oriented measures. There do appear to be data and there is no insuperable conceptual problem in constructing a more relevant health sector accounting scheme. Whether something comparable could be done in space and defense is not clear at the moment. Suggestions for possible attacks on the second question, measuring the technological distance between firms and industries, have been advanced in the body of this paper and will not be repeated here. They too appear to be feasible.

At the empirical-econometric level we need studies that compare and carefully contrast results at different levels of aggregation in an attempt to detect and measure the importance of social returns to R&D. We also need studies that pay much more attention to the estimation of the various lag structures between R&D expenditures and productivity growth, and at the same time recognize the problem of simultaneity and tackle it in a nontrivial manner. In addition, with patent data now available for 55 SIC product fields, a serious effort should be mounted to determine whether they actually measure something of interest and exactly what it may be. Especially, one should be able to tell whether there is any connection between the rate of patent activity and subsequent productivity growth in the various industries.

This is a large order, but we are talking about a major source of economic growth and about one of the few variables (R&D) which public policy can affect in the future (and has affected in the past). Hence it is of the utmost importance that we improve our knowledge in this area. It will not be easy, but it can be done, and it should not take a very large increase in research resources to accomplish at least some of it.

References

Agnew, C. E. and Wise, D. E. "The Impact of R&D on Productivity: A Preliminary Report." Paper presented at the Southern Economic Association Meetings. Princeton: Mathtech, Inc., 1978.

Ben-Zion, U. "The Investment Aspect of Nonproduction Expenditures: An Empirical Test." Unpublished manuscript, 1977.

Berndt, E. and Christensen, L. "Testing for a Consistent Aggregate Index of Labor Input." *The American Economic Review,* Vol. 44 (1974), pp. 391–404.

Brown, M. and Conrad, A. "The Influence of Research on CES Production Relations" in M. Brown, ed., *The Theory and Empirical Analysis of Production,* Studies in Income and Wealth, Vol. 3, New York: Columbia University Press for NBER, 1967, pp. 275–340.

Chase Econometrics Associates Inc. "The Economic Impact of NASA R&D Spending." Bala Cynwyd, Pa.: 1975.

Chow, G. "Technological Change and the Demand for Computers." *The American Economic Review,* Vol. 57 (1967), pp. 1117–1130.

Diewert, E. "Aggregation Problems in the Measurement of Capital." University of British Columbia Discussion Paper No. 77–09, 1977.

Evenson, R. E. and Kislev, Y. *Agricultural Research and Productivity.* New Haven: Yale University Press, 1975.

Fisher, F. M. "The Existence of Aggregate Production Functions." *Econometrica,* Vol. 37, No. 4 (1969), pp. 553–577.

Gordon, R. J. "The Disappearance of Productivity Change." Harvard ED Report No. 105. Mimeographed, 1968.

Griliches, Z. "Research Cost and Social Returns: Hybrid Corn and Related Innovations." *Journal of Political Economy* Vol. 66, No. 5 (1958), pp. 419–431.

———. "The Sources of Measured Productivity Growth, U.S. Agriculture, 1940–1960." *Journal of Political Economy* (August 1963).

———. "Distributed Lags: A Survey." *Econometrica* (January 1967).

———. "Research Expenditures and Growth Accounting" in B. R. Williams, ed., *Science and Technology in Economic Growth,* London: MacMillan, 1973, pp. 59–95.

———. "Errors in Variables and Other Unobservables." *Econometrica,* Vol. 42, No. 6 (1974), pp. 971–998.

———. "Returns to Research and Development Expenditures in the Private Sector" (1975a) in J. W. Kendrick and B. Vaccara, eds., *New Developments in Productivity Measurement,* Studies in Income and Wealth, Vol. 41, forthcoming. [Reprinted as chap. 3 in this volume.]

———. "Comments on CEA: The Economic Impact of NASA R&D Spending." Mimeographed, 1975b.

———. "Economic Problems of Measuring Returns to Research" in Y. Elkana et al., eds., *Toward a Metric of Science: The Advent of Science Indicators,* New York: John Wiley & Sons, Inc., 1977.

———, ed. *Price Indices and Quality Change.* Cambridge: Harvard University Press, 1971.

Griliches, Z. and Ringstad, V. *Economies of Scale and the Form of the Production Function.* Amsterdam: North-Holland Publishing Company, 1971.

Grunfeld, Y. and Levhari, D. "A Note on External Economies." Mimeographed, 1962.

Jorgenson, D. W. and Griliches, Z. "The Explanation of Productivity Change." *Review of Economic Studies,* Vol. 34, No. 3 (1967), pp. 249–283.

——— and ———. "Issues in Growth Accounting: A Reply to E. F. Denison." *Survey of Current Business* (May, Part II, 1972).

Kendrick, J. W. *Postwar Productivity Trends in the U.S., 1948–1969.* New York: Columbia University Press for NBER, 1973.

Mansfield, E. "Basic Research and Productivity Increase in Manufacturing." *The American Economic Review,* Vol. 70 (1980), pp. 863–873.

Mansfield, E., Rapaport, J., Romero, A., Wagner, S., and Beardsley, G. "Social and Private Rates of Returns from Industrial Innovations." *Quarterly Journal of Economics,* Vol. 91, No. 2 (1977), pp. 221–240.

Milton, H. S. "Cost-of-Research Index, 1920–1970." *Operations Research* (1972), pp. 1–17.

Mundlak, Y. "Estimation of Production and Behavioral Functions from a Combination of Cross Section and Time Series Data" in C. Christ et al., eds., *Measurement in Economics,* Studies in Mathematical Economics and Econometrics in Memory of Yehuda Grunfeld, Stanford: Stanford University Press, 1963.

——— and Hoch, I. "Consequences of Alternative Specifications of Cobb-Douglas Production Functions." *Econometrica,* Vol. 33 (1965), pp. 814–828.

National Science Foundation. "A Price Index for Deflation of Academic R&D Expenditures." NSF 72–310. Washington, D.C., 1972.

———. *Research and Development in Industry, 1975.* NSF 77–324. Washington, D.C.: 1977.

Nelson, R. and Winter, S. "Neoclassical vs. Evolutionary Theory of Economic Growth: Critique and Prospectus." *Economic Journal,* Vol. 84, No. 336 (1974), pp. 886–905.

Nerlove, M. *Estimation and Identification of Cobb-Douglas Production Functions.* Chicago: Rand McNally & Company, 1965.

Pakes, A. and Schankerman, M. A. "The Rate of Obsolescence of Knowledge, Research Gestation Lags, and the Private Rate of Return to Research Resources." Harvard Institute of Economic Research, Discussion Paper 659, October 1978. [Published as "The Rate of Obsolescence of Patents, Research Gestation Lags, and the Private Rate of Return to Research Resources" in Z. Griliches, ed., *R&D, Patents, and Productivity,* Chicago: University of Chicago Press, 1984, pp. 73–88.]

Raines, F. "The Impact of Applied Research and Development on Productivity." Washington University Working Paper No. 6814, 1968.

Rymes, T. K. *On the Concept of Capital and Technical Change.* Cambridge: Cambridge University Press, 1971.

Schankerman, M. "The Determinants, Rate of Return, and Productivity Impact of Research and Development." Unpublished Ph.D. dissertation, Harvard University, 1979.

Sharpe, W. F. *The Economics of Computers.* New York: Columbia University Press, 1967.

Terleckyj, N. E. *Effects of R&D on the Productivity Growth of Industries: An Exploratory Study.* Washington, D.C.: National Planning Association, 1974.

———. "Direct and Indirect Effects of Industrial Research and Development on the Productivity Growth of Industries" (1975) in J. W. Kendrick and B. Vaccara, eds., *New Developments in Productivity Measurement,* Studies in Income and Wealth, Vol. 41, forthcoming.

———. "Output of Industrial Research and Development Measured as Increments to Production of Economic Sectors." Paper given at the 15th Conference of the International Association for Research in Income and Wealth, York, England, 1977.

Williams, B. R. *Science and Technology in Economic Growth.* London: MacMillan, 1973.

II R&D and Productivity at the Firm Level: The Evidence

3 Returns to Research and Development Expenditures in the Private Sector

3.1 Introduction

In late 1965, the Bureau of the Census and the Office of Manpower Studies of the National Science Foundation asked me to consider a project to analyze the available historical data on company research and development expenditures together with other data for the same companies collected in different Census inquiries. During 1966–67, a plan of work was outlined, cut down to size, and agreed upon. The Census undertook to develop a company record, edited for consistency, to produce regressions and related outputs free of disclosures for individual companies, and to pass on the reasonableness of the various series employed. Only Census employees were to have (and have had) access to individual company data, and the treatment of outliers was in accordance with the usual criteria employed by the Census. The process of matching the same companies in different data sets and over time turned out to be quite a difficult and time-consuming task. Because the results were slow in coming, and in the context of severe budgetary cuts, the Office of Manpower Studies of the NSF bowed out as a direct partner in this study in 1968. The rest of the financing for this project still came from the National Science Foundation, but in the form of a direct research grant to me rather than as a continuation of the

Reprinted from *New Developments in Productivity Measurement and Analysis,* edited by John W. Kendrick and Beatrice N. Vaccara, pp. 419–54 (Chicago: University of Chicago Press, 1980). © 1980 by the National Bureau of Economic Research. All rights reserved.

A large number of people were essential and helpful in initiating and carrying through this work. I am grateful to, among many others, Max Conklin, Owen Gretton, L. Jack Owen, Walter Heller, Milton Eisen, and Ruth Rynyan at the Bureau of the Census; to Thomas Hogan, Pat Riley, Ken Sanow, and James Blackman at the National Science Foundation; and to Paul Ryan, Ruth Helpman, and Bronwyn Hall at Harvard University, for help, encouragement, and research assistance. I am indebted to the National Science Foundation for the financial support of this project both through the budget of the Office of Economic and Manpower Studies and through grants no. G-1812, GS-712, GS-2762X, GS-39865X, and SOC 73-05374-A01.

in-house research partnership. The funding crisis and other workload pressures on the Census delayed the completion of the data match until 1970. During this long gestation period the project was greatly reduced in scope by abandoning the idea of extending the match to such additional company data sources as the IRS and Compustat tapes and by limiting the number and range of variables to be included in the final data base. First regression results for a restricted set of equations and variables became available in early 1971, and final corrected runs were delivered in 1972. This is the first report based on the results of this project. I am solely responsible for the interpretation and analysis of the results and for the delay since mid-1972.

The original universe of this study consists of large (1000-plus employees) R&D-performing U.S. manufacturing companies. There were 1,154 such companies in 1964. Our final sample is based on data for 883 such companies, accounting for about 90% of total sales and over 92% of total R&D expenditures of all firms in this universe (see table 3.1 for more detail). Since large firms account for most of the reported R&D expenditures in industry, our sample accounted for 91% of all the R&D performed in industry in 1963 including the R&D performed outside our universe of large companies. Thus, in spite of quite a few companies for which some or many of the data are missing, the coverage of our sample is rather complete, especially in comparison to other micro-data sets of this kind.

The data base consists of individual company time series on research and development expenditures (company-financed and total), on the number of research scientists and engineers, and on total company employment and sales—all based on the 1957–65 annual NSF-Census R&D surveys—and of additional company data on value added, assets, depreciation, and other economic magnitudes, based on the match with the 1958 and 1963 Census of Manufactures and Enterprise statistics. Because of problems of handling confidential data I received only matrices of correlation coefficients and standard deviations for the various variables in the data base, broken down into six rather broad industry groupings, and never had access to the actual individual observations. The restriction of this study to variables contained in the original data sets and the associated inability to add such things as prices, stock valuations, or concentration ratios, the availability of data only in the form of moment matrices, the relative shortness of the available time series, and the lack of detailed industrial breakdown, all severely limit the range of questions that can be asked and largely predetermine the feasible modes of analysis.

When this study was initiated in the mid-1960s, my own interests centered on sources of productivity growth and on estimating the contribution of non-market factors to growth using production function models and econometric estimation techniques. The study reported below bears the marks of this interest. It focuses on estimating the coefficient of cumulated R&D expenditures in company-level production functions or its equivalent in company productivity growth equations. Because the data are for individual companies, this study

Table 3.1   Sample Coverage in 1963: R&D-Performing Companies with 1,000 or More Employees

SIC Industry	Number of Companies			Total Sales (billions of dollars)			Total R&D Expenditures (millions of dollars)		
	Population	Sample	Coverage Ratio	Population	Sample	Coverage Ratio	Population	Sample	Coverage Ratio
1. 28, 29, 13: Chemicals and petroleum	134	110	.82	52.6	48.4	.92	1,556	1,294	.83
2. 34, 35: Fabricated metal products and machinery	257	187	.73	32.1	23.7	.74	1,111	958	.86
3. 34, 48: Electrical and communication equipment	134	102	.76	28.2	23.2	.82	2,866	2,579	.90
4. 371, 373–9: Motor vehicles and other transport equipment	55	34	.62	32.0	29.6	.92	1,090	1,062	.97
5. 372, 19: Aircraft and missiles	53	31	.58	17.4	16.8	.97	4,712	4,619	.98
6. All others	521	419	.80	97.8	90.5	.93	1,137	922	.81
Total	1,154	883	.77	260.1	232.2	.89	12,472	11,434	.92

Source: Unpublished census tabulations.

can explore only the magnitude of *private* returns to such expenditures. It cannot deal with the very important issue of externalities—returns that accrue to other firms and to society at large and are not captured by the original investors. In a later report I shall try to deal with this problem by comparing the estimates presented here with those derivable from aggregate industry and economy-wide time series. Here we'll limit ourselves, however, to what direct information can be gleaned from the data at hand.

The next section of this paper outlines the theoretical model used and the statistical problems associated with its estimation. The variables used in this study are described in section 3.3 and the main results are summarized in section 3.4. Section 3.5 digresses to consider the relation of R&D to firm size. Concluding remarks are contained in section 3.6, while more detail on the matching process and data construction can be found in the Appendix.

3.2   Models and Problems

Both the theoretical and empirical literature on the relationship between research and productivity have been reviewed recently by several authors (cf. Griliches 1973a; Mansfield 1967, 1972; and Nordhaus 1969, among others) and we shall not go over the same ground again here except to present the simplest possible model of this process which will serve as the framework of our estimation efforts below.

This model, which is common to most analyses of the contribution of research to productivity growth, can be summarized along the following lines:

(1) $$Q = TF(C, L),$$

(2) $$T = G(K, O),$$

(3) $$K = \sum w_i R_{t-i},$$

where Q is output (sales, or value added), C and L are measures of capital and labor input, respectively, T is the current level of (average) technological accomplishment (total factor productivity), K is a measure of the accumulated and still productive (social or private) research capital ("knowledge"), O represents other forces affecting productivity, R_t measures the real gross investment in research in period t, and the w_i's connect the levels of past research to the current state of knowledge.[1]

For estimation purposes, the F and G functions are usually specialized to the Cobb-Douglas form and O is approximated by an exponential trend. The whole model then simplifies to

---

1. Note that in writing equations (1) and (2) in this fashion we have implicitly assumed the separability and ultimate neutrality of the research process from the production process. Since theoretical generalization is cheap, we could have extended the model to make the coefficients of C and L also dependent on K, but our data could not sustain such complications.

(4) $$Q_t = Ae^{\lambda t} K_t^\alpha C_t^\beta L_t^{1-\beta},$$

where A is constant, λ is the rate of disembodied "external" technical change, and constant returns to scale have been assumed with respect to the conventional inputs (C and L). Equations like this have been estimated by Griliches (1964) from several agricultural cross-sections, and by Evenson (1968) and Minasian (1969) from combinations of time series and cross-section data for agricultural regions and chemical firms, respectively. Alternatively, if one differentiates the above expression with respect to time and assumes that conventional inputs are paid their marginal products, one can rewrite it as

(5) $$f = q - \hat{\beta}c - (1 - \hat{\beta})l = \lambda + \alpha k,$$

where f is the rate of growth of total factor productivity, lower-case letters represent relative rates of growth of their respective upper-case counterparts [$x = \dot{X}/X = (dX/dt)/X$], and $\hat{\beta}$ is the estimated factor share of capital input.[2] Equation (5) is a constrained version of (4). Versions of such an equation were estimated by Evenson (1968) for agriculture and by Mansfield (1965) for manufacturing industries, among others. In either form, the estimates of α have tended to cluster around .05 for public research investments in agriculture (Evenson and Griliches) and around .1 for private research investments in selected manufacturing industries (Mansfield, Minasian, and Terleckyj).

Up to now I have been deliberately vague as to the operational construction of the various variables. The difficulties here are myriad. Perhaps the two most important problems are the measurement of output (Q) in a research-intensive industry (where quality changes may be rampant), and the construction of the unobservable research capital measure (K). Postponing the first for later consideration, we note that $K_t = \Sigma w_i R_{t-i}$ can be thought of as a measure of the distributed lag effect of past research investments on productivity. There are at least three forces at work here: the lag between investment in research and the actual invention of a new technique or product, the lag between invention and the development and complete market acceptance of the new technique or product, and the disappearance of this technique or product from the currently utilized stock of knowledge due to changes in external circumstances and the development of superior techniques or products by competitors (depreciation and obsolescence). These lags have been largely ignored by most of the investigators. The most common assumption has been one of no or little lag and no depreciation. Thus, Griliches and Minasian have defined $K_t = \Sigma R_{t-i}$ with the summation running over the available range of data, while Mansfield assumed that since R has been growing at a rather rapid rate, so also has K (i.e., $\dot{K}/K \approx \dot{R}/R$). Evenson (1968) has been the only one to investigate this question econometrically, finding that in the aggregate data for U.S. agriculture, an "in-

---

2. To the extent that research inputs are included among the conventional input measures, they have already been imputed in the average private rate of return.

verted V" distributed lag form fitted best, with the peak influence coming with a lag of five to eight years and the total effect dying out in about ten to sixteen years. There is some scattered evidence, based largely on questionnaire studies (see Wagner 1968), that such lags are much shorter in industry, where most of research expenditures are spent on development and applied topics.[3]

Because of the difficulties in constructing an unambiguous measure of K, many studies have opted for an alternative version of equation (5), utilizing the fact that

$$\alpha = \frac{dQ}{dK}\frac{K}{Q}$$

and

$$\alpha k = \frac{dQ}{dK}\frac{K}{Q}\frac{\dot{K}}{K} = \frac{dQ}{dK}\frac{\dot{K}}{Q},$$

allowing one to rewrite (5) as

(5′) $$f = \lambda + \alpha k = \lambda + \rho I_R/Q,$$

where ρ is the rate of return to research expenditures (the marginal product of K) while I_R/Q is the net investment in research as a ratio to total output. In practice, to make some connection between gross and net investment in research one needs information about its "depreciation" which, if available, would have allowed us to construct a measure of K in the first place.

While our models are written as if the main point of research expenditures is to increase the physical productivity of the firm's production process, most of the actual research in industry is devoted to the development of new products or processes to be sold and used outside the firm in question. Assuming that, on average, the outside world pays for these products what they are worth to it, using sales or value added as our dependent variable does in fact capture the private returns to such research endeavors. However, the observed private returns may underestimate the social returns because, given the competitive structure of the particular industry, the market price of the new product or process will be significantly below what consumers might have been willing to pay for it. On the other hand, part of the increase in sales of an individual firm may come at the expense of other firms and not as the result of the expansion of the market as a whole. Also, some of the increase in prices paid for a particular new product may come from changes in the market power of a particular firm induced by the success of the research program. Moreover, some of the gains in productivity or in the sales of new products may be based on the research results of other firms in the same or some other industry. Such

---

3. In the U.S. about three-fourths of all expenditures on R&D in industry have been spent on development and most of the rest on "applied research." Only about 5% of the total R&D expenditure has gone to "basic" research. Thus, one should not expect long lags *on the average.*

factors could result in the observed private returns overestimating the social returns significantly. We cannot say much about the net impact of such forces on the basis of the data at hand. It requires a detailed comparison of the individual firm results with estimates based on industry and economy-wide returns to research, a topic beyond the scope of this paper. But since expected private returns are presumably a determinant of private investment flows into this activity, the estimates presented below may be of some interest even if they cannot answer the social-returns question unequivocally.

Another important problem arises as soon as we write down a system of equations, such as (1)–(3), a problem that will stay with us throughout this paper. Ideally, we would like to distinguish between capital and labor used to produce current "output" and capital and labor used in research (the production of future knowledge and the maintenance of the current stock). In fact, we are usually unable to observe these different input components and are forced to use totals for C and L in our investigations. This leads to a misspecification of equation (4) or (5). Moreover, if components of L and C are weighted in proportion to their current returns, the resulting estimates of the contribution of K (or R) represent, errors in timing apart, excess returns above and beyond the "normal" remuneration of such factors of production.

Given the limited range of our time series, we decided early on a *two-pronged* research strategy: (a) Concentrate on estimating versions of equation (5) based on average *rates of growth* for the whole 1957–65 period. (b) Estimate equation (4) based on the 1963 cross-section levels. Equation (5) has the advantage that, dealing with rates of growth, one essentially differences out permanent efficiency differences across firms and does not allow them to influence the final results. Equation (4) has the advantage that it does *not* ignore the cross-sectional differences in levels, which are a major source of variance in the data and of intrinsic interest themselves. Given our limited data base, additional compromises had to be made in the definition and the choice of variables which are best discussed after we describe, in the next section, the available data and the variables constructed from them.

3.3 Data, Variables, and Caveats

Table 3.1 gives some detail on our sample and its coverage. We have data on 883 large R&D-performing companies, divided into six industrial groupings.[4] Unfortunately, the industrial groupings are rather coarse and the number of companies in some of them is rather small, especially in the motor vehicles and aircraft and missiles groups. Most of our attention will be devoted, therefore, to

---

4. See Appendices B and C for details on the criteria for inclusion of companies in the sample and the methods of imputation for missing data. The Standard Industrial Classification code of a company is determined by its main activity, and its entire research and development operations are classified in that industry.

the combined total industry results, though, for comparison purposes, we will also present the individual industry group results and comment on them.

Our data base was limited to the short list of the R&D survey variables on the matched historical R&D tapes (i.e., R&D expenditures—company and total, sales, total employment, and the employment of scientists and engineers) and the limited number of variables that could be matched to them from the 1958 and 1963 Census of Manufacturers and Enterprise Statistics schedules. Moreover, since the original data could not be released except in the form of moment matrices for selected variables, an irreversible decision had to be made about the choice and functional form of the variables to be included in them. The choice was guided by the following research strategy decision: Given the fact that we have only relatively short time series at hand and assuming that much of the individual annual fluctuations in these series are of a transitory nature, our analysis will concentrate on *two* dimensions of these data—average *rates of growth* over the whole observation period (1957–65) and *levels* in 1963.

Thus, a major subset of the variables included in this study are *rates of growth* computed from regressions of the natural logarithms of the annual observations in the historical R&D tapes on a time-trend. They are the estimated slope coefficients (b's) from $\ln X = a + bt$ type equations, fitted to the whole 1957–65 period or to the sub-period of available data, provided that four or more years of data were available to compute such time-trend regressions.

Appendix table 3A.1 lists the sixty variables for which moment matrices were released by the Census Bureau. These variables can be divided roughly into the following sets: (1) potential dependent variables; (2) various measures of R&D growth and intensity; (3) measures of physical capital and its age composition; (4) measures of total company employment; (5) quality of data measures; (6) other background variables. In what follows we shall discuss only the variables used intensively in this study.

The major dependent variable used in the growth rates section of this study is BPT (number 41 in table 3A.1), or partial productivity growth, computed as the difference between the estimated rate of growth of total company sales in 1957–65 (31. BS) and the product of the rate of growth of total company employment (32. BE) and the average share of labor (total payroll) in sales (12. ALSS), in 1958 and 1963. That is, BPT = BS − ALSS · BE is a partial approximation to equation (5) with βc taken to the right-hand side:

$$(5'') \qquad q - (1 - \beta)l \approx \text{BPT} \approx \lambda + \alpha k + \beta c + u,$$

where ALSS is an approximation to $(1 - \beta)$, λ is the average exogenous rate of productivity growth, c is the rate of growth of physical capital, and u is a catchall mnemonic for all other systematic and random factors affecting productivity. Because we have no explicit measure of the growth of company physical capital, we could not construct an explicit total factor productivity measure (f) and use the direct version of equation (5). The procedure of using each individual firm's labor share as an approximation to its output-labor elasticity has the virtue of allowing this elasticity to differ across firms, adjusting thereby for rather wide differences in vertical integration across firms.

The missing company rate of growth of physical capital is approximated by two variables: the ratio of accumulated depreciation to the total stock of physical capital in 1963 (6. Age C = [gross fixed assets − net fixed assets]/gross fixed assets) and the depreciation rate (7. D = depreciation charged in 1963/gross fixed assets in 1963). These two proxy variables (Age C and D) taken together should approximate rather well the unobserved true rate of growth of fixed capital, assuming that it remained reasonably constant over the period in question. Moreover, it can be shown that the estimated coefficient of D should be on the order of β, the elasticity of output with respect to physical capital.[5]

Our major measure of the growth in research capital (k) is the estimated rate of growth in total company expenditures on research and development during 1957–65 (34. BTRD). Note that we are approximating the rate of growth in the *stock* of research capital by the rate of growth in gross *investment* in this type of activity. For variables whose initial level is rather low while the rate of growth of investments is rather high, the assumption of proportionality in these rates of growth $(\dot{K}/K \approx \dot{R}/R)$ is not a bad one (cf. Mansfield 1965).[6] Other

---

5. Let g be the rate of growth of fixed investment and d its depreciation rate. If g has been approximately constant and d can be taken as (or approximated by) a fixed declining balance scheme, then

$$\text{Age } C = \frac{\text{Gross Stock} - \text{Net Stock}}{\text{Gross Stock}} = 1 - \frac{g}{g + d - dg} \approx \frac{d}{g + d}.$$

Fluctuations in Age C can then be approximated by a second-order Taylor expansion as

$$\text{Age } C \approx \overline{d/(g + d)} - \overline{d/(g + d)} \cdot g + \overline{g/(g + d)} \cdot d,$$

where bars indicate an evaluation at the mean levels of these variables. Now, in the function we need βg, where β is the elasticity of output with respect to fixed capital. Substituting a_1 Age $C + a_2 d$ for it, and ignoring constants, we get:

$$a_1 = -\beta \frac{\overline{(g + d)^2}}{d} \quad \text{and} \quad a_2 = \beta \overline{g/d}.$$

Since $g/d \approx 1$, the estimated coefficient of d should be close to β, while the estimated coefficient of Age C (a_1) should be on the order of a quarter of β (assuming $g \approx d \approx .06$). Note that this construction made no allowance for differences in capital utilization among firms or overtime. The available data base contains no information on this topic.

6. Assume no depreciation and let research expenditures R grow at a constant rate ρ. Then the rate of growth of K, say, g, is given by

$$g_t = R_t/K_{t-1} = R_0(1 + \rho)^t / \sum R_{t-1-i}$$

$$= R_0(1 + \rho)^t / R_0 \sum (1 + \rho)^{t-1-i}$$

$$= (1 + \rho) / \sum [1/(1 + \rho)]^i$$

$$= (1 + \rho) / 1 /[1 - 1/(1 + \rho)] = \rho.$$

measures of R&D growth include the rate of growth in company-financed (excluding federally supported) R&D expenditures (35. BCRD) and the rate of growth in the *number* of scientists and engineers engaged in research and development (33. BSE). In addition we also use, in various contexts, the average total R&D to sales ratio (28. AR/S, average of 1958 and 1962) as a measure of research intensity, the ratio of company funds to total cumulated R&D expenditures during 1957–62 (24. FP62) as a measure of the composition of R&D funds, and the logarithm of total cumulated R&D expenditures over the 1957–62 period (54. LGK62) and the logarithm of the average number of research scientists and engineers during 1957–62 (53. LGANSE) as measures of the absolute size of the company research endeavor.

In the level regressions, the main dependent variable is the logarithm of value added in 1963 (51. LGVA63) and the main independent variables are a measure of capital services in 1963 (46. LGC2 = the logarithm of the sum of depreciation plus rentals plus 8% of net fixed assets and inventories), employment in the manufacturing establishments of the company (47. LGEM63), and the previously described cumulated R&D variable (54. LGK62). Among other variables used we should note the company's (five-digit) specialization ratio in 1963 (18. SPR63), the fraction of the total company labor force that is employed in establishments classified as manufacturing in 1963 (11. M), and several "quality of data" variables: a dummy variable for no imputations (42. DNI), and the standard errors for the computed trend growth rates for sales (36. SBS) and for total R&D (37. SBTRD). A number of other variables are used occasionally, especially as instruments in the context of allowing for simultaneity. They will be identified as we go along. Of some intrinsic interest, however, is an estimate of the overall company profitability rate in 1963 (20. NRR), computed as value added in 1963 minus total manufacturing payroll, minus equipment rentals, and minus depreciation, all divided by net fixed assets plus inventories.

As these variables are introduced and described, several problems and difficulties immediately come to mind. First, note that in the growth-rate equations the basic data are for the company as a whole and not just for its manufacturing component, and that the dependent variable is based on the growth of sales rather than of value added. In the level equations we try to stick to the manufacturing portion of these companies, but the division of the labor force into these components is far from perfect and no separate data were available on fixed assets for the manufacturing establishments only. All of the variables except

---

Allowing for depreciation and a variable past would make ρ an underestimate or an overestimate of g depending on whether K_0, the level of accumulated stock at the beginning of the period, was relatively small or large. For total U.S. industry during this period (1957–65), taking initial level estimates for 1948 from Kendrick (1976), extrapolating the NSF figures back from 1953 to 1948, and assuming a depreciation rate of 10% per year, gives a g of .10 instead of the observed ρ of about .07, or a 30% underestimate of g when using ρ. However, an allowance for the rising relative costs of research (deflation of these figures) would bring the two together rather closely.

employment and the various ratio variables are in undeflated current or historical prices. Since we have no explicit information about the specific product mix of the various companies we could, at best, construct only industry-wide deflators. But then all companies within an industry would be treated alike and additively (given our largely linear-in-the-logarithms framework), affecting only the constants in the various equations. Hence, the whole deflation adjustment can be subsumed and allowed for by including separate industry dummy variables (the I's, 1–5) in the overall regressions.

Another major issue is one of lags, timing, and possible simultaneity. In the growth equations we use the growth in R&D over the whole 1957–65 period as an independent variable. On the whole, we believe that we gain more by averaging over a longer period than we lose by introducing a possible simultaneous-equation bias due to contemporaneous correlation between the disturbances in the output and R&D-determining equations. Given our data base, we did not have enough of a history to experiment with fancier lag structures. We shall attempt to check our results below for robustness with respect to the simultaneity problems by (a) using intensity rather than growth measures of R&D, and (b) estimating equation (5″) using instrumental variable methods. Similar problems of interpretation and the possibility of bias arise also in the level equations where our measure of accumulated research capital is the simple unweighted sum of total R&D expenditures for the whole 1957–62 period, allowing for little lag and no depreciation.

To recapitulate, we have to use makeshift proxies for the growth in both physical and research capital. We confound price changes with quantity changes in our productivity measures, and our treatment of lags and simultaneity is both crude and cavalier. Nevertheless, it is about the best that we could do with these data. It is our belief that in spite of their shortcomings and in spite of our many simplifications and dubious assumptions, our data are interesting and rich enough, and the underlying relationships are strong enough, to show through and yield valuable insights into the R&D process and its effects on productivity and growth.

3.4   The Main Results

The relationship between the rate of growth of partial productivity during the 1957–65 period and measures of growth in fixed capital and in R&D is investigated, for the combined sample, in table 3.2. Under the assumption of relatively constant rates of growth of fixed capital, the ratio of (gross − net)/gross stock and the depreciation rate together act as a proxy for the unobserved rate of growth of fixed capital. Each of the regressions includes five industry dummy variables, allowing for separate industry intercepts and for differential rates of price inflation in these industries. In addition to trying out various R&D variables, some of the regressions also include a set of "quality of data" variables: the estimated standard errors of the rate of growth of sales (SBS)

Table 3.2 **All Industries Combined: Growth Rates 1957–65**
Dependent Variable BPT = BS − ALSS × BE,
Partial Productivity Growth, $N = 883$

| Reg. No. | Coefficients of (standard errors) | | | | | | |
	Age C	D	R&D Variables	LGANSE	Other Variables[a]	R^2	S.E.
				BTRD			
1	−.069 (.011)	.334 (.077)	.076 (.013)		I's	.105	.0561
2	−.074 (.016)	.350 (.064)	.073 (.011)	−.003 (.001)	I's SBTRD−, DNI−	.113	.0559
3	−.052 (.016)	.286 (.061)	.074 (.010)		I's, SBS+, SBTRD−, DNI−	.402	.0459
				BCRD			
4	−.070 (.019)	.343 (.075)	.063 (.012)		I's	.096	.0564
5	−.054 (.016)	.301 (.061)	.063 (.010)	−.002 (.001)	I's, SBS+, SBTRD−, DNI−	.399	.0460
				BSE			
6	−.072 (.019)	.345 (.076)	.087 (.014)		I's	.109	.0560
7	−.055 (.015)	.294 (.061)	.087 (.011)		I's, SBS+, SBTRD−, DNI	.409	.0456

[a]Coefficients that are statistically significant at the conventional .05 level are identified by their respective signs.

Age C   = (gross fixed assets − net fixed assets)/gross fixed assets in 1963
D   = Depreciation rate, depreciation charged in 1963/gross fixed assets in 1963
BS   = Rate of growth of sales, 1957–65
BE   = Rate of growth of employment, 1957–65
BTRD   = Rate of growth of total R&D expenditures, 1957–65
BCRD   = Rate of growth of company R&D expenditures, 1957–65
BSE   = Rate of growth in the employment of scientists and engineers, 1957–65
LGANSE = Logarithm of the average number of scientists and engineers, 1957–62
SBS   = Standard error of the estimated rate of growth of sales
SBTRD   = Standard error of the estimated rate of growth of total R&D expenditures
DNI   = Dummy variable = 1 when there were "no imputations" in the data
I's   = Industry dummy variables (five)

and of R&D (SBRD), and a dummy variable signifying a record with no imputations (DNI).

For all firms combined, both the fixed capital and the R&D growth variables are "highly significant" and of the right sign. Total R&D growth is a somewhat better variable than company R&D growth, while the growth in the number of scientists and engineers is marginally better than either one of the dollar measures. The implied elasticity of output with respect to cumulated R&D is about .07 and there is an indication (in the more detailed results not reported here) of some diminishing returns to the absolute size of the research program (LGANSE) and of a negative impact of variability in it (SBTRD). The overall fit is low and a large fraction of the variance is accounted for by the "quality of data" variables.

Table 3.3 summarizes the results for the individual industry groups. They are roughly similar except that the .07 estimate for the combined cross-section can be seen to be an average of a somewhat higher elasticity (.1) for the

Table 3.3   **Dependent Variable: Partial Productivity Growth, BPT = BS − ALSS × BE, 1957–65, by Industry**

		Coefficients of alternative research variables, standard errors of the coefficients, R^2's and standard errors of the regressions (other variables included: Age C, D, SBS, SBTRD, DNI)	
Industry	BTRD	BCRD	BSE
1. Chemicals and petroleum $N = 110$	.093 (.038) .230 (.042)	.090 (.038) .229 (.042)	.089 (.042) .220 (.042)
2. Metals and machinery $N = 187$	.102 (.022) .209 (.043)	.087 (.023) .179 (.044)	.123 (.023) .237 (.042)
3. Electric equipment $N = 101$	.106 (.030) .405 (.040)	.055 (.019) .384 (.040)	.093 (.029) .393 (.040)
4. Motor vehicles $N = 34$	.126 (.070) .491 (.036)	.143 (.055) .543 (.034)	.044 (.083) .435 (.038)
5. Aircraft $N = 31$	.107 (.077) .229 (.042)	.034 (.050) .183 (.044)	.250 (.064) .491 (.034)
6. Other $N = 419$	.052 (.015) .556 (.047)	.051 (.015) .555 (.047)	.062 (.016) .559 (.047)

Note: See notes to table 3.2 for definitions of variables.

research-intensive industries and a somewhat lower coefficient (.04) for the rest (the "other" half of the sample).

A complementary analysis of the problem can be had by looking at the *levels* of productivity and their relationship to the cumulated total of past R&D expenditures (K62). Table 3.4 presents estimates of such 1963 cross-sectional production relationships. They are surprisingly reasonable, and the estimated coefficient of cumulated R&D is rather close to that derived from the time series (growth rates) regressions. At the individual industry level the estimated coefficients are somewhat lower, suggesting that the time series results may be a bit biased upward due to the simultaneity between the growth in research and in sales. But the differences are not statistically significant, as we shall show below. There is no evidence in these data of increasing returns to firm size as such, while both specialization (SPR) and average *plant* (but not firm) size (LSE) are positively related to productivity.

There are interesting consistencies between the estimates given in tables 3.2 and 3.3 and those of table 3.4, though each is based on a very different cut across the data base. We noted before (in footnote 5) that the coefficients of *D* in table 3.2 are approximate estimates of the physical capital elasticity, and that the coefficients of Age *C* should be on the order of a quarter of (and of opposite sign to) the coefficients of *D*. Both estimates are of the right order of magnitude (about .33 and .07, respectively). Moreover, they are not too far from the directly estimated coefficients of log C2 in table 3.4, which hover around .4. Similarly, the R&D coefficient is about .07 in the growth equations in table 3.2, and about .06 in the level equations in table 3.4, for all industries combined. Since both the dependent and independent variables are quite different, this consistency reinforces our belief that this is the right order of magnitude for this coefficient.

We can check in greater detail whether the data are mutually consistent by estimating a combined multivariate regression, imposing the pairwise equality of the *D* and log C2 and of the BTRD and log K62 coefficients and testing whether these restrictions are rejected by the sample. Table 3.5 presents the original independent estimates, industry by industry, and the estimated constrained cross-equation coefficients. It also gives the computed chi-square values for the tests of these restrictions. It is clear, at a glance, that except for the two small sample industries (4 and 5), the different estimates are quite close. In no case do the tests reject the hypothesis that the estimates arise from a population having these parameter values in common.

A basic difficulty with the results presented in tables 3.2, 3.3 and 3.5 is the likelihood of simultaneity between the productivity and R&D *growth* measures. One way of guarding against this possibility is to treat BTRD as an endogenous variable and use instrumental variable methods to estimate its coefficient in equation (5″). The results of doing so are given in table 3.6. The instruments used are basically intensity and level variables as of 1957 and

| | Coefficients of (standard errors) | | | | | |
Industry	Log C2	Log EM	Log K62	Other Variables in Regression[a]	R^2	S.E.
1. Chemicals and petroleum	.381 (.067)	.538 (.097)	.115 (.040)	Age C−, SPR+, DNI, LSE	.893	.391
2. Metals and machinery	.455 (.050)	.282 (.048)	.075 (.022)	Age C, SPR, DNI+, LSE+	.895	.305
3. Electric equipment	.534 (.065)	.439 (.071)	.029 (.020)	Age C, SPR+	.950	.272
4. Motor vehicles	−.048 (.106)	1.067 (.117)	.063 (.042)	Age C, SPR, DNI	.981	.233
5. Aircraft	.176 (.072)	.795 (.090)	.037 (.034)	Age C, SPR, DNI	.987	.173
6. Other	.414 (.028)	.542 (.035)	.045 (.012)	Age C, M−, SPR+, DNI	.920	.299
All industries combined						
a.	.422 (.018)	.435 (.022)	.069 (.009)	I's	.918	.330
b.	.376 (.021)	.527 (.026)	.061 (.008)	I's, Age C−, M−, SPR+, LSE+	.922	.322

Note: See the notes to table 3.2 for the definition of the other variables. The number of observations is the same as in tables 3.2 and 3.3.

[a]Coefficients that are statistically significant at the conventional .05 level are identified by their respective signs.

VA63 = Value added in 1963

C2 = Capital services in 1963; depreciation plus rentals plus 8% of net fixed assets and inventories

EM = Total employment in manufacturing establishments

SPR = 1963 company industry (five-digit) specialization ratio

M = Fraction of total company employment in manufacturing establishments

LSE = Logarithm of the average size of establishment in 1963 (total employment / number of establishments)

LFP = Logarithm of the fraction of cumulated research expenditures (by 1963) that were financed by company funds; FP = "fraction private"

Table 3.5 Constrained Multivariate Regression Estimates: (a) Growth Rates (BPT) and (b) Levels (LVA63) Combined

	Coefficients of R&D			Coefficients of Capital			Estimated Chi-square
	Unconstrained			Unconstrained			
Industry	(a) BTRD	(b) LK62	Constrained	(a) Deprec.	(b) LC2	Constrained	
1	.122 (.030)	.186 (.041)	.140 (.023)	.303 (.241)	.360 (.047)	.355 (.045)	1.66
2	.098 (.023)	.093 (.021)	.085 (.014)	.235 (.165)	.453 (.049)	.449 (.042)	2.42
3	.077 (.033)	.031 (.020)	.041 (.016)	.320 (.111)	.507 (.064)	.456 (.054)	2.70
4	.025 (.060)	.043 (.038)	.028 (.028)	.284 (.137)	.017 (.072)	.074 (.059)	3.10
5	.114 (.063)	.032 (.031)	.048 (.024)	−.143 (.363)	.196 (.065)	.176 (.058)	1.80
6	.054 (.021)	.044 (.011)	.046 (.009)	.535 (.178)	.467 (.024)	.471 (.024)	.20
7. Total	.072 (.013)	.069 (.009)	.067 (.007)	.324 (.074)	.454 (.022)	.422 (.017)	1.60

Notes: Estimated standard errors are given in parentheses. Other variables in equations: (a) DNI, Age C; (b) LEM63, and industry dummies in the total (industry 7) equation.

Estimated chi-square: Twice the difference in the estimated log likelihood between the unconstrained and constrained multivariate regressions. The expected value of this statistic under the null hypothesis of the validity of the two cross-equations restrictions is 2. The critical value of χ^2 with two degrees of freedom is 6 at the .05 significance level and 4.6 at the .1 level. The estimated chi-squares are thus not even close to the critical values.

Table 3.6   Alternative Estimates of the Coefficient of R&D, by Industry

Industry	OLS	TSLS
1	.122	.110
	(.030)	(.048)
2	.098	.232
	(.023)	(.069)
3	.077	.099
	(.033)	(.072)
4	.096	.117
	(.067)	(.094)
5	.114	.113
	(.063)	(.072)
6	.054	.011
	(.021)	(.035)
7 All (combined)	.072	.139
	(.013)	(.049)

Notes: Dependent variable: BPT.
Included independent variables in addition to BTRD: Age C, D, DNI. Also SBTRD for industry 4. Industry dummies in the combined (all industries) equation.
Instruments (excluded independent variables): M, AV/S, AI/V, SCE58, SPR63, GRR, FP62, AR/S, SE/E, SBTRD, LGW58, LGANSE, ALVA. In industry 4, SBTRD is not used as an instrument. In industry 6, the instruments were AI/V, GRR, SE/E, SBTRD, LTRD57, LGFP62, K/SC, and LGVA57. (See table 3A.1 for definitions.)

1963, which should be less correlated with the disturbances in the 1957–65 growth equations. On the whole, the results are very encouraging. Except for industries 2 and 6, the TSLS results are similar to the original ones, indicating little simultaneity bias. Only in industry 6 do the TSLS results not yield a significant R&D coefficient. If anything, the overall TSLS results give somewhat higher estimates for the R&D coefficient, indicating that our main problem may not be simultaneity but error (random noise) in the R&D data.

To the extent that the simultaneity problem is the result of too close a contemporaneity of the sales growth and R&D growth variables one could deal with it by either shortening the period over which the R&D growth is estimated or by using intensity variables such as R&D as a percentage of sales, or number of engineers and scientists as a fraction of total employment, instead of the suspect growth rates. While the results of doing so are somewhat more difficult to interpret, on the whole they do support the finding of a significant and apparently nonspurious influence of R&D on productivity growth. For example, in industry 6 (all others) where the instrumental-variables approach did not yield a significant R&D coefficient, if instead of BTRD we use LGK62/LTRD57 we get a significant coefficient on the order of .01 (.004). Assuming a constant rate of growth of R&D between 1957 and 1962, this stock over initial flow variable approximates the rate of growth of R&D times 3 (ignoring constants).[7] Thus, the implied coefficient of the rate of growth of R&D over the shorter period is about .03, not much less than the earlier estimate of .04. Alternatively, if one substitutes the ratio of research scientists and engineers to total employment (29. SE/E), one gets a coefficient of .38 with a standard error of .21. The intensity variables do a better job for all industries combined, the substitution of the average R&D to sales ratio (28. AR/S) resulting in a coefficient of .07 (.02).

Another way of asking a similar question is to relate profitability rates to past research investments. Assume profits consist of two types of returns $\Pi \approx r_1C + r_2K$, where r_1 is the rate of return on physical capital and r_2 is the rate of return on "knowledge" capital. Then regressing the observed profit rate $\Pi/C = r_1 + r_2 K/C$ on the ratio of cumulated R&D to fixed capital would provide an estimate r_2. Unfortunately, because we really don't have the right numbers we can only approximate such an estimate. Since the returns to R&D are distributed over time, we'd like to have a time series in profitability or some estimate of permanent or average profits. Actually, we don't have a perfect measure even for one year. What we do have is gross profits (called by Telser [1972] the "contribution to overhead") in one year (1963) as a ratio to total domestic assets. This variable (19. GRR) is computed by subtracting total payrolls and equipment rentals from value added and dividing the result by total domestic assets. It is an estimate of the gross company rate of return, before depreciation and corporate taxes. Also, bypassing the problems involved in the measurement of the stock of R&D capital (K) discussed earlier, we do not have an explicit measure of K/C. It was not one of the variables included in our matrices. But we do have log K/C and can use that to approximate it. In addition, there will be a problem in interpreting the resulting r_2 estimates, since past and current R&D expenditures are treated as current expense and subtracted from profits rather than capitalized, while the equipment used in the R&D process is already included in the total fixed capital measure (C). Thus, the resulting estimates are to some extent a measure of the *excess* rate of return, above and beyond that already imputed to the conventional factors used in the R&D process.

With these reservations out of the way, we can turn to table 3.7, which pres-

---

7. If we assume that $R_t = R57 (1 + \rho)^{t-57}$, then $K62 = \sum^{62} R_t = R57 \sum^5 (1 + \rho)^i = R57 (6 + 15\rho + 20\rho^2 + \ldots)$. Ignoring terms of order ρ^3 and higher and assuming that $\rho \approx .1$ and hence $20\rho^2 \approx 2\rho$, gives

$$\log K62/R57 \approx \log 6 (1 + 17\rho/6 + \ldots)$$

$$\approx \log 6 + \log (1 + 3\rho \ldots)$$

$$\approx \log 6 + 3\rho.$$

The first term goes into the constant, implying that the estimated coefficient of log K62/R57 should be multiplied by about 3 to convert it into a coefficient of ρ.

Table 3.7   Relationship between Company Profitability (GRR) and Past
Research Investment (K62), by Industry

Industry	Coefficients of (standard errors)		R^2 and S.E.	Implied Rate of Return to R&D Investments[a]	
	log K62/C1 (1)	log C2 (2)	(3)	Total (4)	Company[b] (5)
1	.077 (.018)	−.039 (.018)	.344 .241	.93	1.03
2	.055 (.013)	−.041 (.014)	.112[c] .204	.25	.28
3	.015 (.010)	−.021 (.013)	.037 .148	.02	.03
4	.046 (.017)	−.014 (.015)	.191 .121	.23	.29
5	.104 (.036)	−.079 (.029)	.332 .227	.05	.17
6	.010 (.005)	−.033 (.008)	.041 .155	.23	.26
7 (combined total)	.033 (.007)	−.034 (.005)	.136 .185	.17	.19

Definitions: Log K62/C1: logarithm of cumulated total R&D as a fraction of total domestic assets in 1963; log C2: logarithm of capital services as of 1963; dependent variable: 19. GRR: approximate company gross rate of return in 1963; S.E.: estimated residual standard error.
[a]Evaluated at the ratio of arithmetic means for K62 and C2.
[b]Column (4) divided by the FP62 ratio.
[c]Also contains a significant SPR variable.

ents the results of such regressions for the six separate industrial groupings and the total sample. In addition to the log K/C measure, we include also a measure of absolute size (log C2)[8] and industry dummies (in the combined regression). The estimated coefficients of log K/C are always positive and significant, except in the case of industry 3. Since we used log K/C instead of K/C as our variable, we have to multiply the resulting coefficient by C/K to get at an estimate of r_2. Evaluating it at the approximate arithmetic means of C and K, i.e., at $\overline{C/K}$, gives the numbers in column (4).[9] Dividing these numbers in turn by the ratio of average company-financed to total R&D (24. FP62) translates them into rates of return to company-financed R&D. These are listed

8. We use log C2 instead of log C1 to reduce the possible spurious relationship between the various measures. But the results of using log C1 are very similar to those reported here.
9. Because we were not given the actual means for our samples, but only means rounded to lower class interval boundaries, we cannot really use the supplied geometric means to evaluate anything (since being off by 1 on a natural logarithm is to be off by a factor of 2.7). But since the arithmetic means are very large, rounding introduces little error there.

in the last column of table 3.7. On the whole the estimates appear to be both reasonable and high. The highest rates of return are estimated for the chemical, drugs, and petroleum industry group. Metals and machinery, motor vehicles, and all other industries show a rather high overall rate of return, in excess of 20%. Allowing for a depreciation rate of 10% still would leave an *excess* rate of return above 10%, or about double that earned by physical capital during the same period.

Two industries, 3 (electrical equipment) and 5 (aircraft and missiles), yield the lowest estimates. These industries have the highest federal involvement in their research activity. The fraction that company-financed R&D is of the total was .65 in industry 3 and only .28 in industry 5 in 1962. The relative specificity of federally supported R&D may explain the estimated low rates of return in these industries. Since together these two industries accounted for over 60% of total R&D in 1963 (see table 3.1), they have a strong depressing effect on the estimated rate of return for the total combined sample. Still, an *excess* gross rate of return of 19% on average company R&D investment is no small matter.

3.5   R&D and Firm Size

There are a number of important policy issues connected with the question of optimal size of an R&D program which cannot really be dealt with in this study. Nevertheless, we do have some negative results which are worth reporting.

The question of the relationship between firm size and research productivity has been recently analyzed by Fisher and Temin (1973) who show that one can tell very little, a priori, about this relationship, and that one cannot conclude much from an observed relationship between firm size and research *inputs*. Roughly speaking, it may pay a large firm to engage in more research, pushing it to a point where its marginal return is lower than that for a smaller firm. We cannot, then, conclude that just because a firm is doing relatively more research it would be a good idea to transfer additional resources to it from the smaller firms.

Actually, we can also look at the relation of R&D output to firm size, not just R&D input. The results presented earlier, however, are rather negative. There is no indication of significant increasing returns to scale in the productivity *level* results summarized in table 3.4. For most company-level production function regressions the estimated sum of coefficients *including* the coefficient of cumulated R&D is unity or less. There is some evidence that more specialized (i.e., less diversified) companies having plants of larger than average size are more efficient, but there is no evidence of increasing returns to total company size as such (except possibly in industries 1 and 4).

Nor is there any evidence of increasing returns to the relative size of the research program as such. In the productivity growth rate equations, shown in table 3.2, and in comparable estimates (not shown) for individual industry groups, an absolute measure of the level of R&D investments such as LGK62 or LGANSE always has a negative sign, and this negative relation is usually statistically significant. Similarly, the estimated functional form used in the rate-of-return regressions in table 3.7 (GRR on LGK62/LGC1) implies diminishing productivity with respect to the absolute size of the R&D programs.

There are several reasons why these findings should not be taken seriously as a positive proof of diminishing returns to R&D: some of our variables are subject to errors of measurement which could lead to downward biases in our estimates. Also, the use of rates of R&D *investment* growth as measures of R&D *stock* growth may overestimate the latter for large companies with a long R&D history, and the estimated negative coefficients for the cumulated R&D levels may be due to nothing more than an adjustment for such a specification bias. But the point to be made is that we have found no prima facie evidence that the *rate of growth* of productivity is higher in larger companies with larger R&D programs or that the *level* of productivity is proportionately higher in the largest companies.

Nor is it clear that the larger companies invest more than proportionately in R&D.[10] Ours is the first set of data which allows a look at this question at the micro level for a relatively large number of companies (almost all of the universe). In table 3.8 we present regressions which summarize, for the whole sample, the relationship between different measures of R&D and company size. The major measure of company size used is ALVA—average of the logarithm of value added in 1957 and 1963. The first measure examined is the logarithm of total cumulated R&D (LGK65) over the whole available period (1957–65).[11] The crude results, regression 1, indicate that larger companies did spend relatively more, and significantly so, on R&D than smaller companies. But once we allow for data difficulties (DNI) and differences in specialization (SPR), this relationship evaporates. What remains (in regression 3) is a strong indication that fixed capital-intensive firms tend also to be R&D-intensive. There is also some indication that larger plant firms (LSE) are more R&D-intensive, but not larger companies as such.

The other regressions reported in table 3.8 examine in turn the relationship to firm size of cumulated company (as against total, which also includes federally financed) R&D in 1962 (LGCK62), the average R&D investment to value-added ratio in 1957 and 1963 (AR/V), the average company R&D to value-added ratio (CAR/V), and the log of the fraction that cumulated company R&D was of total cumulated R&D in 1962 (LFP62). The conclusion is the same: Overall there is little evidence of anything more than just a proportional rela-

---

10. While the relationship of R&D inputs to size does not in general imply much about the relationship of R&D output to size (see Fisher and Temin 1973), for the specific model outlined in section 3.2 of this paper which is homogeneous in R&D and non-R&D input, a more than proportionate increase in input would also imply a more than proportionate increase in output.

11. Value added in 1957 was estimated from value added in 1958 using the relative change in total sales between these years.

Table 3.8   Relationship of R&D to Company Size, All Industries Combined

Dependent Variable	ALVA	LC2/ALVA	Other Variables	R^2	S.E.
LGK65					
1	1.203		I's	.656	1.202
	(.037)				
2	1.024		I's, DNI+, SPR−	.692	1.138
	(.040)				
3	1.010	.248	I's, DNI+, SPR−, LSE	.697	1.129
	(.090)	(.080)			
LGCK62					
1	1.149		I's	.615	1.173
	(.036)				
2	.967	.202	I's, DNI+, SPR−, LSE+	.661	1.104
	(.088)	(.077)			
AR/V					
1	.006		I's	.198	.124
	(.004)				
2	.004	+.035	I's, DNI, SPR, LSE+	.223	.123
	(.010)	(.009)			
CAR/V					
1	−.003		I's	.05	.093
	(.003)				
2	−.003	+.017	I's, LSE+	.061	.092
	(.007)	(.006)			
LFP62	LVA63	LC2/VA63			
	−.062	.077			
	(.035)	(.031)	I's, DNI+, SPR+	.400	.446

Definitions :

$$\text{LGK65} = \log \sum_{57}^{65} \text{Total R\&D}; \quad \text{LGCK62} = \log \sum_{57}^{62} \text{Company R\&D}$$

$$\text{AR/V} = \tfrac{1}{2}\left[\left(\frac{\text{Total R\&D}}{\text{Value Added}}\right)57 + \left(\frac{\text{Total R\&D}}{\text{Value Added}}\right)63\right]$$

$\text{ALVA} = \tfrac{1}{2}\,(\log \text{VA57} + \log \text{VA63}),$ Average of log value added

$\text{CAR/V} = $ similar for company R&D

$\text{LFP62} = \text{LGCK62} - \text{LGK62}$

tionship between R&D and size. There is some evidence that federally financed R&D is biased towards larger, more diversified companies, and that total R&D investments are not uniformly distributed across industries and companies. Capital-intensive, large-plant companies tend to invest somewhat more in R&D, which may be related to technological differences and the differential profitability of R&D investments across industries. But holding such differences constant, none of the measures yields any evidence for the proposition that the largest firms invest more than proportionately in R&D. They do invest *more,* but not relatively to their size.

In table 3.9 we examine the relationship of the R&D to value-added ratio to company size for each of our six industry groupings separately. Again, once capital intensity is controlled for, there is no significant relationship of R&D intensity to size. The results of using only the company-financed R&D ratio as the dependent variable (not shown here) are similar. In short, in our population of already very large companies (1000-plus employees) there is no indication that either the intensity of R&D investments or their productivity is related positively to company size.

3.6 Discussion and Suggestions for Further Research

In spite of various reservations, we have found a rather consistent positive relationship between various measures of company productivity and investments in research and development. In particular, Cobb-Douglas-type production function estimates based on both levels (1963) and rates of growth (1957–65) indicate an overall elasticity of output with respect to R&D investments of about .07, which can be thought of as an average of .1 for the more R&D-intensive industries such as chemicals and .05 for the less intensive rest of the universe. These findings are consistent with the earlier findings of Mansfield and Minasian, but are based on a much larger and more recent data base.

It is rather hard to convert the estimated $\alpha = .07$ into an estimate of the rate of return to R&D investments. Accepting our estimates and the validity of our measures, and using the elasticity formula to derive the implied marginal product estimate yields .27 as the overall estimate of the average gross excess rate of return to R&D in 1963. This is an average for 1963 because it is based on a function fitted across all the firms in our sample and because it is evaluated at the average total cumulated R&D to value-added ratio in 1963 in our sample ($K/V = .26$).[12] It is "gross" because neither our measures of output or of input allow for any depreciation of past R&D investments, and it is "excess" because the conventional labor and fixed capital measures already include the bulk of the current R&D expenditures once.

While our industry groupings differ in the estimated level of this elasticity, they also differ markedly in their R&D intensity, which actually results in much less difference in the estimated rates of return than one might have thought to start out with. Taking tables 3.5 and 3.6 together, one might conclude that α is about .1 or higher for industries 1 and 2, between .05 and .1 for industries 3, 4, and 5, and less than .05 for industry 6. Since the average K/V

12. The average K suffers from conflicting biases. It contains nothing for pre-1957 R&D investments and hence it is too low, but it allows no depreciation in the past accumulation and hence is too high. The two effects are likely to cancel each other out, at least as of 1963. For total industrial R&D, taking Kendrick's (1976) estimates for 1948 cumulated R&D capital as a benchmark and assuming a 10% annual depreciation rate yields a stock estimate of K as of 1963 only about 6% higher than what we get by just summing from 1957 to 1962.

Table 3.9   Relationship of R&D Intensity to Company Size by Industry,
                   Dependent Variable: AR/V

Industry and Regression		Coefficient of (standard error)		R²	S.E.
		ALVA	LC2/ALVA		
1	a	−.002 (.004)		.004	.043
	b	−.002 (.007)	−.008 (.006)	.021	.043
2	a	.013 (.007)		.017	.091
	b*	−.002 (.018)	.081 (.015)	.176	.083
3	a	.005 (.026)		.000	.311
	b	.006 (.081)	.171 (.078)	.047	.305
4	a	.010 (.003)		.304	.025
	b	.011 (.007)	.006 (.007)	.322	.025
5	a	.064 (.032)		.009	.239
	b	.057 (.102)	.124 (.090)	.174	.236
6	a	−.000 (.001)		.000	.025
	b	−.000 (.003)	−.000 (.003)	.000	.025

*Also includes DNI.

ratios for these industries are .23, .23, .6, .16, 1.4, and .09, respectively, the implied rates of return are approximately .43, .43, .08, .31, .04, and .44, respectively (taking α as .1 for industries 1 and 2, .05 for industries 3, 4, and 5, and .04 for industry 6). Thus, except for industries 3 and 5, the resulting estimates of the private rates of return to total R&D are on the order of 30 to 40%. These estimates are larger than, but not inconsistent with, those presented in table 3.7, based on an entirely different dependent variable (GRR). There, too, the two industries with the largest federal involvement in the financing of R&D (3. electrical equipment and 5. aircraft and missiles) yield the lowest rate-of-return estimates.[13]

13. In general these estimates are of the same order of magnitude as those reported by Griliches (1973a) and Terleckyj (1974) based on regressions of productivity growth on R&D investment ratios for aggregate interindustry data in the U.S. The first study, based on eighty-five manufactur-

It is interesting to note that we have stumbled on this impact of federally financed R&D in the interpretation of our results rather than in the econometric analysis itself. In our regressions we were unable to discover any direct evidence of the superiority of company-financed R&D as against federally financed R&D in affecting the growth in productivity. It may well be the case that within any company a dollar is a dollar, irrespective of the source of financing, but that in these two specific industries the externalities created by the large federally financed R&D investments and the constraints on the appropriability of the results of research that may have been associated with such investments have driven down the realized private rate of return from R&D significantly below its prevailing rate in other industries.[14]

In general, this paper can be viewed as another link in a chain of a rather limited number of investigations supporting the argument that R&D investments have yielded a rather high rate of return in the recent past. In addition, we find no evidence for, and some evidence against, the notion that larger firms either have a higher propensity to invest in R&D or are more effective in deriving benefits from it.

There is little point in reiterating the various reservations outlined earlier. Some of the difficulties are inherent in the attempt to measure and discuss "research" and "productivity" as if they were clear and unequivocal concepts. But many of the problems, particularly those dealing with timing effects, spillovers, and externalities, could yield to more data and better data analysis. It would be very useful to have more detail on the firms at hand, especially information on the distribution of their research expenditures, on other measures of research output such as patents granted and papers published, on income received from royalties, and on money spent on advertising. All of this is feasible; it requires "only" the additional matching of IRS, SEC, and Patent Office and scientific abstracting services data bases. It would also help to know, for

---

ing industries, yielded estimates of 32 to 40% for the rate of return to R&D. The second study, based on twenty manufacturing industries, yielded an estimated rate of return of 37% to company-financed R&D and essentially zero to federally financed R&D. Both studies were based on R&D data for 1958 only. While the results reported above are of the same order of magnitude, I have not been able to replicate this type of equation on these data and get coefficients of the same order of magnitude. The best equation for the combined sample was

$$BPT = .135\,AR/V - .042\,K/V + \text{(constant, } \Gamma\text{'s, Age } C, D); \qquad R^2 = .089$$

$$(.028) \qquad\qquad (.008) \qquad\qquad\qquad\qquad S.E. = .058\,,$$

implying a rate of return of about a half of that discussed above and a depreciation rate of 31%, if it were to be believed. Besides pointing to the difference in time periods and the use of aggregate versus micro data, I do not have a satisfactory way of reconciling these results at the moment.

14. This may explain why the aggregate studies cited in the previous footnote found much higher returns to company-financed R&D investments relative to federally financed ones than we did. Another way of looking at it is that in industries with a high rate of federally financed R&D expenditures the rate of depreciation (obsolescence) of the previously accumulated R&D capital is much higher. Again, this would be a difference which wouldn't be observed at the firm level. It is external to the firm but internal to the industry.

tracing out and following up potential externalities, more about the exact industrial structure of individual firms and their product mix. Finally, it should be relatively easy and quite useful to extend this study, as is, to the 1966–74 period. Such an extension would be particularly interesting since it would allow us to observe a period during which R&D growth largely came to an end for many firms (at least in real terms). Besides helping us to find out something about the structure of lags and the rate of depreciation in such data, it would also, for the first time, break sharply the confounding collinearity between growth in R&D and the growth that occurred in almost all of the other economic variables during the 1956–65 period.

Even without new data, we have not yet exhausted what can be learned from the data at hand. Additional analysis of the data on the number of scientists and engineers as against R&D dollar totals should prove illuminating. This distinction between federally and company-financed R&D has not really been explored in depth yet. Finally, a detailed comparison of the individual industry results with industry aggregates, focusing on the potential externalities (external to the firm but internal to the industry), is required before any strong conclusion could be drawn about *social* rates of return from our estimates of *private* rates of return to R&D.

Appendix A

Table 3A.1   Variables in the R&D Study (Total N = 883)

Variable			Overall Sample	
Number	Name	Definition	Mean (approximate)	Standard Deviation
1	ID1	Industry dummy: Chemicals and petroleum SIC 28, 29, 13	$N = 110$	
2	ID2	Metals and machinery SIC 34, 35	$N = 187$	
3	ID3	Electrical equipment and communication SIC 36, 43	$N = 102$	
4	ID4	Motor vehicles and transportation SIC 371, 373–9	$N = 34$	
5	ID5	Aircraft and missiles SIC 372, 19	$N = 31$	
6	AGE C	(gross fixed assets − net fixed assets) divided by gross fixed assets (in 1963)	.5	.105

Table 3A.1 (continued)

Variable			Overall Sample	
Number	Name	Definition	Mean (approximate)	Standard Deviation
7	D	Depreciation ratio: Depreciation charged in 1963 divided by gross fixed assets in 1963	.06	.028
8	D/V	Depreciation to value-added ratio, 1963	.06	.057
9	C3	Total domestic assets, 1963	260×10^6	766×10^6
10	S57	Sales in 1957	200×10^6	62×10^6
11	M	Ratio of employment in manufacturing establishments to total company employment	.80	.17
12	ALSS	Average share of total payroll in sales (average of the ratios for 1958 and 1963)	.30	.11
13	ALSV	Average share of labor in value added (average of payroll to value added for 1958 and 1963)	.50	.16
14	AV/S	Average ratio of value added to sales (1958 and 1963)	.50	.16
15	AI/V	Average ratio of investment (total capital expenditures) to value added (1958 and 1963)	.07	.07
16	VA63	Value added in 1963	120×10^6	361×10^6
17	SCE58	Average number of employees per establishment in 1958	350	751
18	SPR63	1963 company industry (five-digit) specialization ratio	60	27
19	GRR	Gross rate of return in 1963: Value added minus total manufacturing payroll minus equipment rentals divided by gross domestic assets	.26	.20
20	NRR	"Net" rate of return: Value added minus manufacturing payroll, minus equipment rentals, minus depreciation, divided by net *fixed* assets plus inventories	.50	.62
21	LGS63	Log total sales in 1963	10.00	1.20
22	LGS57	Log total sales in 1957	10.00	1.29
23	K62	Cumulated total R&D expenditures, 1957–62	50×10^6	272×10^6
24	FP62	Fraction private 62: Cumulated company R&D expenditures 1957–62 divided by K62	.90	.23
25	FP65	Fraction private 65: Cumulated company R&D expenditures 1957–65, divided by K65	.90	.23

(continued)

Table 3A.1 (continued)

| Variable | | | Overall Sample | |
Number	Name	Definition	Mean (approximate)	Standard Deviation
26	AR/V	Average R&D to value-added ratio, 1957 and 1963	.05	.14
27	K/V	Cumulated R&D in 1962 to value-added in 1963 ratio	.26	.51
28	AR/S	Average (1957 and 1962) R&D to sales ratio	.03	.09
29	SE/E	Average (1957 and 1962) scientists and engineers to total employment ratio	.02	.04
30	CAR/V	Company R&D to value-added ratio 1957 and 1962 average	.03	.09

Rates of growth (b's), computed from regressions of log $y = a + bt$, for the period 1957–65

31	BS	Rate of growth of sales	.06	.074
32	BE	Rate of growth of employment	.023	.065
33	BSE	Rate of growth of scientists and engineers employment	.05	.14
34	BTRD	Rate of growth of total R&D	.08	.15
35	BCRD	Rate of growth of company R&D	.08	.16
36	SBS	Standard error of estimate rate of growth of sales	.014	.015
37	SBTRD	Standard error of estimate rate of growth of total R&D	.035	.038
38	R/V57	Total R&D to value-added ratio, 1957	.05	.21
39	LTRD57	Log total R&D, 1957	6.0	2.25
40	LCRD57	Log company R&D, 1957	6.0	2.13
41	BPT	Partial productivity growth 1957–65: BS − ALSS × BE	.05	.06
42	DNI	Dummy variable 1 if no imputations in the data, zero otherwise	.6	
43	LGE63	Log total employment, 1963	8.0	1.04
44	E57	Total employment, 1957	9,000	26,358
45	LGC1	Log gross fixed assets 1963	10.00	1.48
46	LGC2	Log capital services in 1963; capital services: Depreciation and rentals and 8% of net fixed assets and inventories	8.00	1.32
47	LGEM63	Log manufacturing employment, 1963	8.00	1.04
48	LGFM57	Log manufacturing employment, 1957	8.00	1.12
49	LGW58	Log average "wage" in 1958 (wage = payroll per employee)	1.6	.20

Table 3A.1   (continued)

Variable			Overall Sample	
Number	Name	Definition	Mean (approximate)	Standard Deviation
50	LGW63	Log wage rate in 1963	1.8	.20
51	LGVA63	Log value added in 1963	10.00	1.15
52	LGSCE63	Log average scale of establishments in 1963	5.00	1.0
53	LGANSE	Log average number of scientists and engineers, 1957–62	3.5	1.90
54	LGK62	Log cumulated R&D through 1962	8.0	2.1
55	LGK65	Log cumulated R&D through 1965	9.0	2.0
56	LGFP62	Log 1962 cumulated company R&D as a fraction of total cumulated R&D	−.18	.57
57	T63	Log absolute total factor productivity level in 1963: LGVA63 − ALSV × LGEM63 − (1 − ALSV) LGC2	2.0	.34
58	GVA	Growth in value added, 1957–63: (LGVA63 − LGVA57)/6	.06	.074
59	GPT	Growth in partial productivity 1957–63: [GVA − ALSV × (LGEM63 − LGEM57)]/6	.05	.058
60	GSCE	Growth in average scale of establishments: (LGSCE63 − LGSCE58)/5	−.02	.09

Note: Industry group 6 is "All others," $N = 419$. All dollar figures are in thousands. Additional variables constructed from the above set:

K/SC	= 54 − 53, log of cumulated R&D per scientist
LGCK	= 56 + 54, log of cumulated company-financed R&D, 1962
K/C	= 54 − 45, log of the cumulated R&D to fixed capital ratio
LGVA57	= 51 − 6 × 58, log of value added, 1957
ALVA	= 51 − 3 × 58, average of log value added in 1957 and 1963

Value added in 1957 estimated by extrapolating value added in 1958 using the percentage change in sales between 1957 and 1958.

Appendix B
Criteria Used for Inclusion of a Company in the Griliches-NSF-Census Bureau Project

1. Only companies with 1,000 or more employees in one or more years and filing annual reports on Research and Development (Form RD-1 or RD-2) were included. The list was further limited to companies classified in manufac-

turing, Petroleum (SIC 13), and Communications (SIC 48). This is the area included under the term "manufacturing" in the Annual Survey of Research and Development in Industry conducted by the Census Bureau for the National Science Foundation.

2. Subsequently, in the final tabulations, only those companies for which we had R&D reports for four or more years during the period 1957–65 were retained.

3. All companies included were matched to the 1963 and 1958 Enterprise Statistics data. Company data in the Griliches-NSF-Census study are combined and classified according to the 1963 enterprise company composition and industry code. A few R&D companies of relatively small size, not matched to the enterprise lists, were dropped.[15]

4. During the search and edit routine, all cases outside four standard deviations of the various tests were rechecked by clerical and professional staff. A few small cases that could not be explained were dropped from the project.

Appendix C

Memorandum to Mr. Owen
23 November 1971
Attachment C

Imputation and Estimation Methods for Griliches-NSF-Census Project

1. Imputation of R&D data. Our primary data file contained nine years of data, 1957 through 1965, for five items reported in R&D surveys: sales, employment, employment of scientists and engineers assigned to R&D work, total R&D expenditures, and federal R&D expenditures. For each company in the survey, for each of these items, we imputed zero values as follows:

Let X represent year with a value of 80 for 1957, 90 for 1958, etc.

Let Y represent one of the R&D variables.

15. Comments on the R&D-Enterprise match: The 1958 enterprise data were placed in the 1963 format. Mergers and acquisitions during the period were reflected by the addition of two or more 1958 enterprise records to equal one 1963 enterprise record. No case came to light where a single 1958 record represented two or more 1963 records. According to the R&D survey instruction, respondents should report for the entire company. However, the results of the instructions have weaknesses that are avoided in the enterprise statistics (1958 and 1963) by a match to lists of related employer identification numbers and associated employment data. The R&D-enterprise match served to update the R&D company composition data, and to establish changes in broad industry classes, based upon Census company industry codes developed in the processing of the economic census data.
Since any four years of R&D data were sufficient to include a company, it was possible for a company with no R&D reported in 1958 or 1963 to be included in the sample. A few such cases did turn up in the development of the matched R&D-enterprise data.

For each nonzero Y, we cumulated N, ΣX, ΣY, ΣX^2, and ΣXY.

Then, $A = \Sigma Y/N$ and $B = (N\Sigma XY - \Sigma X\Sigma Y)/(N\Sigma X^2 - (\Sigma X)^2)$.

Each zero value of Y was imputed from its matching year value by $Y = A + B(X - \bar{X})$; and each imputed value was flagged.
Negative imputed values were set to zero.

This is a straight-line imputation procedure; its effects were partially as follows:

a) items totally not reported were left at zero and flagged as imputed;

b) items reported in only one year had that value imputed for all years.

2. Estimation of regression variables.

a) Federal R&D values were reset to zero if imputed and any federal R&D greater than total R&D was set equal to the total R&D value.

b) In the following description the numbers in parentheses refer to field positions in the primary data record, Attachment A. The variable abbreviation follows Griliches's document of 13 May 1971 as amended by notes of meetings and other conversations. Only those variables whose derivation is not direct from the Griliches definition are described below. In all cases not explicitly covered below, the calculation of a ratio with a zero value for numerator or denominator would result in a zero value for the ratio.

   i. If $(50) = 0$, Age $C = 0$.

   ii. If R&D sales for 1957 and 1958 were not reported or 0, S57 = (21) and V57 = (39); i.e., no 1957 to 1958 ratio adjustment.

   iii. If R&D employment for 1957 or 1958 was not reported or 0, EM57 = (29) × M; i.e., no 57 to 58 adjustment.

   iv. For ALSS, ALSV, AV/S, and AI/V, which require an averaging of two ratios, if either ratio was zero, the other ratio is used and not averaged. If both ratios were 0, the variable would be zero and the case listed.

   v. For AR/V, CAR/V, and R/V, which require averaging of a ratio involving a 1962 R&D item and a ratio involving a 1957 R&D item, if the 1962 data were missing, we used 1961; if that was also missing we used 1960; and, similarly, for 1957 we substituted 1958 and 1959. If all three early years were missing, the resulting zero ratio would have been averaged.

   vi. For AR/S and SE/E, which require an averaging of a ratio of two 1962 R&D items and a ratio of two 1957 R&D items, if either 1962 item were missing we would use 1963, if 1963 were missing we would use 1964, and if both of these were missing we would set that ratio to zero; similarly, we would substitute 1958 and 1959 for 1957. If both ratios were zero, the case would be listed.

   vii. Growth rates and standard errors of the growth rates for the following R&D variables were computed: sales, employment, scientists and engineers employment, total R&D expenditures, and company R&D expenditures. For each variable, for the nine-year period, we let X represent year with a value of 1 through 9, and Y represent the log of the variable for nonzero values. For nonzero values of Y we obtained the following counts and sums: N, $\sum X$, $\sum Y$, $\sum X^2$, $\sum Y^2$, $\sum XY$. If N was less than 4 we set the growth rate and the standard error of the growth rate to zero, and set a dummy variable to one; otherwise

the dummy variable $= 0$;

the growth rate,

$$b = (N\sum XY - \sum X \sum Y)/[N\sum X^2 - (\sum X)^2],$$

and the standard error of the growth rate

$$= \text{SQRT} ([N\sum Y^3 - (\sum Y)^2 - b(N\sum XY - \sum X \sum Y)]/$$
$$\{(N - 2)[N\sum X^3 - (\sum X)^2]\}).$$

viii. If BS or BE could not be calculated, BPT $= 0$.

ix. The log of a variable with a value of zero would be set to zero.

References

Evenson, R. 1968. The contribution of agricultural research and extension to agricultural production. Ph.D. diss., University of Chicago.

Fisher, F. M., and Temin, P. 1973. Returns to scale in research and development: what does the Schumpeterian hypothesis imply? *Journal of Political Economy* 81:56–70.

Griliches, Z. 1964. Research expenditures, education, and the aggregate agricultural production function. *American Economic Review* 54:961–74.

———. 1973a. Research expenditures and growth accounting. In B. R. Williams, ed., *Science and technology in economic growth*, pp. 59–95. London: Macmillan.

———. 1973b. Productivity and research. In National Commission on Productivity, *Conference on an agenda for economic research on productivity*. Washington: Government Printing Office.

Kendrick, J. W. 1976. *The formation and stocks of total capital*. National Bureau of Economic Research, General Series 100. New York: Columbia University Press.

Mansfield, E. 1965. Rates of return from industrial research and development. *American Economic Review* 55:310–22.

———. 1967. *Econometric studies of industrial research and technological innovation*. New York: W. W. Norton.

———. 1972. The contribution of research and development to economic growth in the United States. In National Science Foundation, *R&D and economic growth productivity*, NSF 72–303. Washington: Government Printing Office.

Minasian, Jora R. 1962. The economics of research and development. In National Bureau of Economic Research, *The rate and direction of inventive activity.* Princeton: Princeton University Press.

———. 1969. Research and development, production functions, and rates of return. *American Economic Review* 59 (Proceedings issue): 80–85.

National Science Foundation. 1959. *Methodology of statistics on research and development,* NSF 59–36. Washington: Government Printing Office.

———. 1970a. *Research and development in industry, 1968,* NSF 70–29. Washington: Government Printing Office.

———. 1970b. *National Patterns of R&D Resources, 1953–71,* NSF 70–44. Washington: Government Printing Office.

Nordhaus, W. 1969. *Invention, growth, and welfare: a theoretical treatment of technological change.* Cambridge: MIT Press.

Telser, L. 1972. *Competition, collusion and game theory.* Chicago: Aldine-Atherton.

Terleckyj, N. E. 1960. Sources of productivity advance. Ph.D. diss., Columbia University.

———. 1974. *Effects of R&D on the productivity growth of industries: an exploratory study.* Washington: National Planning Association.

Wagner, L. U. 1968. Problems in estimating research and development investment and stock. In ASA, *1968 Proceedings of the business and economic statistics section,* pp. 189–97. Washington: ASA.

4   Productivity, R&D, and Basic Research at the Firm Level in the 1970s

This paper reports new results on the relationship of research and development (R&D) expenditures, especially expenditures on basic research, to productivity growth in U.S. manufacturing firms during the 1970s. It is based on a unique data set, the National Science Foundation (NSF) R&D-Census match, containing information on R&D expenditures, sales, employment, and other detail for approximately 1000 largest manufacturing firms from 1957 through 1977. It updates my earlier work (1980) on the precursor of this data set, replicates some of Edwin Mansfield's (1980) work on the contribution of basic research to productivity growth using a larger, more recent, and more representative sample of firms, and complements similar work by myself and J. Mairesse (1983, 1984) based on a publicly accessible but more limited data set.

Two topics are explored in some detail: 1) Is there any evidence of a decline in the returns to industrial R&D expenditures, a decline in their "fecundity" in the 1970s as compared to earlier time periods? 2) Is there evidence that basic research is a relatively more important component of R&D and that there may have been an underinvestment in this component?

A few background facts are worth stressing at this point. In the United States, total R&D expenditures in industry peaked (in real terms) around 1968, dropped slightly in the early 1970s and recovered somewhat in the late 1970s. Relative to total sales, R&D expenditures in industry declined from 4.2 percent in 1968 to a trough of 2.6 percent in 1979 and then recovered to 3.7 percent by 1982. This pattern masks a strong divergence between the trends in federally and privately supported industrial R&D. Federally supported R&D fell

Reprinted from the *American Economic Review* 76, no. 1 (March 1986): 141–54.

I am indebted to NSF Grant no. SES-82-08006 for the support of this work, to Douglas Dobas and Bronwyn H. Hall for making the data gathering effort possible, and to David Body for research assistance. I have also benefited from comments of seminar participants at the NBER and Yale University.

from 2.1 percent of manufacturing sales in 1967 to 0.7 percent in 1979 and has only recently begun to recover, while company-financed R&D stayed essentially constant (relative to industry sales) with almost all of the fluctuation coming from the decline in federal support (NSF, 1983; 1984). During the same period, the economy experienced one of the sharpest and most prolonged recessions of the postwar period and a large and pervasive productivity slowdown. Hardest hit were the primary metals, motor vehicles, and other heavy, energy-related industries. On the whole, these were the less R&D intensive industries, resulting in a largely accidental correlation between R&D intensiveness and the productivity slowdown. (See my 1980b paper and my article with F. Lichtenberg, 1984, for more discussion of these issues.)

The remainder of the paper is organized as follows. First, I describe the data set with its advantages and limitations and present some overall comparative statistics. Second, I outline briefly the framework that underlies the computations to be performed. The results are presented and discussed, and the paper closes with some conclusions, caveats, and suggestions for further research.

4.1   Previous Work and the Current Data Set

The current project is an extension of work originally begun in the mid-1960s. That work was based on the matching of R&D data collected on behalf of the NSF by the Bureau of the Census during 1957–65 with additional company data from the 1958 and 1963 Census of Manufactures and Enterprise Statistics. The universe consisted of large (1000 or more employees) U.S. manufacturing companies performing R&D. The final sample of 883 of such companies accounted for over 90 percent of total sales and R&D expenditures of all firms in this universe.

The main finding of that work (see my 1980a paper) was a rather consistent and positive relationship between various measures of company productivity and its investments in research and development. The Cobb-Douglas-type production functions, estimated on both levels (1963) and rates of growth (1957–65) yielded an elasticity of output with respect to R&D investments of about .07 and an implied average gross excess rate of return of 27 percent (as of 1963), a significantly lower rate of return to federally financed R&D expenditures, and no clear evidence of significant scale effects either in R&D investment policies or the returns from it.

In trying to extend the earlier study to the more recent time period, it became clear that the earlier work could not be simply updated because much of the earlier data was lost and a new data set had to be created instead. The basic objective was to create a matched body of data on most of the large R&D performing corporations in the United States, making it possible to analyze both the determinants and consequences of R&D spending *over time*. For this purpose a time-series record has been created for each company consisting of the major variables in the annual R&D survey for each of the years 1957–77, supplementary R&D information for selected years (1962, 1967, 1972, and 1975), data from the Enterprise Statistics (i.e., company level questionnaires) for 1967, 1972, and 1977, and a few additional items from the Census of Manufactures establishment record summaries for 1967 and 1972. The data set began with all the "certainty" companies in the NSF R&D survey as they existed in 1972. There were approximately 1100 such companies, but a "complete" record is available only for a much smaller number.[1]

Table 4.1 lists the sample size, means, and standard deviation for the major variables as of 1972 and their growth rates from 1966 to 1977. It is intended to describe three aspects of these data: 1) the general characteristics (means and standard deviations) of the sample as of 1972; 2) average rates of growth of the major variables of interest during the 1967–77 period; and 3) how these measures change when the sample is changed to select observations according to the availability of the requisite information.

Turning to the last topic first, note that we tend to lose smaller and more R&D intensive firms as the sample gets more restrictive. The first column of Table 4.1 corresponds to the most liberal criterion: a firm had to exist in 1972 and report positive R&D. Column 2 requires both the ability to compute a growth rate for the 1967–77 period (i.e., at least five good time-series observations) and a successful match to the 1972 Census of Enterprise data (NCK–1). In column 3, I add the requirement of a successful match to the 1977 Census data, while in column 4 the subsample is based on a match with the 1967 and 1972 Census data instead. The major differences occur in the transition from column 1 to column 2 where trying to match to the Census we lose a relatively large number of smaller firms for which there are still data in the R&D survey files. The firms that can be also found in the 1977 Census are slightly larger and have had a somewhat higher rate of growth in employment, R&D, and productivity. The firms that also existed in 1967 are even larger but have on average grown somewhat more slowly than those that existed in the 1972–77 period. If we look at two of the major variables of interest, partial productivity growth and the ratio of basic to total R&D, there is almost no difference in their means across the relevant columns (2, 3, and 4), and hence it is unlikely that subsequent conclusions will be subject to a serious sample selection bias. I will, therefore, ignore this topic here.

Looking at the levels of the variables in 1972, we see that the average firm in the sample is quite large (5000+ employees), employs close to one hundred R&D scientists and engineers, and is making only a relatively modest invest-

---

1. The universe of this data match consists of all "certainty" cases in the 1972 R&D survey; i.e., the basic definition is the population of companies as they existed in 1972 (as against 1962 in the earlier study) and the requirement of "certainty" assures that the Census Bureau tried to collect consistent data for these firms for more than one year. The "certainty" cases correspond closely to the earlier restriction to companies with 1000 or more employees, though it is a bit more inclusive. See my paper with Bronwyn Hall (1982) and Hall (1984) for more detail on sample definition and variable construction.

Table 4.1 **Major Variables in 1972 and 1966–77 Growth Rates by Subsample: Means and Standard Deviations[a]**

	Data Set, Selection Criteria, and Sample Size			
Variable	1972 R&D Survey Universe (N = 1105) (1)	1966–77 Growth Rate Computable and Matched to 1972 Census (N = 652) (2)	(2) and Matched to 1977 Census (N = 491) (3)	(2) and Matched to 1967 Census (N = 386) (4)
A. Levels in 1972				
Sales in Million Dollars	146	205	223	236
	(1.61)	(1.43)	(1.40)	(1.44)
Total Employment	4038	5570	6212	6698
	(1.48)	(1.27)	(1.30)	(1.31)
R&D Scientists and	89	74	82	106
Engineers	(1.66)	(1.70)	(1.71)	(1.72)
R&D in Million Dollars	2.3	3.0	3.4	4.3
	(1.74)	(1.78)	(1.77)	(1.83)
R&D to Sales Ratio (RS)	.051	.033	.032	.035
	(.131)	(.064)	(.051)	(.048)
Company R&D/Sales	.028	.022	.023	.025
Ratio (CRS)	(.069)	(.026)	(.026)	(.026)
Basic to Total R&D	.025	.026	.026	.027
Ratio (BR)	(.074)	(.071)	(.075)	(.073)
Value-Added, Million		100	113	121
Dollars		(1.32)	(1.31)	(1.34)
Gross Fixed Assets		115	124	147
Million Dollars		(1.67)	(1.59)	(1.65)
B. Growth Rates 1966–77				
Employment Growth		.012	.015	.006
		(.046)	(.041)	(.040)
Partial Productivity		.025	.026	.025
Growth (BPT)		(.036)	(.034)	(.035)
Total R&D Growth,		−.001	.003	−.007
Deflated (BTRD)		(.079)	(.074)	(.070)
Scientists and Engineers		.008	.012	.004
Growth		(.087)	(.084)	(.078)
Company R&D Growth,		.004	.008	−.000
Deflated (BCRD)		(.081)	(.076)	(.071)

Notes: Col. 1: "Certainty" firms in the NSF R&D Survey with positive R&D in 1972; Col. 2: Growth rates for 1966–77 computable (at least 5 years of good data on sales, employment, and R&D) and a successful match to the 1972 Enterprise Census (NCK–1); Col. 3: (2) and a successful match to the 1977 Census (NCK–1); Col. 4: (2) and a successful match to the 1967 Census and growth rates computable for 1957–65; Partial productivity growth = deflated sales growth − (share of labor compensation in total sales) × growth in employment; Sales deflated by NIPA based output price indexes at the 2–3 digit SIC level. R&D deflator based on the methodology suggested by Jaffe (NSF 1972), from my 1984 comment. Geometric means and standard deviations (shown in parentheses) of the logarithms (approximate coefficient of variation) except for growth rates or ratios.

ment of its own money (about 2.5 percent of sales) in R&D, with very little of that, less than 3 percent, being devoted to basic R&D. This picture is somewhat misleading, however. The actual distribution of firms is quite skewed, with a small number of larger firms spending much larger amounts on both total and basic R&D. Looking at growth rates one can observe that on average these firms grew only moderately during this period: about 1 percent per year in total employment, about 2.5 percent per year in partial productivity, and almost zero growth in deflated R&D expenditures (though a slightly positive rate of growth in the number of R&D scientists and engineers). Here again, while on average there is little movement, there is a great deal of variability at the individual firm level. The standard deviations of the rates of growth of partial productivity and total R&D are 3.5 and 8 percent per annum, respectively, with many firms growing much faster (and also much slower) than the average.

Looking at some of the R&D ratios over time, not reported in Table 4.1, one cannot see any significant decline in the rate of private investment in R&D. While the total R&D to sales ratio falls from .042 in 1962 to .035 in 1972 and again from .032 in 1972 to .029 in 1977 for firms in subsamples 4 and 3, respectively, the company-financed R&D to sales ratios (*CRS*) are essentially unchanged (.025 in 1962 and 1972 in subsample 4 and .023 in 1972 and 1977 in subsample 3). On the other hand, while the basic research ratio (*BR*) fell only modestly from .033 to .031 between 1962 and 1972, and from .027 to .023 between 1972 and 1977, coupled with the decline in the overall total R&D to sales ratio, this implies about a 40 percent reduction in the relative intensity of industrial investment in basic research, relative to industry sales. Almost all of this decline came from the overall decline in federally financed R&D which declined from about 55 percent of total R&D in industry in 1965 to about 35 percent in 1982. The federal government financed about 32 percent of all basic research in industry in 1967 but only 19 percent in 1982 (see NSF, 1983 and 1984). The reduction was so steep that basic research in industry declined not only relatively (to sales) but also absolutely, from a peak of $813 million in 1966 (in 1977 dollars) to a trough of $581 million in 1975 and did not surpass the 1960s levels until the early 1980s. How one interprets the consequences of such a decline depends on one's view of the relative productivity of governmentally financed R&D expenditures in industry, a topic I will be exploring below.

4.2   The Analytical Framework and Econometric Results

The work reported here focuses primarily on the analysis of productivity growth for these companies, using a rather simple Cobb-Douglas production function approach:

(1) $$Q_t = Ae^{\lambda t}K_t^{\alpha}C_t^{\beta}L_t^{1-\beta},$$

where Q is output (sales, or value-added), C and L are measures of capital and labor input, respectively, $K = \sum_i w_i R_{t-i}$ is a measure of the accumulated and still productive research capital ("knowledge"), R_t measures the real (deflated) gross investment in research in period t, and the w_i's connect the levels of past research to the current state of knowledge. In addition, λ measures the rate of disembodied "external" technical change (where t is time in years), A is a constant, and constant returns to scale have been assumed with respect to the conventional inputs (C and L).

A number of serious difficulties arise when one turns to the operational construction of the various variables (see my 1979 article for more detailed discussion). Perhaps the two most important problems are the measurement of output (Q) in a research-intensive industry (where quality changes may be rampant), and the construction of the unobservable research capital measure (K). Turning to the second problem first, note that $K_t = \sum_i w_i R_{t-i}$ can be thought of as a measure of the distributed lag effect of past research investments on productivity. There are at least three forces at work here: the lag between investment in research and the actual invention of a new technique or product; the lag between invention and the development and complete market acceptance of the new product; and its disappearance from the currently utilized stock of knowledge due to changes in external circumstances and the development of superior techniques or products by competitors (depreciation and obsolescence). There is some scattered evidence, based largely on questionnaire studies, that such lags are rather short in industry, where most of research expenditures are spent on development and applied topics, and where the private returns from R&D become obsolete much faster due to the erosion of a firm's specific monopoly position (Ariel Pakes and M. Schankerman, 1984).

While my models are written as if the main point of research expenditures is to increase the physical productivity of the firm's production process, most of the actual research in industry is devoted to the development of new products or processes to be sold and used outside the firm in question. Assuming that, on average, the outside world pays for these products what they are worth to it, using sales or value-added as the dependent variable does, in fact, capture the private returns to such research endeavours. However, the observed private returns may underestimate the social returns because, given the competitive structure of the particular industry, the firm is unlikely to appropriate all of these returns. On the other hand, part of the increase in the revenues of a particular firm may come at the expense of other firms, or from changes in the market power induced by the success of its research program. I cannot say much about the net impact of such forces on the basis of the data at hand. This would require a detailed comparison of the individual firm results with estimates based on industry and economy-wide returns to research, a topic beyond the scope of this project. But since expected private returns are a determinant of private investment flows into this activity, they are of some interest even if one cannot answer the social returns question unequivocally.

This framework can be extended to ask whether different types of R&D (private vs. federal, or basic vs. applied) are equally "potent" in generating productivity growth. One way of answering this question is to look at the "mix" of R&D expenditures and ask if it matters for the question at hand. Let there be two types of R&D expenditures, R_1 and R_2, and let us assume that the overall analysis is in terms of the logarithm of total R&D expenditures but that we believe that R_2 should have been weighted more, given a δ premium (or discount). That is, the right variable is

$$(2) \qquad R^* = R_1 + (1 + \delta)R_2 = R(1 + \delta s),$$

where $s = R_2/R$ is the "share" of R_2 in total $R = R_1 + R_2$. Then the $\alpha \log R^*$ term can be approximated by $\alpha \log R^* \simeq \alpha \log R + \alpha\delta s$. The sign and significance of the mix term s will give us some clue about the size and magnitude of the δ term.

A similar argument can be made also in the context of a growth-rate formulation. Let lower case letters denote growth rates. Then $r = (1 - s)r_1 + sr_2$ while $r^* = (1 - s)r_1 + (1 + \delta)sr_2$. If, as is mostly the case in our data, the growth rates of r_1 and r_2 are roughly equal, then $r^* = r(1 + \delta s)$, and again, the coefficient of the mix term s provides us with some information about the "premium" or "discount" on R_2 since αr^* can be approximated by

$$(3) \qquad \alpha r^* \simeq (\alpha + \delta\bar{s})r + (\alpha\bar{r}\delta)s .$$

Given the peculiarities of my data set—its unbalanced nature (many missing observations towards the beginning and end of the period), the availability of capital and value-added only for Census years, the desire to preserve comparability with the earlier study, and the difficulty of doing elaborate programming inside the Census Bureau, I focus primarily on two major dimensions of the data: levels (in 1967, 1972, and 1977) and growth rates, and eschew any attempt at a complete annual data analysis. The annual data are summarized by computing average growth rates for two subperiods 1957–65 (corresponding to the earlier study period) and 1966–77, based on regressions of the logarithms of the relevant variables on time trends (solving thereby the missing years problem within each of these subperiods).

In implementing such a framework of analysis one has to deal with several serious data problems: missing data, erroneous data and possible erroneous matches, and mergers. Except for R&D data, no special effort was made to replace missing values by various imputation procedures. It was my notion that the basic data set represents what the Census did collect, what we actually know, and that any imputation procedure should be done only in the context of a particular research project where its implications for the final analysis could be interpreted. As far as the R&D data are concerned, the Census used the shuttle nature of the original questionnaires to fill in many of the original blanks. To the extent that there remain missing values which are not due to the fact that the whole company is missing before or after some date, they were interpolated on the basis of the estimated growth rates (which require at least five good data points within each subperiod). For other variables, missing values were not imputed. It was not possible, within the constraints of this project, to develop optimal imputation procedures. This would have required several repeated passes at the original numbers. Instead, the analysis is based either on reduced "clean" samples or on "pairwise present" correlation coefficient matrices.

From an econometric point of view, we have to deal with the problem of firm effects (or firm-specific left-out variables) and the possibility that the relationships being estimated may not stay constant either across firms or across time. The first is handled by analyzing first differences or growth rates, transformations that eliminate any unchanging effects from the data. The second problem, the problem of differences across firms, is handled in part by calculating a measure of "partial" productivity growth $[BPT = y - (1 - \hat{\beta})l]$, using individual firm data on the share of labor in total costs. One can also estimate separate and different parameters for the various industry groupings and include some of the other variables available in the record which might distinguish one firm's environment and response pattern from another's (such as its specialization ratio, size, or vertical integration). The main hypothesis under investigation, that the returns to R&D investments may have declined over time, is tested both by comparing estimates based on the more recent data with the earlier results, and by allowing and testing for systematic changes in the estimated relationships between the three available cross sections.

Let us look now at the first set of substantive results. Table 4.2 reports the results of estimating cross-sectional production functions (equation (1)) separately for each Census year, adding to the standard capital and labor variables a measure of total R&D capital accumulated by the firm and two R&D mix variables: the fraction of total R&D that was spent on basic research and the fraction of accumulated R&D that had been financed privately. All the reported estimates allow for 18 to 20 (depending on the subsample) separate industry intercepts. Columns 1 and 3 report estimates that are based on the same number of firms and use the same dependent variables, differing only by the year of observation. Column 2 presents additional estimates for 1972 based on different sample and dependent variable definitions with the main intent being to show that the major conclusions are insensitive to such differences. There are three major points to be made about these estimates. The first is that the stock of R&D capital contributes significantly to the explanation of cross-sectional differences in productivity and there is little evidence of a decline in its coefficient over time.[2] There is a minor rise in the estimated coefficient from 1967

---

2. Here and subsequently, all statements about statistical "significance" should not be taken literally. Besides the usual issue of data mining clouding their interpretation, the "samples" analyzed come close to covering completely the relevant population. Tests of significance are used

Table 4.2   NSF-Census Study: Cross-Sectional Production Functions, Log Value-Added
                   Dependent Variable[a] U.S. Firms: 1967, 1972, 1977

Variables	(1)		(2)		(3)[b]	
	1967	1972	1972	1972	1972	1977
ln Employment	.604	.622	.623	.586	.578	.611
	(.045)	(.046)	(.035)	(.038)	(.038)	(.039)
ln Capital Services	.224	.199	.161	.234	.254	.291
	(.041)	(.044)	(.032)	(.036)	(.036)	(.035)
ln R&D Stock (db)	.113	.135	.165	.126	.115	.089
	(.023)	(.026)	(.019)	(.019)	(.018)	(.017)
Basic Research (BR)	.396	.340	.274	.499	.517	.401
	(.240)	(.261)	(.215)	(.191)	(.189)	(.189)
Company-Financed	.190	.247	.068	.133	.138	.044
Research (FP)	(.097)	(.106)	(.100)	(.088)	(.088)	(.084)
N	386	386	652	491	491	491
SEE	.312	.336	.390	.312	.309	.290

Notes: ln Employment = log (total employment − employment of scientists and engineers); ln Capital
Services = log of (depreciation plus interest on net assets plus machinery and equipment rentals); ln R&D
Stock (db) = log of the "stock" of total R&D expenditures based on a 15 percent per year declining
balance depreciation assumption; BR = basic research as a fraction of total R&D; 1972 in the 1977
equation, 1967 in 1967 and 1972. FP = fraction of R&D stock "private," company-financed R&D stock
as a ratio to the total R&D stock, as of *t*. All equations include also a constant term and industry dummies.
The number of industry dummies used depends on the data set and varies between 18 and 20. Standard
errors are shown in parentheses.

[a] Value-added and materials used in research in 1967 and 1972.

[b] Value-added only.

to 1972 and a somewhat larger but not really significant decline from 1972 to
1977. Given this particular measure of R&D capital, based on a 15 percent per
year declining balance depreciation formula (the results are insensitive to the
particular formula used), the implied average (at the geometric mean of the
sample) gross rate of return to R&D investment rises in a similar fashion from
.51 in 1967 to .62 in 1972 (in col. 1) and falls from .39 in 1972 to .33 in 1977
(in col. 3). In either case the estimated rate of return is quite high and there
does not appear to be any dramatic fall in it over time.

The second major finding is the significance and rather large size of the
basic research coefficient. It seems to be the case that firms that spend a larger
fraction of their R&D on basic research are more productive, have a higher
level of output relative to their other measured inputs, including R&D capital,
and that this effect has been relatively constant over time. If anything, it has
risen rather than fallen over time. Using the formulation of equation (2) implies
a very high premium on basic versus the rest, a $\hat{\delta}$ of between 2.5 to 4.5, a

here as a metric for discussing the relative fit of different versions of the model. In each case, the
actual magnitude of the estimated coefficients is of more interest than their precise "statistical significance."

several hundred percent premium on basic research. Before I explore the implications of this result, I want to examine other dimensions of these data and see whether similar effects can be observed there too.

The last major result of interest is the significant positive coefficient on the privately vs. federally financed R&D mix variable. This variable is of most import for the older more established firms in subsample 4 (Table 4.1) but its sign is consistent throughout, indicating a positive premium on privately financed R&D, or equivalently a discount as far as federally financed expenditures are concerned. Here the implied premium is smaller, between 50 and 180 percent, but still quite large.

All the above results were based on cross-sectional level regressions that are subject to a variety of biases, the main one being the possibility that "rich" successful firms are both more productive and can afford to spend more of their own money on such luxuries as R&D and especially the basic variety. One can reduce somewhat the possibility of this type of bias by focusing on firm-growth rates, the changes that occurred, rather than on their levels. To the extent that firms have idiosyncratic productivity coefficients that may be also correlated with their accumulated R&D levels, considering growth rates is equivalent to doing a "within" firms analysis, one that eliminates such fixed effects from the analysis. The next two tables present, therefore, the results of analyzing the growth in the partial productivity of these same firms during the whole 1966–77 period.

Table 4.3 presents the results of estimating partial productivity equations in

Table 4.3		Growth Rate of Partial Productivity, 1966–77			
				$N = 652$	
Variables		$N = 911$		(with industry dummies)	
Constant	.019	.009	.012	—	—
BTRD 6677	.107		.117	.119	
	(.014)		(.017)	(.016)	
BCRD 6677		.095			.106
		(.014)			(.015)
BR72	.056	.056	.059	.035	.034
	(.017)	(.017)	(.019)	(.018)	(.018)
FP72	.011	.019	.017	.022	.030
	(.005)	(.005)	(.006)	(.007)	(.007)
SEE	.0383	.0384	.0337	.0305	.0307

Notes: Dependent variable: *BPT* 6677 = trend growth rate of deflated sales minus the trend growth of total employment multiplied by the share of payroll in total sales. *BTRD* = trend growth of deflated total R&D expenditures; *BCRD* = same for company-financed R&D expenditures; *BR* = basic research expenditures as a fraction of total research expenditures; *FP* = ratio of company-financed R&D stock to total; *SEE* = residual standard error. All equations contain also a term reflecting the variance of R&D and terms representing the growth of physical capital: age composition and depreciation as of 1972.

the largest possible sample for which 1966–77 growth rates were computable ($N = 911$) and in the subsample with a successful 1972 Census match. Here again we find my three main results confirmed: the R&D growth term and the two mix variables, the basic research ratio, and the fraction of research financed privately all contribute significantly to the explanation of productivity growth.

On the assumption that the growth rate in the stock of R&D is roughly proportional to the growth in deflated R&D itself, the coefficient of *BTRD* should be estimating the same number as the coefficient of the R&D stock variable in Table 4.2. The results are in fact surprisingly close: about .12 in Table 4.3 as against .09 to .17 in Table 4.2. Moreover, there seems to have been no decline in this coefficient relative to the earlier 1957–65 period. In my previous study (1980a), I estimated the same coefficient to be .073. In the current replication and extension of this sample a similar equation for 1957–65 yields a *BTRD* coefficient of .086. Thus, if anything, the coefficient of R&D went up between the early 1960s and the early 1970s.

The second major finding of interest is the positive and significant basic research coefficient. It is hard to interpret its magnitude since the approximation outlined in equation (3) breaks down when the average growth rate of deflated R&D and of basic R&D is close to zero or negative. Consider, however, the following illustrative calculation. Raising the *BR* ratio by one standard deviation, from .026 to .097 at the mean, would increase the rate of growth of partial productivity by close to half a percent per year ($.071 \times .059 = .0042$). This same increase would raise the growth of total R&D by .107 for one year and would contribute a once-and-for-all increase in the level of productivity of .0125. Discounting the more "permanent" effect of basic research by a real interest rate of .05 yields an "equivalent" one-year effect of .084, or a 7 to 1 ratio in favor of basic research! If one allows for industry dummies which in this formulation represent separate industry trend rates of disembodied technical change, the effect of basic research is cut by about 50 percent, implying perhaps that a significant fraction of the estimated effect comes from spillovers that diffuse throughout the industry. Note that it is the only coefficient that is affected substantively when separate industry dummies are allowed for. Nevertheless, even a 3.2 to 1 ratio is quite high!

The third finding is the significant positive premium on company-financed R&D. Here too the implied premia are quite high, but given that the mix variable is defined in terms of stocks rather than flows, the calculations are more cumbersome. Consider starting from a zero growth position and a .7 ratio of private to total R&D stock. To move this fraction from .7 to .75, one would need to raise the private stock by 29 percent and the overall stock by 20 percent (without reducing absolutely the stock of federally financed R&D capital). There are different possible investment paths that would achieve this goal and would have somewhat different present value consequences. If one roughly doubled the rate of privately financed R&D expenditures, from the previous replacement level of .105 (.7 × .15) to .205, one could achieve this target in slightly over two years. Ignoring discounting, this would lead to a once-and-for-all growth in productivity of .024, due to the growth in the total stock of R&D *and* a .0011 permanent increase in the rate of growth due to the shift of the fraction private ratio from .7 to .75. The present value of this second term is about .022, or of the same order of magnitude as the first term. That is, raising the stock of R&D by 20 percent but shifting it all into the private component doubles the effect of such dollars.

There are problems, however, with such an interpretation. If private R&D expenditures contribute more to productivity growth, one might have thought that when they are substituted for the total R&D growth measure, they might fit better and also have a higher coefficient. But that is not the case as can be seen from the results presented in columns 2 and 5 of Table 4.4. The total R&D measure does a little bit better both in terms of fit and in the overall size of its coefficient, implying that the contribution of federal dollars is not zero. That is perhaps what one should expect. Most of the direct output of federal research dollars is "sold" back to the government at "cost plus" and is unlikely to show up as an increase in the firm's own productivity. Thus all that one could expect to measure here are the within-firm spillover effects of such expenditures. What we may be detecting is that such effects are indeed present and positive, but we should not have expected them to be of the same order of magnitude as would be the case for the firm's own investments in improving its productivity or profitability.

There are a number of econometric questions that can be raised about the robustness and sensitivity of such results. I will discuss only a few of these here. The most obvious question arises from the fact that even though I allowed, in the growth rates version, for separate firm intercepts and different industry trends, I am still assuming common R&D and the conventional capital

Table 4.4   **Growth Rate of Partial Productivity, by Industry, 1966–77 (Matrix 6, Total $N = 991$)**

Coefficients of	Coefficients by the Estimated t-Ratio			
	<-1.5	$-1.5-0$	$0-1.5$	$1.5+$
BTRD		2	7	10:Miscellaneous, Industrial Chemicals, Drugs, Stone & Glass, Machinery, Electronics, Electrical Equipment, Transportation Equipment, Scientific Instruments, Non-Manufacturing
BR72		5	8	6:Wood & Paper, Other Chemicals, Oil, Machinery, Aircraft, Non-Manufacturing
FP72	2	6	7	4:Oil, Rubber, Electronics, Aircraft

Notes: All equations contain also a term reflecting the variance of R&D and terms representing the growth of physical capital: age composition and depreciation as of 1972.

coefficients across rather different industries. This is done from necessity rather than as a virtue. Estimating the same models industry by industry reduces the sample sizes drastically and raises greatly the relative noise level, making it rather hard to interpret the resulting estimates. Nevertheless, these estimates, which are summarized in Table 4.4, are quite consistent with the earlier story: 17 out of the separately estimated 19 coefficients for the R&D growth variable are positive and more than half of them are statistically significant at conventional significance levels. Similarly, the coefficients of the basic research ratio variable are positive in 14 of my 19 industries and significant in over a third of them. The fraction private variable is less robust to the division of the sample into industries, with more than half of the coefficients still positive, but only 4 of them are statistically significant within particular industries. Two of these industries are indeed the ones where one would expect to find such an effect, aircraft and electronics, industries where the bulk of federal monies is spent. Nevertheless, it seems that the effect that is being caught by the fraction private variable has an important industry component, something that had been already noted in my earlier study (1980a), as does also the effect associated with the basic research variable, though to a lesser extent.

A number of other versions were computed using the growth in capital services rather than the depreciation and age composition variables that had been used to keep the results comparable to the earlier study, and the growth in R&D "capital" rather than the flow (and also different definitions of such capital). I also estimated versions using the "intensity" form for the R&D variable, to make it more comparable to other studies in the literature (my paper with Lichtenberg, 1984; Mansfield, 1980; and others).[3] By and large the results of these alternatives were somewhat weaker but not substantively different. Perhaps the most interesting alternative estimate is the intensity version using the growth of capital between 1967 and 1972 as its capital measure:

$$BPT6677 = \ldots.243ACRS + .045ABR + .180DLCS$$

(4)
$$(.069) \qquad (.024) \qquad (.130)$$

$$SEE = .0316$$
(Subsample 4)

where $ACRS$ is the average company R&D to sales ratio, averaged over 1967 and 1972, ABR is a similar average basic to total R&D ratio, and $DLCS$ is the rate of growth in deflated capital services between 1967 and 1972. This version

---

3. The intensity version uses the fact that $\alpha = (\partial Q/\partial K)\, K/Q$ and reexpresses $\alpha \dot{K}/K$ as $\rho[R/Q]$, where $\rho = \partial Q/\partial K$ is the marginal product (gross rate of return) of R&D capital and it has been assumed that $\dot{K} = R - \delta K \simeq R$, i.e., either $\delta \sim 0$ (no depreciation) and/or initial K very small. This formulation has the advantage that it does not impose the assumption of a constant *elasticity* across different firms, replacing it instead by the, possibly more plausible, assumption of the constancy of rate of return.

is closest in form to the equation estimated by Mansfield on much smaller samples. The basic results are similar, however. Basic R&D is a significant contributor to productivity growth with an implied basic to company premium of about 5 to 1 (given an average R&D to sales ratio of .035).

The final set of results to be presented here, in Table 4.5, relate to the relative profitability of our firms in 1972 and 1977. The dependent variable, *GRR*, is the ratio of gross profits (value-added minus labor costs and plus R&D) to total gross fixed assets. The independent variables include the ratio of R&D capital (undepreciated) to total fixed assets and our ubiquitous R&D mix variables: the basic research and fraction private ratios. Even though the dependent variable is quite different, the overall results are rather similar to the earlier ones. The R&D capital variable is positive and almost always statistically significant though its coefficient is a bit low if it is to be interpreted as a rate of return to it. The basic research variable is both large and significant though possibly too large to be credible. Given that the ratio of total R&D capital to total fixed assets is only about .05 on average, the 1972 coefficients imply a δ of about 30 to 60. The fraction private ratio also contributes positively to profitability but its effect largely disappears once industry differences are allowed for. The results for 1977 are weaker than those for 1972, the residual variance is significantly higher, but they too suggest the importance of basic research even in this context.

Table 4.5   **Gross Profit Rate Regressions**
GRR = (Value-Added-Payrolls + R&D)/Gross Assets

| Dependent Variable and Sample Size | Constant | Coefficients of | | | |
		R&D Capital to Total Fixed Assets Ratio	Basic R&D Ratio	Fraction Private	*SEE*
*GRR*72					
N = 652 (a)	.144	.088	.344	.107	.262
	(.049)	(.012)	(.144)	(.048)	
(b)		.060	.187	−.012	.237
		(.013)	(.138)	(.052)	
N = 491 (a)	.117	.080	.514	.154	.264
	(.052)	(.013)	(.139)	(.051)	
(b)		.061	.366	.074	.227
		(.015)	(.138)	(.057)	
*GRR*77					
N = 491 (a)	.341	.031	.402	.033	.313
	(.064)	(.019)	(.187)	(.068)	
(b)		.004	.261	−.028	.292
		(.022)	(.187)	(.077)	

Notes: (a) Regressions do not contain industry dummies; (b) do.

A similar analysis was performed using an estimate of the net rate of return as the dependent variable, subtracting depreciation from the numerator of *GRR* and using a net stock concept for the denominator and also in the definition of the R&D capital variable. While the fit was significantly worse when using this definition of the dependent variable, the overall results were rather similar. The net return version was also available for 1967 and the results using it indicate a relatively constant and significant coefficient for the basic research ratio while the coefficient of the total R&D stock rises from 1967 to 1972 and then falls again in 1977 (from .11 to .16 and down to .06). It is doubtful whether these fluctuations represent real trends or, more likely, reflect the larger noise level in the 1977 data and the changing composition of these samples. In any case, the profitability regressions are consistent with the productivity level and productivity growth rate based results described earlier (Tables 4.2, 4.3, and 4.4).

4.3   Discussion and Summary

There are three major findings in this paper: R&D contributed positively to productivity growth and seems to have earned a relatively high rate of return; basic research appears to be more important as a productivity determinant than other types of R&D; and privately financed R&D expenditures are more effective, at the firm level, than federally financed ones. These findings are not entirely new. The first finding has been documented in a number of earlier studies (see my 1980a,b papers; my article with Mairesse, 1984; A. N. Link, 1981a; and others). What is new in this paper in this regard is a confirmation of this finding on a much larger and more recent data set. It also presents evidence for the view that this effect has not declined significantly in recent years, in spite of the overall slowdown in productivity growth and the general worry about a possible exhaustion of technological opportunities.[4]

The evidence for a "premium" on basic research is much more scarce. The major previous paper suggesting this type of a result is Mansfield (1980), which uses aggregate data for 20 industries for 1948–66 and data for 16 firms during 1960–76, and finds a significant premium on basic research, on the order of 2 to 1 at the industry level and 16 to 1 at the firm level. (See also Link, 1981b, for similar results for 1973–78 based on data for 55 firms.) In this paper I get similar though somewhat smaller effects at the firm level, using a much larger and more representative sample. I also find that differences in levels of

---

4. The finding that the coefficients in a logarithmic regression have not declined over time does not dispose of the possibility that there could have been an overall loss in accumulated knowledge capital due to accelerated obsolescence. A proportional decline in the effectiveness of past capital or in the rate that R&D is converted into new knowledge capital need not show up as decline in the slope coefficient, it would get absorbed into the shifting constant. Disproportionate shifts should, however, have an impact on the estimated slope coefficient. Also, a pure obsolescence shock to old knowledge capital would have called forth an increase in the rate of R&D expenditures, something which has not been observed in the data. I am indebted to M. N. Baily for this point.

productivity and profitability are related to differences in the basic research intensity of firms.

Such findings are always subject to a variety of econometric and substantive reservations. In this context the two major related issues are simultaneity and the question of how major divergences in private rates of return persist for such long periods. It is possible to argue that it is not R&D, or its basic research component, that causes firm "success" as measured by productivity and profitability, but rather that success allows firms to indulge in these types of luxury pursuits. It is difficult to argue about causality on the basis of what are essentially correlational data. It is possible to use simultaneous equation techniques to estimate such models, but then the argument shifts to the validity of the exogeneity assumption for the particular instruments. In the context of my specific data set, it is hard to think of any valid instruments except for possibly lagged values of the same variables, which raises some problems of its own. The best evidence for the notion that these results are not entirely spurious is provided by the growth rates where the individual firm levels are partialed out of the analysis. But, here too, one could argue about the impact of common unanticipated "luck" elements. Unfortunately, it is unlikely that one could use lagged growth rates as instruments, since there is very little correlation in growth rates over time at the firm level. While an attempt will be made in further work with these data to estimate more extended simultaneous equations versions of such models, I am not too optimistic as to what can be accomplished in this regard. The evidence presented here should not be interpreted as "proving" that R&D, and especially its basic component, are important for productivity growth but rather as presenting some prima facie evidence in support of such an interpretation. In this sense it is an exercise in economic rhetoric (Donald McCloskey, 1983).

It is even more difficult to respond to the theoretical a priori argument that such results cannot be true since they imply widely differing rates of return to different activities under the control of the same firm. One's response to this depends on one's views as to the prevalence of equilibria in the economy. While it is likely that major divergences in rates of return are eliminated or reduced in the long run, the relevant runs can be quite long. R&D as a major component of firm activity was undergoing a diffusion process in the 1950s and 1960s and may not have reached full equilibrium even by the end of our period. This may be especially true of the basic research component where the risks are much greater and the uncertainty introduced by changing government policies and the changing economic environment make it quite difficult to decide what is the right level for it.

A somewhat different version of this argument would claim that the world is indeed in approximate equilibrium but that different firms face different opportunities for doing research, basic or otherwise, are in different ecological niches, and hence have different coefficients in their "production functions." This would explain why different firms are observed to spend different amounts on R&D while actually earning about the same rate of return on it. When a constant coefficients production function is fit to such data, it will fit because it is approximating a market equilibrium relation. If the level of R&D invested were independent of the coefficient, then such a function would just reproduce its average share and not produce any evidence of excess returns. But if, as is reasonable, R&D is invested optimally with firms which have better opportunities, higher coefficients, investing more, this will induce a positive correlation between R&D and its individual coefficient and lead to an upward bias in the estimated "average" coefficient.[5] The resulting "larger" coefficient, larger than the observed factor share, will be interpreted, wrongly, as implying a higher rate of return than is actually prevailing at the individual level.

This argument may be recognized as a version of the earlier attacks on the Cobb-Douglas production function combined with a random coefficients interpretation of the same phenomenon. In its extreme form it is testable. Since there are time-series data available for individual firms, one could try to estimate individual firm parameters and check whether they are in fact distributed as is predicted by this particular argument. While individual parameters are unlikely to be well estimated, given the relative shortness of the available time-series, the parameters of the distribution of such coefficients might be estimable with more precision. I intend to pursue this possibility in future work.

To restate again the major points of the paper: a newly available body of data on all the major firms performing R&D in the United States has been examined and evidence has been presented for the proposition that R&D contributes significantly to productivity growth, that the basic research component of it does so even more strongly, and that privately financed R&D expenditures have a significantly larger effect on private productivity and profitability than federally financed R&D. These findings are open to a number of reservations. Nevertheless, they do raise the issue that the overall slowdown in the growth of R&D and the absolute decline in basic research in industry which occurred in the 1970s may turn out to have been very costly to the economy in terms of foregone growth opportunities.

References

Bound, John et al., "Who Does R&D and Who Patents?," in Z. Griliches, ed., *R&D, Patents, and Productivity,* Chicago: University of Chicago Press, 1984, 21–54.

5. A positive correlation is not enough, by itself, for a positive bias. The weight of an individual firm slope coefficient in the cross-sectional estimate is proportional to the *square* of the deviation of R&D stock from its mean. A positive correlation between levels does not translate itself directly into a positive correlation between the level of one variable and the square of the other, except for certain skewed distributions. Since we do not observe the individual coefficients directly, it is rather difficult to check out this conjecture.

Griliches, Zvi, "Issues in Assessing the Contribution of R&D to Productivity Growth," *Bell Journal of Economics,* Spring 1979, *10,* 92–116. [Reprinted as chap. 2 in this volume.]

———, (1980a) "Returns to Research and Development Expenditures in the Private Sector," in J. W. Kendrick and B. Vaccara, eds., *New Developments in Productivity Measurement,* NBER Studies in Income and Wealth No. 44, Chicago: University of Chicago Press, 1980, 419–54. [Reprinted as chap. 3 in this volume.]

———, (1980b) "R&D and the Productivity Slowdown," *American Economic Review, Proceedings,* May 1980, *70,* 343–48.

———, "Comment" on Edwin Mansfield, "R and D and Innovation: Some Empirical Findings," in Z. Griliches, ed., *R&D, Patents, and Productivity,* Chicago: University of Chicago Press, 1984.

——— and Hall, B. H., "Census-NSF R&D Data Match Project: A Progress Report," in *Development and Use of Longitudinal Establishment Data,* Economic Research Report, ER-4, Bureau of the Census, 1982, 51–68.

——— and Lichtenberg, F., "R&D and Productivity Growth at the Industry Level: Is There Still a Relationship?," in Z. Griliches, ed., *R&D, Patents, and Productivity,* Chicago: University of Chicago Press, 1984, 465–96. [Reprinted as chap. 9 in this volume.]

——— and Mairesse, J., "Comparing Productivity Growth: An Exploration of French and U.S. Industrial and Firm Data," *European Economic Review,* April 1983, *21,* 89–119. [Reprinted as chap. 7 in this volume.]

——— and ———, "Productivity and R&D at the Firm Level," in Z. Griliches, ed., *R&D, Patents, and Productivity,* Chicago: University of Chicago Press, 1984, 339–74. [Reprinted as chap. 5 in this volume.]

Hall, Bronwyn H., "Historical R&D Panel: 1957–77. Public Use Correlation, Matrices Tape Documentation," unpublished, September 1984.

Link, A. N., (1981a) *Research and Development Activity in U.S. Manufacturing,* New York: Praeger, 1981.

———, (1981b) "Basic Research and Productivity Increase in Manufacturing: Additional Evidence," *American Economic Review,* December 1981, *71,* 1111–12.

McCloskey, Donald N., "The Rhetoric of Economics," *Journal of Economic Literature,* June 1983, *22,* 481–517.

Mansfield, Edwin, "Basic Research and Productivity Increase in Manufacturing," *American Economic Review,* December 1980, *70,* 863–73.

National Science Foundation (Jaffe, S. A.), "A Price Index for Deflation of Academic R&D Expenditures," NSF 72–130, Washington: USGPO, 1972.

———, *Trends to 1982 in Industrial Support of Basic Research,* NSF 83–302, Washington: USGPO, 1983.

———, *National Patterns of Science and Technology Resources,* NSF 84–311, Washington: USGPO, 1984.

Pakes, Ariel and Schankerman, M., "The Rate of Obsolescence of Knowledge, Research Gestation Lags, and the Private Rate of Return to Research Resources," in Z. Griliches, ed., *R&D, Patents, and Productivity,* Chicago: University of Chicago Press, 1984, 209–32.

5   Productivity and R&D at the Firm Level

5.1   Motivation and Framework

5.1.1   Introduction

Because of worries about domestic inflation and declining international competitiveness, concern has been growing about the recent slowdowns in the growth of productivity and R&D, both on their own merit and because of their presumed relationship. This paper tries to assess the contribution of private R&D spending by firms to their own productivity performance, using observed differences in both levels and growth rates of such firms.

A number of studies have been done on this topic at the industry level using aggregated data, but ours is almost the first to use time-series data for a cross section of individual firms, that is, panel data.[1] The only similar study at the firm level is Griliches's (1980a) use of pooled NSF and Census data for 883 R&D performing companies over the 1957–65 period. This study had to rely on various proxies (and on corresponding ad hoc assumptions) for the measurement of both physical (C) and R&D (K) capital. Furthermore, because of confidentiality requirements, the data were provided only in moment-matrices

This chapter is coauthored with Jacques Mairesse and is reprinted from *R&D, Patents, and Productivity,* edited by Zvi Griliches, pp. 339–74 (Chicago: University of Chicago Press, 1984). © 1984 by the National Bureau of Economic Research. All rights reserved.

A first draft of this paper was presented at the Fifth World Congress of the Econometric Society at Aix-en-Provence, August 1980. This work is part of the National Bureau of Economic Research Program of Productivity and Technical Change Studies. The authors are indebted to the National Science Foundation (PRA79–1370 and SOC78–04279) and to the Centre National de la Recherche Scientifique (ATP 070199) for financial support. The authors are also thankful to John Bound, Bronwyn Hall, and Alan Siu for very able research assistance.

1. M. Ishaq Nadiri and his associates have done important related investigations. In their work at the firm level they have estimated factor demand equations (including demand for R&D) but did not pursue the direct estimation of production functions (see, for example, Nadiri and Bitros 1980).

form, which made it both impossible to control for outliers and errors and difficult to deal with the special econometric problems of panel data. In spite of these limitations, the results were very (and somewhat surprisingly) encouraging, yielding an elasticity of output with respect to R&D capital of about .06 in both the time-series and cross-section dimensions of the data.

A major goal of our work described in this paper was to confirm these findings using a longer and more recent sample of firms, while paying more attention to the definition and measurement of the particular variables and to the difficulties of estimation and specification in panel data. In spite of these efforts, under close scrutiny our results are somewhat disappointing. This paper includes, therefore, two very different parts: section 5.2 documents the various estimates in detail, while section 5.3 attempts to rationalize and circumvent the problems that are evident in these estimates. First, however, we shall set the stage in this first section by explaining our data and our model. A more detailed description of the variables used and a summary of results using alternative versions of some of these variables can be found in the appendix.

5.1.2   The Data and Major Variables

We started with the information provided in Standard and Poor's Compustat Industrial Tape for 157 large companies which have been reporting their R&D expenditures regularly since 1963 and were not missing more than three years of data. Because of missing observations on employment and of questionable data on other variables, we first had to limit the sample to 133 firms (complete sample), and then, in response to merger problems, to restrict it further to 103 firms (restricted sample). The treatment of mergers has an impact on our estimates. These two overlapping samples are fully balanced over the twelve-year period, 1966–77.[2]

Our sample is quite heterogeneous, covering most R&D performing manufacturing industries and also including a few nonmanufacturing firms (mainly in petroleum and nonferrous mining). Since the number of firms is too small to work with separate industries, we have dealt with the heterogeneity problem by dividing our sample into two groups: *scientific firms* (firms in the chemical, drug, computer, electronics, and instrument industries) and *other firms*.

The measurement of the variables raises many conceptual issues as well as practical difficulties. These problems have been discussed at some length in Griliches (1979, 1980a), and we shall only allude to the most important ones in our context. We think of the unobservable research capital stock (K) as a measure of the distributed lag effect of past R&D investments on productivity:

---

2. We also considered two corresponding subsamples (96 firms and 71 firms) with no data missing for the entire eighteen-year (1960–77) period. We focus in this paper on the larger, shorter samples because of potential errors in our R&D measures in the earlier years. Most of the interpolation and doctoring of R&D expenditures (for missing observations or changes in definition) occurred in the years before 1966. Also, we had to estimate an initial R&D capital stock level in 1958 by making various and somewhat arbitrary assumptions whose impact vanishes by 1966.

$K_{it} = \sum_{\tau} w_{\tau} R_{i(t-\tau)}$, where R is a deflated measure of R&D, and the subscripts t, $(t - \tau)$, and i stand for current year, lagged year, and firm, respectively. Ideally, one would like to estimate the lag structure (w_{τ}) from the data, or at least an average rate of R&D obsolescence and the average time lag between R&D and productivity. Unfortunately, the data did not prove to be informative enough. Various constructed lag measures and different initial conditions made little difference to the final results. We focused, therefore, on one of the better and most sensible looking measures based on a constant rate of obsolescence of 15 percent per year and geometrically declining weights $w_{\tau} = (1 - \delta)^{\tau}$.

We measure output by deflated sales (Q) and labor (L) by the total number of employees. There is no information on value added or the number of hours worked in our data base. This raises, among other things, questions about the role of materials (especially energy in the recent period) and about the impact of fluctuations in labor and capacity utilization and the possibility that ignoring these issues may bias our results—see section 5.3 where we address these questions and the related question of returns to scale. Sales are deflated by the relevant (at the two- or three-digit SIC level) National Accounts price indexes.[3] We assume that intrasectoral differences in price movements reflect mostly quality changes in old products or the development of new products. Accordingly (and to the extent that this assumption holds), we are in principle studying here the effects of both process- and product-oriented R&D investments.

Finally, we have used gross plant adjusted for inflation as our measure of the physical capital stock (C). This variable (as in some of our previous studies) performs reasonably well; however, it tends to be collinear over time with the R&D capital stock K, especially for some sectors and subperiods. We have tried various ways of adjusting gross plant for inflation and have also experimented with age of capital and net capital stock measures. Since random errors of measurement are another issue, we made various attempts to deal with the errors in variables problem by going to three-year averages. All these experiments resulted in only minor perturbations to our estimates.

Table 5.1 provides general information on our samples and variables, while more detail is given in the appendix. Note the much more rapid productivity growth and the higher R&D intensiveness in the "scientific firms" subsample.

5.1.3   The Model and Stochastic Assumptions

Our model, which is common to most analyses of R&D contributions to productivity growth (see Griliches 1979, 1980b), is the simple extended Cobb-Douglas production function:

3. At least two problems arise in applying these price indexes to our data. First, our firms are diversified and a significant fraction of their output does not fall within the industry to which they have been assigned. Second, observations are based on the companies' *fiscal* years which often do not coincide with price index calendar years. Experiments performed to investigate these problems indicated that our conclusions are not affected by them. We used 1978 Business Segment data to produce weighted price indexes for about three-quarters of our sample, with the results changing only in the second decimal place. Similarly, a separate smoothing of the price indexes, to put them into fiscal year equivalents, has very little impact on the final results.

Table 5.1   Sample Composition and Size, R&D/Sales Ratio, and Labor Productivity Growth Rate[a]

SIC Industry Classification	Complete Sample			Restricted Sample		
	Number of Firms	R&D Sales (%)	Productivity Growth Rate (%)	Number of Firms	R&D Sales (%)	Productivity Growth Rate (%)
Scientific firms:						
28(−283)—chemicals	19	3.4	6.7	16	3.6	5.1
283—drugs	19	6.5	3.3	10	7.5	4.6
357—computers	10	5.3	7.8	6	5.3	8.0
36—electronic equipment	14	4.6	3.3	10	4.7	3.8
38—instruments	15	5.5	3.6	15	5.5	3.6
Subtotal	77	5.0	4.3	57	5.2	4.7
Other firms:						
29—oil	6	0.7	5.1	6	0.7	5.1
35(−357)—machinery	13	2.8	0.7	10	2.8	0.7
37—transportation equipment	8	2.2	1.8	8	2.2	1.8
Other manufacturing—mostly 20–32–33	20	2.3	0.2	17	2.3	0.8
Nonmanufacturing—mostly 10	9	2.0	−0.6	5	2.2	0.5
Subtotal	56	2.2	0.9	46	2.2	1.5
Total	133	3.8	2.9	103	3.8	3.3

[a]The restricted sample excludes firms with large jumps in the data, generally caused by known merger problems.

$$Q_{it} = Ae^{\lambda t}C_{it}^{\alpha}L_{it}^{\beta}K_{it}^{\gamma}e^{e_{it}},$$

or in log form:

$$q_{it} = a + \lambda t + \alpha c_{it} + \beta \ell_{it} + \gamma k_{it} + e_{it},$$

where (in addition to already defined symbols) e_{it} is the perturbation or error term in the equation; λ is the rate of disembodied technical change; α, β, and especially γ are the parameters (elasticities) of interest—in addition to the weights w_{τ} or the rate of obsolescence δ implicit in the construction of the R&D capital stock variable.

One could, of course, also consider more complicated functional forms, such as the CES or Translog functions. We felt, based on past experience and also on some exploratory computations, that this will not matter as far as our main purpose of estimating the output elasticities of R&D and physical capital (α and γ), or at least their relative importance (α/γ), is concerned. However, two related points are worth making.

First, an important implication of our model in the context of panel data is that in the cross-sectional dimension differences in levels explain differences in levels, while in the time dimension differences in growth rates explain differences in growth rates. An alternative model would allow γ to vary across firms and impose the equality of marginal products or rates of return across firms, $\partial Q/\partial K = \rho$, implying that the rate of growth in productivity depends on the intensity of R&D investment (rewriting $\gamma \dot{k} = (\partial Q/\partial K)(K/Q)(\dot{K}/K) = \rho \dot{K}/Q = \rho(R - \delta K)/Q \simeq \rho R/Q$ for small δ). We have not pursued such an alternative here, but we may consider it again in future work.[4]

Second, we also have the choice of assuming constant returns to scale (CRS) in the Cobb-Douglas production function: $\alpha + \beta + \gamma + \mu = 1$, or not—which amounts to estimating the regression

$$(q_{it} - \ell_{it}) = a + \lambda t + \alpha(c_{it} - \ell_{it}) + \gamma(k_{it} - \ell_{it}) + (\mu - 1)\ell_{it} + e_{it},$$

with $(\mu - 1)$ left free or set equal to zero. In our data the constant returns to scale assumption is accepted in the cross-sectional dimension, but is rejected in the time dimension in favor of significantly decreasing returns to scale. Because of the large effects of this restriction on our estimates of γ, we shall report the estimates obtained both with and without imposing constant returns to scale.

A distinct issue, which may explain why not assuming constant returns to scale and freeing the coefficient of labor in the regressions causes a problem, is that of simultaneity. Actually, it seems to provide a better explanation of our results than left-out variables or errors of measurement. We have, therefore, estimated a two, semireduced form, equations model in which output and employ-

---

4. An important practical advantage of this alternative approach is that by assuming $\delta = 0$ a priori it does not require the construction of an R&D capital stock. See Griliches (1973), Terleckyj (1974), and Griliches and Lichtenberg (1984) for estimates based on this approach.

ment are determined simultaneously as functions of R&D and physical stocks, based on the assumption of short-run profit maximization and predetermined capital inputs. These estimates yield plausible estimates of the relative influence of R&D and physical capital on productivity in both the cross-sectional and time dimensions. We elaborate on this line of research in section 5.3.

These different specification issues are, of course, related to the assumptions made about the error term, e_{it}, in the production function. When working with panel data, it is usual to decompose the error term into two independent terms: $e_{it} = u_i + w_{it}$, where u_i is a permanent effect specific to the firm and w_{it} is a transitory effect. In our context u_i may correspond to permanent differences in managerial ability and economic environment, while w_{it} reflects short-run changes in capacity utilization rates, in addition to other sources of perturbation. The habitual and convenient way to abstract from the u_i's is to compute the *within-firm regression* using the deviations of the observations from their specific firm means: $(y_{it} - y_{i.})$, which is equivalent to including firm dummy variables in the total regression using the original observation (y_{it}). The way to eliminate the w_{it}'s (in a long enough sample) is to compute the *between-firm regression* using the firm means $(y_{i.})$. The least-squares estimates of the *total regression* are in fact matrix-weighted averages of the least-squares estimates of the within and between regressions. If most of the variability of the data is between firms rather than within, as is the case here, the total and between estimates will be very close.[5]

Another manner of viewing the decomposition of the overall error into permanent and transitory components, and of interpreting the between and the within estimates, is to consider them as providing cross-sectional and time-series estimates, respectively. Both estimates will be consistent and similar if the u_i's and the w_{it}'s are uncorrelated with the explanatory variables. Very often, however, the two are rather different, implying some sort of specification error. This is, unfortunately, our case. Following the early work of Mundlak (1961) and Hoch (1962), the general tendency is to hold the u_i's responsible for the correlations with the explanatory variables and to assume that the within estimates are the better, less biased ones.[6] This leads to the discarding of the information contained in the variability between firms, which is predominant (at least in our samples), relying thereby only on the variability within firms over time, which is much smaller and more sensitive to errors of measurement. In fact, there are also good reasons for correlations of the w_{it}'s with the explanatory variables and, therefore, putting somewhat more faith in the between estimates. These reasons have been sketched in Mairesse (1978); they will be considered further in section 5.3 when we discuss the potential influence of misspecifications on our results.

---

5. An independent year effect $v_t (e_{it} = u_i + v_t + w_{it})$ can also be taken into account by adding year dummies instead of a time trend to the regression.
6. The model is then equivalent to the so-called fixed effects model.

5.2   Overall and Detailed Estimates

5.2.1   First Look at Results

Our first results were based on the complete sample of 133 firms for the 1966–77 period and various variants of our variables, especially R&D capital. Although the use of different measures had little effect, disappointing our hope of learning much about the lag structure from these data, the actual estimates looked reasonably good even if far apart in the cross-section and time dimensions. Table 5.2 gives the total, between, and within estimates (and also the within estimates with year dummies instead of a time trend), using our main variants for output, labor, and physical and research capital, both with and without the assumption of constant returns to scale. The total estimates of the elasticities of physical and R&D capital (α and γ) are about .30 and .06, respectively, similar to Griliches's (1980a) previous estimates. The more purely cross-sectional between estimates are nearly identical to the total estimates, .32 and .07, respectively. This follows from the fact that most of the relevant variability in our sample is between firms (about 90 percent, see table 5A.1 in the appendix). The time-series within estimates are, however, rather different: α being about .15 and γ about .15 or .08 depending on whether constant returns to scale are imposed or not. It is also clear that using separate year dummy variables instead of a linear trend makes little difference.

Unfortunately, these first results did not improve with further analysis; on the contrary. While the measurement of variables (within the range of our experimentation) does not really matter, trying to allow for sectoral and period differences and cleaning the sample of observations contaminated by mergers sharply degraded our within estimates of the R&D capital elasticity γ. The pattern of results already evident in table 5.2 is much amplified, especially in the time dimension: a tendency of the estimated γ's to be substantial, whenever the estimated α's seem too low; and a tendency for them to diminish or even to collapse when constant returns to scale are not imposed. We shall now document these different problems in detail before considering their possible causes and solutions.

5.2.2   Alternative Variable Definitions and Sectoral Differences

One of the original aims of this study was to experiment with various ways of defining and measuring physical and R&D capital. Using all the information available to us, we tried a number of different ways of measuring these variables but to little effect. The resulting differences in our estimates, even when they were "statistically significant," were nonetheless quite small and not very meaningful. In particular, they did not alter the order of magnitude of our two parameters of interest, α and γ. The various measures we tried turned out to be very good substitutes for each other and the choice between them had little practical import. Our final choices were based, therefore, primarily on a priori

Table 5.2 Production Function Estimates (complete sample, 133 firms, 1966–77)

Total Regressions

α	γ	$(\mu-1)$	λ	R^2	MSE
0.319	—	—	0.012	0.499	0.099
(0.009)			(0.002)		
0.310	0.073	—	0.011	0.514	0.097
(0.008)	(0.011)		(0.002)		
0.332	0.054	−0.032	0.011	0.524	0.094
(0.009)	(0.011)	(0.005)	(0.002)		

Within Regressions

α	γ	$(\mu-1)$	λ	R^2	MSE
0.232	—	—	0.017	0.402	0.0211
(0.017)			(0.001)		
0.160	0.150	—	0.018	0.422	0.0204
(0.020)	(0.020)		(0.001)		
0.150	0.080	−0.126	0.025	0.437	0.0199
(0.019)	(0.022)	(0.019)	(0.002)		

Between Regressions

α	γ	$(\mu-1)$	R^2	MSE
0.324	—	—	0.522	0.079
(0.027)				
0.317	0.072	—	0.538	0.077
(0.027)	(0.034)			
0.341	0.053	−0.033	0.551	0.075
(0.029)	(0.035)	(0.017)		

Within Regressions with Year Dummies

α	γ	$(\mu-1)$	R^2	MSE
0.250	—	—	0.420	0.0206
(0.017)				
0.176	0.158	—	0.442	0.0198
(0.019)	(0.020)			
0.163	0.091	−0.121	0.455	0.0194
(0.019)	(0.022)	(0.020)		

considerations, external evidence, and convenience. The appendix describes these choices and some of our experiments.

Since our sample consisted of R&D performing firms in rather diverse industries, it was also of interest to investigate the influence of sectoral (industrial) differences. Table 5.3 gives our main estimates separately for firms in research-intensive industries (so-called scientific firms) and the rest of our sample.

Dividing the sample into two allows for much of the heterogeneity, bringing down the sum of square of errors (SSE) by about 20 percent for the total regressions and 10 percent for the within regressions (with the division corresponding to very high F ratios of about 100 and 70, respectively). The two groups are indeed a priori very distinct: as a matter of fact, the average rate of productivity growth is about four times higher for the scientific firms, while the average R&D to sales ratio is about twice as high (see table 5.1).

In spite of this sharp contrast, the differences in our estimates are not that large, except for the estimated time-trend coefficients (rates of technical progress λ). The within estimates of α and γ (and also μ) are, in fact, quite comparable, although the fit is much lower in the "other firms" equation. Yet the total estimates of γ are very large in the scientific firms and insignificant for the other firms. Part of this discrepancy can be accounted for by the higher estimates of α in the other firms group.

Disaggregating to the industrial level decreases the total and within sums of square of errors by another 20 percent or so. The main effect is, however, to worsen the collinearity between R&D and physical capital in the within dimension. Some of the within estimates actually fall apart: two extreme cases being the computer industry with an estimated α of $-.06$ and an estimated γ of .50, and the instruments industry with an estimated α of .49 and an estimated γ of $-.32$. Without a larger sample, we do not really have the option of working at the detailed industrial level.[7]

5.2.3 Differences between Subperiods

Current discussions of "the productivity slowdown" suggest that some of it may be due not only to "the slowdown in R&D," but also to a significant decrease in the efficiency of recent R&D investments (Griliches 1980b); hence, our interest in whether we could find any evidence of a decrease in the R&D capital elasticity γ over time. Table 5.4 shows what happens (for the scientific firms group) when we divide our data into two six-year subperiods, 1966–71 and 1972–77.[8] Table 5.5 explores the resulting differences further by pres-

---

7. An intermediate step, without going fully to the sectoral level, is to allow for separate sectoral time trends and intercepts. While the total and within estimates change only slightly for the scientific firms, the total estimates of γ and α for the other group move up and down respectively, making them less different from those of the scientific group.

8. We also looked at the preceding six-year subperiod (1960–65) for our longer but smaller subsample of firms. The estimates are very similar to those for 1966–71.

Table 5.3   Production Function Estimates Separately for the Scientific and Other Firms (complete sample, 77 and 56 firms, respectively, 1966–77)

	Total Regressions						Within Regressions					
	α	γ	$(\mu - 1)$	λ	R^2	MSE	α	γ	$(\mu - 1)$	λ	R^2	MSE
Scientific firms	0.243	—	—	0.030	0.423	0.088	0.194	—	—	0.033	0.607	0.0170
	(0.012)			(0.003)			(0.020)			(0.002)		
	0.203	0.223	—	0.025	0.570	0.066	0.150	0.111	—	0.032	0.615	0.0167
	(0.011)	(0.013)		(0.003)			(0.022)	(0.026)		(0.007)		
	0.250	0.185	−0.051	0.026	0.604	0.061	0.140	0.021	−0.200	0.044	0.653	0.0151
	(0.011)	(0.013)	(0.006)	(0.002)			(0.021)	(0.026)	(0.020)	(0.002)		
Other firms	0.364	—	—	−0.008	0.609	0.093	0.243	—	—	−0.001	0.172	0.0202
	(0.011)			(0.003)			(0.028)			(0.002)		
	0.365	−0.007	—	−0.008	0.609	0.093	0.169	0.124	—	0.001	0.196	0.0196
	(0.012)	(0.018)		(0.004)			(0.032)	(0.028)		(0.002)		
	0.351	0.010	0.025	−0.008	0.614	0.092	0.133	−0.015	−0.207	0.011	0.223	0.0190
	(0.013)	(0.019)	(0.009)	(0.003)			(0.032)	(0.039)	(0.043)	(0.003)		

Table 5.4   Production Function Estimates for Two Subperiods: 1966–71 and 1972–77 (scientific firms, complete sample, 77 firms)

Periods	Total Regressions						Within Regressions					
	α	γ	(μ − 1)	λ	R^2	MSE	α	γ	(μ − 1)	λ	R^2	MSE
1966–71	0.219 (0.018)	—	—	0.013 (0.009)	0.264	0.103	0.250 (0.029)	—	—	0.011 (0.004)	0.307	0.0115
	0.169 (0.016)	0.241 (0.019)	—	0.007 (0.007)	0.463	0.076	0.106 (0.033)	0.250 (0.034)	—	0.013 (0.004)	0.380	0.0103
	0.235 (0.017)	0.189 (0.019)	−0.068 (0.009)	0.008 (0.007)	0.528	0.067	0.113 (0.030)	0.040 (0.036)	−0.307 (0.029)	0.041 (0.004)	0.501	0.0083
1972–77	0.273 (0.016)	—	—	0.033 (0.007)	0.434	0.071	0.083 (0.028)	—	—	0.043 (0.003)	0.459	0.0080
	0.242 (0.014)	0.207 (0.017)	—	0.029 (0.006)	0.578	0.053	−0.012 (0.034)	0.225 (0.047)	—	0.041 (0.003)	0.486	0.0076
	0.269 (0.015)	0.183 (0.017)	−0.032 (0.008)	0.028 (0.006)	0.594	0.051	−0.023 (0.034)	0.175 (0.057)	−0.076 (0.050)	0.044 (0.004)	0.488	0.0076

Table 5.5   Analysis of Subperiod Differences (scientific firms, complete sample, 77 firms)

Periods	Within Degrees of Freedom	Rates of Growth, (within standard deviations), [% within variability]				Within Regressions ($\mu = 1$)					
		$q - l$	$c - l$	$k - l$	l	α	γ	λ	γ ($\alpha = 0.25$)	λ ($\alpha = 0.25$)	γ ($\alpha = 0.25$) ($\lambda = 0.025$)
1966–77	847	4.3 (0.22) [100.0]	6.2 (0.33) [100.0]	3.0 (0.22) [100.0]	4.6 (0.28) [100.0]	0.15	0.11	0.032	0.06	0.027	0.08
1966–71	385	3.3 (0.14) [19.0]	9.1 (0.25) [27.6]	4.5 (0.20) [38.3]	6.3 (0.24) [33.4]	0.11	0.25	0.013	0.17	0.003	0.09
1972–77	385	5.1 (0.13) [17.0]	4.3 (0.19) [15.1]	2.4 (0.13) [15.8]	2.4 (0.13) [10.2]	−0.01	0.23	0.041	0.02	0.034	0.08
Between subperiods	77	4.7 (0.58) [64.0]	6.2 (0.81) [57.3]	2.9 (0.50) [45.9]	4.2 (0.69) [56.4]	0.25	−0.02	0.032	−0.02	0.032	0.07

enting the within estimates for the two subperiods (as well as the overall period and "between subperiods") and comparing the estimated γ when α and λ are constrained to .25 and .025, respectively. Table 5.5 also lists the rates of growth of the main variables, their within standard deviations, and the decomposition of their within variability for the subperiods (the overall period and "between subperiods").

As might be expected, the total estimates differ only slightly, while the within estimates change a lot. Yet the striking feature is not a decrease in the estimated γ but rather in $\hat{\alpha}$. The decomposition of variance shows, however, that by breaking down our data into two subperiods we keep only about half of the within variability in the overall period (the other half being between subperiods). Our capital stock variables as well as the time variable itself are slowly changing, trendlike variables, and there is not enough variability in them to allow us to estimate all of their coefficients separately and precisely. What we get are relatively wide gyrations in the estimated coefficients α, γ, and λ, with some of them going down as the others go up. If we impose a reasonable a priori value of $\alpha = .25$, which corresponds to estimating the impact of R&D capital on total factor productivity (TFP), we do indeed get a large decline in γ, from .17 in the first period to effectively zero in the second. However, this decline is associated with a correspondingly large increase in λ, from .003 to .034. Since such an acceleration in "disembodied" technological change goes against all other pieces of information available to us, we reestimate again, imposing also an a priori $\lambda = .025$. With this new restriction everything falls into place: $\hat{\gamma}$ being estimated at approximately .08 for both subperiods (as well as between subperiods and for the overall period).

This, of course, does not mean that we have strong evidence that γ is about .08, but only that one should not interpret the data as implying a major decline in γ over time. What the data tell us is that one cannot tell and that there is not enough independent variation in the subperiods to estimate the contribution of physical capital, R&D capital, and trend separately. If, however, we are willing to impose a priori, reasonable values on α and λ, then the implied $\hat{\gamma}$ is both reasonable and stable. Moreover, the imposition of such constraints is not inconsistent with the data; while they are not "statistically" accepted given our relatively large sample size, the actual absolute deterioration in fit is rather small, the standard deviation of residuals changing by less than .01.[9]

This may not be all that surprising considering the other major fact that emerges from table 5.5: our "scientific firms" did not actually experience a productivity slowdown in 1972–77 relative to 1966–71 (as against the experience of manufacturing as a whole). There was a slowdown in the growth of both physical and R&D capital, but this was associated with an *acceleration*

---

9. Our estimated regression standard errors are about .1 in the within dimension, implying that we explain annual fluctuations in productivity up to an error whose standard deviation is about 10 percent. Imposing the a priori values of α and λ increases this error by less than one additional percent.

in labor productivity growth and, hence, also in total factor productivity growth. (The latter rises from about 0.6 percent in the first period to about 3.8 percent in the second.)[10] Given these facts, it is not surprising that correlation of productivity growth with capital input growth tends to vanish, leading to a collapse of the estimated α and γ. These strange events are not limited to the firms in our sample, they also actually happened in the science-based industries as a whole, as can be seen by examining the aggregate data collected by NSF and the BLS.[11] (Average TFP growth in "scientific" industries increases in these data from about 0.8 percent in 1966–71 to 3.2 percent in 1972–77.) If anything, the puzzle is why there was so little "exogenous" productivity growth in 1966–71. One possible answer would invoke errors of measurement in the dating of physical and R&D investments (longer lag structures); another might be based on different cyclical positions of the endpoints of these two periods. In any case, since there is no evidence that there has been a significant productivity slowdown in R&D intensive industries, it is unlikely that whatever slowdown did occur could be attributed to the slowdown in R&D growth.[12]

5.2.4   The Problem of Mergers

Starting from our original sample of 157 firms, we first eliminated 24, primarily because of missing observations (in the number of employees generally and in gross plant occasionally) or obvious large errors in the reported numbers. In the case of one or two missing observations we "interpolated" them. In some instances we managed to go back to the original source and obtain the missing figure or correct an error. Fortunately, most firms did not present such difficulties, and the construction of our "complete sample" was straightforward enough. We were still left with the important issue of mergers. About one firm out of five in our "complete" sample (as many as twenty among the seventy-seven "scientific" firms) appeared to be affected (at least for one year over the 1966–77 period) by considerable and generally simultaneous "jumps" (80 percent or more year-to-year increases) in gross plant, number of employees,

---

10. This is computed from the average yearly rates of growth given in table 5.5, using .65, .25, and .1 as relative weights for labor, physical capital, and R&D capital, respectively.

11. The data are taken from sources given in Griliches (1980b). The numbers that correspond to those of table 5.5 are:

Scientific Industries Aggregate: Based on NSF and BLS Statistics (average yearly rates of growth)

Subperiods	$q - \ell$	$c - \ell$	$k - \ell$	ℓ
1960–65	4.3	2.0	8.2	2.8
1966–71	3.3	7.4	6.3	0.9
1972–77	3.8	2.0	0.6	2.3

Although the definitions and measures are quite different, and although our firms are much faster growing than the scientific industries as a whole, the growth patterns are very similar.

12. For possible contrary evidence, see Scherer (1981) who emphasizes the impact of R&D on productivity growth in the R&D *using* rather than R&D *doing* industries.

and sales. We have been able to check and convince ourselves that most of these jumps do, in fact, result from mergers, although some may be the result of very rapid growth. Since the problem was of such magnitude (as is bound to be the case in a panel of large companies over a number of years), we had to be careful about it.

One way of dealing with this problem is simply to drop the offending firms. This results in what we have called the "restricted" sample. An alternative is to create an "intermediate" sample in which a firm before and after a major merger is considered to be two different "firms." If mergers were occurring precisely in a given year, we would have as many observations in the intermediate sample as in the complete one (and more "firms" but some of them over shorter periods), and we would eliminate only the "variability" corresponding to the "jumps." In fact, we lost a few observations because some mergers affect our data for more than one year (primarily because we chose gross plant at the beginning of the year as our measure of capital for the current year) or because they occur in the first or last years of the study period (since we decided not to have "firms" with less than three years of data in the intermediate sample). Estimates for the restricted sample and its complement, the "merger" sample, are given in table 5.6 for the scientific firms group. (Estimates for the other group behave similarly, although there were fewer mergers there.) Table 5.7 provides more detail, showing separately the results for the complete, intermediate, and restricted samples and decomposing the merger group into "jump" and "no-jump" periods. To facilitate interpretation, it also presents estimates of γ based on constraining α to .25 and λ to .025, and it lists the rate of growth, the standard deviations, and the variance decomposition of the main variables.[13]

The total estimates (reported in table 5.6) manifest their usual stoutness, remaining practically unchanged whatever the sample. The within estimates are, on the contrary, very sensitive, and the estimated γ collapses, declining from .11 to .05 and $-.03$ in the complete, intermediate, and restricted samples, respectively (even when constant returns to scale are imposed; see table 5.7). It is clear from table 5.7 that the merger firms are responsible for the difference. They correspond to a major part of the within variability of our variables

---

13. The variance decomposition of a variable y for a firm i going through a merger at the end of year t_0 is identical to its decomposition into the two subperiods before and after the merger, the "jump" component corresponding to the between subperiods component. It can be written

$$\sum_{t=1}^{T} (y_{it} - y_{i.})^2 = \sum_{t=1}^{t_0} (y_{it} - y_{i.}^{(1)})^2 + \sum_{t=t_0+1}^{T} (y_{it} - y_{i.}^{(2)})^2$$
$$+ t_0(y_{i.}^{(1)} - y_{i.})^2 + (T - t_0)(y_{i.}^{(2)} - y_{i.})^2,$$

where $y_{i.}$, $y_{i.}^{(1)}$, and $y_{i.}^{(2)}$ are the respective means of y_{it} over the whole period $(1, T)$, the before merger period $(1, t_0)$, and the after merger period $(t_0 + 1, T)$. The practical way to run the regressions corresponding to the jump component is simply to substitute $(y_{i.}^{(1)} - y_{i.})$ and $(y_{i.}^{(2)} - y_{i.})$ for $(y_{it} - y_{i.})$ in the before and after merger years.

Table 5.6 Separate Production Function Estimates for the Restricted and the Merger Samples (57 and 20 firms respectively, scientific firms, 1966–77)

Samples	Total Regressions						Within Regressions					
	α	γ	$(\mu - 1)$	λ	R^2	MSE	α	γ	$(\mu - 1)$	λ	R^2	MSE
Restricted	0.264	—	—	0.032	0.510	0.075	0.221	—	—	0.035	0.737	0.010
	(0.012)			(0.003)			(0.025)			(0.002)		
	0.230	0.210	—	0.028	0.645	0.054	0.239	−0.034	—	0.035	0.737	0.010
	(0.011)	(0.013)		(0.003)			(0.030)	(0.028)		(0.002)		
	0.278	0.170	−0.048	0.028	0.671	0.050	0.211	−0.062	−0.112	0.041	0.745	0.010
	(0.012)	(0.014)	(0.006)	(0.003)			(0.030)	(0.028)	(0.025)	(0.002)		
Merger	0.204	—	—	0.021	0.235	0.117	0.200	—	—	0.021	0.379	0.034
	(0.032)			(0.007)			(0.036)			(0.004)		
	0.146	0.292	—	0.017	0.462	0.093	0.117	0.270	—	0.020	0.437	0.031
	(0.028)	(0.029)		(0.005)			(0.038)	(0.055)		(0.004)		
	0.171	0.265	−0.064	0.020	0.524	0.073	0.114	0.135	−0.229	0.042	0.506	0.027
	(0.027)	(0.028)	(0.011)	(0.006)			(0.036)	(0.057)	(0.040)	(0.005)		

Table 5.7   Analysis of Merger Differences (scientific firms, 1966–77)

Samples	Within Degrees of Freedom	Rates of Growth, (within standard deviations), [% within variables]				Within Regressions ($\mu - 1$)					
		$q - 1$	$c - 1$	$k - 1$	l	α	γ	λ	γ ($\alpha = 0.25$)	λ ($\alpha = 0.25$)	γ ($\alpha = 0.25$) ($\lambda = 0.025$)
Complete (1)	847	4.3 (0.22) [100.0]	6.2 (0.33) [100.0]	3.0 (0.22) [100.0]	4.6 (0.28) [100.0]	0.15	0.11	0.032	0.06	0.027	0.08
Intermediate (2)	783	4.7 (0.21) [82.5]	5.8 (0.26) [58.6]	3.7 (0.21) [79.6]	3.2 (0.20) [49.2]	0.19	0.05	0.035	0.01	0.033	0.09
Restricted (3)	627	4.7 (0.21) [67.3]	6.1 (0.27) [50.4]	3.4 (0.22) [63.6]	3.2 (0.21) [42.6]	0.24	−0.03	0.035	−0.04	0.045	0.05
Merger (4) = (1) − (3)	220	3.3 (0.24) [32.7]	6.5 (0.45) [49.6]	2.0 (0.26) [36.4]	8.6 (0.41) [57.4]	0.12	0.27	0.020	0.18	0.012	0.11
"Jump" (5) = (1) − (2)	64	0.0 (0.33) [17.5]	11.5 (0.76) [41.4]	−4.8 (0.36) [20.4]	21.9 (0.72) [50.8]	0.20	0.11	0.011	0.07	0.006	0.02
"No-jump" (6) = (2) − (3)	156	4.7 (0.20) [15.2]	4.5 (0.22) [8.2]	4.9 (0.21) [16.2]	3.1 (0.17) [6.6]	−0.18	0.65	0.019	0.30	0.017	0.23

(much of it being from the "jumps"). Moreover, they seem to account for the significant, positive within estimates of γ in our complete sample, especially through their "no-jumps" component. In other words, R&D seems most effective for firms growing rapidly through mergers, and both phenomena (mergers and R&D growth) are apparently related.

Merger firms have higher R&D than physical capital growth rates during their nonmerger ("no-jumps") periods, while the opposite is true for nonmerging ("restricted") firms. The labor productivity growth rates are about equal for both, but they are much more closely related to R&D growth for the merger firms. Actually, not enough variability is left to estimate the separate contributions of the two capital terms and the time trend term precisely. If one imposes $\alpha = .25$ and $\lambda = .025$ a priori, one gets back from the restricted subsample a reasonable though still low estimate of $\hat{\gamma} = .05$. The intermediate sample, however, is the most relevant one from our point of view, yielding a much higher $\hat{\gamma} = .09$, which can be interpreted as a weighted average of about .2 for the merger firms and .05 for the rest.[14]

Such a finding raises questions that deserve additional analysis: Who are these "merger" firms and why would their R&D investment be more successful? What kind of selectivity is at work here? How does one expand this type of analysis to allow for different R&D-related success rates by different firms? A random coefficient model does not, at first thought, appear to be the most appropriate way to go. Unfortunately, given the small size of our sample, we cannot pursue these questions further here.

Our tentative conclusion is that we should *not* exclude the merger firms from our sample entirely. These are firms whose R&D has apparently been very effective. Throwing them out would seriously bias our estimates of the contribution of R&D to productivity downward.

5.3 Misspecification Biases or an Exercise in Rationalization

5.3.1 Three Possible Sources of Bias

Our within estimates of the production function are unsatisfactory in the sense that they attribute unreasonably low coefficients to the physical and research capital variables and imply that most of our firms are handicapped by severely diminishing returns to scale. The simplest explanation is to impute these "bad results" to a major misspecification of our model. The trouble is that when we start thinking about possible misspecifications, many come to mind. The most important appear to be: (1) the omission of labor and capital intensity of utilization variables, such as hours of work per employee and hours of operation per machine; (2) the use of gross output or sales rather than value

14. Here also the imposition of the a priori values of $\alpha = .25$ and $\lambda = .025$ does not result in an economically meaningful deterioration of fit.

added or, alternatively, the omission of materials from the list of included factors; (3) overlooking the jointness (simultaneity) in the determination of employment and output.[15]

These three misspecifications are similar in the sense that they all imply the failure of the ordinary least-squares assumption of no correlation between the included factors, c, ℓ, k, and the disturbance e in the production function, resulting in biases in our estimates of the elasticities of these factors (and in our estimate of the elasticity of scale). In all three cases the correlation of the disturbance e with the labor variable ℓ is likely to be relatively high in the time dimension, affecting especially our within estimates.

If we consider the "auxiliary" regression connecting e to c, ℓ, k:

$$E(e) = b_{ec.\ell k}c + b_{e\ell.ck}\ell + b_{ek.c\ell}k$$

(where we suppress for simplicity the constant and trend terms by taking deviations of the variables from the appropriate means, i.e., respectively, $[y_{it} - y_{.t}]$ and $[y_{it} - y_{.t} - y_{i.} + y_{..}]$ for the total and within regressions), the specification biases in our estimates can be written in the following general form:

$$E(\hat{\alpha} - \alpha) = \text{bias } \hat{\alpha} = b_{ec.\ell k},$$

$$E(\hat{\beta} - \beta) = \text{bias } \hat{\beta} = b_{e\ell.ck},$$

$$E(\hat{\gamma} - \gamma) = \text{bias } \hat{\gamma} = b_{ek.c\ell}.$$

If we assume more specifically that the physical and research capital variables c and k are predetermined and that only the labor variable is correlated with e, we can go one step further and formulate the biases in α and γ as proportional to the bias in β (see Griliches and Ringstad 1971, appendix C):

$$\text{bias } \hat{\alpha} = -(\text{bias } \hat{\beta})b_{\ell c.k},$$

$$\text{bias } \hat{\gamma} = -(\text{bias } \hat{\beta})b_{\ell k.c}.$$

There is no good reason why the coefficients $b_{\ell c.k}$ and $b_{\ell k.c}$ should be both small, or one much smaller than the other, or very different for the within and total estimates. One will expect them to be positive and less than one, but large enough to result in a significant transmission of an upward bias in $\hat{\beta}$ into downward biases in both $\hat{\alpha}$ and $\hat{\gamma}$. One would also expect the absolute biases in $\hat{\alpha}$ and $\hat{\gamma}$ to be of the same order of magnitude and, therefore, to have a much

---

15. Three other possible misspecifications are the following: (4) ignoring the possibility of random errors in our measures of labor and capital; (5) assuming wrongly that firms operate in competitive markets; and (6) ignoring the peculiar selectivity of our sample. We shall allude briefly to (4) and (5) in what follows, but continue to ignore the selectivity issue, postponing the investigation into this topic to a later study based on a much larger post-1972 sample.

larger relative effect on $\hat{\gamma}$ than on $\hat{\alpha}$ (assuming that the true γ is small relative to the true α). For example, a bias of $-.1$ might reduce $\hat{\alpha}$ from a true .3 to .2 but could wipe out $\hat{\gamma}$ if its true value were .1.

We can actually estimate such bias transmission coefficients in our sample. They are relatively large and of comparable magnitude, on the order of .3 to .4.[16]

To the extent that the correlation between labor and the disturbance in the production function is the main problem, we are left with the evaluation of the bias in labor elasticity and the question of whether we can ascertain the "within" bias to be positive and sizeable in contrast to a small "total" bias. This is much more difficult, and we have to consider specifically our three possible misspecifications. We shall say a few words about the first two and then concentrate on the simultaneity issue. This issue seems most important, and we have been able to progress further toward its solution by considering a simultaneous equations model composed of the production function and a labor demand function, and by estimating what we call the semireduced form equations for this model.

Consider first the omission of the hours worked per worker variable h (or machine hours operated per machine) and let the "true" model be:

$$q = \alpha c + \beta(\ell + h) + \gamma k + \varepsilon,$$

where labor is measured by the total number of hours of work.

The disturbance in the estimated model is then $e = \varepsilon + \beta h$, and we get for the labor elasticity bias: bias $(\hat{\beta}) = b_{e\ell.ck} = \beta b_{h\ell.ck}$. Cross-sectionally, hours per worker h should be roughly uncorrelated with any of the included variables c, ℓ, and k and, hence, cause no bias in the between regression or in the total regression (which is similar since the between variances of the variables dominate their total variance). In the time dimension, however, short-run fluctuations in demand (say a business expansion) will be met partly by modifying employment (hiring) and partly by changing hours of work (increase in overtime). Hence, $b_{h\ell.ck}$ should be positive and rather large (perhaps .5 or higher), and therefore the within estimate of $\hat{\beta}$ should be biased upward and substantially so (perhaps by $.6 \times .5 = 0.3$). Considering then that the within correlations of h with c and k are likely to be negligible, we have seen that a significant downward bias should be transmitted to the within estimates of $\hat{\alpha}$ and $\hat{\gamma}$ (about $-.3 \times .4$ or $-.3 \times .3 \simeq -.1$).

16. The auxiliary regression of ℓ on c and k giving these coefficients is precisely what we shall call our semireduced form labor equation; tables 5.8, 5.9, and 5.10 provide their exact values for our various samples. Note that since the order of magnitude of the sum of these coefficients is less than one, we cannot explain the downward biases in $\hat{\alpha}$ and $\hat{\gamma}$ and also in the returns to scale $\hat{\mu}$ solely by the transmission of an upward bias in $\hat{\beta}$. Our second misspecification example, the omission of materials, does not assume that c and k are predetermined and hence that the biases are only caused by the correlation of ℓ and e; it provides, as we shall see below, a rationalization of the decreasing returns to scale estimates in the within dimension.

The same type of analysis applies to the exclusion of materials as a factor in the production function (or to not using value added but gross output or sales to measure production). The total estimates of $\hat{\alpha}$, $\hat{\beta}$, and $\hat{\gamma}$ should all move up roughly in proportion to the elasticity of materials δ [by $1/(1 - \delta)$], while the within estimates $\hat{\alpha}$, $\hat{\beta}$, and $\hat{\gamma}$ will be raised in lesser proportions, with the plausible result of a negligible bias in the total and a large downward bias in the within estimates of the scale elasticity.

This time let the "true" model be:

$$q = \alpha c + \beta \ell + \gamma k + \delta m + \varepsilon$$

(i.e., a generalized Cobb-Douglas production function where materials come in as another factor). Estimating a gross output equation ignoring m assumes implicitly that materials are used in fixed proportion to output. This may be a belief about the technical characteristics of the production processes (the form of the production function) or the consequence of assuming that materials are purchased optimally and that their price relative to the price of output remains roughly constant over firms and over time. In any case, omitting m where it should be included means that the error in the estimated model is $e = \varepsilon + \delta m$, resulting in the following biases for our estimates:

$$\text{bias } \hat{\alpha} = \delta b_{mc.\ell k}, \text{ bias } (\hat{\beta}) = \delta b_{m\ell.ck}, \text{ bias } (\hat{\gamma}) = \delta b_{mk.c\ell}.$$

Across firms, in the between dimension, it is quite likely that the sum of the auxiliary regression coefficients b's will not depart far from unity, so that the sum of estimates $\hat{\alpha} + \hat{\beta} + \hat{\gamma}$ will approach the relevant true scale elasticity $\mu = \alpha + \beta + \gamma + \delta$. If the proportionality assumption of q and m holds well enough, then the b's would be more or less proportional to the corresponding elasticities and the relative biases roughly the same:

$$\hat{\alpha} = \alpha/(1 - \delta), \hat{\beta} = \beta/(1 - \delta), \hat{\gamma} = \gamma/(1 - \delta).$$

Over time, however, it is more likely that material usage may change less than proportionally, since it will respond incompletely or with lags to short-run output fluctuations. Hence, the sum of the b's might be much less than one in the within dimension, causing the misleading appearance of decreasing returns to scale. As a plausible example, we can take

$$b_{mc.\ell k} = b_{mk.\ell c} = 0, \text{ and } b_{m\ell.ck} = .5,$$

and if the true coefficients are $\alpha = .15$, $\beta = .3$, $\gamma = .05$ and $\delta = .5$ ($\mu - 1 = 0$), we get the following within estimates when m is omitted:

$$\hat{\alpha} = .15, \hat{\beta} = .55, \hat{\gamma} = .05, \text{ and } \hat{\mu} - 1 = -.25.$$

Turning to the problem of simultaneity and assuming that firms try to maximize their profits in the short run, given their stocks of physical and R&D

capital, the true model will consist of a production function and a labor demand function:

$$q = \alpha c + \beta \ell + \gamma k + e,$$

$$q = \ell + w + v,$$

where w is the real price of labor, and v is a random optimization error. We can assume that the errors in the two equations (e and v) are independent or, more generally, that they are of the following form: ($e + f$) and ($v + f$), where e and f are respectively the parts of the disturbance in the production function transmitted and not transmitted to the labor variable. The OLS bias in $\hat{\beta}$ can be written as

$$E(\beta - \hat{\beta}) = b_{e\ell.ck} = (1 - \beta)R,$$

where

$$R = \sigma_e^2 / [\sigma_e^2 + \sigma_w^2 (1 - r_{w.ck}^2) + \sigma_v^2]$$

is the ratio of the random transmitted variance in the production function to the sum of itself and the independent variance in the labor equation. Thus, to get some notion about the value of R and the bias in $\hat{\beta}$, we need to discuss the potential sources of variation in e, v, and w.

Schematically, we can think of the disturbance in the production function as consisting of: (1) long-term differences in factor productivity between firms; (2) short-run shifts in demand which are being met (partly) by changes in (unmeasured) utilization of labor and capital; and (3) errors of measurement in the deflators of output, errors arising from the use of gross rather than net output concepts, and errors arising from the use of sales rather than output concepts. Only items (1) and (2) matter as far as the formulas are concerned since (3) (errors of measurement) is not really transmitted to labor. Moreover, only (1) matters in the cross-sectional (between) dimension under the assumption that (2) cancels out over time, while only (2) matters in the time (within) dimension.

Similarly, the independent variation in the labor equation can be partitioned into: (4) the independent variation in real wage and (5) other short-run deviations from the profit-maximizing level of employment because of implicit contracts, shortages, or mistaken expectations. It is probably the case that most of the factor price variation to which firms respond is either permanent and cross-sectional or is common to all firms in the time dimension and hence is captured by the time dummies or trend coefficients. Thus, we anticipate that (4) manifests itself largely in the between dimension while (5) is all that is left in the within dimension.

On the basis of the estimated variances and covariances of the residuals for the semireduced form equations to be discussed below, we can give the following illustrative orders of magnitude (for $\beta \sim .6$):

$$\sigma^2_{(1)} = \sigma^{2(B)}_e = .004, \ \sigma^2_{(2)} = \sigma^{2(W)}_e = .002,$$

$$\sigma^2_{(3)} = \sigma^{2(B)}_f + \sigma^{2(W)}_f = .04 + .008,$$

$$\sigma^2_{(4)} = \sigma^{2(B)}_{w.ck} = .04, \ \sigma^2_{(5)} = \sigma^{2(W)}_v = .002.^{17}$$

The R would equal $(.004/.044) \sim .10$ in the between dimension and $(.002/.004) \sim .50$ in the within dimension. With a true β of .6, the OLS between and within estimates $\hat{\beta}$ would be respectively biased upward by about .04 and .20.

5.3.2   The Semireduced Form Estimates

If one takes the simultaneity story seriously, it is not surprising that the OLS within estimates of the production function are unreasonable. We should be estimating a complete simultaneous equations system instead. We cannot do that, unfortunately, lacking information on factor prices. But we can estimate semireduced form equations (i.e., reduced form equations omitting factor price variables) which may allow us to infer the relative size of our two parameters of interest α and γ.

Let the true production function be (ignoring constants, time trends, or year dummies)

$$q = \alpha c + \beta \ell + \gamma k + \delta m + e,$$

where both c and k are assumed to be predetermined and independent of e, while q, ℓ, and m are endogenous, jointly dependent variables. Short-run profit maximization in competitive markets implies:

$$q - \ell = w + v, \ q - m = p + \varepsilon,$$

where w and p are the real prices of labor and of materials, respectively, and v and ε are the associated optimization errors. Solving for q, ℓ, and m yields:

$$q = \frac{1}{1 - \beta - \delta} [\alpha c + \gamma k + e - \beta(w + v) - \delta(p + \varepsilon)],$$

$$\ell = \frac{1}{1 - \beta - \delta} [\alpha c + \gamma k + e - (1 - \delta)(w + v) - \delta(p + \varepsilon)],$$

$$m = \frac{1}{1 - \beta - \delta} [\alpha c + \gamma k + e - \beta(w + v) - (1 - \beta)(p + \varepsilon)].$$

---

17. The variances of the residual e' and v' in our semireduced form production and labor equations are respectively:

$$[\sigma^2_e + \beta^2(\sigma^2_w + \sigma^2_v)]/(1 - \beta)^2 + \sigma^2_f, \ \text{and} \ (\sigma^2_e + \sigma^2_w + \sigma^2_v)/(1 - \beta)^2,$$

Since materials and factor prices are unobserved in our data, we have to drop the last equation and lump w and p with the other error components in these equations. We are thus left with two semireduced form equations for output and labor. Coming back for the sake of coherence to our previous notations of the production function with m solved out $[\alpha = \alpha/(1 - \delta), \ldots, e = e - \delta(p + \varepsilon)/(1 - \delta)]$, we can rewrite these two equations more simply:

$$q = \frac{1}{1 - \beta}(\alpha c + \gamma k) + e',$$

$$\ell = \frac{1}{1 - \beta}(\alpha c + \gamma k) + v',$$

where $e' = [e - \beta(w + v)]/(1 - \beta)$ and $v' = [e - (w + v)]/(1 - \beta)$.

The semireduced form equation should provide unbiased estimates of $\alpha/(1 - \beta)$ and $\gamma/(1 - \beta)$ to the extent that factor prices w and p are more or less uncorrelated with the capital variables c and k. This condition seems quite plausible in the within dimension. There is little independent variance left in w and p in the within dimension after one takes out their common time-series components with time dummies or a trend variable. In the between dimension, however, one would expect that w and p might vary across firms and be positively correlated with c and k, leading to downward biases in $\alpha/(1 - \beta)$ and $\gamma/(1 - \beta)$ in both equations (and more so in the labor equation).

Tables 5.8, 5.9, and 5.10 present estimates of such semireduced form equations comparable to the production function estimates reported in the earlier tables 5.2–5.7: total and within estimates for all firms and for scientific and other firms separately; for the two subperiods 1966–71 and 1972–77 (and between these two subperiods); for the restricted and merger samples (and the merger-no-jump sample). Since the "theory" of the semireduced form equations implies that corresponding coefficients should be the same in the two equations, we also present the constrained system (SUR) estimates.

A first look at the results shows that they are in the right ball park. They are not very strikingly different in the two dimensions, and most remarkably, the within estimates of the research capital coefficient are quite significant and rather large. Also, the corresponding estimates in the two equations are rather close. Given the large number of degrees of freedom, all differences are "statistically" significant, but constraining the coefficients to be equal in the two equations results in a negligible loss of fit, changing the systemwide R^2 only in the third (or second) decimal place.

A more careful examination confirms, more or less, our previous production function findings. The estimates for the two, scientific and other firms, are

---

while the covariance is $[\sigma_e^2 + \beta(\sigma_w^2 + \sigma_v^2)]/(1 - \beta)^2$. For a given β, we can thus derive estimated values of σ_e^2, $(\sigma_w^2 + \sigma_v^2)$, and σ_f^2. However, these values are extremely sensitive to the value of β chosen and to small differences in the variances and covariance of the semireduced form equations residuals.

Table 5.8   Semireduced Form Equations Estimates (complete sample, 1966–77)

Different Regressions		Total Regressions			Within Regressions		
		$\alpha/(1-\beta)$	$\gamma/(1-\beta)$	System R^2	$\alpha/(1-\beta)$	$\gamma/(1-\beta)$	System R^2
All firms ($N = 133$)	Output	.574 (.010)	.296 (.014)	.873	.407 (.022)	.265 (.027)	.559
	Labor	.415 (.013)	.416 (.017)		.400 (.021)	.288 (.026)	
	Constrained	.554 (.010)	.311 (.014)	.857	.403 (.019)	.278 (.024)	.558
Scientific firms ($N = 77$)	Output	.488 (.013)	.378 (.017)	.910	.321 (.025)	.291 (.031)	.711
	Labor	.464 (.019)	.375 (.024)		.283 (.025)	.423 (.030)	
	Constrained	.490 (.013)	.378 (.017)	.909	.301 (.023)	.395 (.028)	.706
Other firms ($N = 36$)	Output	.544 (.018)	.380 (.024)	.860	.510 (.037)	.067 (.052)	.340
	Labor	.290 (.021)	.558 (.029)		.559 (.036)	.122 (.051)	
	Constrained	.506 (.018)	.407 (.024)	.802	.536 (.033)	.096 (.041)	.337

Table 5.9 Semireduced Form Equations Estimates for Subperiods: 1966–71 and 1972–77 and between Subperiods (scientific firms, complete sample)

Different Regressions		Total Regressions			Within Regressions		
		$\alpha/(1-\beta)$	$\gamma/(1-\beta)$	System R^2	$\alpha/(1-\beta)$	$\gamma/(1-\beta)$	System R^2
Subperiod 1966–71	Output	0.480 (0.019)	0.363 (0.025)	0.902	0.350 (0.036)	0.164 (0.047)	0.582
	Labor	0.482 (0.027)	0.341 (0.035)		0.437 (0.043)	0.230 (0.057)	
	Constrained	0.480 (0.019)	0.363 (0.025)	0.902	0.371 (0.035)	0.180 (0.046)	0.571
Subperiod 1972–77	Output	0.500 (0.018)	0.394 (0.023)	0.917	0.060 (0.046)	0.622 (0.071)	0.418
	Labor	0.447 (0.026)	0.408 (0.033)		0.107 (0.040)	0.579 (0.062)	
	Constrained	0.506 (0.018)	0.392 (0.022)	0.915	0.093 (0.039)	0.592 (0.059)	0.417
Between subperiods	Output				0.413 (0.022)	0.264 (0.024)	0.830
	Labor				0.259 (0.020)	0.464 (0.022)	
	Constrained				0.320 (0.019)	0.385 (0.027)	0.822

Table 5.10   Semireduced Form Equations Estimates for the Restricted, Merger, and Merger No Jump Samples (scientific firms, 1966–77)

Different Regressions		Total Regressions			Within Regressions		
		$\alpha/(1-\beta)$	$\gamma/(1-\beta)$	System R^2	$\alpha/(1-\beta)$	$\gamma/(1-\beta)$	System R^2
Restricted sample	Output	0.521 (0.014)	0.343 (0.019)	.923	0.500 (0.038)	0.146 (0.037)	.730
	Labor	0.481 (0.022)	0.343 (0.029)		0.392 (0.035)	0.281 (0.034)	
	Constrained	0.527 (0.013)	0.343 (0.017)	.921	0.433 (0.033)	0.230 (0.032)	.725
Merger firms	Output	0.402 (0.028)	0.484 (0.031)	.896	0.208 (0.042)	0.434 (0.059)	.714
	Labor	0.461 (0.038)	0.438 (0.042)		0.179 (0.045)	0.572 (0.063)	
	Constrained	0.407 (0.028)	0.480 (0.031)	.895	0.196 (0.038)	0.492 (0.053)	.709
Merger: no-jumps sample	Output	0.460 (0.028)	0.414 (0.032)	.925	−0.117 (0.083)	0.652 (0.106)	.519
	Labor	0.521 (0.039)	0.355 (0.045)		0.178 (0.077)	0.372 (0.098)	
	Constrained	0.468 (0.027)	0.405 (0.031)	.924	0.049 (0.066)	0.495 (0.085)	.504

close, given the collinearity between c and k, which causes the much lower within estimate of $\gamma/(1 - \beta)$ for the other firms group to be largely counterbalanced by the higher estimates of $\alpha/(1 - \beta)$. The estimates for the two subperiods are also quite comparable, since the higher within estimates of $\gamma(1 - \beta)$ for 1972–77 can be explained, similarly, by the lower estimate of $\alpha/(1 - \beta)$. Also, the merger firms do not seem to behave as differently as it appeared earlier. The within estimates of $\gamma/(1 - \beta)$ for the nonmerger firms are significant, and the discrepancy between the estimates for the two types of firms may also be a result of the collinearity between c and k.

The remaining difficulty with our semireduced form estimates is their absolute size. It is different from our a priori expectations. If the true coefficients of the production function were $\alpha = .15$, $\beta = .3$, $\gamma = .05$, and $\delta = .5$, or in value-added terms $\alpha = .3$, $\beta = .6$, and $\gamma = .1$, the semireduced form coefficients should be about .75 and .25, respectively. The estimated physical capital coefficients should be about .75 and .25, respectively. The estimated physical capital coefficient is much smaller, being about .5 at best, while the estimated R&D coefficient is of the expected order of magnitude but often higher. Although the total and within estimates do not differ too strikingly, it should be noted that the estimated sum $(\alpha + \gamma)/(1 - \beta)$ is about .8 or .9 cross-sectionally and about .5 to .7 in the time dimension. This is quite similar to what happened to our production function returns to scale estimates.

We can think of two possible explanations for these shortfalls: (1) errors in variables, and (2) failure of the perfect competition assumption.

To the extent that errors in measurement are random over time (which is a difficult position to maintain for *stock* variables), their effects can be mitigated by averaging and by trying to increase the signal-to-noise ratio in the affected variables. The between subperiods estimates given in table 5.9 represent an attempt to accomplish this by using differences between two six-year subperiod averages. It is clear from this attempt (and from others not reported here) that averaging does not solve the problem of the absolute magnitude of our estimates. Either our solution for the errors of measurement is not effective (because the errors are correlated over time) or the problem is caused by something else entirely.

The perfect competition assumption is especially dubious for our large firms and short-run context. To explore the consequences of such a misspecification, we have to expand our model by adding a demand equation:

$$q_{it} = \alpha_i + z_t + \eta p_{it} + \phi k_{it} + \varepsilon ,$$

where α_i is a permanent firm demand level variable, z_t is a common industry demand shifter, η is the relative price elasticity of demand (where the price of the firm's products p_{it} is measured relative to the overall price level in the industry), and ϕ is the direct effect of R&D capital on the demand for the firm's products.

Given this model, we reinterpret our output variable as sales (which it really is), make price endogenous, and use the demand equation to solve it out of the system. This yields comparable semireduced form equations, but the coefficients are now

$$\frac{\alpha\left(1 + \dfrac{1}{\eta}\right)}{1 - \beta\left(1 + \dfrac{1}{\eta}\right)} \quad \text{and} \quad \frac{\gamma\left(1 + \dfrac{1}{\eta} - \dfrac{\phi}{\eta}\right)}{1 - \beta\left(1 + \dfrac{1}{\eta}\right)}$$

for physical and research capital, respectively. With $\eta < 0$, the research capital coefficient is seen to be a combination of both its production and demand function shifting effects.

The introduction of the $(1 + 1/\eta)$ terms into these coefficients provides an explanation for the "shortfall" in our estimates. Assuming $\eta = -4$ (i.e., if a firm lowers the relative price of its product by 25 percent, it would double its market share) and $\alpha = .3$, $\beta = .6$, $\gamma = .1$, and $\phi = .1$, implies .4 and .18 as the respective coefficients in the semireduced forms. That is not too far off and the assumptions are plausible enough, but that is about all that we can say. We shall need more data and more evidence from other implications of such a model before we can put much faith in this interpretation of our results.

5.4 Summary and Conclusions

We have analyzed the relationship between output, employment, and physical and R&D capital for a sample of 133 large U.S. firms covering the years 1966 through 1977. In the cross-sectional dimension, there is a strong relationship between firm productivity and the level of its R&D investments. In the time dimension, using deviations from firm means as observations and unconstrained estimation, this relationship comes close to vanishing. This may be due in part to the increase in collinearity between the trend, physical capital, and R&D capital in the within dimension. There is little independent variability left there. When the coefficients of the first two variables are constrained to reasonable values, the R&D coefficient is both sizeable and significant. Another reason for these difficulties may be the simultaneity of output and employment decisions in the short run. Allowing for such a simultaneity yields rather high estimates of the importance of R&D capital relative to physical capital. Our data do not enable us, however, to answer any detailed questions about the lag structure of the effects of R&D on productivity. These effects are apparently highly variable, both in timing and magnitude.

Appendix
Variables and Additional Results

In this appendix we present more information on our sample and summarize the results of various additional computational experiments.

Table 5A.1 lists means, standard deviations, and growth rates for our major variables, and indicates that most of the observed variance in the data (90+ percent) is between firms, rather than within firms and across time. It also underscores the fact that these firms are rather large, with an average of more than 10,000 employees per firm.

Table 5A.2 compares our main measure of physical capital stock C to four alternatives: C', CA, CN, and CD. C is gross plant adjusted for inflation, which we assume to be proportional to a proper capital service flow measure. Since our adjustment for inflation is based on a rough first-order approximation, assuming a fixed service life, a linear depreciation pattern, and an estimate of the age of capital (AA) from reported depreciation levels, we also tried different variants of it.[18] C' is one of them in which we assume the same average service life for plant and equipment of sixteen years for all our firms. The fit is somewhat improved, but the changes in the estimates are only minor. Actually, using the reported gross plant figure without any adjustment does not make that much difference either. CA is our C measure taken at the end of the year instead of the beginning of the year. The fit is slightly improved, and the within estimates of α are increased a little. This could indicate that end of the year measures are appropriate but may also reflect a simultaneity bias arising from the contemporaneous feedback of changes in production on investment. CN and CD are net plant and depreciation adjusted for inflation, respectively. CN can be advocated on the grounds that in some sense it allows for obsolescence and embodied technical progress, and CD on the grounds that it is nearer in principle to a service flow measure. CN results in a small decrease of the within estimate of α and a corresponding increase in γ, while CD results in an increase in both total and within estimates of α with no noticeable effect on γ. We have also run regressions including an age of capital variable, AA. While our estimates of α and γ are not affected by its inclusion, this variable in conjunction with our gross capital measure C (but not so in conjunction with the net capital measure CN) is clearly significant both in the cross-sectional and time dimensions, tending to indicate a rate of embodied technical progress of 5.5 percent per year (see Mairesse 1978).

Table 5A.2 also gives the estimates obtained with an alternative measure of

---

18. To be precise C_t is computed as reported gross plant $\times P(72)/P(t - AA_t)$, where P is the GNP price deflator for fixed investment and AA_t (the average age of gross plant) is computed as reported gross plant minus reported net plant (i.e., accumulated depreciation) divided by an estimate of the average service life LL_t. LL_t itself is computed as the five-year moving average of reported gross plant/reported depreciation.

Table 5A.1   Characteristics of Variables, Complete Sample (133 firms)[a]

Main Variables[b]	Scientific Firms (77)					Other Firms (56)				
	Geometric Mean	Standard Deviation	Percent Variability		Rate of Growth (%)	Geometric Mean	Standard Deviation	Percent Variability		Rate of Growth (%)
			Between	Within				Between	Within	
Q Deflated sales	297.0	1.66	95.1	4.9	8.9	442.8	1.74	97.9	2.1	3.9
L Number of employees	10.4	1.63	97.4	2.6	4.6	12.5	1.52	97.6	2.4	2.9
C Gross plant adjusted for inflation	188.4	2.12	95.3	4.7	10.8	295.7	2.11	97.3	2.7	8.4
K R&D capital stock computed using a 0.15 rate of obsolescence	58.1	1.64	95.7	4.3	7.6	39.6	1.53	82.3	17.7	4.4
Q/L Deflated sales per employee	28.7	0.39	71.6	28.4	4.3	35.3	0.49	89.8	10.2	0.9
C/L Gross plant adjusted per employee	18.1	0.85	86.6	13.4	6.2	23.6	1.05	93.2	6.8	5.4
K/L R&D capital stock measure per employee	5.6	0.70	90.6	9.4	3.0	3.2	0.67	87.5	12.5	1.5

[a]Standard deviations and the decomposition of the variance are given for the logarithms of the variables.

[b]Deflated sales, gross plant adjusted, and R&D capital stock are in $10^6 and constant 1972 prices. Number of employees is in 10^3 persons.

Table 5A.2   **Production Function Estimates for Different Measures of Physical Capital Stock and Output, All Sectors, Complete Sample (133 firms), 1966–77 (annual and three-year averages)**

Different Regressions[a]	Total Regressions			Within Regressions		
	α	γ	MSE	α	γ	MSE
C	0.310	0.073	0.097	0.160	0.150	0.0204
	0.332	0.054	0.095	0.150	0.080	0.0199
C′	0.323	0.070	0.095	0.180	0.142	0.0202
	0.350	0.048	0.092	0.173	0.069	0.0197
CA	0.322	0.074	0.095	0.201	0.156	0.0201
	0.344	0.054	0.092	0.186	0.101	0.0197
CN	0.304	0.076	0.096	0.124	0.184	0.0204
	0.325	0.050	0.094	0.114	0.115	0.0199
CD	0.361	0.062	0.099	0.194	0.163	0.0202
	0.383	0.044	0.097	0.189	0.086	0.0196
QC	0.305	0.073	0.100	0.102	0.127	0.0229
	0.325	0.055	0.098	0.093	0.060	0.0224
Three-year averages	0.313	0.074	0.091	0.195	0.154	0.0153
	0.336	0.055	0.090	0.187	0.092	0.0149

[a]Constant returns to scale are imposed for estimates reported in the first line of each cell but not in the second.

deflated sales, QC, tentatively corrected for inventory change. The correction, however, is problematic since it is based on all inventories and not just finished products. In any case, QC performs much worse both in terms of fit and in terms of the order of magnitude of the within estimates. Finally, we also list estimates based on three-year averages of the observations. While errors of measurement appear to be a priori an important issue (if they were random and uncorrelated, going to averages should reduce the resulting biases), the changes are not striking and the discrepancy between total and within estimates remains. Yet there is a sizeable increase (about 20 percent) in the within estimate of α, which might reflect an error in the capital-labor ratio accounting for about 30 percent of the observed "within" variance in this ratio.

Because we did not want to give up hope of gaining some evidence on the lag structure of R&D effects, we experimented with a large number of R&D capital stock measures, but mostly in vain. Table 5A.3 compares K, the measure we finally settled on based on a 15 percent depreciation rate, to six rather different alternatives. $K00$ and $K30$ are computed similarly to K but assuming 0 and 30 percent per year obsolescence rates instead. K' and $K'00$ differ from K and $K00$ respectively in assuming that R&D vintages older than eight years are completely obsolete. Since information on R&D is available only from 1958 (i.e., for eight years before 1966), this is also a way to test our initial condition assumption. In the K and $K00$ measures, the 1958 R&D capital levels are based on extrapolating R&D expenditures back to 1948, using the 1958–63

Table 5A.3   Production Function Estimates Based on Different Measures of R&D Capital, Complete Sample (133 firms), 1966–77

Alternative R&D Capital Measures[a]	Total Regressions			Within Regressions		
	α	γ	MSE	α	γ	MSE
K	0.310	0.073	0.097	0.160	0.150	0.0204
	0.332	0.054	0.095	0.150	0.080	0.0199
K'	0.311	0.075	0.096	0.173	0.119	0.0206
	0.333	0.057	0.094	0.153	0.064	0.0199
K00	0.309	0.059	0.098	0.152	0.172	0.0202
	0.334	0.040	0.095	0.154	0.081	0.0199
K'00	0.311	0.070	0.097	0.178	0.106	0.0207
	0.333	0.051	0.095	0.158	0.050	0.0200
K30	0.311	0.079	0.096	0.167	0.137	0.0204
	0.332	0.061	0.094	0.147	0.084	0.0198
KP	0.311	0.065	0.097	0.195	0.070	0.0209
	0.334	0.046	0.095	0.165	0.027	0.0200
K and $P_{-34}, P_{-56}, P_{-78}, P_{-9+}$	0.318	0.070	0.094	0.149	0.205	0.0197
	0.340	0.051	0.092	0.152	0.120	0.0196

[a]First line regressions assume constant returns to scale, second line regressions do not.

individual firm R&D growth rate shrunk toward the overall industry rate. KP is also a summation of past R&D expenditures over eight years but with a very different peaked lag structure: $w_{-1} = w_{-8} = 0.05$, $w_{-2} = w_{-7} = 0.10$, $w_{-3} = w_{-6} = 0.15$, and $w_{-4} = w_{-5} = 0.20$. Finally, $K, P_{-34}, P_{-56}, P_{-78}, P_{-9+}$ is one of the free-lag version experiments we have attempted. The P variables are the following proportion of past R&D expenditures (over two years plus the tail) to total cumulated expenditures (with a .15 rate of obsolescence): $(R_{-3} + R_{-4})/K$, $(R_{-5} + R_{-6})/K$, $(R_{-7} + R_{-8})/K$, $(R_{-9} + R_{-10} + \ldots)/K$. Hence, the coefficients of the P's should give an indication of how far the respective true weights are from the assumed declining weights in K: 1, .85, .72, .61, .52, . . . , etc.

As was the case for the different physical capital measures, the total estimates are almost unaffected by all this experimentation, while the within estimates are more sensitive. The initial conditions seem to matter very slightly, showing some influence of a truncation remainder or tail effect. The within regressions with the K and K00 measures perform a little better in terms of fit than those with the corresponding K' and K'00 measures (which assume no effective R&D before 1958), and the estimated γ is a bit higher. The assumption about the order of magnitude of the rate of obsolescence δ is even less important. Still, there is some tenuous evidence here for a rather rapidly declining lag structure. The KP measure (which assumes a peaked lag structure) has the lowest fit and the lowest within γ, while the "free lag" version in the neighborhood of the K measure performs best on both grounds. The estimated P coefficients (within) are:

$$P_{-34} : -0.35, \quad P_{-56} : -0.17, \quad P_{-78} : -0.10, \quad P_{-9+} : 0.05,$$

$$(0.09) \qquad (0.07) \qquad (0.07) \qquad (0.02)$$

implying that around lag 3 and 4 the weight of past R&D is about .22 rather than .57, around lag 5 and 6 it is .24 rather than .41, around lag 7 and 8 it is .20 rather than .30, and around lag 11 it is .22 rather than .17. That is, there is a reasonably strong immediate effect in the first two years which then drops sharply and stays constant through most of the rest of the observable range.

References

Griliches, Z. 1973. Research expenditures and growth accounting. In *Science and technology in economic growth,* ed. B. R. Williams, 59–83. London: Macmillan.

———. 1979. Issues in assessing the contribution of research and development to productivity growth. *Bell Journal of Economics* 10, no. 1:92–116. [Reprinted as chap. 2 in this volume.]

———. 1980a. Returns to research and development expenditures in the private sector. In *New developments in productivity measurement and analysis,* ed. J. Kendrick and B. Vaccara, 419–61. NBER Conference on Research in Income and Wealth: Studies in Income and Wealth, vol. 44. Chicago: University of Chicago Press. [Reprinted as chap. 3 in this volume.]

———. 1980b. R&D and the productivity slowdown. *American Economic Review, Proceedings Issue* 70, no. 2:343–48.

Griliches, Z., and F. Lichtenberg. 1984. R&D and productivity growth at the industry level: Is there still a relationship? In *R&D, patents, and productivity,* ed. Zvi Griliches, 465–96. Chicago: University of Chicago Press. [Reprinted as chap. 9 in this volume.]

Griliches, Z., and V. Ringstad. 1971. *Economies of scale and the form of the production function.* Amsterdam: North-Holland.

Hoch, I. 1962. Estimation of production function parameters combining time-series and cross-section data. *Econometrica* 30:34–53.

Mairesse, J. 1978. New estimates of embodied and disembodied technical progress. *Annales de l'INSEE* 30–31:681–719.

Mundlak, Y. 1961. Empirical production function free of management bias. *Journal of Farm Economics* 43:44–56.

Nadiri, M. I., and G. C. Bitros. 1980. Research and development expenditures and labor productivity at the firm level: A dynamic model. In *New developments in productivity measurement and analysis,* ed. J. Kendrick and B. Vaccara, 387–412. NBER Conference on Research in Income and Wealth: Studies in Income and Wealth, vol. 44. Chicago: University of Chicago Press.

Scherer, F. M. 1981. Interindustry technology flows and productivity growth. Working paper, Northwestern University.

Terleckyj, N. E. 1974. *Effects of R&D on the productivity growth of industries: An exploratory study.* Washington, D.C.: National Planning Association.

6 Productivity Growth and R&D at the Business Level: Results from the PIMS Data Base

The recent slowdown in productivity growth in the United States and elsewhere has increased interest in understanding its determinants. Among the determinants commanding attention have been expenditures for research and development. R&D investment has attracted attention because a slowdown in its growth seemed to coincide with the productivity slowdown, and because earlier studies of the R&D-productivity connection had found R&D to be an important determinant of productivity growth. Recent work on R&D and productivity growth, however, presents a relatively mixed picture. While studies on 1950s and 1960s data generally found positive effects, productivity equations for the 1970s found the coefficient alternately collapsing (Griliches 1980; Agnew and Wise 1978; Scherer 1981; Terleckyj 1980) and reviving (Griliches and Lichtenberg 1984; Scherer 1981), depending on the data used and, in particular, on the level of aggregation. Where disaggregated data were explored, a relatively sizeable effect of R&D was found, even in the turbulent 1970s.

This paper presents the results of a study of productivity growth and R&D in the 1970s using data on narrowly defined "business units" within a firm. The principal focus of the analysis is estimation of the productivity of R&D at the margin. Estimates are developed under different assumptions about technology, industry effects, and changes in the return to R&D over time. Our R&D data are classified into process and product expenditures, and we examine the effect of proprietary technology and technological opportunity on R&D productivity.

The results reported below suggest a significant relationship between R&D and the growth of productivity; in versions using total factor productivity as the

This chapter is coauthored with Kim Clark and is reprinted from *R&D, Patents, and Productivity*, edited by Zvi Griliches, pp. 393–416 (Chicago: University of Chicago Press, 1984). © 1984 by the National Bureau of Economic Research. All rights reserved.

dependent variable, the estimated marginal product or rate of return is about 18 percent. There is no evidence in these data of a deterioration in the productivity of R&D in the 1970s. Irrespective of model specification, trends in the R&D coefficient are substantively and statistically insignificant. We also find some evidence that, all else equal, a shift in the mix toward more product R&D lowers the measured rate of growth of productivity, and that R&D has its biggest effect on productivity in those businesses where major technical changes have occurred within the recent past.

The paper has three parts. We discuss the data used and present summary information about our key variables in section 6.1. Particular attention is paid to the reported price indexes. Estimates of price changes in the PIMS data are compared with estimates based on government surveys. Section 6.2 sets out the analytical framework and presents estimates of the effect of R&D on productivity under several model specifications. The paper concludes in section 6.3 with a brief summary and some suggestions for further work.

6.1   The Data Set

The data we use are drawn from the PIMS project of the Strategic Planning Institute (SPI).[1] The Institute is composed of over 1,500 member companies which participate in the project by supplying annual data on individual businesses within the company. Our sample covers 924 U.S. manufacturing businesses over the period 1970–80.

A "business" in the PIMS lexicon is a unit of a firm "selling a distinct set of products to an identifiable set of customers in competition with a well-defined set of competitors." Businesses tend to be synonymous with operating divisions of a company but may be defined in terms of product lines within divisions. In addition to annual income statements and balance sheets, each business provides information on several measures of market structure, technology, previous competitive experience, and competitive strategy. Along with its panel structure and level of detail, the richness of the PIMS data set makes it a potentially valuable source of information on the determinants and impact of R&D.

But richness has its price. Several aspects of the data must be kept in mind when interpreting the evidence presented below. In the first place, we are not dealing here with typical or representative firms. The companies in the project tend to be large, diversified corporations; many are found in the *Fortune* 500; and almost all of them are found in the *Fortune* 1,000. The analysis thus deals with the impact of R&D on productivity among firms that may not be representative of all firms in a given sector, but which probably account for a significant fraction of the assets and people employed.

---

1. A description of the PIMS data can be found in Schoeffler (1977). For an analysis of R&D and profitability using the PIMS data, see Ravenscraft and Scherer (1981).

The unit of observation is a further problem. Although SPI provides guidelines for defining "business units," the choice is left to the company and will depend on the availability of data and the company's assessment of the usefulness of the definition.[2] In a related fashion, much of the structural data is subject to the company's assessments and perceptions. Of course, a good deal of the information requested by SPI is available through accounting systems and is subject to uniformity of definition and guidelines developed and imposed by SPI. But variables, like the number of competitors or the relative quality of the business's products, depend to some extent on the respondent's perceptions.

Finally, the self-reported character of the data and their use in comparative modeling raise questions about their quality and integrity. Two considerations suggest that the quality of the data is reasonably high. First, the information requested is of value to the business itself (e.g., its market share), and it seems reasonable to suppose that the firm is in a position to know and has expended effort to acquire accurate data. Second, a firm's participation in the project is motivated by a desire to use the data in the strategic planning models developed by SPI. Considerable effort is made to preserve confidentiality and ensure quality: only the firms themselves have access to their own data; sensitive variables (e.g., profits) are only reported in disguised or ratio form; analysts at SPI run the data through an elaborate procedure to check for consistency, and gross errors are followed up with the company.

6.1.1   Major Variables

The annual income statement and balance sheet provided by each firm can be used to construct measures of productivity, R&D, and capital. We use sales, deflated by an index of product prices, as the basic measure of output. Although available information permits calculation of value added, we found that treating materials as a separate factor of production fit the data much better. The output price index and an index of materials prices are provided by the business under guidelines set forth by SPI. The guidelines define the relevant concept of output price as a weighted average of the business's selling prices, holding the mix of products constant. Since the quality of the output and productivity series depends on the quality of the output price indexes, they are examined below in more detail.

Information on labor input is limited. The only variable available to us is the number of employees, and that is only available on a disguised basis and thus can only be used in ratio form. There are no data on hours per employee, nor are the data broken down by occupation or type of employment. Output per employee and capital-labor ratios are defined for all employees, including sales and managerial personnel, as well as those engaged in R&D activities and

---

2. Definition of a business as developed in the PIMS guidelines is based on the concept of a "strategic business unit." This concept is spelled out in more detail in Abell and Hammond (1979).

production. These variables are not adjusted for differences in quality, since no wage data or data on education or other characteristics are available.

Estimates of the real stock of capital are derived from information on the firm's balance sheet and annual investment. The value of plant and equipment in the firm is reported at historical cost, but each firm provides an estimate of the replacement value of gross plant and equipment in the initial year of its participation in the survey. This gives an initial capital stock value in current prices. Since firms may enter the sample in different years, we restate the initial value in current prices into constant (1972) dollars using the deflator for business fixed investment (BFI) from the National Income and Product Accounts. Subsequent investment in plant and equipment is deflated by the BFI price index and added to the initial year stock. The investment series we use is net of retirements, but we have not subtracted out reported depreciation.[3] To provide a comparative perspective, we shall estimate the models using gross book value of capital as well as the stock of capital adjusted for inflation as described above.

As with most data sets, information on R&D comes in the form of current spending. Expenditures on research and development are treated as an expense in the PIMS accounting system and are, therefore, reported in the income statement. Businesses are asked to include in this category all expenses (material, labor, etc.) incurred to improve existing products or to develop new products, and all expenses to improve the efficiency of the manufacturing process. Total R&D expenditures are thus classified into product and process categories. How that split is implemented, however, is left to the business to decide. All R&D expenses are specific to the business and exclude charges for research and development done in a central corporate facility. They may, however, include expenses shared with other businesses but conducted below the corporate level.

Table 6.1 presents definitions, means, and standard deviations of the basic variables used in the analysis. The sample covers 924 businesses, with a total of 4,146 observations; not all firms are present in each year, so the design of the sample is unbalanced. Data on real sales, materials, and capital per employee show a substantial amount of variability around relatively high average rates of growth. In real terms, sales per employee grew at an annual rate of 4 percent in these data, while capital and materials per person grew at rates between 3.5 and 4.0 percent. The data on newness of the capital stock (ratio of net to gross book value) suggest that, on average, productivity growth occurred during a period in which the capital stock was aging.

---

3. The nominal investment series is calculated as the difference in the gross book value of plant and equipment. It thus reflects both gross investment and retirements. Estimates of real capital can be obtained in other ways. One possibility is to estimate the age of capital using the ratio of accumulated depreciation to annual depreciation, and then to adjust current book values based on changes in the BFI deflator since the year the average piece of capital (determined by the age calculation) was purchased. For an example of this approach, see Griliches and Mairesse 1984. Their results, as well as our own estimates reported below, suggest that the R&D estimates are relatively insensitive to adjustments of this sort.

Table 6.1   **Means and Standard Deviations U.S. Manufacturing Businesses, PIMS Data Base, 1971–80**

Variable	Definition	Mean	Std. Dev.
(1) Rates of Growth (in percent):			
$(s - l)$	real sales per employee	3.95	17.33
p	output price index	7.40	9.10
$(m - l)$	real purchases per employee	3.93	22.31
p_m	materials price index	9.17	12.42
$(g - l)$	gross book value of plant and equipment per employee	7.32	19.22
$(c - l)$	gross plant and equipment per employee in 1972 \$	3.55	17.00
util	rate of capacity utilization	2.71	16.62
new	ratio of net to gross book value of plant and equipment	−1.15	12.54
(2) R&D Variables (in percent):			
RQ(−1)	ratio of total R&D expenses to average of current sales and sales lagged one period	2.21	3.76
RMIX	ratio of product R&D expenses to total R&D expenses	65.49	29.94
(3) Proprietary Technology and Technological Opportunity:			
DPROD	= 1 if business derives significant benefit from proprietary products (patents etc.) = 0 otherwise	0.21	—
DPROC	= 1 if business derives significant benefit from proprietary processes (patents etc.) = 0 otherwise	0.21	—
DTECH	= 1 if there have been major technological changes in product or process of the business or its major competitors in last eight years = 0 otherwise	0.28	—

Variables measuring R&D intensity and mix are listed in part 2 of table 6.1. These data are of a reasonable order of magnitude and imply that the businesses in the sample cover a wide range of R&D intensities. As in data collected at other levels of aggegation, the majority of R&D (65 percent) is devoted to improving old or developing new products. Although the sample covers most of the two-digit industries, almost half of the observations are from businesses in chemicals, electrical and nonelectrical machinery, and instruments.

We have used the PIMS data to calculate R&D intensity for these two-digit industries, as well as for primary and fabricated metal products, and compared them to data published by the National Science Foundation (NSF). This comparison, presented in table 6.2, shows the same ranking of industries by R&D intensity in the two data sets. Since the NSF is a company-based data set, and since the mix of subindustries within the two-digit industries may not be identical, differences in the R&D-to-sales ratio in the two series are to be expected. But the two sources yield intensity estimates that are quite similar. Only in machinery (SIC 35) does a sizeable discrepancy emerge.

We make no attempt to estimate the stock of R&D capital, but rather use R&D intensity to capture the effects of R&D on productivity. To allow for lagged effects and to break any spurious correlation induced by the presence of lagged output as an independent variable, we define R&D intensity as:

$$RQ(-1) = \frac{R_{-1}}{\frac{1}{2}(S + S_{-1})},$$

where R_{-1} is R&D expenditure in the previous period, and S indicates total sales. Other measures, including R&D intensity lagged one and two periods, and an instrumental variable procedure, had no effect on the results. We shall report only the estimates with $RQ(-1)$.

Part 3 of table 6.1 provides information on three variables that we use as indicators of previous technical activity. The first two indicate whether the business "derives significant benefit" from proprietary products or processes, either through patents or what the SPI guidelines call "trade secrets." The last variable indicates whether "major" technological change (either product or process) had occurred in the business or in its major competitors in the last eight years. These questions are asked only once (when the business enters the PIMS project) so that the dummy variables are constant over time. The data suggest that a sizeable fraction of the businesses have carried out R&D projects that have led to patents or some other form of proprietary products or processes. An issue we examine below is whether R&D capability defined in this way affects the current connection between R&D investments and productivity.

The mean growth rates of the basic variables are of a reasonable order of magnitude, but a somewhat more detailed look at the data, particularly at the

Table 6.2   **R&D Expenditures as a Percent of Sales in PIMS and NSF Data[a] for Selected Two-Digit Industries, 1974**

Industries (SIC)	PIMS	NSF
Chemicals (28)	2.8	3.0
Primary metals (33)	0.5	0.5
Fabricated metal prod. (34)	1.3	1.1
Machinery (35)	2.0	3.8
Electrical equipment (36)	3.5	3.5[b]
Instruments (38)	4.8	5.2

Source: NSF = National Science Foundation; PIMS = Calculated from PIMS data base.

[a]NSF data pertain to company expenditures on R&D; the PIMS data pertain to business level R&D, excluding R&D performed in corporate research laboratories.

[b]The NSF data for electrical equipment include data on communication (SIC 48).

output price series, seems in order. Although our focus is productivity, the measures of output underlying the analysis are only as good as the price indexes used to deflate nominal sales. A full-scale analysis of the data is beyond the scope of this paper, but we can provide some perspective by comparing rates of change of prices in the PIMS data with those found in the statistics published by the government. To do that we have focused on price changes in a group of industries where the number of observations available in the PIMS data set is sufficient to justify comparison with the published figures.

Table 6.3 presents annual rates of price change for nine two-digit SIC industries over the period 1971–79. Each cell in the table contains three entries. The first is the percentage change in the two-digit industry deflator calculated by the Bureau of Economic Analysis as part of the National Income and Product Accounts. The second entry is the average percentage change in the price indexes of PIMS firms in the corresponding two-digit industry. The last number is the number of PIMS firms in the industry in that year. The comparisons in table 6.2 are necessarily rough. Because the mix of four-digit industries underlying the PIMS two-digit calculations is different than the mix used in the BEA calculations, it is not reasonable to expect the two sources to yield identical estimates. However, to the extent that similar economic forces affect the constituent four-digit industries in similar ways, a two-digit level comparison should give us some idea of comparability.

Perhaps the most noticeable aspect of the BEA/PIMS comparison in table 6.3 is the similar pattern of change over time. Both data sets generally show small changes in prices in the first three years, followed by an explosion in 1974–75, with rates of price increases running as high as 25–30 percent in some industries. In the latter part of the period, the rate of change is once again much smaller, although higher than the rates found at the beginning of the decade.

Amidst this broad pattern of similarity there are clear differences between the published data and the data from PIMS. In most of the industries, for example, the 1974–75 explosion in prices shows up earlier in the PIMS data, but lasts longer in the BEA estimates.[4] A comparison of the sums of the rates of change in the two years (1974–75) yields values much closer together than comparisons of the years taken individually. Even before the oil shock and the expiration of controls, the two data sets show different patterns in some years in several industries. In fact, the comparisons before the oil shock are much more diverse than those made in the 1976–79 period. Although differences are present in the latter period, the large discrepancies found in the 1971–74 period are less frequent. This pattern may reflect the influence of wage-price controls on reporting practices or the different sources of inflationary pressure in the two periods.

---

4. The use of these data to deflate industry level output would change the estimated pattern of the productivity slowdown quite a bit. It would imply a much slower rise in the 1971–73 period and much less of a fall in 1975.

Table 6.3 Comparison of Rates of Price Change in the PIMS Data Set and the National Income Accounts for Selected Two-Digit Manufacturing Industries

Industry (SIC)	Data Set	1971	1972	1973	1974	1975	1976	1977	1978	1979
(1) Food (20)	BEA	1.5	-4.4	-7.4	15.4	22.7	-2.5	6.6	5.4	4.0
	PIMS	4.0	4.3	9.5	18.5	13.9	2.6	4.5	6.6	11.6
	N	29	35	41	49	40	33	27	17	11
(2) Chemicals (28)	BEA	1.1	-.2	-.8	11.0	12.4	4.2	2.8	4.5	2.7
	PIMS	-0.5	0.2	5.3	23.2	16.0	4.7	5.2	6.0	11.0
	N	75	89	108	95	94	91	55	36	15
(3) Rubber and plastics (30)	BEA	3.2	1.4	-1.0	6.9	9.5	4.9	5.3	4.4	4.3
	PIM	-0.7	-0.6	1.5	18.3	8.2	3.5	4.4	5.6	4.6
	N	22	29	37	46	43	32	21	17	12
(4) Stone, clay, and glass (32)	BEA	9.1	3.2	2.0	6.8	13.5	7.0	8.5	10.0	5.8
	PIMS	3.6	3.9	3.8	15.2	14.4	7.8	7.7	8.1	4.7
	N	15	23	30	36	36	38	34	22	7
(5) Primary metals (33)	BEA	3.1	8.6	-1.8	24.5	20.2	2.8	8.5	9.1	10.9
	PIM	0.5	2.3	10.3	29.2	12.4	2.0	5.2	9.7	9.4
	N	13	16	29	28	32	31	31	26	7
(6) Fabricated metals (34)	BEA	7.3	3.3	3.1	15.9	19.2	1.4	4.8	6.9	5.5
	PIMS	5.5	4.8	6.2	17.1	9.6	6.0	6.3	7.6	9.1
	N	12	25	42	56	63	57	49	36	34
(7) Nonelectrical machinery (35)	BEA	3.7	0.9	1.1	5.6	17.8	3.2	7.3	7.0	6.2
	PIMS	4.9	3.5	5.5	13.7	10.3	6.9	7.2	7.0	7.4
	N	42	60	84	95	100	91	71	45	23
(8) Electrical equipment (36)	BEA	3.0	-0.2	-0.3	4.8	12.5	3.0	5.1	3.8	6.7
	PIMS	0.7	1.4	2.3	12.7	8.7	5.4	5.2	6.2	8.5
	N	51	67	78	62	62	61	53	34	26
(9) Instruments (38)	BEA	1.4	-0.2	-0.6	-.08	9.0	6.2	1.7	6.5	4.0
	PIMS	1.1	2.0	3.2	9.4	8.3	4.9	5.4	4.1	5.3
	N	21	27	31	33	41	41	30	15	7

Source: BEA = Bureau of Economic Analysis, unpublished data, National Income and Product Accounts; PIMS = SPI/PIMS data set.

6.2 Empirical Analysis

The connection between R&D and productivity growth is studied in the context of a fairly conventional model. In its simplest form, output (Q) of the ith business at time t is assumed to be a function of the stock of capital (C), the number of employees (L), accumulated investment in R&D (K), and a factor accounting for disembodied technical change ($Ae^{\lambda t}$), as in

(1) $$Q_{it} = Ae^{\lambda t}Q(K_{it}, L_{it}, C_{it}).$$

It is standard procedure to assume that K_{it} can be represented by a distributed lag of past investments in R&D with the weights presumed to depend on the way in which past activities affect the current state of technical knowledge.

Assuming the production function is Cobb-Douglas and separable in R&D, we can totally differentiate (1) and rearrange terms to derive an expression in terms of rates of growth:

(2) $$q_i = \lambda + \gamma k_i + \alpha c_i + (1 - \alpha)\ell_i,$$

where γ and α are output elasticities with respect to R&D and capital, and lowercase letters have been used to indicate relative rates of growth of their uppercase counterparts (e.g., $k = (dK/dt)/K$). Note that we have assumed constant returns to scale with respect to the conventional measures of capital and labor. Rearranging terms yields a productivity equation:

(3) $$(q - \ell)_i = \lambda + \gamma k_i + \alpha(c - \ell)_i,$$

Where $(q - \ell)_i$ is the growth rate of labor productivity, and $(c - \ell)_i$ is the rate of growth of the capital-labor ratio.

The effect of R&D is measured by γ; estimation in this context requires data on the growth of the stock of R&D capital. If, however, investments in R&D do not depreciate, then data on R&D intensity can be used to capture the R&D effect. If R_{it} is R&D expenditures in year t, then $k_{it} = R_{it}/K_{it}$, and $\gamma k_{it} = \rho(R_{it}/Q_{it})$, where ρ is the marginal product of R&D. Under competitive assumptions, ρ can also be interpreted as the rate of return.[5] Because employment and capital employed in R&D have not been segregated explicitly, this is an excess return to R&D expenditures. Further, it is a private return because the data pertain to individual businesses. Returns accruing to other firms and investors are not captured here.

Equation (3) provides a starting point for empirical analysis, but several adjustments seem warranted. In the first place, the model as specified ignores the

---

5. If R&D investments depreciate, as they most likely do, especially as far as private returns are concerned (see Pakes and Schankerman 1984) then the equation is misspecified by leaving out a term of the $-\delta K/Q$ form. Since K/Q and R/Q are likely to be positively correlated, this omission may bias the estimated R/Q coefficient downward, possibly by a rather large amount (since the R/Q coefficient in the K/Q auxiliary equation is likely to be significantly above unity).

role of intermediate products in production by implicitly assuming that materials (including purchases of intermediate products and energy) are proportional to output.[6] This problem can be dealt with by using information on purchases to expand the input list. It is, of course, possible to use data on materials to calculate a value-added version of output. But this too makes assumptions about the nature of the production process (e.g., materials are used in fixed proportion) which may not apply across all firms. While we have used materials in both ways, treating them explicitly as an input yields much better statistical results, and we shall focus on such results in the empirical work reported below. The variable we use is total purchases deflated by an index of materials prices.[7]

One of the reasons for adding materials as an input is our view that the technology of production is likely to vary across firms and industries. If that is true, estimation of (3) without adjustment could lead to misleading inferences about R&D. A first cut at this problem is to add a set of industry dummies so that parameter estimates are based on variation in productivity and its determinants within industries, with each industry having its own value of λ. Firm-specific variations in technology can be introduced by casting the estimation problem in a total factor productivity framework. Instead of estimating the output elasticities of capital and materials directly, we can use the observed factor shares for each business as an approximation (the two are identical in competitive equilibrium).

After rewriting the R&D variable in intensity form, adding materials and industry dummies and using factor shares, equation (3) becomes:

$$(4) \qquad f_i = \sum_{j=1}^{N} \lambda_j D_j + \rho(R_{it}/Q_{it}),$$

where j indexes industries, D is an industry dummy, and f_i is defined as:

$$(5) \qquad f_i \cong q_i - \alpha_i c_i - \delta_i m_i - (1 - \alpha_i - \delta_i)\ell_i.$$

The parameters α_i and δ_i are respectively the shares of capital and materials in the sales of the ith firm. To better approximate equilibrium values, we have averaged each firm's share over the sample period. Material's share can be calculated directly, since it is simply the value of purchases divided by sales. No data are provided on the wage bill, however, hence capital's share was estimated as depreciation plus profits divided by sales.[8] Profits are defined gross

6. As Griliches and Mairesse (1984) show, failure of the proportionality assumption may induce bias into the estimated R&D effects.

7. The data set contains no breakdown of purchases into energy and other intermediate inputs; use of aggregate purchases implicitly treats materials and energy as interchangeable.

8. The use of total profits in the calculation of the share of physical capital is likely to overstate capital's share, since some of the returns that accrue to R&D will be counted as return to capital. The error thus introduced may lead to a downward bias in the estimate of the rate of return to R&D. If total profits include returns to physical capital and the stock of R&D capital, so that

of R&D expenditures (we treat R&D as an investment), but net of marketing expenses.[9]

The specification of the basic productivity equation is based on what is essentially a long-term perspective. It is assumed that movements in total factor productivity reflect movements in the production frontier caused by R&D investment and disembodied technical change. In practice, businesses may deviate from the frontier, not only because of errors in optimization, but because of disequilibrium phenomena associated with fluctuations in demand and consequent changes in utilization.

One way to incorporate such factors into the model is to assume that the production function (and thus productivity growth) is composed of a long-term and a short-term component. R&D and disembodied technical change are assumed to affect only the long-term component in the manner specified in (4). The short-term component is specified to be a simple linear function of capacity utilization. Cast in growth rate form, these assumptions introduce the rate of change of capacity utilization as a variable in the analysis.

6.2.1   The Main Results

Estimates of several versions of the basic productivity model are presented in table 6.4. The dependent variable in columns (1)–(4) is the rate of growth of real sales per employee, while the growth of total factor productivity (TFP) is examined in columns (5) and (6). In addition to R&D intensity, the model includes variables measuring the R&D mix, the growth of capacity utilization, the newness of the capital stock, and the percent of employees unionized. Capital and materials per employee are included as independent variables in (1)–(4) and are incorporated into the dependent variable in the TFP regressions.

Irrespective of specification, the estimates in table 6.4 show a significant effect of R&D on the growth of productivity. In column (1), the model yields an estimated rate of return to R&D investment of 0.18 with a standard error of 0.05. The utilization rate as well as capital and materials per employee are significantly related to sales per employee. Correcting capital for inflation appears to have little effect on the estimated R&D effect. When the growth of gross book value per employee is substituted for $c - \ell$ in column (1), for example, the estimated return to R&D is still 0.18.

The newness variable has a negative sign, while unionization's impact is statistically insignificant. It is possible that the sign of the newness variable reflects measurement problems as well as the differential effects of newer capital. Although capital has been adjusted for inflation, the procedure relies on

---

$\Pi = rC + \rho K$, then the estimated share of capital will be equal to the true share plus the elasticity of output with respect to R&D capital (note that $\rho K/Q = \gamma$). Use of the estimated share in a total factor productivity framework introduces $-\gamma_i c_i$ into the error term. If c and $RQ(-1)$ are positively correlated, estimates of ρ will be downward biased.

9. In those cases where profits in a given year were negative for a given firm, the average share for that firm was calculated excluding the negative year.

Table 6.4   Estimates of Alternative Productivity Model Specifications (standard errors in parentheses)

Independent Variables	Specification[a]					
	Real Sales (1)	Real Sales (2)	Real Sales (3)	Real Sales (4)	TFP (5)	TFP (6)
CONS	0.49 (0.51)	2.13 (1.32)	0.88 (0.52)	2.34 (1.35)	1.08 (0.52)	2.53 (1.35)
RQ(−1)	0.18 (0.05)	0.18 (0.05)	0.19 (0.05)	0.19 (0.05)	0.20 (0.05)	0.20 (0.05)
RMIX	−1.42 (0.59)	−1.22 (0.61)	−1.16 (0.60)	−1.11 (0.62)	−1.22 (0.60)	−1.15 (0.62)
$c - l$	0.25 (0.01)	0.25 (0.01)	—	—	—	—
$m - l$	0.45 (0.01)	0.44 (0.01)	—	—	—	—
$(c - l)^{*b}$	—	—	1.17 (0.06)	1.17 (0.06)	—	—
$(m - l)^{*b}$	—	—	1.05 (0.02)	1.05 (0.02)	—	—
util	0.32 (0.01)	0.32 (0.01)	0.28 (0.01)	0.28 (0.01)	0.28 (0.01)	0.28 (0.01)
new	−0.05 (0.01)	−0.05 (0.01)	−0.04 (0.01)	−0.03 (0.01)	−0.03 (0.01)	−0.03 (0.01)
%UN	0.01 (0.01)	0.01 (0.01)	0.01 (0.01)	0.01 (0.01)	0.01 (0.01)	0.01 (0.01)
Ind. effect[c]	no	yes	no	yes	no	yes
R^2	0.587	0.591	0.574	0.577	0.148	0.154
SEE	11.1	11.1	11.3	11.3	11.3	11.3
d.f.	4,138	4,119	4,138	4,119	4,140	4,121

[a]The dependent variable in columns (1)–(4) is real sales per employee; in columns (5)–(6) the dependent variable is TFP (total factor productivity), calculated as described in the text.

[b]$(c - l)^*$ is $(c - l)$ multiplied by capital's share; $(m - l)^*$ is $(m - l)$ multiplied by material's share.

[c]Industry effects are captured by two-digit SIC dummies.

estimates of replacement value in the first year of participation in the survey. To the extent that the correction fails to remove the effects of inflation, the rate of increase in the stock of capital will be overstated, a problem likely to be more serious for newer equipment. In fact, when column (1) is estimated with the book value of capital, the newness variable remains negative but increases by 30 percent. It is also possible that the negative sign remaining after the inflation correction is the result of adjustment costs of new capital. The integration of new equipment into existing plants or the start-up of new facilities may require time and effort to bring on line and may be disruptive to existing operations.

Measurement problems may also be a factor in the estimates of product-process mix effects. The coefficients on *RMIX* indicate that an increase in product R&D's share in total R&D investment is associated with a lower rate of productivity growth. High shares of product R&D may indicate a high rate of new product introduction which may be associated with lower rates of productivity growth for two reasons: First, much like new equipment, new products tend to be disruptive to established production processes. Product introductions generally involve a start-up and debugging phase of varying length in which new equipment or new tasks are specified and learned. Productivity growth is likely to suffer as a result. Second, where new products are an important aspect of competition, the business may adopt a relatively adaptable and flexible process technology. The firm is likely to avoid equipment and processes dedicated to a specific product and thus somewhat rigid. Some sacrifice in productivity is likely in the interests of flexibility. Although some of this should be picked up in the capital-labor ratio, this variable is likely to be too broad and rough to capture the distinctions we have in mind. It is well known, for example, that a highly capital-intensive machine shop can be quite flexible in adapting to new products. The R&D mix effect may, therefore, be an indication of the type of technology and the importance of new products.

While these possibilities are interesting, too much should not be made of the mix effect. The distinction between product and process R&D is likely to involve a good deal of arbitrariness. This arises because the guidelines are vague and because the distinction may not be meaningful at this level. Not only are process and product efforts jointly pursued on a project basis, and thus difficult to disentangle, but even pure product development can change the efficiency of the process. A new product design, for example, may lead to a reduction in the number of operations required or in a simplification of tasks, so that labor input is reduced even without any capital investment. Furthermore, if higher product R&D is associated with new products, and if firms base their price index on a fixed set of products, the reported rates of inflation may overstate the extent of price change. Output and productivity growth may, therefore, be understated. The fact that the standard errors on *RMIX* are relatively large, given the number of observations, lends some support to the importance of measurement error.

Finding a significant effect of R&D on productivity is unaffected by the specifications changes introduced in columns (2)–(6). Column (2) adds two-digit industry dummies, which allows each industry to have its own trend term. Estimation within industries has little effect on the results. In column (3), a new version of the capital and materials variables is used. The new variables are the rates of growth of capital and materials per employee multiplied by their average shares in sales. If the technology were Cobb-Douglas and the businesses were fully competitive, then coefficients on the new variables should equal unity. The materials and capital coefficients are significantly different from one in a statistical but not substantive sense, implying that the Cobb-Douglas specification is not too far off the mark. It is clear that the fit of the equation deteriorates only marginally when the average shares are imposed, and these changes, with or without industry effects, have little impact on the estimated return to R&D investment.

The same is true of the TFP equations in columns (5) and (6). We estimate that R&D had a return of 20 percent in the TFP results, slightly higher than the estimate in columns (1) and (2) but essentially similar to the earlier results. The other coefficients are little changed as well, although the newness variable declines from $-.05$ to $-.03$. As before, the industry dummies have no effect on the results.

6.2.2   Proprietary Knowledge, R&D Capability, and Technological Opportunity

Estimates of R&D's effect on productivity in table 6.4 are obtained under the assumption of a common effect across businesses. While differencing has eliminated fixed firm effects from the production function formulation, firms may also differ in their ability to translate R&D effort into actual products or processes. The productivity of R&D investment may depend on the "opportunity" for technical change in the firm's product or process. Some firms participate in industries where the scientific knowledge related to the product or process technology is rich and growing, while others use techniques where the possibility of new understanding is much more limited. Moreover, where the potential for innovation is high, firms may differ in their ability to exploit those opportunities because of differences in organization or management skill.

The likelihood of interfirm differences in technical opportunity and R&D capability suggests that the average effect of R&D in table 6.4 may mask significant variation across firms. A simple way to model the distinction between R&D effort (expenditures on R&D) and R&D output (new products or processes) and consequent gains in productivity is to assume that ρ is a function of the firm's R&D capability (or technical opportunity). If we assume that past R&D success is an indicator of that ability and if we are willing to specify a linear relationship between ρ and past success, we can write

$$(6) \qquad\qquad \rho = b_0 + b_1 P,$$

where b_0 and b_1 are parameters, and P indicates previous R&D success (e.g., patents). It seems reasonable to allow for the possibility that past R&D success may affect productivity independent of the current R&D effort. The total factor productivity model then becomes

$$(7) \qquad f_i = \lambda + b_0(R/Q)_{it} + b_1(R/Q)_{it}P_i + dP_i,$$

where the effects of utilization, unionization, newness, and industry have been suppressed.

Although we have no data on the number of patents the businesses have produced, we have three variables that provide some indication of R&D capability and technological opportunity. The first two are dummy variables based on answers to the question: Does this business derive significant benefit from (1) proprietary products and/or (2) proprietary processes? Patented products or processes are included in the definition, but firms are also instructed to consider processes (products) regarded as proprietary but not patented. The broader definition seems reasonable, since the decision to seek a patent depends not only on the significance of the invention or development and potential gains, but also on the costs of the legal process. Moreover, the firm may derive significant benefit from R&D results that are not clearly patentable.

The third variable is based on the question: Have there been major technological changes in the products or processes of this business or its major competitors within the last eight years? Inclusion of the firm and its competitors in the definition means that the variable provides information about the potential for change and development in the technology used in the industry, whether or not the firm itself has experienced a major change. The fact that a firm or its competitors have experienced a major change in technology can be interpreted in several ways. To the extent that an affirmative answer refers to the firm, one could infer that the firm has the capability to apply R&D and make use of the results. A similar conclusion would apply to competitors. However, the change in technology could have come through the purchase of equipment or licensing of new techniques rather than the firm's own R&D effort. Whatever the source of change, the fact that it has occurred implies the existence of further opportunities for technical development.

It is important to note, however, that asking a business about the occurrence of technical change may be equivalent to asking it about the productivity of its R&D investments. In that sense, inferences about the effects of technological opportunity based on the technical change variable may have little substantive content, since the estimated coefficient would be little more than a reflection of how accurately the businesses answered the question. While the possible tautology between our measure of technical opportunity and R&D productivity remains in the analysis to follow, it is mitigated to some extent by the fact that R&D investments are measured in the previous period, while changes in technology may have occurred sometime in the previous eight years.

It would clearly be useful to have more information about what firms have in mind when they answer yes to the technical change question. The PIMS guidelines warn respondents only to answer in the affirmative if there is no doubt that a major change has occurred. The meaning of the variable measuring technical change and proprietary products and processes deserves more analysis, but the nature of the data and the confidentiality provisions of the PIMS project make an in-depth analysis difficult and beyond the scope of this paper.[10]

Table 6.5 presents estimates of the TFP model after inclusion of our measures for R&D capability and technical opportunity. Although the results in line (1) with the proprietary product/process dummies show little change in the R&D effect, the new dummy variables are statistically and substantively significant. Furthermore, the sign pattern—negative on product, positive on process—is reminiscent of the R&D mix effect noted above. When the dummy variables are interacted with R&D intensity in line (2), however, we find little evidence of a significant relationship between R&D productivity and proprietary technology. Each of the interaction terms has the same sign as its dummy variable counterpart, but the coefficients are not statistically significant.

Lines (3) and (4) present TFP estimates with the technological change variable. While there appears to be no relationship between TFP growth and $DTECH$, there is a strong connection between $DTECH$ and R&D intensity; the coefficient on $RQDTECH$ is 0.24 and statistically significant. Moreover, the coefficient on $RQ(-1)$ in line (4) (which measures the R&D effect in businesses where $DTECH = 0$) is close to zero. If interpreted literally, the results imply that R&D has no effect on productivity in businesses where technical opportunities are apparently low. The connection between $DTECH$ and R&D intensity links these finding with results reported by Griliches and Mairesse (1984), where R&D's largest effect on productivity was in R&D intensive firms. While interesting and worthy of further analysis, the statistical evidence in line (4) can be overinterpreted. It is useful to note that the addition of $DTECH$ and its interaction with $RQ(-1)$ has little effect on the explanatory power of the equation.

---

10. While our ability to be precise about the substantive content of these variables is limited, we have examined them for internal consistency. A comparison of mean R&D intensity in samples selected on the basis of the presence or absence of technical change ($DTECH$) and proprietary technology ($DPROD$, $DPROC$) shows that firms with $DTECH = 1$ are almost twice as R&D intensive as their $DTECH = 0$ counterparts. A similar difference exists for firms where $DPROD$ or $DPROC$ equals one. We also found that 45 percent of firms with $DPROD = 1$ answer yes to the question about major technical change; for firms with $DPROD = 0$, the number is 23 percent. The results for $DPROC$ are almost identical. This kind of consistency also shows up in analysis by industry. Not only are changes in technology correlated with proprietary products and processes within industries, but the industrial focus of major technical change is consistent with other information. The industries with high mean values of $DTECH$—paper, chemical, plastics, transportation equipment (including aerospace), instruments, and electrical equipment—are industries where major changes in technology have occurred.

Table 6.5 The R&D Effect, R&D Capability, and Technological Opportunity[a] (standard errors in parentheses)

Specification/ Dependent Variable	CONS	RQ(−1)	DPROD	DPROC	DTECH	RQ DPROD	RQ DPROC	RQ DTECH	R^2	SEE	d.f.
(1) TFP	0.26 (0.33)	0.19 (0.05)	−1.21 (0.48)	1.11 (0.48)	—	—	—	—	0.149	11.3	4,139
(2) TFP	0.38 (0.36)	0.13 (0.07)	−1.06 (0.56)	0.69 (0.55)	—	−.05 (.10)	.15 (.10)	—	0.149	11.3	4,137
(3) TFP	0.24 (0.34)	0.19 (0.05)	—	—	0.05 (0.40)	—	—	—	0.147	11.4	4,140
(4) TFP	0.58 (0.37)	0.02 (0.08)	—	—	−0.51 (0.47)	—	—	0.24 (0.10)	0.148	11.3	4,139

[a]Each equation includes *util*, *new*, and *%UN*, in addition to the variables listed.

6.2.3   Time Effects

Attention has been focused in recent years on possible changes in the productivity of R&D over time. Using aggregated industry data (two-digit SIC) from the 1970s, a number of researchers have documented the collapse of what had been a relatively strong R&D effect. Griliches (1979), Terleckyj (1980), Scherer (1981), and Kendrick and Grossman (1980) all find little evidence in two-digit level data that R&D affected productivity in the post-1973 period. Once the data are disaggregated, however, some R&D effect emerges. Griliches and Lichtenberg (1984), for example, find that the strong relationships found in the 1960s persisted into the later period.

Figure 6.1 presents a profile of the growth rates of TFP in the PIMS data and in published data on manufacturing. The published TFP estimates were prepared by Kendrick and Grossman (1980). Their output measure is based on real value added, and labor input is total hours worked. The TFP series from the PIMS data shows a downward trend over the 1970s, accompanied by sharp fluctuations associated with the business cycle. A similar pattern is apparent in the published data, although the timing and magnitude of cyclical swings in the 1974–76 period are somewhat different. These differences likely reflect differences in price indexes as noted earlier and differences in output and input definitions.

We examine the question of a decay in the potency of R&D in table 6.6, where estimates of the TFP model with a time trend and time-R&D interaction are presented. The specification also includes the variables measuring proprietary technology. Line (1) provides a base case, with the time trend entered separately without interaction with R&D intensity. It is evident that TFP growth slowed over the period covered by the data. The coefficient on *TIME*, negative and statistically significant, implies an average decline of .2 percent per year. The productivity of R&D, however, shows no tendency to decline. In line (2), the *TIME*-R&D interaction term is negative, but its standard error is quite large, and its actual value is quite small. The estimate of -0.171, for example, implies a decline of 1.7 percentage points in the rate of return over the decade of the 1970s. Evaluated at the midpoint of the time period, the implied rate of return in line (2) is 0.18, quite close to the estimate in line (1).

Lines (3) and (4) present estimates of the TFP model in the sample of firms where *DTECH* = 0 and in the sample where *DTECH* = 1. Looking first at line (3), there is some indication of a sizeable drop in R&D productivity, but the evidence is quite weak. The interaction term shows a decline of 4.8 percentage points per year in the return to R&D, but the standard error is relatively large. At the midpoint of the time period, the estimated return to R&D is -5 percent. When line (3) is reestimated without the time trend or the interaction term, the return to R&D is 1.3 percent with a standard error of 8.2.

In line (4) a very different picture emerges. As the estimates in table 6.5 indicated, R&D investment has a substantial impact on TFP growth in busi-

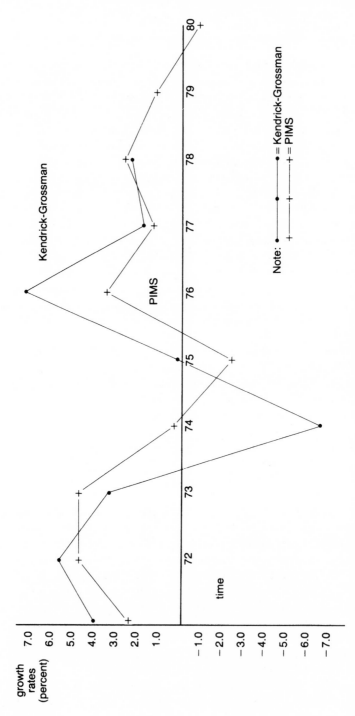

Fig. 6.1 Growth rates of total factor productivity in PIMS and Kendrick-Grossman, 1977–80

Table 6.6   Trends in the Productivity of R&D (standard errors in parentheses)

Specification[a] and Sample	CONS	RQ(−1)	TIME	RQTIME (× 10²)	DPROD	DPROC	Rate of Return on R&D at Midpoint[b]	R^2	SEE	d.f.
Total Sample:										
(1) TFP	401.0 (157.8)	0.17 (0.05)	−0.20 (0.08)	—	−1.31 (0.49)	1.06 (0.48)	0.17	0.150	11.3	4,138
(2) TFP	393.3 (177.8)	3.56 (36.0)	−0.20 (0.09)	−0.171 (1.83)	−1.30 (0.49)	1.06 (1.48)	0.18	0.150	11.3	4,137
Tech Change Samples:[c]										
(3) TFP; DTECH = 0	386.2 (220.6)	9.471 (76.03)	−0.20 (0.11)	−4.798 (3.85)	−0.54 (0.59)	0.52 (0.59)	−0.05	0.156	10.7	2,995
(4) TFP; DTECH = 1	79.9 (380.2)	−6.00 (46.79)	−0.04 (0.19)	0.317 (2.37)	−2.42 (0.91)	2.25 (0.91)	0.26	0.148	12.8	1,133

[a]Lines (3) and (4) are based on observations for firms with DTECH = 0 and DTECH = 1, respectively.

[b]The midpoint of the time period was 1975; the rate of return in that year is equal to the coefficient on RQ(−1) plus the quantity 1975 times the coefficient on RQTIME.

[c]All equations include new, util, and %UN.

nesses where a major change in technology has occurred. In 1975, for example, the estimated return to R&D in line (4) is 26 percent. The interaction term implies a small increase of 0.3 percentage points per year in the return to R&D, but, once again, the standard error is enormous.

The evidence thus suggests that if one looks at businesses where technological opportunity apparently is high and where most of the R&D-productivity effect occurs, there is little statistical support for the notion that the return to R&D declined in the 1970s. In the rest of the sample, where the average return to R&D is very small, there is stronger support for a decline in R&D productivity, but the data do not provide us with a very precise estimate. Further analysis and data may help to clarify trends in the return to R&D in businesses where technological opportunity is low, but for now the evidence is inconclusive.

6.3   Conclusions and Implications

The estimates presented in tables 6.4–6.6 suggest that R&D investment has a significant positive effect on the growth rate of total factor productivity. All of the specifications examined yielded estimates of an 18–20 percent rate of return to R&D investment. We also found an important connection between the potency of R&D and technical opportunity. And while use of proprietary process technology appears to increase TFP growth, there is only weak statistical evidence of a relationship between the returns to R&D and the use of proprietary processes. Finally the notion that the potency of R&D declined in the 1970s finds little support in these data. Irrespective of model specification or sample used, the coefficient of the time and R&D intensity interaction is both small and statistically insignificant.

The fact that R&D investment continued to have a strong positive effect on productivity growth in the 1970s means that R&D may have played a role in the slowdown of productivity growth. From the early 1970s to the late 1970s, for example, the mean R&D-to-sales ratio fell from 2.7 to 1.9 percent in the PIMS data. With a rate of return to R&D of 20 percent, this would imply a decline of TFP growth of 0.16 percentage points, or about 10 percent of the decline observed over the period. We have found, however, that most of the effect of R&D comes in businesses where technological opportunity is high. Among those firms, a somewhat different perspective emerges. In that group, R&D intensity fell from 3.9 to 3.0 percent, while at the same time TFP growth fell from 4.1 to 3.0 percent. With a return to R&D of about 24 percent, the fall in R&D intensity could explain close to 20 percent of the decline in productivity growth in the high technical opportunity sector.

6.3.1   Further Work

Our analysis has uncovered some interesting relationships and left a number of issues open for further research. One of these issues is the mix between product and process R&D. Both the R&D mix variable and the variable indicating the use of proprietary products had negative effects on productivity growth. This suggests the possibility of some interesting connections between the product development process, choice of technology, and growth of productivity. Analysis of these questions in the PIMS data (and probably in other data sets as well) will have to confront serious measurement problems, especially difficulties in the measurement of prices and output.

There is also the possibility of improving the statistical methodology. All of the estimates presented here are based on ordinary least squares. Except for the use of growth rates, which sweeps out fixed effects, we have ignored the panel structure of the data. Using growth rates does eliminate an important source of autocorrelation, but other forms of covariation in the residuals of a given business may be present and could affect our estimates. If the sample were balanced, there would be little difficulty in applying some form of generalized least squares. An unbalanced design, however, calls for an approach accounting for the differences in numbers of observations within a business over time in calculating the relevant covariance matrix.

Finally, we have not examined explicitly the effect of R&D on costs, prices, and profits. It is well known that under competition the production function and TFP have a dual representation in the cost function as the difference between the sum of share-weighted input price growth rates and the growth of the output price. Although we have no data on the "price" of R&D, its effect in a price-side version of the TFP equation can be estimated using R&D intensity.

References

Abell, D. F., and J. S. Hammond. 1979. *Strategic market planning: Problems and analytical approaches.* Englewood Cliffs, N.J.: Prentice-Hall.

Agnew, C. E., and D. E. Wise. 1978. The impact of R&D on productivity: A preliminary report. Paper presented at the Southern Economic Association Meetings. Princeton, N.J.: Mathtech, Inc.

Griliches, Z. 1979. Issues in assessing the contribution of research and development to productivity growth. *Bell Journal of Economics* 10, no. 1:92–116. [Reprinted as chap. 2 in this volume.]

———. 1980. R&D and the productivity slowdown. *American Economic Review* 70, no. 2:343–48.

Griliches, Z., and F. Lichtenberg. 1984. R&D and productivity growth at the industry level: Is there still a relationship? In *R&D, patents, and productivity,* ed. Zvi Griliches, 465–96. Chicago: University of Chicago Press. [Reprinted as chap. 9 in this volume.]

Griliches, Z., and J. Mairesse. 1984. Productivity and R&D at the firm level. In *R&D, patents, and productivity,* ed. Zvi Griliches, 339–74. Chicago: University of Chicago Press. [Reprinted as chap. 5 in this volume.]

Kendrick, J. W., and E. Grossman. 1980. *Productivity in the United States: Trends and cycles.* Baltimore: The Johns Hopkins University Press.

Pakes, A., and M. Schankerman. 1984. The rate of obsolescence of patents, research gestation lags, and the private rate of return to research resources. In *R&D, patents, and productivity,* ed. Zvi Griliches, 73–88. Chicago: University of Chicago Press.

Ravenscraft, David, and F. M. Scherer. 1981. The lag structure of returns to R&D. *Applied Economics* 14, no. 6:603–20.

Scherer, F. M. 1981. Research and development, patenting, and the microstructure of productivity growth. Final report, National Science Foundation, grant no. PRA-7826526.

Schoeffler, Sidney. 1977. Cross-sectional study of strategy, structure, and performance. In *Strategy + structure = performance,* ed. Hans B. Thorelli, 108–21. Bloomington: Indiana University Press.

Terleckyj, Nestor E. 1980. *R&D and the U.S. industrial productivity in the 1970s.* Paper presented at the International Institute of Management Conference on Technology Transfer, Berlin.

7 Comparing Productivity Growth: An Exploration of French and U.S. Industrial and Firm Data

7.1 Introduction

The United States, France, and many other industrial countries experienced a significant slowdown in the growth of productivity in the recent decade. This slowdown exacerbated inflationary pressures and contributed to the growing pessimism about the prospects for future economic growth. Its causes are still unclear and controversial. It makes a difference from a policy response point of view whether it was caused by insufficient investment, by rising energy and raw materials prices, or by a decline in the fecundity of R&D and the exhaustion of technology opportunities.[1]

In this paper we bring a comparative perspective to the analysis of some of these issues. To accomplish this we had to assemble and construct consistent and comparable data sets for French and United States manufacturing industries and firms. After a discussion of the respective data sets and a description of the extent of the slowdown in productivity growth in the two countries and the great variability in it, we turn to an analysis of the potential causes of such fluctuations. At the industrial level, we focus on the contribution of capital

This chapter is coauthored with Jacques Mairesse and is reprinted from the *European Economic Review* 21, Zvi Griliches and Jacques Mairesse, "Comparing Productivity Growth: An Exploration of French and U.S. Industrial and Firm Data," 89–119, 1983, with kind permission from Elsevier Science, NL Sara Burgerhartstraat 25, 1055 KV Amsterdam, The Netherlands.

This work is part of the National Bureau of Economic Research Program on Productivity and Technical Change Studies. We are indebted to the National Science Foundation (PRA79-13740, PRA81-08635, and SOC78-04279) and to the Centre National de la Recherche Scientifique (ATP 070199) for financial support, to Sumanth Addanki, Phillipe Cuneo, Bronwyn H. Hall and Alan Siu for research assistance and Martin Baily, Michael Bruno, and Robert J. Gordon for comments on the first draft of this paper.

1. See Denison (1979) and Nordhaus (1982) for a more detailed discussion of some of these issues.

and the rise in material prices to an explanation of the observed productivity slowdown. At the firm level we look also more closely at the potential effect of R&D expenditures on productivity growth. A number of tentative conclusions close the paper.

7.2 Productivity Growth at the Industry Level

7.2.1 Data and Basic Facts

In this section we focus on comparing total factor productivity growth rates in manufacturing industries at the approximate 2-digit level in both France and the United States. Our industry breakdown (described in the appendix table 7A.1) is somewhat unorthodox. It is the result of trying to match the U.S. SIC classification to the French NAP classification, and was chosen primarily on the basis of the availability of the French data, and secondarily because of our interest in R&D (which led us to subdivide several industries). It differs from the usual 2-digit SIC scheme in the U.S. mainly by the separation of drugs and "parachemicals" from the other chemicals, the aggregation of several minor industries, and the exclusion of the petroleum refining industry from manufacturing so defined.

The French estimates are based on national accounts publications, augmented by various unpublished data from the "branch" (establishment level) and "sector" (company level) accounts. The U.S. estimates were aggregated from the 4-digit SIC level detail data base constructed by Fromm et al. (1979) on the basis of the Census Annual Surveys of Manufactures and National Income Accounts based detailed deflators. Both data sets yield a gross output measure (shipments adjusted for inventory changes) in constant (1972) prices and divide inputs into three categories: labor (man-hours), capital (gross capital stock in constant prices), and purchased materials (intermediate consumption including energy inputs). With each input and output measure we associate a set of price indexes and cost shares. For each of our fifteen industries, in both countries, we compute Tornquist Divisia total input indexes and use them to construct Total Factor Productivity (TFP) indexes for the 12-year period, 1967–78, and for two sub-periods, 1967–73 and 1973–78. The final results of these rather extensive computations are given in table 7.1 and illustrated in fig. 7.1.

For the period as a whole, the rate of growth of total factor productivity was higher in France than in the U.S., and this was also true for *each* industry separately. The median difference was on the order of one percent per year with larger differences occurring in the "heavy" industries (Primary Metals, Fabricated Metals, Machinery, and Aircraft and Boats). In both countries productivity growth slowed significantly in the second sub-period, though here the results are much more variable across industries. For aggregate manu-

Table 7.1   Total Factor Productivity Growth Rates in Manufacturing Industries; France and the United States (percent per year)

Industry	1967–78			1967–73			1973–78			Change		
	FR	US	FR−US	FR	US	FR−US	FR	US	FR−US	FR	US	FR−US
1. Paper and allied products	1.0	0.8	0.2	0.5	1.8	−1.3	1.5	−0.4	2.0	1.0	−2.3	3.3
2. Chemicals (excluding drugs)	1.5	0.3	1.2	1.8	3.7	−2.0	1.1	−3.7	4.8	−0.7	−7.5	6.8
3. Rubber, misc. plastic products	0.9	0.1	0.8	1.0	1.9	−0.9	0.9	−2.0	2.9	−0.1	−4.0	3.9
4. Stone, clay, and glass products	1.5	0.1	1.4	2.3	1.0	1.4	0.5	−0.9	1.4	−1.9	−1.9	0.0
5. Primary metal industries	1.0	−0.7	1.7	1.7	0.2	1.5	0.2	−1.8	2.0	−1.5	−2.0	0.5
6. Fabricated metal products	1.4	−0.4	1.8	1.9	0.5	1.3	0.7	−1.5	2.3	−1.1	−2.0	0.9
7. Machinery and instruments	1.9	0.1	1.8	3.2	1.1	2.1	0.3	−1.2	1.5	−2.9	−2.3	−0.6
8. Electrical equipment	2.6	1.9	0.7	2.9	1.7	1.2	2.3	2.1	0.2	−0.6	0.3	−0.9
9. Automobile and ground transport	1.8	1.1	0.7	2.6	2.1	0.5	0.9	−0.1	1.0	−1.7	−2.1	0.5
10. Aircraft, boats, and space vehicles	3.4	−0.4	3.7	2.7	−0.9	3.6	4.2	0.3	3.9	1.4	1.2	0.2
11. Textiles and apparel	1.4	0.8	0.6	2.0	0.9	1.1	0.7	0.7	0.0	−1.3	−0.2	−1.2
12. Wood, furniture, and misc. products	1.6	0.1	1.5	2.0	0.9	1.1	1.2	−0.8	2.0	−0.8	−1.7	0.9
13. Printing and publishing	0.6	0.3	0.2	−0.4	0.7	−1.1	1.7	−0.1	1.8	2.1	−0.7	2.8
14. Drugs	0.9	0.9	0.1	1.1	1.4	−0.3	0.7	0.3	0.4	−0.4	−1.1	0.7
15. Leather	1.1	−0.2	1.2	1.9	−0.4	2.3	0.1	0.1	0.0	−1.8	0.5	−2.3
Aggregates												
Aggregate manufacturing	1.7	0.4	1.3	2.2	1.2	1.0	1.2	−0.5	1.7	−0.9	−1.6	0.7
Sectors included in micro study	2.0	0.8	1.2	2.5	1.8	0.7	1.4	−0.5	1.8	−1.2	−2.3	1.1
Sectors not included in micro study	1.5	0.2	1.3	1.9	0.8	1.1	1.1	−0.5	1.6	−0.8	−1.4	0.6

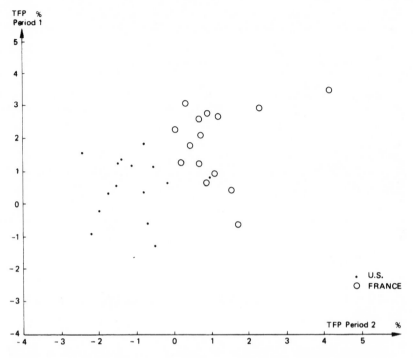

Fig. 7.1   Total factor productivity; fifteen manufacturing industries in France and the U.S., comparison across periods (1: 1967–73, and 2: 1973–78)

facturing the deceleration was somewhat larger in the U.S. (by about 0.7 percent).[2]

If we divide the periods so that they are equal in length and independently constructed, i.e., if we use 1967 to 1972 as our first period, we can do an analysis of variance on the resulting sixty TFP growth numbers, using country, period and industry as classification categories. This yields the following estimates: an average TFP growth rate (in both countries across all industries) of 0.8, an average French advantage over the U.S. of 1.5 percent per year, and an average deceleration of 1.0 percent between the two periods. In terms of contribution to the total variance in TFP growth, the most important factors are country and period, with computed F statistics of 25 and 11, respectively (the 0.05 critical value of the F statistic with 1 and 43 degrees of freedom is about 4). Surprisingly, industrial differences contribute relatively little (the computed $F = 1$ contrasted to a critical $F_{0.95}$ (14,43) of about 2), though individually two industries (electrical equipment and aircraft) have significantly

2. This conclusion depends on the exact choice of time periods. If 1972 is chosen to divide the two time periods instead of 1973, the magnitude of the deceleration is essentially the same in both countries. The U.S. peaked more in 1973.

above average TFP growth rates. This is a rather unfortunate finding from our point of view, since we had hoped to find consistent and significant differences in the rate of productivity growth across industries which might have provided clues to causes of the productivity slowdown. In fact, no consistent industrial differences emerged, either within or across countries.

If we look at the numbers for the more recent sub-period in table 7.1, the biggest difference between the two countries in TFP growth occurs in the chemical (excluding drugs) industry, while the smallest are in textiles, leather, electrical equipment and drugs. It should be noted here that some of these differences may be spurious, the result of errors in the basic data. The biggest potential source of error comes from the price indexes, which could be both erroneous and improperly associated with the relevant industry output. One becomes suspicious of the numbers when one notices that in the U.S. chemical industry capital grew by 5.7 percent per year during 1973–78, materials purchased grew at 9.6 percent, while output went up by only 3.1 percent per year. The other numbers could be wrong, but the suspicion falls on the output number and the associated price index, especially when we note that it had the highest rate of growth of all the industrial price indexes—13.2 percent per year.[3] At this moment, however, we have no way of checking what are basically ingredients of the national income accounts computations. We do want to warn the reader not to place too much confidence in the various numbers; there may still be quite a bit of error left in them.[4]

Looking at table 7.2, which lists the components of the TFP calculation for aggregate manufacturing, we observe that output growth in France was significantly higher in the 1967–73 period (7 vs. 4 percent), and fell by more in the 1973–78 period than in the U.S., to roughly equivalent levels (about 2 percent per year). Throughout both periods, fixed capital was growing faster in France than in the U.S., at the rate of 1 to 2 percent more per year. The big puzzle is in the behavior of man-hours. In the earlier period their growth is small and roughly parallel but diverges sharply during 1973–78. In France labor use declines at about −2 percent per year, while in the U.S. it rises at over 1 percent per year, in the face of a severe output growth slump.[5] There is also a divergence in the materials use story. Materials use is growing much faster in France during the first period and the drop in the second period is much

3. See appendix table 7A.2 for this detail.

4. While there is agreement on the general outlines of the slowdown, there remains much disagreement among various sources about its exact magnitude, especially at the more detailed industrial level. TFP estimates for manufacturing industries at the 2-digit SIC level have been computed in the U.S. by Gollop and Jorgenson (1980) through 1973, and by Kendrick and Grossman (1980) and APC (1981) through 1979. They vary quite a bit from each other (in the 1967–73 overlap period the correlations between these estimates and between them and ours is only on the order of 0.5). Some of the discrepancies could be explained by the use of different data bases (revised vs. unrevised, Census vs. NIPA) and some by differences in methodology (value added vs. gross output, Divisia vs. fixed weight indexes), but the size of some of them remains a puzzle. Within the confines of this paper we cannot pursue this further, but we hope to return to it in the sequel.

5. This difference is smaller if we look at employment rather than man-hours.

Table 7.2   Growth Rates of Output, Inputs and Prices, and Levels of Factor Shares; French and U.S. Manufacturing Industries, 1967–78[a]

Variable	1967–78			1967–73			1973–78			Change		
	FR	US	FR–US	FR	US	FR–US	FR	US	FR–US	FR	US	FR–US
Output	4.8	3.2	1.6	7.4	4.1	3.3	1.8	2.1	-0.3	-5.6	-2.0	-3.6
Capital	5.5	3.9	1.6	6.1	4.0	2.1	4.7	3.8	0.9	-1.4	-0.2	-1.2
Employees	0.3	0.4	-0.1	1.5	0.4	1.2	-1.1	0.4	-1.5	-2.6	0.0	-2.6
Man-hours	-0.6	1.0	-1.6	0.8	0.8	0.0	-2.2	1.2	-3.4	-3.0	0.4	3.4
Intermediate consumption	4.5	3.1	1.4	7.4	3.5	3.9	1.2	2.6	-1.4	-6.2	-0.9	-7.1
Price of output	7.1	6.0	1.1	4.6	3.5	1.0	10.2	9.0	1.3	5.6	5.5	0.1
Imputed price of capital	4.9	5.1	-0.2	5.9	4.2	1.7	3.8	6.2	-2.4	-2.1	2.0	-4.1
Price of labor (wage)	13.6	7.2	6.3	10.8	6.2	4.6	17.0	8.5	8.5	6.2	2.3	3.9
Price of interm. cons.	7.4	6.6	0.8	4.9	4.2	0.7	10.5	9.6	0.9	5.6	5.4	0.2
Share of capital in output	0.14	0.23	-0.09	0.15	0.23	-0.09	0.13	0.24	-0.10	-0.02	0.01	-0.03
Share of labor	0.31	0.27	0.05	0.31	0.28	0.03	0.31	0.25	0.06	0.00	-0.03	0.03
Share of interm. cons.	0.54	0.50	0.04	0.54	0.49	0.05	0.55	0.51	0.04	0.01	0.02	-0.01
Labor productivity (man-hours)	5.4	2.2	3.2	6.6	3.3	3.3	4.0	0.9	3.1	-2.6	-2.4	-0.2
Total factor productivity	1.7	0.4	1.3	2.2	1.2	1.0	1.2	-0.5	1.7	-1.0	-1.7	0.7

[a]Growth rates shown are percent per year; factor shares are period geometric averages.

sharper than in the U.S. (from over 7 to about 1 percent per year versus a drop from 3.5 to only 2.5 in the U.S.).

Looking at the price side, average output price inflation was slightly higher in France, by about 1 percent per year, but not strikingly so. This is true also of material prices, which rose slightly faster in France. The big discrepancy, however, is again in labor. Wages appear to have grown much faster in France, accelerating in the second period to a rate *double* that in the U.S. While the real cost of both labor and materials remained roughly constant in the U.S. in the second period (and rose only gradually in the first), in France real labor costs were rising sharply in both periods (at a rate of 6 to 7 percent per year). This may provide a "push" type explanation for the more rapid productivity growth in France than in the U.S. though the causality is far from clear here.[6]

7.2.2 Looking for Causes of the Slowdown: Capital and Materials

There are three potential explanations of the productivity slowdown and the shortfall of the U.S. relative to other countries in this regard which we can explore with our data: differences in investment, a differential rise in materials (and energy) prices, and different R&D policies. Those who claim that part of the productivity slowdown can be explained by a shortfall in the rate of capital investment must have in mind a model in which the contribution of capital to output growth exceeds its factor share for some reason or other (disequilibrium, taxation, or the embodiment of technical change).[7] While capital stock was growing somewhat faster in France than in the U.S., the TFP calculations already take this into account, to a first order of approximation. One way to check on this is to take apart the TFP calculation and ask whether output growth was faster (slower) in sectors which experienced above (below) average growth in capital input.

Define the "production function" as

$$q = \lambda + \alpha l + \beta c + \gamma m + e,$$

where q, l, c, m and λ denote rates of growth of output, labor, capital, materials and disembodied technical change, respectively; α, β, and γ are the respective input elasticies of output, and e is a disturbance term. Approximating the relevant elasticities by their corresponding factor shares, we estimate

$$q = a_{jt} + b_1(s_l l) + b_2(s_c c) + b_3(s_m m) + e,$$

where the constants (technical change terms) are allowed to differ across countries (i) and periods (t). If the TFP calculations are roughly right, the estimated

---

6. These facts have been noticed before. See, for example, Sachs (1979).

7. They may be thinking primarily of the behavior of output per man-hour, a measure that does not take into account the contribution of the other inputs. Some of the fluctuations in output per man-hour are due to differential movements in capital and/or materials. The concept of total factor productivity attempts to allow for this by including all the major inputs in its definition of total input, weighting them in proportion to their share in total factor costs.

b's should be around unity. If an input is in some sense "more important" than that, it should show up with a coefficient significantly above unity.

The results reported in table 7.3A do not support the capital (or materials) story.[8] Only the labor coefficient exceeds unity significantly and even this result disappears when we exclude the chemical industry with its dubious 1973–78 numbers from the U.S. equation. The capital coefficients are not significantly different from unity, either in the direct production function estimates, or the partial productivity versions, where we first treat labor and then both labor and materials as endogenous variables, constraining their elasticities to equal their factor shares, and subtracting them from the left-hand side.[9] If anything, the coefficient of capital is lower in France than in the U.S., which is exactly the opposite of what would have been needed to provide an explanation for the more rapid productivity growth in France. This is even more obvious when we try to explain cross-country differences in sectoral output growth. There, the estimated capital coefficient actually turns negative, though not significantly so, implying that output was growing faster in France than in the U.S., in industries where the relative capital growth was lower.[10]

As far as materials are concerned, while the direct coefficients are sometimes higher than unity, the differences are not statistically or economically significant. The materials story, suggested especially by Bruno (1981), is based on the notion that in the short-run their elasticity of substitution is less than unity and that a response to a sharp rise in their price is more costly to output growth than is implied by the standard formulae. This can be tested either by looking at the estimated coefficient of materials in the "production function" framework, or by substituting the real price of materials for the more endogenous materials quantity variable.[11]

Treating materials as a separate input with an elasticity of substitution

8. To reduce dependence, these regressions are based on a partition of the data into two non-overlapping periods, 1967–72 and 1973–78. The results are similar when other partitionings, 1967–73 or 1972–78, are used instead.

9. It makes little sense to think of input changes as exogenous in this context of rather aggregate changes over five-year periods. The regressions should be interpreted as a data summary device and not as structural estimates of *the* production function. The partial productivity regressions try to focus on the contribution of specific inputs by constraining the other coefficients to reasonable a priori values.

10. These results are robust to the exclusion of the chemicals industry with its possibly bad U.S. numbers from these regressions and to the use of slightly different time periods.

11. One should note that our definition of purchased materials includes also materials purchased from the same and other manufacturing industries and is not a net "outside" materials concept. The computed materials price changes understate, therefore, the true magnitude of changes in the price of "outside" materials. But the computed share of all "materials" overstates their overall importance, with the product of the two being essentially unaffected by this distinction. Let the computed p_m (rate of growth in materials prices) be $p_m = (1 - d)p_q + dp_0$, where p_q and p_0 are the rates of growth of the industry's own price level and of outside materials prices respectively and d the share of purchases of "outside" materials in total expenditures on materials. Then the variable we use, $s_m(p_m - p_q) = s_m d(p_0 - p_q) = s_0(p_0 - p_q)$, is the same as if we had used the "outside" definition of materials. Our conclusions should, therefore, be robust with respect to the exact definition of "materials" and the boundaries of the various industries. (We are grateful to Michael Bruno for this remark.)

Table 7.3A   **Primal Productivity Regressions: Output, Productivity and Price Growth Regressions; Fifteen Manufacturing Industries in the United States and France, 1967–72 and 1973–78**[a]

Dependent variable and country	Coefficients (standard errors) of			$[s_m/(1 - s_m)]$ $\times (p_m - p_q)$	Residual standard error
	$s_l l$	$s_c c$	$s_m m$		
I. *Output, q*					
U.S.	2.21	0.93	0.62		1.21
	(0.47)	(0.43)	(0.26)		
U.S.[b]	1.13	0.44	1.23		1.20
	(0.58)	(0.58)	(0.22)		
France	1.36	0.32	1.14		1.18
	(0.52)	(0.54)	(0.21)		
Combined[b]	1.11	1.08	1.37		1.08
	(0.26)	(1.9)	(0.16)		
France−U.S.[b]	1.52	−0.43	1.26		1.24
	(0.60)	(0.47)	(0.29)		
II. *Partial productivity, $q - s_l l$*					
U.S.		0.90	1.11		1.33
		(0.47)	(0.19)		
France		0.46	1.21		1.17
		(0.50)	(0.19)		
France − U.S.		−1.15	1.25		1.49
		(0.56)	(0.17)		
III. *Partial productivity, $q - s_l l - s_m m$*					
U.S.		1.01			1.31
		(0.42)			
France		0.64			1.17
		(0.47)			
IV. *Mixed partial productivity, $q - [s_l/(1 - s_m)]l$*					
U.S.		0.92[d]		0.64	1.34
		(0.23)		(0.25)	
France		1.06[d]		0.44	1.46
		(0.28)		(0.14)	
Combined IV[c]		0.87[d]		−0.22	n.c.
		(0.23)		(0.32)	

[a] q, l, c, m and p's are rates of growth of output, labor, capital, materials and of the relevant output and input price indexes [$x = (\log X_t - \log X_{t-5})/5$].
    s_k's are the average (beginning and end period) estimated factor shares of the respective inputs.
    Combined equations estimated using generalized least squares, allowing a freely correlated disturbance matrix (4×4) between countries and time periods across industries. I.e., four separate equations (2 periods × 2 countries) are estimated, with the relevant coefficients constrained to be the same across equations.
    All equations contain separate unconstrained country and period constant terms.
    n.c. stands for not computed.
[b] Excludes the chemicals industry.
[c] Combined IV treats $[s_m/(1 - s_m)](p_m - p_q)$ as endogenous, using $[s_m/(1 - s_m)]p_m$ and $[s_m/(1 - s_m)]p_l$ as additional instrumental variables.
[d] The variable here is $[s_c/(1 - s_m)]c$.

Table 7.3B   **Dual Price Regressions: Output, Productivity and Price Growth Regressions; Fifteen Manufacturing Industries in the United States and France, 1967–72 and 1973–78**

	$s_l p_l$ or $(s_l/s_c)(p_m - p_q)$	$s_c p_c$	$s_m p_m$ or $(s_m/s_c)(p_m - p_q)$	Residual standard error
I. Output price, p_q				
U.S.	1.36	0.65	1.67	1.13
	(0.49)	(0.26)	(0.24)	
France	0.96	0.56	0.79	1.20
	(0.28)	(0.57)	(0.19)	
II. Partial price equation, $p_q - s_c p_c$*				
U.S.	2.01		1.55	1.09
	(0.34)		(0.19)	
France	0.82		0.79	1.11
	(0.21)		(0.16)	
III. Factor price frontier, $p_c - p_q$*				
U.S.	−0.60		0.33	3.99
	(0.69)		(0.54)	
France	0.22		0.04	4.66
	(0.12)		(0.11)	

*Estimated jointly using the SUR procedure.

$\sigma < 1$ between itself and the aggregate of other inputs (value added, consisting of capital and labor) one can write the equation to be estimated as

$$q - \frac{\alpha}{1 - \gamma} l = \frac{\lambda}{1 - \gamma} + \frac{\beta}{1 - \gamma} c - \frac{\gamma\sigma}{1 - \gamma} [p_m - p_q] + e,$$

where, in addition to the symbols defined above, p_m and p_q are the growth rates of materials and output prices, respectively.[12] When such an equation is estimated, it yields invariably the wrong sign for the coefficient of the weighted real price of materials $[(s_m/(1 - s_m)](p_m - p_q)$ implying that productivity improved in industries where real material prices rose more rapidly. This could be due to errors in the measurement of industrial output prices, since both the construction of the output variable and the real materials price variable depend on the same output price deflators. An attempt was made to get around this problem by treating $p_m - p_q$ as endogenous and using p_m and p_l (the growth rate of wage rates) as additional instruments. This yielded a negative but not statistically significant coefficient for the real price of materials, with an estimated σ of about 0.2.

Actually, it is not all that surprising that we cannot get much from the materi-

12. See Bruno (1981, eq. 8).

als story since the basic facts go the wrong way.[13] The growth in material use fell more sharply in France than in the U.S. and hence cannot account for the sharper productivity deceleration in the U.S. Nor is there any evidence that real materials prices were rising more rapidly in the U.S. or accelerated more there; if anything, the opposite appears to be the case. Thus, whatever explanation they may provide for the short-term timing of such movements, the rise in material prices cannot explain the persistent and increasing difference between French and U.S. productivity growth.[14]

Another way of looking at the relationships between our variables is to look at the dual price side. Treating output price as dependent, one can write

$$p_q = -\lambda + \alpha p_l + \beta p_c + \gamma p_m + \varepsilon,$$

where, in addition to the terms defined above, p_l and p_c are rates of growth in labor and capital price indexes, and ε is a disturbance. Table 7.3B presents the results of such regressions where, as before, factor shares replace α, β and γ, and the estimated coefficients should be on the order one. Estimates of a "factor price frontier" equation,

$$p_c - p_q = \lambda/\beta - (\alpha/\beta)(p_l - p_q) - \gamma/\beta(p_m - p_q) + \varepsilon,$$

which endogenize the price of capital (using the real return to capital as the dependent variable), are also reported in this table. In the direct price equations there is a stark contrast between the U.S. and France. In the U.S. labor cost and especially material price increases where transmitted to product prices *more* than proportionally, more than could have been predicted by their relative importance in total costs. In France, material price increases appear to have had less than their predicted impact on product prices. When factor price frontier equations are estimated, with the real return to capital as the dependent variable, real material prices invariably come out with the wrong sign. Somehow, the spuriousness introduced by errors in the output price deflators appears to dominate. This is another manifestation of a problem that is endemic to such data—real factor price differences are rather small across industries within any one country, small relative to the size of transitory and erroneously measured movements in output prices.

One way of reducing the endogeneity of the right-hand terms in the factor price frontier equation is to solve out both the output price and the endogenous capital return measure from the right-hand side of this equation. This leads to the estimation of "partial price equations" with $p_q - \beta p_c$ as the dependent variable, i.e.,

---

13. Moreover, our data are not very powerful in this respect. The real price of materials varies surprisingly little over five-year periods. It appears that most of the materials price changes were passed through to output prices within this length of time.

14. Most of the evidence presented in Bruno (1981) for the materials story is based on aggregate *annual* time series for different countries. France is not considered explicitly and the results for the U.S. are not as good as for some of the other countries.

$$p_q - \beta p_c = \lambda + \alpha p_l + \gamma p_m + \varepsilon .$$

These equations (listed in the middle of table 7.3B) also imply an above average transmission of wage and materials price changes to output prices in the U.S. relative to France. If factor prices have had a special role in this story, it has been their differential impact in the two countries. Thus, they cannot provide a unified explanation for the events in both countries.

7.2.3   The Role of R&D

We cannot really analyze the contribution of R&D to productivity growth in any detail in this section because there are no R&D time series at the industry level in France. We do have, however, French data on R&D expenditures and employment by industry for 1975 and we can use similar U.S. data (see appendix table 7A.3) to investigate whether differences in productivity growth are related to differences in R&D intensity. An earlier study [Griliches and Lichtenberg (1984)] found that one can attribute only very little of the productivity slowdown in the U.S. to the retardation that occurred in the growth of R&D in the late 1960s. This study utilized a more detailed industrial breakdown and showed that the relationship between TFP growth and the R&D to sales ratio did not deteriorate in the 1970s. Moreover, it indicated that the R&D to sales ratios remained relatively stable across industries between the 1960s and 1970s (r^2 for the correlation of R/S in 1964–68 and 1969–73 across twenty-seven manufacturing industries was 0.97). Assuming a similar stability in France, we may use the 1975 data to proxy also for the unavailable earlier data.

If we combine all of our data for the two countries, two periods, and fifteen industries ($N = C \times T \times I = 60$), and estimate a common R&D coefficient in the two countries, using a seemingly unrelated regression framework, we get the following equation:

$$TFP = 0.23 \ DUS1 - 1.02 \ DUS2 + 1.49 \ DF1 + 0.76 \ DF2 + 0.28 \ R/S,$$

$$(0.31) \qquad (0.37) \qquad (0.31) \qquad (0.29) \qquad (0.09)$$

$$SEE = 1.10 ,$$

where $DUS1$ is the U.S. constant term (average rate of TFP growth) in the first period, and similarly for the other terms, while R/S is the ratio of company financed R&D expenditures to total sales in the respective countries.[15] The estimated R&D coefficient implies a 28 percent excess gross rate of return to R&D investment. It is excess because much of the R&D input is already

---

15. The OLS estimates, although less precise, are very similar to the SUR estimates. When we use total R&D to sales ratio (or R&D employment to total employment ratio) instead of company R&D to sales ratio, we obtain rather poor and statistically insignificant estimates for the U.S. These are due mainly to one outlier, the U.S. aircraft, boats and space vehicles industry, which had very low TFP growth rates (the lowest in the first period) and the highest total R&D to sales ratio (of which 80 percent is federally funded). When this industry is left out of the sample all estimates

counted once in the construction of labor and capital and it is gross because no allowance has been made for possible depreciation of R&D capital [see Griliches (1979), Schankerman (1981) and Cuneo-Mairesse (1983) for a more detailed interpretation of such coefficients].

When we allow for separate country coefficients we get the following equation instead:

$$TFP = 0.30 \ DUS1 - 0.94 \ DUS2 + 1.42 \ DF1 + 0.68 \ DF2$$

$$(0.33) \qquad (0.38) \qquad (0.36) \qquad (0.33)$$

$$+ \ 0.23 \ R/S(US) + 0.33R/S(F), \qquad SEE = 1.11.$$

$$(0.12) \qquad (0.14)$$

The difference between the U.S. and French coefficient is substantial but not statistically significant.

The estimated R/S coefficient for the U.S. (0.23) is comparable to what we found in the earlier study. If we accept such a rate of return or even if it were twice as high, this still would not account for much of the deceleration of TFP in the U.S., since the decline in R&D to sales ratio was in fact rather small.[16] Nor can our estimates account for the differences in TFP growth between France and the U.S., since the R&D to sales ratios tend to be lower at the industry level in France than in the U.S. We shall re-examine this conclusion, however, in the next section where the available micro data contain more information on firm R&D expenditures over a longer time period.

7.3   Productivity Growth at the Firm Level

7.3.1   Data and Basic Facts

In this section we examine the growth of productivity at the firm level. Because of our interest in assessing the contribution of R&D to productivity, we have been assembling data on R&D performing firms in both France and the U.S.[17] Data problems and the desire for comparable and adequately sized samples limited the study period to 1973–1978 and to five manufacturing industries for which we had a sufficient number of firms (at least 30) in each of the countries: Drugs, Chemicals (excluding Drugs), Electronics, Electrical Equipment (excluding Computers), and Machinery. The exact definition of

---

become comparable. Earlier work has also shown that productivity growth in the U.S. is more closely related to company R&D expenditures than to the federally financed components of total R&D.

16. The total R&D to sales ratio in U.S. manufacturing declines from about 4.4 percent in the mid-1960s to 3.1 in the mid-1970s. The decline is much smaller, however, for company financed R&D, from a peak of 2.2 percent in 1969 to a low of 2.0 in the mid-1970s.

17. See Griliches and Mairesse (1981) and Cuneo and Mairesse (1983) for a description of earlier work and for more detail on these data.

these five industries in terms of the two- or three-digit French NAP or U.S. SIC classifications is indicated in table 7A.4 in the appendix. It differs somewhat from our aggregate industry breakdown. The "parachemical" firms were brought together with the chemical firms (rather than with the drug firms), and the medical instrument firms were added to the "drug" industry. The electronics and electrical equipment firms are treated separately, and computer and (non-medical) instrument firms have been excluded, since there were too few of them in France.

Our samples correspond best to the subtotal of the four aggregate industries (2 + 7 + 8 + 14) given separately in table 7.1 of the previous section. The number of firms is relatively small ($N = 185$) in the French sample and only somewhat larger ($N = 343$) in the U.S. one, but these firms do account for about 25 and 85 percent of the total number of employees in these four aggregate industries in France and the U.S., respectively. They are not a representative sample from these industries, however. This occurs, first, because we include only firms which actually perform R&D and, second, because our data cleaning efforts result in additional selection. In particular, firms which grew through major mergers have been excluded.[18]

That the use of similar selection procedures in both countries yields a much lower coverage for the French sample than the U.S. one is rather interesting. Only about a third of the French firms (in terms of the number of employees) in these industries have significant levels of R&D expenditures as against most of the firms in the U.S. This difference in the industrial structure of the two countries also accounts for the observed discrepancy between the R&D to sales ratios at the firm and industry levels in the two countries. (See the data sources appendix for more details.)

In addition to constructing our samples along the same lines for both countries, we also defined and measured our main variables as similarly as possible. Output is defined as deflated sales. The industrial level of the sales deflators depends on their respective availability in the two countries (eleven different price indices for the French and twenty-five for the U.S. data).[19] Labor is measured by the total number of employees and gross physical capital stock by the book value of gross plant adjusted for inflation (based on a rough estimate of the average age of the capital stock). An R&D capital stock variable is constructed as a weighted sum of past R&D expenditures, using a 15 percent rate of depreciation and all of the pre-1973 information on R&D that we could get for our firms.[20] Because materials purchases and labor costs are not separated

18. We recognized "major mergers" by large jumps in the data such as the doubling of gross plant, sales or the number of employees. This eliminated about 50 firms from the French sample and 80 from the U.S. one.

19. For the U.S. sample firm-specific price indices were also computed as weighted averages of sectoral indices, the weights being obtained from the information on sales by different business segments within a company in 1978. Using such firm specific price indices did not alter our results in any significant way.

20. We were able to use R&D data as far back as 1963 for two-thirds of the French sample, and at least back to 1968 for practically all the firms of the French sample and most of the firms in the

for most U.S. firms (they are lumped together in the item "cost of good sold"), it was not possible to treat materials as a separate factor of production and estimate a TFP index similar to that computed at the industry level. We focus, therefore, on labor productivity Q/L and on an approximate TFP measure $Q/[L^{0.75}C^{0.25}]$, which assumes the proportionality of materials to value added and uses constant labor and physical capital cost shares.[21] We also put more emphasis on econometric estimates of the contribution of physical investment and R&D to labor productivity growth, using a standard Cobb-Douglas production function framework to allow factor elasticities to diverge from their corresponding cost shares.

Table 7.4 presents means and standard deviations of the growth rates of our main variables between 1973 and 1978 and of their levels as of 1974. It also reports their weighted growth rates and compares them to the corresponding aggregate growth rates.[22] The standard deviations of the rates of growth of labor productivity are 4.9 and 4.2 percent per year in the French and U.S. samples, respectively, and the corresponding interquartile ranges are $[-0.1; 6.0]$ and $[-1.8; 3.4]$. In fact, when one looks at any histogram of individual rates of growth, or any plot of them, the scatters overlap widely across countries. This is illustrated in figs. 7.2 and 7.3 which show for both samples the histogram of $q - n$ (labor productivity growth rate) and the plot of $q - n$ against $c - n$ (capital stock per employee growth rate).

Another interesting point is that the dispersion of growth rates, even though quite large in its own terms, is rather small (about a tenth) relative to the dispersion of the corresponding levels. Moreover, growth rates and levels are almost uncorrelated, Gibrat's law of proportionate and independent growth holding also for productivity and not just for the growth in size (number of employees or sales), as it is usually formulated.[23] These two features are reflected in the long period stability of firm rankings by absolute productivity in spite of the great variability in their productivity growth rates.

Looking at the average growth rates of our variables and comparing unweighted to weighted averages, it appears that smaller firms are growing faster than larger ones in the U.S., while no such differential tendency is apparent in

---

U.S. sample. We tried also alternative measures of R&D capital, retrapolating R&D series on the basis of the corresponding industry growth rates instead of using all the firm information whenever possible and adopting a 30 percent rate of depreciation. The means of such different measures differ of course appreciably (and thus the estimates exhibited in table 7.4 for our main measures are only roughly indicative) but the estimated regression coefficients (elasticities) are practically unchanged.

21. Using specific country and industry cost shares of labor and physical capital (rather than 0.75 and 0.25) to compute an alternative TFP variable did not affect our results significantly.

22. Table 7A.4 in the appendix gives similar detail for the five industry sub-samples.

23. For example, the correlation between the 1973–78 growth in labor productivity and its level in 1974 is only -0.05 and -0.07 in the French and U.S. samples, respectively, while the correlation between the growth rate in employment and its level is only -0.02 and -0.15. Gibrat's "law" asserts that percentage growth rates are independent of both levels and previous growth rates; i.e., the logarithms of levels follow a random walk. See Marris (1979) for references on this and related literature.

Table 7.4   **Characteristics of the Main Variables in the French ($N = 185$) and U.S. ($N = 343$) Samples**

| Main variables | Rates of growth of variables over 1973–78 (except R/S for which the 1974 level is given) | | | | Levels of variables in 1974[a] | |
| | Unweighted sample means (standard deviations) | | Weighted sample means [corresponding aggregate estimates] | | Unweighted sample means (standard deviations) | |
	FR	US	FR	US	FR	US
Deflated sales per employee, $q - n$	3.2 (4.9)	0.7 (4.2)	3.6 [3.5]	2.2 [1.9]	25.8 (0.4)	33.5 (0.4)
Gross plant adjusted per employee, $c - n$	5.6 (4.9)	5.0 (6.5)	5.5 [6.9]	5.9 [3.3]	9.8 (0.5)	14.6 (0.6)
R&D capital stock per employee, $k - n$	5.9 (6.7)	3.7 (7.9)	5.8	3.6	3.8 (1.0)	3.0 (0.8)
Number of employees, n	0.4 (4.4)	2.5 (7.1)	0.8 [−0.4]	0.8 [1.8]	0.9 (1.3)	3.0 (1.7)
Total factor productivity, TFP	1.8 (4.8)	−0.5 (4.1)	2.2 [1.8]	0.8 [1.1]		
R&D to sales ratio in 1971, R/S	4.8 (4.4)	2.6 (2.0)	3.7 [2.6]	2.9 [3.0]		

[a]Levels of deflated sales, gross-plant adjusted, R&D capital stock are in millions of dollars. An approximate rate of 5 francs for 1 dollar has been used to convert the French figures. Levels of numbers of employees are in thousand persons. The sample means are the geometric sample means, while the standard deviations are the log-standard deviations.

France. This is particularly striking when we look at the number of employees, but is also true for the growth in sales and capital. Some of this may be explained by differences in the size (and also in the range of sizes) of French and U.S. firms: the geometric means of the number of employees being 900 in France and 3000 in the U.S.[24]

Given all the discrepancies that could have arisen from the selection of our samples and the measurement of our variables, the agreement between our "micro" and "macro" numbers is rather surprising. The weighted sample means and the corresponding four industries aggregates are not that far apart. In France, the growth of R&D firms has been apparently more rapid than that for the corresponding industries as a whole, which is not surprising. Curiously,

24. The arithmetic means of the number of employees are 2,100 and 12,600 in the French and U.S. samples, respectively. While the growth in employment was about the same in France for firms with less than 2,000 employees and for those with more than 2,000 employees, in the U.S. the respective growth rates were 3.6 and 1.7 percent.

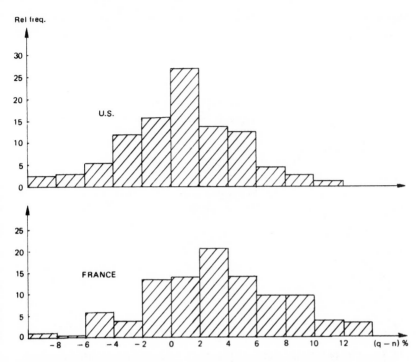

Fig. 7.2   Frequency distributions of labor productivity growth rates; French and U.S. samples, 1973–78

Note: France: Mean = 3.20, standard deviation = 4.85, interquartile range = 6.12. United States: Mean = 0.73, standard deviation = 4.17, interquartile range = 5.20.

the reverse seems to be the case for the U.S., R&D firms having a somewhat lower growth in employment (although they invested more) and a lower growth of sales than the corresponding industries. We have already noted the remarkable difference between our "micro" and "macro" R&D to sales ratios. French firms performing R&D have been investing relatively more in research and development than their U.S. counterparts, but since they constitute a much smaller proportion of the totals the opposite is true for the corresponding industries taken as a whole. The unweighted and weighted average R&D to sales ratios are 4.8 and 3.7 percent, respectively, for the French sample, 2.6 and 2.9 percent for the U.S. sample, while the corresponding industry estimates are 2.6 and 3.0 percent, respectively.[25]

In spite of such differences, a comparison of the 1973–78 productivity growth rates in the two countries yields essentially the same picture as before. Both labor and total factor productivity (based on our rough calculation with

25. The large difference between the unweighted and weighted ratios in France implies a difference in the R&D intensity of small and large firms: 5.1 percent in firms with less than 2,000 employees, 3.8 percent for those with more than 2,000 employees.

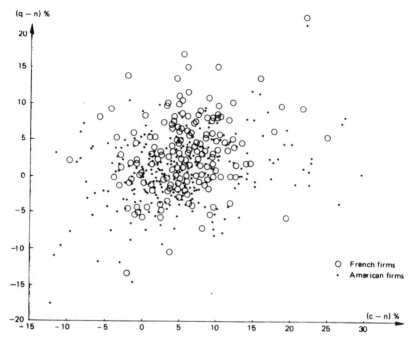

Fig. 7.3   Plot of labor productivity growth rates against the growth in capital-labor ratios; French and U.S. samples, 1973–78

a capital share of 0.25) increased much faster in France than in the U.S., by 1.5 to 2.0 percent per year.

We should, finally, remark on the comparison of productivity levels in the two countries given in table 7.4 using five francs for one dollar as an approximate rate of conversion. Though productivity growth has been more rapid in France, labor productivity levels are still below those in the U.S. by about as much as 25 percent on the average. Part of this gap may be due to differences in physical capital intensity and the scale of enterprises between the two countries.

7.3.2   Assessing the Contribution of R&D to Productivity Growth

In an attempt to assess the contribution of R&D as well as that of physical capital to productivity growth, we find it convenient to pool the French and U.S. samples together. This is not unreasonable since the standard deviations of our variables and the correlations between them are rather similar in both samples. Among different ways of handling such panel data, we chose to analyze differences in firm growth rates between 1973 and 1978. This has the advantage that the general economic situation in these two years was good in both countries, in contrast to the 1975–76 recession years. Compared to using year-to-year growth rates, it also has the advantage of reducing biases due to measurement errors in the variables (diminishing the ratio of error to true variance). In doing so, we discard all the cross-sectional information in our data panel, relying only on its time series components. As we know from the literature on the econometrics of panel data and from previous work, cross-sectional estimates often differ from time series estimates. In our earlier studies [see Griliches-Mairesse (1981) and Cuneo-Mairesse (1983)], they actually provide more sensible estimates of the elasticity of output with respect to R&D capital. Despite that, we do not report here on such cross-sectional estimates to keep the analysis parallel to the first section.

Let us denote by $q - n$, $c - n$ and $k - n$ the annual rate of growth between 1973 and 1978 of labor productivity, physical, and R&D capital–labor ratios respectively (dropping for simplicity the firm subscripts i); and by COU, IND, SIZ the appropriate set of dummy variables indicating whether or not firms belong to one of the two countries, one of the five industries, or one of four size groups (which we defined to control for the different range in the number of employees in the French and U.S. samples). The following types of regressions were estimated:

$$(q - n) = \beta \cdot (c - n) + \delta \cdot (k - n) + DUM + e,$$

or

$$(q - n) = \beta \cdot COU \cdot (c - n) + \delta \cdot COU \cdot (k - n) + DUM + e,$$

or

$$(q - n) = \beta \cdot COU \cdot IND \cdot (c - n) + \delta \cdot COU \cdot IND \cdot (k - n)$$
$$+ DUM + e,$$

where the slope coefficients are first constrained to be constant across countries and industries and then free to differ across countries and also across industries, and where DUM denotes either the set of dummy variables COU, IND, $IND \cdot COU$, SIZ (thirteen independent ones) or only the sub-set COU, SIZ (five independent ones). When the full set of dummy variables is included, the regressions are based only on intra-country and intra-industry growth differences. When the industry dummies and their interactions are excluded, the regressions are based also on inter-industry growth differences and are therefore more similar to those computed in section 7.2. To relate these regressions even more closely to the previous analysis and because we did not find evidence of a statistically significant contribution of $k - n$ (the growth in R&D capital) to productivity growth, we used also an R&D intensity variable ($R/S74$) instead of the R&D capital measure. We used the R&D to sales ratio as of 1974 instead of a comparable 1973 ratio, so as to avoid any spurious correlation with the 1973–78 growth rate in labor productivity $q - n$. The substitution of R/S for $k - n$ implies a different specification of the production function, one that assumes a constant marginal product for R&D rather than a constant elasticity across firms or industries [see Griliches-Lichtenberg (1984)]. Our main results are summarized in table 7.5 which gives the estimated parameters of interest for a number of specifications we tested. Starting with the simplest analysis of variance which uses only dummy variables, we find that all the effects are statistically significant. Among the various dummy variables, the country and industry effects are most highly significant while the size effects are less so, implying a slight tendency for faster growth of produc-

Table 7.5   Inter- and Intra-industry Regressions, without and with Industry Dummies (and Possibly Separate Industry Slopes), Respectively: Productivity Growth Differences in Pooled French-U.S. Sample ($N = 185 + 343 = 528$)

Different specifications	Coefficients (standard errors) of			Residual standard error
	$c - n$	$k - n$	R/S	
France and U.S. combined				
Inter-industry estimates	0.17 (0.04)	0.02 (0.03)		4.26
	0.17 (0.03)		0.28 (0.06)	4.18
Intra-industry estimates	0.16 (0.03)	0.03 (0.03)		3.99
	0.17 (0.03)		0.12 (0.06)	3.99

	Coefficients (standard errors) of				Residual standard error
	$(c - n)$		R/S		
	FR	US	FR	US	
France and U.S. separately					
Inter-industry estimates	0.19 (0.06)	0.16 (0.04)	0.31 (0.07)	0.19 (0.11)	4.18
Intra-industry estimates, with different industry slopes — Drugs	0.20 (0.09)	0.08 (0.10)	0.27 (0.15)	0.41 (0.23)	
Chemicals	0.40 (0.19)	0.03 (0.09)	0.00 (0.23)	−0.10 (0.36)	3.99
Electronics	−0.04 (0.18)	0.21 (0.06)	0.12 (0.11)	−0.06 (0.19)	
Electrical equipment	0.13 (0.14)	0.15 (0.10)	0.45 (0.24)	−0.44 (0.33)	
Machinery	0.21 (0.13)	0.25 (0.06)	−0.55 (0.38)	0.11 (0.27)	

tivity in larger firms. The country-industry interactions are just on the border of statistical significance.

In addition to such country and industry effects, physical capital growth also contributes significantly to the growth in labor productivity, especially when constrained to have the same average elasticity in all five industries. The evidence is weaker when different industries are considered separately. But the discrepancies in the estimated elasticities by industries and countries are not statistically significant, and we can maintain the hypothesis of a common elasticity. Given the small size of our industry sub-samples, we cannot really discern differences in elasticities across industries.

In contrast to physical capital, growth in R&D capital is not significant at all, even when we impose a constant elasticity across industries. These negative results may be due to our turbulent sample period [see Griliches-Mairesse (1981)] and also to problems of measurement. Double counting of R&D-related employees and R&D-related capital expenditures in our actual measure of labor and physical capital stock may obscure the relation between productivity and R&D investments. In the French sample, where we can correct for some of these problems, we obtain much more sensible looking estimates, with an estimated output elasticity of R&D capital δ of about 0.1 [see Cuneo-Mairesse (1983)].

On the other hand, the R&D to sales ratio does turn out to contribute significantly to the explanation of the interindustry differences in productivity growth. When it is restricted, however, to the explanation of intra-industry differences, the contribution of R/S dwindles to insignificance. In the inter-industry regressions, the estimated coefficient of R/S (ρ), which can be interpreted as the marginal product or gross rate of return of R&D, is 0.28, while in the intra-industry regressions (those containing industry dummy variables) it is only 0.12. Part of the discrepancy might be attributable to externalities, the fact that R&D performed by a particular firm may benefit other firms in the same industry. Unfortunately, the evidence of an intra-industry effect becomes especially weak when we relax the constraint that the coefficient ρ be the same in the different industries. Nonetheless, to end on a positive note, it is quite encouraging that the contribution of R&D to productivity growth is confirmed by our analyses at both the industrial and the firm levels. It may even be a bit of luck that the estimated order of magnitude of the overall gross rate of return to investment in R&D comes out so close in both cases: about 0.25, somewhat more perhaps in France and less in the U.S.

7.4   Conclusions

Analyzing the French and U.S. industrial data we confirmed both the fact of faster productivity growth in France and the pervasiveness of the recent productivity slowdown. Looking at the individual industry experiences did not yield any new clues about its sources, but it did reject some old ones. Three explanations of the slowdown were examined and were found not to bear on the differences in productivity growth across the two countries. It has been alleged by some that the productivity slowdown has resulted from insufficient physical investment and this argument has been also used to justify policies that would subsidize savings and investment. The evidence we examined does not indicate any close relationship between investment and the growth in productivity. Industries with above (below) average growth in physical capital did not have an above (below) average growth rate of total factor productivity. The rise in materials and energy prices has also been implicated in the productivity slowdown, working either via a low short-run substitutability of materials for other inputs and/or complementarity between equipment and energy. The evidence we examined at the individual industry level does not support this view. Industries that experienced above average growth in the price of materials, and/ or had been more materials-intensive, did not appear to have suffered differentially. The notion that the productivity slowdown is associated with the decline in the growth of R&D expenditures has also been quite prevalent and has led to various proposals (and legislation in the U.S.) to subsidize or provide special tax treatment for R&D. While we did find some modest evidence of a positive effect of R&D on productivity, it could account for only very little of the aggregate cross-country differences, since the overall R&D investment intensities were not higher in France than in the U.S.

Looking at the individual firm data did not change these conclusions. The major impression that emerged was one of variance. At the firm level, the estimated output elasticity of physical capital is positive and statistically significant but does not exceed its factor share in either country. Thus, there is no evidence for the notion that investment in fixed assets is more important in accounting for changes in labor productivity than is already implied in the usual total factor productivity calculations. Because a much smaller proportion of firms in an industry do R&D in France than in the U.S., it turns out that the French sample is more research-intensive than our U.S. one, while the reverse is true at the aggregate level for the corresponding industries. Nevertheless, the estimated R&D effects are statistically significant and of comparable magnitude at both the micro- and macro-level; they cannot account, however, for much of the observed difference in productivity growth.

This is our first look at the comparative performance of manufacturing industries and firms in France and the U.S. It is obvious that we have still many unsolved problems and puzzles, both in the quality of the underlying data and in our understanding the substance of what has happened. But we have made a beginning and hope that others will be encouraged to pursue such comparative studies further.

Appendix
Data Sources at the Industry and the Firm Level

The French industrial data come from the National Accounts data bases. Gross output, materials (intermediate consumption) and their associated price indexes and the total number of employees by industry are taken from "Les comptes de l'industrie" [*Les Collections de l'INSEE* no. C55 (1977), C76 (1979), C92 (1981)]. Hours of work are obtained by multiplying the average total number of employees, over the year, by the average number of hours worked per week by production workers in the same years. The latter is taken from the INSEE national accounts data bank. For a description of the methods used in constructing capital stock, see J. Mairesse, "L'evaluation du capital fixe productif: Methodes et resultats" [*Les Collections de l'INSEE* no. C18–19 (1972)]. The numbers are taken from INSEE national accounts data bank. The share of labor in gross output is computed from the labor share in value added data, available in "Les comptes d'entreprises par secteurs" [see *Les Collections de l'INSEE* no. C78 (1979)] by multiplying them by $(1 - s_m)$, where s_m is the share of materials in gross output. The estimates from the "sectoral" national accounts (based on firms data) are not quite coherent with the other estimates from the "branch" national accounts (more or less based on establishments data). But at our national level of industrial aggregation and for our purpose of computing TFP estimates, the possible discrepancies are negligible.

The U.S. industrial data are aggregated from the 4-digit SIC level data base constructed by the Penn-SRI-Census project [Fromm et al. (1979)] and updated and extended at the NBER by Wayne Gray and Frank Lichtenberg. The basic data come from the Census Annual Surveys of Manufactures, while the price series are based on the underlying detailed national income deflators. Labor input (total hours) is computed by dividing total payrolls in operating establishments by the average hourly wage rate of production workers. It can be interpreted as an estimate of total man-hours in production-worker equivalent units. The capital stock data were constructed by Fawcett and Associates for Penn-SRI by perpetual inventory methods from Census sources. Output and input price indexes are based on unpublished detailed National Income deflators and tabulations. The price index of intermediate consumption was revised at the NBER by using the 1972 I-O table and I-O sector level price indexes constructed by the Bureau of Labor Statistics. The total labor costs were revised at the NBER by adding the payrolls of Central and Auxiliary Offices for Census years and interpolating in the intercensal years.

One source of discrepancies between the French and U.S. industrial data sets is that the latter are based on Census sources and not on NIPA conventions. In particular, in the U.S. Census, the notion of "materials" does not include all intermediate consumption, excluding especially purchased services. Since the capital share (s_c) is computed residually, it is somewhat too high in the U.S.,

Table 7A.1   **France-U.S. Joint Classification of Manufacturing Industries**

Ind.	Niveau 40	Niveau 90 (NAP)	French industries	2–3 digits (SIC)	U.S. industries
1.	T21	50	Papier-Carton	26	Paper and allied products
2.	T11	171, 172, 43	Chimie de base. Fibres synthétiques	28 (less 283, 284, 285, 289)	Chemicals (excluding drugs and pharmaceuticals)
3.	T23	52, 53	Caoutchouc—Matières plastiques	30	Rubber, miscellaneous plastic products
4.	T09, T10	14, 15, 16	Matériaux de construction—Verre	32	Stone, clay and glass products
5.	T07, T08	09, 10, 11, 12, 13	Minerais et métaux ferreux et non-ferreux	33	Primary metal industries
6.	T13	20, 21	Fonderie, travail des métaux	34	Fabricated metal products
7.	T14	22, 23, 24, 25, 34	Construction mécanique	35, 38 (less 357)	Machinery and instruments (excluding computers)
8.	T15A, T15B	27, 28, 291, 292, 30	Matériels électriques et életroniques professionnels et equipement menagers	36, 357	Electrical equipment (including computers)
9.	T16	311, 312	Automobile et transport terrestre	37 (less 372, 373, 376)	Automobile and ground transportation equipment
10.	T17	26, 32, 33	Constructions navales et aéronautique, armement	372, 373, 376	Aircraft, boats and space vehicles
11.	T18	441, 442, 443, 47	Textile, habillement	22, 23	Textiles and apparel
12.	T20	48, 49	Bois, meubles, industries diverses	24, 25, 39	Wood, furniture and miscellaneous products
13.	T22	51	Presse, imprimerie, édition	27	Printing and publishing
14.	T12	18, 19	Parachimie, pharmacie	283, 284, 285, 289	Drugs and parachemicals
15.	T19	451, 452, 46	Cuir et chaussures	31	Leather

Table 7A.2A Growth Rates of Output and Inputs, and Price of Output[a]

| | Q | | | | C | | | | L | | | | M | | | | PQ | | | |
| | 1967–73 | | 1973–78 | | 1967–73 | | 1973–78 | | 1967–73 | | 1973–78 | | 1967–73 | | 1973–78 | | 1967–73 | | 1973–78 | |
Ind.	FR	US	FR	US	FR	US	FR	US	FR	US	FR	US	FR	US	FR	US	FR	US	FR	US
1.	6.6	4.6	0.9	1.8	6.0	3.7	4.5	3.8	0.7	0.4	-2.9	0.4	8.3	3.3	-0.6	2.3	5.6	3.1	11.8	9.6
2.	10.0	7.3	1.4	3.1	7.3	4.2	1.8	5.7	0.4	0.4	-1.1	2.1	11.8	4.1	0.5	9.6	3.0	0.3	11.8	13.2
3.	9.2	8.8	2.5	2.0	8.2	7.7	3.0	5.6	4.3	4.7	-1.5	3.3	11.0	7.6	3.3	3.6	3.3	2.0	12.4	9.8
4.	7.8	3.7	0.7	1.7	7.6	2.3	4.7	2.5	-0.5	1.5	-3.0	1.0	9.0	3.9	0.8	3.7	5.0	4.7	11.4	9.8
5.	5.1	3.3	0.4	-1.5	4.1	2.7	4.6	1.7	-1.3	0.6	-1.7	-0.8	4.6	4.3	0.1	0.2	6.8	4.6	9.5	11.9
6.	5.2	2.4	-0.2	0.2	6.0	3.9	3.6	3.6	0.7	0.5	-3.0	1.2	4.5	2.0	-0.3	1.1	5.7	4.4	12.1	11.0
7.	8.8	4.5	0.2	2.3	8.5	5.2	7.3	5.2	1.1	1.3	-2.6	3.0	8.2	3.8	-0.3	3.0	4.2	3.5	10.9	9.9
8.	9.6	5.0	6.2	5.3	8.7	6.8	10.2	4.7	3.2	0.6	-0.6	2.0	8.5	3.3	5.1	3.3	2.3	1.8	6.3	5.6
9.	10.3	7.5	3.3	3.0	8.6	3.2	6.9	5.4	4.0	4.2	-0.1	1.3	9.2	6.1	3.0	3.0	4.5	3.3	12.7	8.6
10.	7.9	-4.7	5.9	1.1	2.3	3.2	1.9	0.0	0.3	-6.2	-1.2	0.8	7.7	-4.0	2.5	1.1	3.5	4.0	9.4	9.3
11.	5.1	3.2	-1.9	1.3	2.8	4.2	0.5	2.8	-1.8	0.7	-4.7	-1.2	5.7	2.5	-2.0	0.7	4.5	3.2	9.2	5.3
12.	7.1	4.9	1.6	1.4	5.8	4.1	5.0	4.4	0.5	2.7	-2.2	0.9	7.4	4.6	0.7	1.9	5.5	6.3	8.7	8.4
13.	4.1	2.7	3.0	2.7	6.6	3.1	2.9	1.9	1.4	0.8	-2.0	2.3	6.0	2.4	2.9	3.9	7.4	4.4	10.5	8.3
14.	9.1	5.6	4.1	4.0	8.1	5.3	7.2	3.8	1.6	1.4	0.2	2.2	11.0	4.1	3.8	4.3	2.4	2.2	9.3	7.8
15.	3.1	-2.0	-2.0	-0.2	2.6	1.9	1.7	0.6	-2.0	-2.9	-3.9	-1.2	2.7	-2.4	-1.5	0.0	5.7	5.1	11.9	6.7

[a]Q, C, L and M are output, capital stock, labor input (man-hours) and intermediate consumption, respectively. The rates of growth of these (real) quantities and the rate of growth of PQ—the price of output—are shown.

Table 7A.2B   Growth Rates of Input Prices and Average Levels of Factor Shares[a]

Ind.	PC 1967–73 FR	US	PC 1973–78 FR	US	PL 1967–73 FR	US	PL 1973–78 FR	US	PM 1967–73 FR	US	PM 1973–78 FR	US	SL 1967–73 FR	US	SL 1973–78 FR	US	SM 1967–73 FR	US	SM 1973–78 FR	US
1.	3.1	5.0	6.3	5.7	11.3	6.8	21.0	9.3	4.8	4.3	11.9	10.6	0.24	0.24	0.26	0.20	0.61	0.53	0.62	0.56
2.	7.0	4.0	5.2	5.4	12.7	6.6	20.1	9.8	1.0	3.1	12.6	10.9	0.23	0.18	0.25	0.14	0.57	0.48	0.56	0.54
3.	5.0	5.1	5.8	1.5	9.5	5.5	17.8	7.5	0.5	2.3	12.8	11.1	0.34	0.28	0.35	0.26	0.47	0.46	0.50	0.49
4.	3.5	6.7	4.5	8.3	13.3	6.7	15.9	8.3	5.0	4.3	12.5	9.8	0.34	0.30	0.33	0.27	0.44	0.42	0.47	0.45
5.	9.7	3.3	-5.5	6.1	12.5	7.1	16.4	10.4	7.3	4.5	10.1	11.0	0.20	0.24	0.21	0.22	0.67	0.60	0.68	0.62
6.	5.4	4.1	5.9	6.8	12.0	6.2	17.5	8.2	5.1	4.6	10.9	11.3	0.38	0.31	0.42	0.28	0.46	0.48	0.43	0.49
7.	2.6	3.5	0.7	6.2	10.0	6.1	16.5	8.2	7.5	4.2	10.6	10.4	0.39	0.32	0.39	0.30	0.44	0.42	0.46	0.43
8.	4.0	1.6	-1.8	6.9	8.8	5.7	13.9	8.1	3.0	3.1	8.7	7.8	0.37	0.32	0.36	0.31	0.45	0.43	0.48	0.44
9.	9.2	8.2	7.6	3.4	12.4	7.1	19.7	9.6	4.3	4.3	11.7	9.5	0.29	0.18	0.31	0.18	0.59	0.65	0.56	0.67
10.	1.4	-6.5	18.9	12.5	8.4	6.5	21.0	8.3	6.1	4.1	10.8	9.7	0.29	0.41	0.28	0.39	0.63	0.41	0.64	0.42
11.	8.5	3.9	2.9	3.4	10.2	5.5	15.0	7.6	4.3	3.5	8.7	6.2	0.31	0.26	0.31	0.25	0.57	0.55	0.59	0.56
12.	6.4	9.3	2.5	3.8	10.0	6.4	14.4	8.1	6.4	6.8	9.5	9.0	0.31	0.28	0.29	0.26	0.55	0.50	0.59	0.52
13.	4.5	4.6	7.6	9.4	10.0	6.4	15.6	6.6	5.7	4.2	11.5	8.7	0.33	0.36	0.33	0.34	0.55	0.33	0.56	0.35
14.	-0.7	2.5	4.1	6.4	7.0	6.6	13.2	8.1	3.0	3.6	10.2	10.0	0.27	0.17	0.22	0.16	0.57	0.38	0.66	0.42
15.	6.8	1.3	9.9	6.0	11.0	5.2	18.9	6.9	6.0	5.8	8.0	7.1	0.31	0.31	0.36	0.29	0.58	0.48	0.52	0.50

[a]PC, PL and PM are the price of capital (imputed), labor (the wage rate) and intermediate consumption, respectively. The rates of growth of these prices and the average levels of SL and SM—the shares of L and M in output—are shown.

Table 7A.3   **Various Measures of R&D Intensity[a]**

Ind.	R&D percent of sales				R&D employees per 1,000	
	Total R&D		Company R&D			
	FR	US	FR	US	FR	US
1.	0.1	0.6	0.1	0.6	0.3	0.8
2.	2.9	3.5	2.7	2.9	5.4	3.5
3.	2.0	1.7	2.0	1.1	2.5	1.4
4.	0.6	0.8	0.6	0.8	0.6	0.7
5.	0.5	0.5	0.5	0.5	1.0	0.6
6.	0.2	0.4	0.2	0.4	0.3	0.5
7.	0.8	2.0	0.8	1.2	1.0	1.0
8.	6.4	7.7	3.5	4.9	6.7	4.9
9.	2.2	3.2	2.2	2.7	2.9	2.5
10.	8.0	12.7	4.4	2.8	9.9	7.2
11.	0.1	0.1	0.1	0.1	0.0	0.1
12.	0.0	0.3	0.0	0.3	0.0	0.3
13.	0.0	0.2	0.0	0.2	0.0	0.2
14.	3.1	3.7	3.2	3.7	6.2	4.5
15.	0.0	0.1	0.0	0.1	0.0	0.0

[a]French R&D numbers are estimated from "Le compte satellite de le recherche, Methodes et series 1970–1976," *Les Collections de l'INSEE* C85 (1979), and U.S. ones are estimated from NSF79.313, *Research and Development in Industries, Detailed Statistical Tables* (1979).

perhaps by as much as a third (see the attempt at reconciliation of value added and GNP originating in the *U.S. Census of Manufacturers,* 1977, Vol. 1, p. XXVII).

The French firm sample is the result of matching two different data sources: INSEE provided us with the balance-sheet and current account numbers (from the SUSE files) while the Ministry of Research and Industry provided the R&D numbers (from the annual survey on company R&D expenditures). The U.S. firm sample is built from the information available in the Standard and Poor's Compustat Industrial Tape. These samples are larger than the ones actually used in Griliches-Mairesse (1981) and Cuneo-Mairesse (1983). More details on the construction and cleaning of the samples, as well as on the definition and measurement of the variables can be found in these two studies.

Table 7A.4   1973–78 Rates of Growth of the Main Variables by Industry in the French and U.S. Firm Samples (1974 Levels for R/S); Unweighted Means with Standard Deviations Given in Parentheses

	Drugs		Chemicals		Electronics		Electrical equipment		Machinery	
FR: Niveau + 90–600 (NAP)	Niveau + 90–600 (NAP)		17 + 18		291		28 + 292 + 30		22 thru 25 + 3407	
US: 3–4 digits (SIC)	283 + 2844 + 3841 + 3843		28 (−283 − 2844)		366 + 367		36 (−366 − 367)		35 (−357)	
Country	FR	US	FR	US	FR	US	FR	US	FR	US
Subsample size	47	57	30	62	37	65	32	47	39	112
Deflated sales per employee, $q - n$	4.5 (4.8)	0.1 (3.7)	2.2 (5.0)	1.1 (3.5)	5.4 (4.7)	3.0 (4.7)	3.2 (4.3)	0.1 (4.0)	0.3 (3.9)	−0.5 (4.0)
Gross plant adjusted per employee, $c - n$	5.7 (6.2)	3.8 (5.8)	5.6 (3.7)	5.7 (5.8)	6.0 (3.6)	4.3 (8.2)	5.1 (5.0)	5.6 (6.0)	5.3 (4.9)	5.3 (6.2)
Total factor productivity, TFP	3.0 (4.7)	−0.1 (3.7)	0.8 (4.8)	−0.3 (3.7)	3.9 (4.7)	1.9 (4.4)	2.0 (4.3)	−0.1 (4.0)	−1.0 (3.7)	−1.8 (3.6)
R&D capital stock per employee, $k - n$	6.5 (6.5)	3.1 (7.1)	4.4 (5.5)	3.5 (7.2)	6.1 (6.2)	3.0 (7.8)	5.0 (6.0)	4.9 (6.9)	6.9 (8.4)	4.1 (9.1)
Number of employees, n	0.2 (4.4)	5.5 (7.2)	0.5 (3.5)	1.2 (5.9)	1.8 (4.5)	3.4 (8.2)	0.6 (4.6)	−0.0 (6.7)	−1.1 (4.5)	2.4 (6.5)
R&D to sales ratio in 1974, R/S	6.4 (3.9)	3.4 (2.4)	3.6 (3.3)	2.6 (1.5)	7.8 (6.0)	3.5 (2.6)	3.2 (3.0)	2.0 (1.8)	2.0 (1.7)	1.9 (1.4)

Table 7A.5   *Sample Comparisons*: **Numbers of Employees (E) in Thousands and R&D to Sales Ratios (R/S) in Percent, for the French and U.S. Samples, for the Corresponding Aggregate Industries, and Also for All "R&D-Doing Firms" in the Two Countries**[a]

	Samples (S)		R&D doing firms (R)		Corresponding industries (I)			Coverage	
	E_S	$(R/S)_S$ (%)	E_R	$(R/S)_R$ (%)	E_I	$(R/S)_I$ (%)	$(RT/S)_I$ (%)	E_S/E_I (%)	E_R/E_S (%)
France (1974)	395	3.7	565	4.3	1,550	2.6	3.3	25	35
U.S. (1976)	4,250	2.9	4,500	2.6	4,900	2.9	4.1	85	90

[a]The estimates for the samples and the corresponding industries are the ones obtained in this study. The estimates for the "R&D doing firms" are computed from "La recherche-developpement dans les entreprises industrielles en 1974" [*Documentation Française*, 1977] and from "Who does R&D and who patents?" [Bound et al. (1984)]. RT/S refers to the ratio of total R&D performed in the industry (whether company or public financed), while R/S refers only to company-financed R&D. These estimates are only indicative and can be misleading for a number of reasons. First, they are not strictly comparable, since computers and non-medical instruments are not included in our samples, while they are part of the corresponding industries. This explains specifically why $(R/S)_S$ appears to be higher than $(R/S)_S$ and $(R/S)_R$ in the U.S. Second, they are not strictly comparable also due to the conglomerateness and the importance of foreign activities of many of our firms, particularly in the U.S., while the industry level numbers are establishment-based and cover only domestic activities. This results in a severe overestimation of the coverage ratios in the U.S., but is not enough to change the finding that the proportion of R&D doing firms in the industries considered is much less in France than in the U.S. Third, the cutoff point between R&D and non-R&D doing firms seems somewhat higher in France than in the U.S. This is not enough, however, to account for the finding that R&D doing firms appear to do relatively more R&D in proportion to their sales in France than in the U.S. Fourth, the picture differs across industries, the coverage and the R&D sales ratios being both much less for machinery than for drugs and chemicals or for electronics and electrical equipment.

References

APC, 1981, Multiple input productivity indexes, Vol. 1, no. 3 (American Productivity Council, Houston, TX).

Bound, J., C. Cummins, Z. Griliches, B. Hall and A. Jaffe, 1984, Who does R&D and who patents? in: Zvi Griliches, ed., R&D, patents, and productivity (University of Chicago Press, Chicago, IL).

Bruno, M., 1981, Raw materials, profits, and the productivity slowdown, NBER working paper no. 660R.

Cuneo, P. and J. Mairesse, 1983, Productivity and R&D at the firm level in French manufacturing, NBER working paper no. 1068.

Denison, E. F., 1979, Accounting for slower economic growth (The Brookings Institution, Washington, DC).

Fromm, G., L. R. Klein, F. C. Ripley and D. Crawford, 1979, Production function estimation of capacity utilization, Unpublished paper.

Gollop, F. M. and D. W. Jorgenson, 1980, U.S. productivity growth by industry, 1947–73, in: J. W. Kendrick and B. N. Vaccara, eds., New developments in productivity: Measurement and analysis, Studies in income and wealth, Vol. 44 (NBER/University of Chicago Press, Chicago, IL).

Griliches, Z., 1979, Issues in assessing the contribution of research and development to productivity growth, Bell Journal of Economics 10, no. 1, 92–116. [Reprinted as chap. 2 in this volume.]

Griliches, Z. and F. Lichtenberg, 1984, R&D and productivity growth at the industry level: Is there still a relationship? in: Z. Griliches, ed., R&D, patents, and productivity (University of Chicago Press, Chicago, IL). [Reprinted as chap. 9 in this volume.]

Griliches, Z. and J. Mairesse, 1981, Productivity and R&D at the firm level, NBER working paper no. 826. [Reprinted as chap. 5 in this volume.]

Kendrick, J. W. and E. Grossman, 1980, Productivity in the U.S.: Trends and cycles (Johns Hopkins University Press, Baltimore, MD).

Marris, R., 1979, The theory and future of the corporate economy and society, Ch. 3 (North-Holland, Amsterdam).

National Science Board, 1980, Science indicators (N.S.B., Washington, DC).

Nordhaus, W. D., 1982, Economic policy in the face of declining productivity growth, European Economic Review 18, no. 1/2, 131–158.

Sachs, J., 1979, Wages, profits, and macroeconomic adjustment: A comparative study, in: Arthur M. Okun and George L. Perry, eds., Brookings papers on economic activity, Vol. 2 (The Brookings Institution, Washington, DC).

Schankerman, M., 1981, The effects of double-counting and expensing on the measured returns to R&D, Review of Economics and Statistics LXIII, no. 3, 454–458.

R&D and Productivity Growth: Comparing Japanese and U.S. Manufacturing Firms

8.1 Introduction

In economic terms, Japan is a large country with a large internal market in addition to its export potential. In an area that is one twenty-fifth the size of the United States, Japan has slightly over half of the population of the United States, and more than one-third of its GNP. Japan's manufacturing sector is relatively larger, with total employment in manufacturing around 42% of that in the United States. One of the major differences between the two countries has been the much faster rate of productivity growth in Japanese manufacturing.

Although the oil crises of 1973 and 1979 affected both economies severely and output and productivity growth slowed in both of them, the productivity of labor in manufacturing continued to increase much faster in Japan than in the United States during the 1970s.[1] These events elicited many comments and studies but mostly at the aggregate macrolevel. Also, while there has been much discussion of the possible role of differential R&D policies in these events, there has been little quantitative examination of the R&D–productivity growth relationship; what there has been has focused largely on aggregate data and single-country analysis.[2] It is our intention to look at these issues using

This chapter is coauthored with Jacques Mairesse and is reprinted from *Productivity Growth in Japan and the United States,* edited by Charles R. Hulten, pp. 317–40 (Chicago: University of Chicago Press, 1990). © 1990 by the National Bureau of Economic Research. All rights reserved.

The authors are indebted to T. Tachibanaki for providing the Japanese data and assisting with their interpretation, to A. Neff for help with Japanese price indexes, to T. Abbott and M. Sassenou for very able research assistance, and to the National Science Foundation (PRA81-08635 and SES82-08006), le Centre National de la Recherche Scientifique, and the National Bureau of Economic Research Program on Productivity and Technical Change Studies for financial support.

1. See, e.g., the *Economic Report of the President* (Council of Economic Advisers 1984, table 3.3).

2. One exception at the macrolevel is Mohnen, Nadiri, and Prucha (1986). After this paper was written we became aware also of the work of Odagiri (1983) and Odagiri and Iwata (1986), who

Japanese and U.S. company data in an attempt to assess the contribution of R&D to productivity in both countries.

This paper can be viewed as a continuation of our previous work on R&D and productivity growth at the firm level in the United States and in France. In analyzing the data for French and U.S. manufacturing we found that differences in R&D effort do not account for much of the observed difference in the average rate of productivity growth or its distribution across industrial sectors or firms (see Griliches and Mairesse 1983, 1984; Cuneo and Mairesse 1984). The availability of similar data for Japan led us to extend these comparisons to that country and the United States, between which the contrasts are even larger.

Our work differs from much of the productivity-comparisons literature by taking the individual firm data as its primary focus. Firm data have the virtue of providing us with much more variance in the relevant variables and a more appropriate level of analysis, the level at which most of our theories are specified. By working with microlevel data we escape many of the aggregation problems that plague macroeconomics. On the other hand, these benefits do not come without cost. Our data bases rarely contain enough variables relevant to the specific circumstances of a particular firm, and the available variables themselves are subject to much higher relative error rates, which are largely averaged out in aggregate data.

The basic approach we follow in this paper is to compute simple productivity-growth measures for individual manufacturing firms both in Japan and the United States for the relatively recent 1973–80 period and relate them to differences in the intensity of R&D effort. We start by describing our data sources and the overall pattern of R&D spending in manufacturing in both countries and by reviewing the major trends in productivity growth across different industrial sectors. We then turn to the discussion of regression results that attempt to account for the differences in labor productivity growth by the differences in the growth of the capital-labor ratio and in the intensity of R&D effort across different firms for total manufacturing as a whole and also separately within specific industrial sectors.

Since, as we shall point out in some detail later on, the Japanese R&D data at the firm level turn out to be especially incomplete, we cannot provide a solution to the original puzzle of differential growth rates, but we still have some interesting facts and several new puzzles to report.

8.2   Comparing R&D Expenditures

Before we look at our R&D data at the firm level, it is useful to compare the industrial distribution of R&D expenditures in both countries. Tables 8.1 and

---

use the same Japanese data base to construct value-added-based TFP growth measures and relate them to firm R&D intensities. Their results for Japan are similar to ours but they make no cross-country comparisons.

Table 8.1   R&D Firms in Manufacturing, Japan, 1976: The Relative Importance of Large Firms (1,000 or more employees) and Their Industrial Distribution

	No. of Employees in Millions and Percentages	Sales in Units of 100 Billion Yen and Percentages	Company R&D Expenditures in Units of 100 Billion Yen and Percentages	No. of Firms	R&D Sales Ratio[a]
All Firms	8.8	1,244	15.14	85,650	.012
R&D firms	59	69	100	11,950	.018
Large firms	41	52	78	1,120	.018
Large R&D firms	39	50	78	1,030	.019
Large R&D-doing firms:					
Total	3.5	623	11.82	1,030	.019
Distribution by industry:[b]					
1. Food & kindred	5.1	9.0	2.2	60	.005
2. Chemicals & rubber	11.0	14.2	16.6	98	.022
3. Drugs	2.3	2.1	5.8	29	.051
4. Primary & fabricated metals	13.7	16.8	9.8	104	.012
5. Machinery	8.0	6.5	6.2	91	.018
6. Electrical equipment	19.1	14.0	30.4	123	.041
7. Transportation equipment	23.7	22.0	20.5	329	.018
8. Instruments	2.1	1.4	2.1	29	.028
9. Other	15.0	14.0	6.4	167	.009

Source: Report on the Survey of Research and Development (Prime Minister's Office 1976).

Note: "Manufacturing" excludes petroleum refining.

[a]Total R&D/total sales (not average of firm ratios).

[b]The numbers in the first three columns are percentages and add up to 100.

8.2 show comparative statistics on the magnitude and industrial distribution c R&D expenditures for manufacturing in both countries, focusing on the rol of "large" firms (firms with more than 1,000 employees).[3] We look primaril at large firms because they account for most of the R&D in either country an also because these are the firms represented in our microdata sets.

Comparing the two tables we can see that large firms are more numerou in the United States, and that, on average, they are also larger (about 10,00 employees per firm versus 3,500 in Japan). Large firms account for 70% c total sales and 65% of total employment in manufacturing in the United State versus 52% and 41%, respectively, in Japan. Similarly, large firms do almo all of the R&D in the United States—94%—but only about three-quarte in Japan.[4]

Allowing for differences in the size of the countries and the size distributio of firms, there is very little difference either in the intensity or the sector distribution of company-financed R&D expenditures in the two countrie There is a big difference, however, in the involvement of government in th financing of R&D performed in manufacturing. In the United States, over third of total R&D has been federally financed while in Japan the state ac counts for less than 2% of the total.[5] Since our microdata reflect only compan financed R&D we shall not be able to discuss the role of public R&D suppo in this context.[6]

While, in absolute terms, large Japanese manufacturing companies spen only about a third as much on R&D as U.S. companies do, the relation of thes expenditures to sales is remarkably similar (about 2%) in both countries. Th distribution of total company R&D by industry and of the intensity of R& effort are also very similar in the two countries. Most of the R&D is don in three sectors: electrical equipment, transportation equipment, and chemic industries.[7] The highest R&D to sales ratios are to be found in the drug an electrical equipment industries, the only noticeable difference being the some what higher relative R&D expenditure in the U.S. instruments industry.

We turn now to the consideration of our firm-level data sources. In bot

3. These numbers come from the national R&D surveys conducted by the Statistics Bureau i the Prime Minister's Office (various years) in Japan and the National Science Foundation (variou years) in the United States.

4. Some of this contrast may be an artifact of different reporting conventions in the two cou tries. A perusal of the individual-firm data seems to indicate that there is less consolidation i Japan, with more units, which in the United States would be treated as subsidiaries, appearing independent firms in the Japanese sources.

5. See Peck (1985) for more discussion of this difference.

6. See Griliches (1980, 1986) for more discussion on this topic.

7. Because we try to have reasonably sized samples in the various "industries," we have aggr gated some of the more detailed statistics into nine industrial "sectors." Thus, sector 2 includ chemical and rubber firms, but not pharmaceutical firms, sector 6 includes computers, electric machinery, and electrical and communication equipment, while sector 9 brings together the textil paper, wood, glass, and miscellaneous manufacturing industries. Petroleum refining is exclude

Table 8.2 **R&D Firms in Manufacturing, United States, 1976: The Relative Importance of Large Firms (1,000 or more employees) and Their Industrial Distribution**

	No. of Employees in Millions and Percentages	Sales in Billions of Dollars and Percentages	Company R&D Expenditures in Billions of Dollars and Percentages	No. of Firms	R&D Sales Ratio[a] Total	R&D Sales Ratio[a] Company Financed
1977 All Firms	21.5	1,275	18.00	295,000	.022	.014
R&D firms	62	63	100	2,835	.035	.022
Large firms	65	70	94	1,910	.030	.019
Large R&D firms	56	61	94	1,140	.035	.022
1976 Large R&D firms:						
Total	11.7	672	15.30	1,137	.036	.023
Distribution by industry[b]						
1. Food & kindred	7.6	12.7	2.0	102	.004	.004
2. Chemicals & rubber	9.7	11.4	13.2	112	.030	.026
3. Drugs	2.3	3.5	6.8	29	.063	.062
4. Primary & fabricated metals	13.1	13.0	4.8	165	.009	.008
5. Machinery	6.7	6.1	5.9	135	.023	.022
6. Electrical equipment	20.0	14.8	30.9	159	.077	.047
7. Transportation equipment	18.3	20.6	25.2	90	.065	.028
8. Instruments	3.5	2.6	6.6	55	.066	.057
9. Other	18.8	16.3	4.7	290	.008	.007

Source: Information for all firms in manufacturing from *Enterprise Statistics: General Report on Industrial Organization* (U.S. Bureau of the Census 1977). R&D related numbers from NSF, *Research and Development in Industry,* 1976 and 1977 issues.

Note: "Manufacturing" excludes petroleum refining.

[a]Total R&D/total sales (not average of firm ratios).

[b]The numbers in the first three columns are percentages and add up to 100.

countries the responses to official R&D surveys are confidential and not publicly available. However, information on individual firms' R&D expenditures is available in their public annual reports or their filings with the respective securities markets regulatory authorities (10K statements in the United States). In Japan such data are collected and organized by the Nihon Keizai Shimbun Corporation and are known as the NEEDS data base. In the United States, the equivalent is Standard and Poor's Annual Industrial Compustat.

We have worked previously with the Compustat data and have created a consistent panel data set based on it.[8] This is, however, our first experience with the NEEDS data, and we had to invest heavily in cleaning them and in trying to understand their construction and provenance. Except for the R&D numbers, as we shall see below, these data seem of comparable quality to the Compustat data for the United States.

The general characteristics of the parallel firm samples that we have constructed are depicted in table 8.3. If we insist on continuous data from 1972 through 1980 with no major mergers or major jumps in the series and require also consistent reporting of R&D expenditures throughout this period, we have complete data for about 400 R&D firms in Japan and slightly over 500 R&D firms in the United States.[9] The U.S. firms are significantly larger, by a factor of four on average. They also seem to be doing much more R&D, even relatively. Here we stumble on our major difficulty with the NEEDS data. The R&D data appear to be badly underreported in this source. If we compare the numbers in table 8.1 with those in table 8.2, we observe that the overall company financed R&D to sales ratio is roughly similar in both countries and only slightly lower in Japan (1.91% vs. 2.3% in the United States for large R&D-performing firms), while the numbers in table 8.3 imply that the U.S. firms are twice as R&D intensive.

It does not take very long to convince oneself that indeed the NEEDS data are heavily deficient in their R&D coverage. Table 8.4 reports coverage ratios for 1981 of the NEEDS R&D numbers relative to the official Japanese R&D survey. While the large firms in the NEEDS sample account for close to 80% of the relevant employment and sales totals, the coverage of R&D expenditures is only slightly above one-third.[10] Looking at the distribution by industrial sec

---

8. See Bound, Cummins, Griliches, Hall, and Jaffe (1984) and Hall, Cummins, Laderman, and Mundy (1988) for a discussion of the construction and description of this data set, which include also a match to the Patent Office data on the number of patents granted to these firms.

9. If we do not require consistent reporting of R&D expenditures we have samples of about 1,000 manufacturing firms in each country. Because of the significant and intermittent nonreporting of R&D one cannot assume that the other firms (the ones not included) are truly "zero R&D" firms. Thus one cannot separate our samples cleanly into R&D and non-R&D firms and compare the results. This has only been possible in a study for France, because it was conducted within the National Institute of Statistics and we had access to the individual data of the French R&D survey (see Mairesse and Cuneo 1985).

10. The coverage ratios in table 8.4 are for the most recent year that we had data for in both the NEEDS and R&D surveys (1981) but they are not much different in the earlier years. There has been little improvement in R&D reporting in the NEEDS data base. The coverage ratios for the

Table 8.3 **Japan and the United States: 1976 Characteristics of the 1972–80 Continuous Samples**

Variable	Japan[a] Total	R&D Reporting Original[b]	R&D Reporting Corrected[c]	United States Total	United States R&D Reporting[d]
N	1,032	394	406	968	525
Average employment, in thousands	2.7	3.4	4.5	13	17
Average sales, in millions of dollars	215	242	345	655	872
Average plant, in millions of dollars	118	128	187	330	434
Average R&D, in millions of dollars	—	3.1	6.9	—	22.7
Average R&D/sales ratio[e]	—	.012	.013	—	.024

[a]From the NEEDS (Nihon Keizai Shimbun) data base. Converted to dollars at $1 = ¥300.

[b]In addition to the 394 continuously R&D-reporting firms in the Japanese sample, there are also 338 firms that reported nonzero R&D expenditures in one or more years in the 1972–80 period.

[c]The data on largest R&D-performing firms in Japan reported in OECD (1984) were used to fill in some missing values and adjust others for apparent underreporting.

[d]In addition to the 525 continuously R&D-reporting firms in the U.S. sample, with no major jumps, there are also 129 firms that reported nonzero R&D expenditures in one or more years in the 1972–80 period.

[e]Average of individual firm R&D to sales ratios.

tor we see that coverage varies from good to reasonable for the chemical, drug, and instruments industries, but that it is abysmal for motor vehicles and transportation equipment and poor for the rest of manufacturing. The magnitude of the problem can be appreciated when it is realized that neither Toyota, Hitachi, Nissan, nor Honda report positive R&D expenditures in the NEEDS data base.

Using information published by the Organization for Economic Cooperation and Development (OECD 1984) on the 20 largest R&D performers in Japan in 1979, we find that of the 18 firms that should be within our definition of manufacturing and are indeed in the NEEDS file, 10 report no R&D whatsoever, 3 report about the same amount of R&D in both sources, and, what may be even more worrisome, 5 companies report significantly less R&D in the NEEDS data base than is reported by the OECD. For example, the reported R&D expenditures of the Sony Corporation differ by a factor of two. If the OECD information is added to the NEEDS data set, total R&D expenditures come close to doubling, and the coverage ratio rises to a respectable 73%.

Thus the problem we face is not only that R&D is missing for some firms,

large firms were 30% and 35% in 1976 and 1981, respectively. Firms that do report their R&D in the NEEDS data base do so continuously and apparently on a consistent basis.

Table 8.4   **Comparison of NEEDS 1981 Data to the Japanese Official 1981 R&**
Survey Coverage in Ratios Expressed in Percentages

	Firms	Employees	Sales	R&D Expenditur
All	1.2	30	46	29
R&D-reporting	4.2	35	38	29
Large firms (1,000 or more employees)	58	79	78	35
Large R&D-reporting firms, total	45	51	49	35
By sector:				
1. Food & kindred	27	30	45	26
2. Chemicals & rubber	65	70	80	92
3. Drugs	71	92	95	98
4. Metals	60	55	70	42
5. Machinery	46	45	54	27
6. Electrical equipment	51	60	69	26
7. Transportation equipment	38	44	38	14
8. Instruments	42	58	73	75
9. Other	42	48	53	29

a problem that we could either ignore or adjust for in some way, but also th the reported figures themselves appear to be inaccurate. They reflect not on real differences in this variable but also differences in reporting practice Since there was nothing else that we could do at this point, we complemente or adjusted the R&D figures for the 18 very large R&D firms for which v had OECD information and proceeded to analyze these data as if they actual mean what they say. The best we can hope for is that the reported R&D num bers are still acceptable proxies for the true figures.[11] We will come back, how ever, to this issue in interpreting the results of our analyses.

A few words should be said at this point about the U.S. R&D data. The indeed seem better. Even though they are not exactly conceptually equivaler the 10K-based reports and the NSF-collected (National Science Foundatio various issues) numbers are not very far apart, especially as far as indust totals are concerned. A recent analysis by the NSF (1985) of data for the 2(largest R&D performers finds the totals in 1981 remarkably close (within 3% though this covers up significant individual variability. Forty-seven percent the firms reported totals within 10% in both sources; 22% were within 10% 25% and only 13% were off by more than 25%. Eighteen percent were n included in the Compustat-based data base, primarily because they were eith

11. Even if the total R&D levels are about right (after correction) and comparable in the tv countries, if the individual observations are subject to much error and different reporting practic (especially for the smaller R&D performers), our subsequent regression-based estimates of importance" of R&D may be significantly biased downward. Actually, however, adjusting R&D data for the 18 large R&D-performing firms, using the OECD (1984) information, had ve little effect on our regression estimates.

privately or foreign owned. Using 1976 totals and adjusting for differences in definition and coverage, we ourselves estimated that the Compustat-based universe contained about 85% of total R&D reported to the NSF, with the major discrepancy arising from the above mentioned absence of privately and foreign owned firms in these data.[12] At the same time, our selection of "continuous R&D" firms preserves about 80% of the total R&D reported in the 1976 large Compustat cross section. Thus, roughly speaking, the firms contained in our U.S. sample account for about 70% of the total company financed R&D as reported to the National Science Foundation.

8.3   Comparing Trends in Productivity Growth

Bearing in mind the limitations of the R&D data, we look now at the productivity record of the firms in our samples for both countries during the 1970s. Tables 8.5 and 8.6 list the sample sizes, averages, and standard deviations for some of our major variables by industrial sector and for manufacturing as a whole. The construction of the major variables is similar for both countries except that in the United States we were able to use 3-digit SIC-level price deflators and business segment information to construct individual firm sales deflators, while for Japan we had to use general 2-digit level deflators.[13] In both countries the gross plant figures were converted from historical to constant prices using the information contained in the net versus gross plant distinction.[14] In neither data set do we have information on hours worked, and materials purchases are available only for Japan.

There are a number of interesting observations to be made on the basis of tables 8.5 and 8.6, some less obvious than others. The major contrast between the two countries is in the employment story and the associated productivity movements. In Japan, total employment declined in eight out of the nine industrial groupings, whereas, in the United States, it rose in all sectors. In fact, real output per firm as measured by deflated sales grew at about the same rate in the United States as in Japan, 3.5% per year on average, with the big difference in the productivity numbers coming essentially from the behavior of the employment series.

The same thing is also true for the growth in the capital-labor ratio, which grew twice as fast in Japan as in the United States, while the capital stock was growing at roughly similar rates in both countries during this same period (about 6.4% per year). It is also interesting to note that in both countries the

12. See Bound et al. (1984) for more detail.

13. The 2-digit deflators for Japan are taken from the Prices Indices Annual issues (Bank of Japan, various years). In previous work, we were able to verify that using 2-digit deflators, instead of more detailed ones, in the case of the United States had very little effect on the regression estimates.

14. See the appendix of Griliches and Mairesse (1984) for more detail on the adjustment of the gross plant numbers for inflation. Using alternative measures for physical capital had little effect on our results.

Table 8.5 Continuous R&D-Reporting Firms Subsample for Japan, 1973–80 Growth Rates (per year) and 1973 Levels: Means (and standard deviations) for Major Variables

Industry	N	Average Employed, 1976 in Thousands[a]	R/S 1973 (estimated)[b]	Average Growth Rates 1973–80			
				Employees	Deflated Sales per Employee	Adjusted Gross Plant per Employee	Approximate TFP[c]
Total	406	4.5 (9.4)	.010 (.013)	-.021 (.038)	.058 (.046)	.085 (.034)	.036 (.045)
1. Food & kindred	22	2.3 (2.3)	.004 (.006)	-.012 (.028)	.029 (.030)	.090 (.032)	.007 (.026)
2. Chemicals & rubber	82	3.0 (3.8)	.011 (.010)	-.023 (.035)	.026 (.027)	.079 (.037)	.006 (.027)
3. Drugs	31	2.4 (2.4)	.037 (.022)	.006 (.030)	.072 (.037)	.082 (.029)	.051 (.036)
4. Metals	41	5.5 (12.9)	.006 (.006)	-.029 (.031)	.035 (.044)	.078 (.029)	.016 (.042)
5. Machinery	48	1.8 (2.5)	.008 (.008)	-.030 (.035)	.067 (.039)	.081 (.032)	.046 (.037)
6. Electrical equipment	67	7.2 (14.4)	.011[d] (.013)	-.017 (.035)	.105 (.035)	.087 (.037)	.084 (.034)
7. Transportation equipment	33	12.3 (17.5)	.001[d] (.005)	-.006 (.033)	.066 (.034)	.084 (.030)	.044 (.031)
8. Instruments	17	2.3 (2.0)	.015 (.017)	-.015 (.055)	.106 (.040)	.101 (.037)	.081 (.035)
9. Other	65	3.0 (3.5)	.004 (.004)	-.039 (.043)	.041 (.042)	.094 (.028)	.017 (.040)

[a]Average employed, 1976 — arithmetic average.

[b]R/S 1973 (estimated) — 1972 through 1974 average R&D divided by average sales in 1972 and 1974.

[c]Approximate TFP (total factor productivity) — growth in deflated value added per employee, .25 (growth is gl. plant per employee)

Table 8.6 Continuous R&D-Reporting Firms Subsample for the United States, 1973–80 Growth Rates (per year) and 1973 Levels: Means (and standard deviations) for Major Variables

Industry	N	Average Employed, 1976 in Thousands[a]	R/S 1973 (estimated)[b]	Average Growth Rates 1973–80			
				Employees	Deflated Sales per Employee	Adjusted Gross Plant per Employee	Approximate TFP[c]
Total	525	16.9 (48.9)	.025 (.023)	.019 (.067)	.016 (.038)	.044 (.051)	.005 (.038)
1. Food & kindred	22	17.0 (17.7)	.006 (.005)	.012 (.042)	.022 (.044)	.042 (.036)	.012 (.041)
2. Chemicals & rubber	71	18.3 (32.5)	.026 (.013)	.014 (.052)	.007 (.034)	.048 (.036)	−.005 (.033)
3. Drugs	44	14.6 (15.1)	.038 (.027)	.040 (.066)	.005 (.033)	.044 (.043)	−.006 (.032)
4. Metals	50	9.5 (18.0)	.012 (.010)	.002 (.053)	.001 (.031)	.045 (.042)	−.010 (.032)
5. Machinery	82	7.8 (12.9)	.024 (.021)	.027 (.074)	.002 (.031)	.046 (.054)	−.009 (.030)
6. Electrical equipment	106	19.4 (51.9)	.035 (.024)	.024 (.080)	.044 (.045)	.046 (.068)	.032 (.047)
7. Transportation equipment	34	66.0 (147.8)	.018 (.013)	.004 (.065)	.003 (.032)	.040 (.049)	−.007 (.028)
8. Instruments	39	10.1 (23.6)	.050 (.032)	.047 (.072)	.030 (.025)	.020 (.040)	.024 (.025)
9. Other	77	9.9 (14.0)	.010 (.007)	.001 (.058)	.012 (.027)	.048 (.048)	−.000 (.026)

[a]Average employed, 1976 − arithmetic average.

[b]R/S 1973 (estimated) − 1972 through 1974 average R&D divided by average sales in 1972 and 1974.

[c]Approximate TFP (total factor productivity) = growth in deflated sales per employee − .25 (growth in plant per employee).

growth of the capital-labor ratio was very similar for the different industrial groupings, varying much less than the growth in the output-labor ratio. This is consistent with the hypothesis that the ratio of real wages to capital user costs moved differently between the two countries but essentially similarly for the different industries within these countries.

If one estimates total factor productivity growth by assuming that value added and sales vary proportionately and that the capital input weight in value added is constant and equal to 0.25 for all firms in both countries, one finds several commonalities and also some contrasts. In both countries the high R&D industries split in their productivity experience: electric equipment and instruments have the highest productivity growth rates while chemicals are among the lowest ones. The major contrasts occur in the machinery, transportation equipment, and drug industries, where there was significant productivity growth in Japan but not in the United States.[15] Only in the food industry did the United States do better than Japan as far as total factor productivity growth is concerned.

Our numbers are not strictly comparable to similar macroestimates, both because they are unweighted firm averages and because many of the firms in our two samples are multinationals with neither their employment nor productivity restricted entirely to the country of origin. Nevertheless, table 8.7 presents the figures on average growth rates of labor and labor productivity that we have gathered at the industry level and for manufacturing as a whole in the two countries, and the corresponding measures from our two total samples.[16] There is no striking inconsistency in the two sets of micro- and macroestimates, but rather a rough agreement in terms of the pattern of differences both across industries and countries. For example, productivity growth is clearly the highest for electrical equipment in the two countries and about the lowest for metals; it is also the case that transportation equipment did quite well in Japan contrary to the United States.[17] It is interesting to note, however, that the overall growth in productivity tends to be more rapid for the firms in our samples than for manufacturing as a whole (the differential being as much as 1.7% per year in Japan and 0.8% in the United States), while the contrast in employment experience is even larger: 2.5% slower growth in our firm data in Japan versus the United States, as against only a 0.8% differential in the national-income-accounts-based industry totals.

15. Using a more appropriate price deflator for the drug companies in Japan than one used for the chemical industry as a whole (which was done in an earlier version of the paper) results in a significant rise in their estimated productivity growth, but it has no effect on regression results that allow for separate industry constants.

16. The macroestimates for Japan are taken from the Annual Reports on National Income Statistics. Those for the United States are constructed from output series based on the Survey of Manufactures and from the price indices used in National Accounts—see Griliches and Lichtenberg (1984) for details. Note that table 8.6 is based on total samples, not just the R&D firms. A comparison of tables 8.5 and 8.6 with 8.7 shows only minor differences between our total sample and the R&D firms subsample.

17. Our numbers are also consistent with the macroevidence given in Jorgenson, Kuroda, and Nishimizu (1987).

Table 8.7   Average Growth Rates, 1973–80, of Labor and Labor Productivity at Company and Industry Level

| | Japan | | | | | United States | | | | |
| | Total Sample | | | National Accounts | | | Total Sample | | | National Accounts | |
Industry	N	Employees	Deflated Sales per Employee	All Persons	Real Output per Person	N	Employees	Deflated Sales per Employee	All Persons	Real Output per Person
Total	1,032	−.024 (.042)	.055 (.047)	−.005	.038	968	.013 (.066)	.012 (.042)	.007	.004
1. Food	82	−.011 (.035)	.034 (.032)	−.003	.049	63	.020 (.052)	.020 (.042)	−.002	.023
2. Chemicals & rubber	149	−.019 (.032)	.026 (.031)	−.009[b]	.039[b]	91	.012 (.056)	.009 (.034)	.007	−.002
3. Drugs	37	.005 (.030)	.071 (.043)			52	.035 (.068)	.003 (.032)	.010	.015
4. Metals	149	−.031 (.035)	.036 (.041)	−.007	.026	135	−.004 (.053)	−.008 (.052)	−.005	−.013
5. Machinery	154	−.028 (.044)	.063 (.037)	−.007	.039	113	.028 (.070)	−.000 (.030)	.023[a]	−.004[a]
6. Electrical equipment	152	−.018 (.036)	.102 (.039)	.003	.083	140	.026 (.081)	.043 (.047)	.022	.051
7. Transportation equipment	79	−.008 (.040)	.063 (.036)	.010	.065	63	−.004 (.066)	−.001 (.043)	−.005	−.009
8. Instruments	33	−.016 (.045)	.102 (.038)	.007	.062	46	.052 (.073)	.026 (.026)		
9. Other	197	−.044 (.049)	.042 (.047)	−.010	.013	265	−.001 (.059)	.012 (.034)	.006	.000

[a]Machinery and instruments.
[b]Chemicals & rubber, and drugs.

8.4 R&D Intensity and Productivity Growth at the Firm Level

The model we consider can be thought of as a modified version of the Cobb-Douglas production function in its growth rate form, with labor productivity being a function of the physical capital–labor ratio and research capital.[18] Because we have only a very short history of research expenditures for most of these firms, it is difficult to construct a reliable research capital measure. We use, therefore, the R&D intensity version of this model instead, in which the beginning period R&D to sales ratio is substituted for the unavailable R&D capital variable.

Let the true equation be

$$(q - l) = \lambda + \alpha(c - l) + \gamma k + \mu l + u,$$

where small lettered variables stand for rates of growth (logarithmic changes): q, l, and c represent output, employment, and physical capital, respectively; k is a measure of accumulated research capital; α, β, γ are the elasticities of output with respect to physical capital, labor, and research capital; $\mu = (\alpha + \beta - 1)$ is the economies of scale coefficient; λ is a constant that reflects, among other things, disembodied technical change; and u is a random disturbance standing in for all other unspecified effects affecting measured productivity growth.

The research capital elasticity γ is equal, by definition, to $(dQ/dK)(K/Q)$. Since $k = dK/K$, we can simplify $\gamma k = (dQ/dK)(K/Q)(dK/K)$ to $\rho(R/Q)$, where $\rho = dQ/dK$ is the marginal product of research capital and R is the level of R&D expenditures. Two points need to be made about this type of simplification: it assumes that R, gross expenditures on R&D, is a good proxy for net investment (dK) in R&D capital. This can be true only if there is no or little depreciation of research capital or if we are in the beginning phases of accumulation and the initial stocks of K are small. Also, it is assumed that ρ rather than γ is constant across firms, that the rate of return ρ is the parameter that is more likely to be equalized across firms.[19]

The equations that we estimate are then of the form

$$(q - l) = \lambda + \alpha(c - l) + \mu l + \rho(R/Q) + u,$$

where the rates of growth of $(q - l)$, $(c - l)$, are generally computed over the seven-year period 1973–80.

---

18. A number of issues are ignored in such a framework, not because they are unimportant, but primarily because there is little that we can do about them here. For example, much of the Japanese progress may be based on imported technology, for which we have no data. However, to the extent that R&D expenditures are required to absorb borrowed or imported technology, this may still be captured, in part, by our measures. We can also do little about the role of government R&D support (there are no data on this at the firm level in either data base) or spillovers in this context (see Griliches 1979 for a discussion of these and other caveats).

19. See Griliches (1979) and Griliches and Lichtenberg (1984) for a related discussion of such models.

The adoption of this specification has two important consequences: first, the estimating equation is expressed in terms of rates of growth of productivity (first differences of the logarithms of the various variables) and thus does not relate differences in productivity levels to differences in R&D capital. This has the advantage of protecting the estimates from potential biases due to (correlated) specific effects but at the cost of ignoring the large variability of the data in the cross-sectional dimension. We know from previous work that results based on this dimension (between-firms) are usually stronger than those based only on the time dimension (within-firms) (see, e.g., Griliches and Mairesse [1984] and Cuneo and Mairesse [1984]). A second consequence is that we relate differences in the rate of growth of productivity to differences in R&D to sales ratios (rather than to the differences in the rate of growth of R&D capital stock).[20]

Several alternative measures of R&D intensity, R/Q, were tried with largely similar results. The final variable chosen, AR/S, relates the average amount of deflated R&D during 1972–74 to the mean (geometric) levels of deflated sales for the period as a whole (average of 1973 and 1980 sales). The numerator of this ratio refers to the beginning of the period and allows, implicitly, for an approximate three-year lag in the effects of R&D.[21] The denominator is positioned in the middle of the period to reduce the spuriousness that may arise when a growth rate is based on a ratio whose denominator is in fact the initial level from which the growth rate is measured.[22] Instead of a unique trend term we include, usually, separate industry dummy variables, which allow for differential industrial trends of disembodied technical change, and also for deflator errors and industrywide changes in capacity utilization. Such equations were also estimated separately for each industrial grouping.

20. There are several difficulties in interpreting the estimated coefficient of R&D intensity, ρ, as the marginal product of or rate of return to R&D. The exact meaning of the estimated ρ depends on the measure of R&D intensity, the measure of output, and what else is included in the equation. Since we use an R&D to sales ratio, ρ should be interpreted as a gross marginal product in terms of output. But leaving material inputs out of the equation brings it closer to a value-added interpretation, which would presumably have resulted in a lower coefficient if value added were substituted for sales in the denominator. On the other hand, leaving out the "depreciation" of the existing R&D capital stock would bias the estimated coefficient downward (on the order of a half). It is also the case that the estimated ρ may be affected by the fact that R&D labor and R&D capital are counted twice, once in the available measures of labor and physical capital and again in the measure of R&D. Hence ρ might be viewed as an excess marginal product or rate of return (above the usual remuneration). Such an interpretation must be qualified however, since it does not apply easily to estimates in the time dimension (see Griliches 1979; Schankerman 1981; Griliches and Lichtenberg 1984; and Cuneo and Mairesse 1984 on these matters). Thus the estimated ρ coefficients are only very distant reflections of the relevant "rate of return" concept.

21. We also tried shorter lags, i.e., by defining the R&D measure as of 1976 (the middle of our period) but this produced significantly worse results in both Japan and the United States. We could not really try for longer lags within the framework of our data bases.

22. Using sales in 1973 or an average of 1972 and 1974 sales as a base does indeed make our results look significantly better. Using the $R/S73$ (estimated) ratio (i.e., $2R73/[S72 + S74]$) in eq. 5 of table 8.8, for example, we get for its coefficient .36 with a t-ratio of 2.6 in Japan and .42 with a t-ratio of 5.5 in the United States. These are significantly higher than the comparable numbers in table 8.8. Since the R&D numerator is the same in both measures, this does imply that our worries about potential spuriousness may not be groundless.

Table 8.8 summarizes our main econometric results. The estimated R&D coefficients in the productivity growth equations are of similar magnitude in both countries. They fall substantially when industry dummies (trends) are allowed for, implying, possibly, the presence of significant interfirm R&D spillovers. The major difference is that, in this case, the coefficients for Japan are not statistically significant at conventional significance levels.

Although significant, the contribution of R&D intensity to the explanation of the variance in productivity growth across firms is rather small, the fit barely improving in the second decimal place. Nor can R&D account for the mean difference in growth rates between the two countries. Both the average R&D intensities and the estimated coefficients are quite close to each other. Nevertheless, if these coefficients are taken at face value, they imply that R&D contributed between 0.4% and 0.6% per year to productivity growth in both countries. This is not a small matter after all.

What is most striking in our results is the lower estimated contribution of physical capital to output growth in the United States. It is about half of what is estimated for Japan.[23] In fact, if we apply the coefficients in table 8.8 (regression 3) to the first row of table 8.5, we can account for about half of the Japan–United States difference in productivity growth by (1) the twice-as-fast rate of growth of the capital-labor ratio in Japan, and (2) its twice-as-large effect on productivity there. The reasons for both of these findings remain to be elucidated.

On the other hand, the Japanese data seem also to imply a much sharper rate of diminishing returns. This last estimate (the $-.24$ coefficient in regression 5) seems rather difficult to believe; it could be due to errors in the Japanese labor variable or to our inability to properly account for the problem of varying capacity utilization and hours of work. In any case, since the Japanese firms reduced their average employment during this period, such "diminishing returns" could not serve as a brake on their productivity growth.

Table 8.9 summarizes our attempts to look at the same issues at the individual industry level. Given the high error rates in the data at the firm level and the relatively small sample sizes, there is little to be seen here. Consistent with our earlier finding that the overall R&D coefficient was not statistically significant in Japan, the individual industry estimates are found to be about half positive and half negative, and only three of them have both the right sign and exceed their estimated standard error. For the United States, the results are only slightly better: seven out of the nine industries have positive R&D coefficients, and three of them are larger than their estimated standard errors. There is little relationship, moreover, in the relative size of these coefficients across the same industry groupings in the two countries (see lower panel of table 8.9).

We made several efforts to improve matters by redefining variables and

---

23. The higher capital elasticity estimate in Japan is consistent with the higher capital share in output reported by Jorgenson, Kuroda, and Nishimizu (1987).

Table 8.8   Productivity (deflated sales per employee) Growth in Manufacturing at the Firm Level as a Function of Growth in the Capital-Labor Ratio and R&D Intensity: Japan–United States Comparisons, 1973–80

| | Coefficients and (Standard Errors) | | | | | | R^2 and (MSE) | |
| | Japan | | | United States | | | | |
Regression	C/L[a]	L[b]	AR/S[c]	C/L	L	AR/S	Japan	United States
1	.372 (.067)			.132 (.032)			.072 (.00198)	.031 (.00141)
2	.377 (.066)		.562 (.229)	.146 (.032)		.410 (.093)	.085 (.00196)	.066 (.00136)
3	.298 (.051)			.152 (.030)			.500 (.00111)	.220 (.00116)
4	.311 (.051)		.302 (.214)	.155 (.029)		.267 (.096)	.502 (.00110)	.251 (.00112)
5	.236 (.052)	−.240 (.049)	.203 (.209)	.107 (.033)	−.080 (.026)	.248 (.096)	.531 (.00104)	.265 (.00110)

Note: Equations 3–5 contain an additional 13 industry dummy variables. Regression 5 includes also the average 1972–74 employment level as a control variable for initial size. Its coefficient is small, positive, and significant for the United States and essentially zero for Japan. MSE is the mean square error of regression residuals.

[a] C/L = growth rate of gross plant in constant prices per employee.

[b] L = growth rate of employment.

[c] AR/S = average R&D to sales ratio. R&D averaged for the years 1972–74, sales at mid-point of the period: geometric average of beginning- (1973) and end-period (1980) sales. Both variables are deflated.

Table 8.9   Distribution of the R/S Coefficients by Industry (regression 4)

	Coefficients			
	<0	0–.5	>.5	Total
t-ratios for Japan:				
<1	3	2		5
>1	1		3	4
Total	4	2	3	9
t-ratios for the United States:				
<1	1	3	1	5
>1	1	1	2	4
Total	2	4	3	9

	Coefficients for Japan			
	<0	0–.5	>.5	Total
Coefficients for the United States:				
<0	1		1	2
0–.5	1	1	2	4
>.5	2	1		3
Total	4	2	3	9

changing the time periods somewhat, but this had little effect. The results are quite robust to the use of net rather than gross physical capital measures or to changes in the averaging procedures for the R&D data. Changing time periods, however, makes more of a difference. Using the slightly shorter 1974–79 period improves the estimates somewhat in Japan but deteriorates them in the United States.[24] This leads us to a disappointing finding: the instability of the productivity-R&D relationship and its sensitivity to the business cycle and macroeconomic supply shocks.

Table 8.10 presents annual estimates of the R&D coefficients using approximate total factor production (TFP) growth as the dependent variable. We use TFP here to avoid adding another source of variation, which would come from allowing also the physical capital elasticity to vary from year to year.[25] What is striking is that, though the exact timing was a bit different, the oil shock–induced sharp recession of 1974–75 hit the R&D-intensive firms disproportionately hard in both countries. It is not clear, however, whether what we see in this table represents a real phenomenon or is just another reflection of the thinness of our data and our inability to estimate the effects of R&D precisely.[26]

24. About half the inflation during our seven-year study period of 1973–80 took place in the first year, 1973–74, and in the last one, 1979–80, as a consequence of the two oil shocks of 1973 and 1979. We thought that the potential errors in price deflators and hence in our productivity measures would thus be smaller for the shorter period 1974–79 and hoped for better results over this period.

25. The estimated physical capital elasticity also varies from year to year. But since the growth in the capital-labor ratio and R&D intensity are nearly uncorrelated, the R&D coefficients are almost unaffected by the constraining of the capital coefficient implicit in the TFP equations.

26. Using average rates of growth over a number of years to estimate the relation of productivity to R&D has the advantage of minimizing the possible biases due to measurement errors and to the

Table 8.10   Coefficients of R&D Intensity in TFP Growth Regressions, by Year, Japan and the United States, 1974–80

Year	Japan	United States
1973–74	−.73	1.50
	(.91)	(.38)
1974–75	−.73	−1.48
	(.91)	(.42)
1975–76	.51	−.58
	(.81)	(.33)
1976–77	.85	.65
	(.70)	(.34)
1977–78	1.01	.35
	(.67)	(.27)
1978–79	.60	1.28
	(.64)	(.29)
1979–80	.55	.38
	(.58)	(.32)

Note: Approximate TFP growth is calculated as: (percent growth in deflated sales per employee) − .25(percent growth in gross plant per employee). All equations contain an additional set of industry dummies and a base year (1973) size variable. The R&D-intensity variable, AR/S, is calculated as the average of 1972–74 R&D divided by the average (geometric) 1973 and 1980 sales (both deflated). It is the same for all years.

8.5   Tentative Conclusions

Japanese manufacturing firms spent about as much of their own money on R&D, relative to their sales, as did similar U.S. firms: about 1.9% versus 2.3%, respectively, in 1976. On the basis of the econometric analysis of our sample of R&D firms, we cannot reject the hypothesis that the contribution of these expenditures to productivity growth was about the same in both countries. There is no strong prima facie evidence for the hypothesis that differences in either the intensity or the fecundity of R&D expenditures can account for the rather large difference in the observed rates of growth of productivity between the two countries.[27] The reasons for this difference must be looked for elsewhere.

We do find two important differences between Japan and the United States that help to account for some of this difference but require an explanation of their own:

1. In spite of their success in growing and exporting, Japanese firms reduced their employment levels significantly during this period while U.S. firms were increasing theirs. This alone is enough to account for the twice-faster growth

timing problem. We expected, therefore, to find instability when looking at this relation on a single year basis, but not to such an extent.

27. Given the high standard errors associated with the Japanese estimates, it is not strong evidence against this hypothesis either.

in the capital-labor ratio in Japanese manufacturing since the capital stock itself has been growing at roughly similar rates in both countries.

2. For reasons that are not well understood, the estimated effect of growth in the capital-labor ratio on firm productivity in manufacturing appears to be twice as large in Japan as in the United States. An exploration of the reasons for this difference awaits better data, another occasion, and perhaps a different approach to the problem.

There are a number of other puzzling findings that we hope to return to in the future: Why did the chemical industry perform so badly during this period in both countries? Why did the drug industry do so badly in the United States during these same years? Is this a real fact or an artifact of poor deflators? While the oil price shocks provide some explanation for the poor performance of the chemical firms along lines outlined by Bruno and Sachs (1985), it is doubtful that they can also explain the experience of the pharmaceutical firms in the United States. Why does the effect of R&D intensity on productivity growth vary so much over the cycle? Is it because it should only be observable at or near full capacity? How can such considerations be incorporated into a more complete analysis of our data?

An improved analysis of the role of R&D expenditures in the growth of Japanese firms will require better data than are currently available to us. The Japanese Statistics Bureau has collected much more extensive and presumably more reliable data on R&D expenditures of firms for many years but as far as we know these data have not been accessible, nor have they been used in their detailed micro form. In the United States, similarly collected data by the National Science Foundation (NSF) and the Bureau of the Census have been matched for different surveys and brought together in a usable data file. The confidentiality problem was solved by performing all of the major data assembly and cleaning operations within the Census Bureau and by releasing only variance-covariance matrices for the major variables across firms and years without disclosing any individual firm information.[28] It would certainly be interesting to launch a similar effort in Japan. Another way of dealing with the confidentiality requirement is to carry out the econometric analysis within the National Statistical Offices themselves, as was the case for our studies for France.[29]

We cannot expect, however, that having better and more reliable data will solve all the problems. What we are looking for are effects that are at best variable, uncertain, and more or less long term in nature and that are also relatively small in magnitude. This does not mean, of course, that these effects are unimportant or that we should not devote more effort in trying to analyze them. But we cannot expect to account for much of the observed growth in productiv-

28. See Griliches (1980, 1986) and Griliches and Hall (1982) for more detail on these data and their construction and for results of analyses using them.

29. Since this was first written we have been informed that such efforts are indeed underway by researchers associated with the Economic Planning Agency in Japan. See Goto and Suzuki (1989).

ity by focusing only on the firm's own R&D investments. The role of research spillovers between firms, sectors, and countries and the impact of other, less formal, ways of generating technical progress, are likely to be quite large and still remain to be measured.

Addendum

After the revision and completion of this paper for this volume, we gained access to new R&D information at the firm level for Japan. We are grateful to Fumio Hayashi for his help in getting these data.

Besides the R&D figures reported in the NEEDS data base and the official R&D survey of the Statistics Bureau of Japan, there exists in fact another R&D survey performed and published by the Nihon Keizai Shimbun Corporation in recent years. This survey is the source of the OECD numbers, which we already used to adjust the NEEDS figures for 18 of the largest R&D firms. In order to check our numbers on a larger scale, we matched these new data to our total sample of 1,032 firms for the fiscal year 1978 or 1979. We found 1,000 firms in common, among which 877 were reporting R&D expenditures. These 877 include our sample of 406 firms that reported R&D consistently from 1972 through 1980 in NEEDS and 471 firms that did not. When we compare the R&D numbers in the two sources for our 406 firms sample, the discrepancy is less than 5% for more than half of the sample; it is less than 50% for another quarter, but it is more than 400% for 48 firms. Contrary to the 18 large R&D adjusted firms, these 48 firms are smaller than average, and it is quite plausible that a major part of their R&D expenditures is external or cooperative and is not declared in NEEDS.

We have adjusted our R&D-intensity variable using the new R&D information (as we already had done with the OECD figures), and we have rerun our main regressions using these adjusted measures for various subsamples: the 406 R&D-reporting firms, among which we consider the 48 R&D-reporting firms with very large R&D discrepancies separately, and the remaining 358 R&D-reporting firms. We have also used the new R&D data for the 471 firms that did not report, or reported intermittently, R&D expenditures in NEEDS. Pooling together this sample and the previous ones, we have two overall samples of 877 (406 + 471) and 829 (358 + 471) firms. The results for the simplest regression (with constant returns to scale and without industry dummies, comparable to regression 2 in table 8.7) are given in table 8A.1.

Using the adjusted R&D-intensity variable does not really improve our estimates. They remain about the same if the 48 firms for which the discrepancies are extreme are excluded, and they look worse if we do include them, the coefficient of R&D being smaller and not significant. Clearly one would like to know more about the 48 problematic firms. The estimates for the additional 471 firms sample and for the pooled 829 firms sample are also very similar to our previous results.

Table 8A.1   Productivity Growth–R&D Intensity Regressions with and without R&D Adjusted Measures for Various Samples of Japanese Firms: 1973–80 (similar to regression 2 in table 8.8)

Various Samples	R&D Measures from NEEDS, Coefficients and Standard Errors			R&D Adjusted Measures, Coefficients and Standard Errors		
	C/L	AR/S	R^2 MSE	C/L	AR/S	R^2 MSE
406 R&D-reporting firms	.38 (.07)	.56 (.23)	.085 .0020	.37 (.07)	.16 (.13)	.075 .0020
48 R&D-reporting firms with very large R&D discrepancies	.00 (.20)	5.22 (2.53)	.090 .0010	−.06 (.21)	.00 (.20)	.002 .0020
358 R&D-reporting firms without very large R&D discrepancies (406 − 48)	.42 (.07)	.48 (.24)	.101 .0019	.42 (.07)	.58 (.21)	.109 .0020
471 nonconsistently R&D-reporting firms	. . .	. . .	. . .	.25 (.050)	.48 (.22)	.060 .0019
877 R&D-reporting (consistently and nonconsistently) firms (406 + 471)	. . .	. . .	. . .	.29 (.04)	.28 (.11)	.063 .0020
829 R&D-reporting (consistently and nonconsistently) firms, without firms with very large R&D discrepancies (358 + 471)	. . .	. . .	. . .	.31 (.04)	.56 (.15)	.077 .0020

On the whole these computations confirm our earlier results. This is reassuring since R&D expenditures are poorly reported in the NEEDS data bank. But it is also unfortunate since one would have hoped for somewhat stronger and more significant estimates with better and more accurate figures. Again the quality of the data is not our only problem.

References

Bank of Japan, Research and Statistics Department. Various years. *Prices indexes annual: Input-output price indexes of manufacturing industry by sector.* Tokyo.

Bound, J., C. Cummins, Z. Griliches, B. H. Hall, and A. Jaffe. 1984. Who does R&D

and who patents? In *R&D, patents, and productivity,* ed. Z. Griliches. Chicago: University of Chicago Press.

Bruno, M., and J. Sachs. 1985. *Economics of worldwide stagflation.* Cambridge, Mass.: Harvard University Press.

Council of Economic Advisers. 1984. *Economic report of the president.* Washington, D.C.: Government Printing Office.

Cuneo, P., and J. Mairesse. 1984. Productivity and R&D at the firm level in French manufacturing. In *R&D, patents, and productivity,* ed. Z. Griliches. Chicago: University of Chicago Press.

Economic Planning Agency, Government of Japan. Various years. *Annual report on national accounts.* Tokyo.

Goto, A., and K. Suzuki. 1989. R&D capital, rate of return on R&D investment and spillover of R&D in Japanese manufacturing industries. *Review of Economics and Statistics* 71(4):555–64.

Griliches, Z. 1986. Productivity, R&D, and basic research at the firm level in the 1970s. *American Economic Review* 76(1):141–54. [Reprinted as chap. 4 in this volume.]

———. 1980. Returns to research and development expenditures in the private sector. In *New developments in productivity measurement and analysis,* eds. J. W. Kendrick and B. Vaccara. NBER Studies in Income and Wealth 44. Chicago: University of Chicago Press. [Reprinted as chap. 3 in this volume.]

———. 1979. Issues in assessing the contribution of R&D to productivity growth. *Bell Journal of Economics* 10, no. 1 (Spring): 92–116. [Reprinted as chap. 2 in this volume.]

Griliches, Z., and B. H. Hall. 1982. Census-NSF R&D data match project. In *Development and use of longitudinal establishment data.* Economic Research Report ER-4. Washington, D.C.: Bureau of the Census.

Griliches, Z., and F. Lichtenberg. 1984. R&D and productivity growth at the industry level: Is there still a relationship? In *R&D, patents, and productivity,* ed. Z. Griliches. Chicago: University of Chicago Press. [Reprinted as chap. 9 in this volume.]

Griliches, Z., and J. Mairesse. 1984. Productivity and R&D at the firm level. In *R&D, patents, and productivity,* ed. Z. Griliches. Chicago: University of Chicago Press. [Reprinted as chap. 5 in this volume.]

———. 1983. Comparing productivity growth: An exploration of French and U.S. industrial and firm data. *European Economic Review* 21(1–2):89–119. [Reprinted as chap. 7 in this volume.]

Hall, B. H., C. Cummins, E. Laderman, and J. Mundy. 1988. The R&D master file documentation. NBER Technical Paper no. 72.

Jorgenson, D. W., M. Kuroda, and M. Nishimizu. 1987. Japan-U.S. industry level productivity comparison, 1960–1979. *Journal of Japanese and International Economics* 1(1):1–30.

Mairesse, J., and P. Cuneo. 1985. Recherche-developpement et performances des entreprises. *Revue Economique* 36(5):1001–41.

Mohnen, P., M. I. Nadiri, and I. Prucha. 1986. R&D, production structure, and rates of return in the U.S., Japanese, and German manufacturing sectors. *European Economic Review* 30(4):749–72.

National Science Foundation. Various years. *Research and development in industry.* Washington, D.C.: Government Printing Office.

———. 1985. A comparative analysis of information on national industrial R&D expenditures. NSF Report 85–311. Washington, D.C.

Odagiri, H. 1983. R&D expenditures, royalty payments, and sales growth in Japanese manufacturing corporations. *Journal of Industrial Economics* 32(2):61–72.

Odagiri, H., and H. Iwata. 1986. The impact of R&D on productivity increases in Japanese manufacturing companies. *Research Policy* 15:13–19.

OECD. 1984. *Science and technology indicators: Resources devoted to R&D*. Paris: Organization for Economic Cooperation and Development.

Peck, M. J. 1985. Government R&D subsidies in the American economy? Discussion Paper no. 35. Economic Research Institute, Economic Planning Agency, Tokyo.

Schankerman, M. 1981. The effects of double-counting and expensing on the measured returns to R&D. *Review of Economics and Statistics* 63(3):454–58.

Statistics Bureau, Management and Coordination Agency. Various years. *Report on the survey of research and development*. Tokyo.

U.S. Bureau of the Census. 1977. Enterprise statistics: General report on industrial organization. ES77–1. Washington, D.C.: Government Printing Office.

III R&D and Productivity at the Industry Level

9   R&D and Productivity Growth at the Industry Level: Is There Still a Relationship?

9.1   Introduction

A previous paper (Griliches 1980) explored the time-series relationship between total factor productivity (TFP) and cumulated past research and development (R&D) expenditures within different "2-1/2 digit" SIC level manufacturing industries. It used the Bureau of Labor Statistics' (BLS) Input-Output (I-O) sector level productivity and capital series and the National Science Foundation's (NSF) applied research and development series by product class as its data base and focused on the potential contribution of the slowdown in the growth of R&D expenditures to the explanation of the recent slowdown in productivity growth in manufacturing. Its main conclusions were: (1) The magnitude of the R&D slowdown together with the size of estimated elasticities of output with respect to R&D stock do not account for more than a small fraction of the observed decline in productivity. (2) When the data are disaggregated by period, almost no significant relationship was found between changes in R&D stock and productivity growth in the more recent 1969–77 period.[1] This led one commentator (Nordhaus 1980) to interpret these results as evidence for the hypothesis of the depletion of scientific opportunities. The paper itself was more agnostic, pointing to the large unexplained annual fluctuations in TFP and arguing that many of the recent observations were affected by unexpected price developments and large swings in capacity utilization and,

This chapter is coauthored with Frank Lichtenberg and is reprinted from *R&D, Patents, and Productivity*, edited by Zvi Griliches, pp. 465–96 (Chicago: University of Chicago Press, 1984). © 1984 by the National Bureau of Economic Research. All rights reserved.

The authors are indebted to the National Science Foundation (grants PRA-79-13740 and SOC-78-04279) and the NBER Capital Formation Program for financial support.

1. These findings were also consistent with the evidence assembled by Agnew and Wise (1978), Scherer (1981), and Terleckyj (1980).

hence, could not be interpreted as being on the production possibilities frontier and as providing evidence about changes in the rate of its outward shift.

A variety of problems were raised by the data and methodology used in that paper, some of which we hope to explore and to improve in this paper. There were, roughly speaking, three kinds of problems: (1) those associated with the choice of a particular R&D series; (2) those arising from the use of a particular TFP series; and (3) those associated with the modeling of the relationship between R&D and subsequent productivity growth. We shall address these topics in turn. To foreshadow our conclusions, we find that the relationship between an industry's R&D intensity and its productivity growth did not disappear. An overall decline in productivity growth has also affected the R&D intensive industries, but to a lesser extent. If anything, this relationship was stronger in recent years. What cannot be found in the data is strong evidence of the differential effects of the slowdown in R&D itself. The time series appear to be too noisy and the period too short to detect what the major consequences of the retardation in the growth of R&D expenditures may yet turn out to be.

9.2   The R&D Data

The major and only source of R&D data at the industrial level of detail are the surveys conducted by the Census Bureau for the National Science Foundation (see, e.g., National Science Foundation 1977). These surveys are based, however, on company reports and on the industrial designation of the company by its main line of activity. There are at least two problems with these data: (1) Many of the major R&D performers are conglomerates or reasonably widely diversified firms. Thus, the R&D reported by them is not necessarily "done" in the industry they are attributed to. (2) Many firms perform R&D directed at processes and products used in other industries. There is a significant difference between the industrial locus of a particular R&D activity, its "origin," and the ultimate place of use of the results of such activity, the locus of its productivity effects. In addition, one should also keep in mind the possibility of pure knowledge spillovers, the cross-fertilization of one industry's research program by developments occurring in other industries.[2]

There are various ways of dealing with such problems. We chose to use the NSF data on applied research and development expenditures by *product class* as the basis for our series.[3] The product-class classification is closer to the desired notion of R&D by industry of *use* and it is available at a reasonable level of SIC detail (twenty-eight distinct "2-1/2" digit groupings). It does attribute the fertilizer research of a "textile" firm to the fertilizer industry (but not

---

2. Cf. Griliches (1979) for a more detailed discussion of these issues.

3. Other ways of dealing with this problem include the use of R&D by product class by industry of origin table (Schankerman 1979), input-output and capital flow of purchase table (Terleckyj 1974), and patents class by industry of origin and use table (Scherer 1981) to redistribute the NSF R&D data.

to agriculture) and the work on bulldozers of an "automotive" firm to the construction equipment industry (but not to construction itself). It is thus based on a notion of proximate rather than ultimate use. Nevertheless, it is much better conceptually than the straight NSF industrial origin classification scheme.[4]

Unfortunately, it is based on much more spotty reporting than the overall R&D numbers. Moreover, after using these numbers in the earlier study, we discovered rather arbitrary and abrupt jumps in the historical series as published by NSF. It appears that when the Census drew new samples in 1968 and 1977, it did not carry through the revisions of the published data consistently backward, leaving large incomparabilities in some of the years for some of the industries. We had to go back to the original annual NSF reports and splice together and interpolate between the unrevised and revised numbers to keep them somewhat comparable over time.[5]

The industrial classification of a particular R&D data set determines the possible level of detail of subsequent analysis. Since the two-digit industrial categories are rather broad, we would like to use finer detail where possible, for example we would like to separate drugs from chemicals or computers from all machinery. This, of course, influences our choice of total factor productivity series.

9.3   The TFP Data

Because we are interested in industrial detail below the usual two-digit level breakdown, we could not use some of the already published and carefully constructed total factor productivity series, such as Gollop and Jorgenson (1980) or Kendrick and Grossman (1980). In the previous paper we used the BLS growth study data based on the input-output classification of 145 sectors (95 of them in manufacturing; see U.S. Department of Labor 1979a) and associated physical capital data series. These data are subject to two major drawbacks: First, the output concept used by BLS is based on the product rather than the

---

4. NSF (1977, p. 70) instructs respondents to the industrial R&D survey to complete the "applied R&D by product field" item on the questionnaire as follows:

Costs should be entered in the field or product group in which the research and development project was actually carried on regardless of the classification of the field of manufacturing in which the results are to be used. For example, research on an electrical component for a farm machine should be reported as research on electrical machinery. Also, research on refractory bricks to be used by the steel industry should be reported as research on stone, clay, glass, and concrete products rather than primary ferrous metals, whether performed in the steel industry or the stone, clay, glass, and concrete industry. Research and development work on an automotive head lamp would be classified in other electrical equipment and supplies, regardless of whether performed by an automotive or electrical company.

In fact, however, the majority of respondents interprets this question as relating to "industry of use" according to a recent internal audit by the Bureau of the Census.

5. This work was done by Alan Siu and is described in more detail in appendix B.

establishment classification, which introduces an unknown amount of incomparability between the output measure and the associated labor and capital measures. The latter are based on the industrial classification of establishments rather than products. Second, the only available output concept is gross output (not value added), and there are no consistent official numbers on material or energy use below the two-digit industry level. The use of gross output and the lack of data on materials introduce a bias of an unknown magnitude that could be quite large during the seventies, when materials and energy prices rose sharply relative to the prices of other inputs.

Because of these problems, we turned to another source of data: the four-digit level, Annual Survey of Manufactures based series constructed by Fromm, Klein, Ripley, and Crawford (1979) as part of a joint Bureau of the Census, University of Pennsylvania, and SRI International (formerly Stanford Research Institute) project.[6] These data cover the years 1959–76 and contain information on material use by industry as well as separate information on energy use since 1971. Several problems also arise with this data set: First, it only goes through 1976. Second, the information on labor input available to us covered only production worker manhours, and we had to adjust it to reflect total employment. Third, the construction of these data is rather poorly documented, so one does not know how some of the numbers were derived or interpolated on the basis of the published sources. Nevertheless, they are very rich in detail and we hope to explore them further in subsequent work.

We used these data, after an adjustment of the labor input, to construct Tornqvist-Divisia indexes of total factor productivity at the relevant levels of aggregation (see appendix A for more detail). Table 9.1 presents estimated rates of growth of TFP between subperiod averages for manufacturing industries according to the breakdown given in the NSF R&D publications. In these data, a clear retardation in the rate of growth for most of the industries is evident already in the late sixties.[7]

Almost all TFP data start with some gross sales or revenues concept adjusted for inventory change and then deflated by some price index to yield a measure of "output in constant prices." Such a measure is no better than the price indexes used to create it. The price indexes are components of the Producer Price Index (PPI) and associated series reprocessed by the U.S. Department of Com-

6. We are indebted to David Crawford for making these series available to us.
7. It should be pointed out that, because of the volatility of the annual TFP series, estimates of the timing and severity of the TFP slowdown (measured by the change in the average annual growth rate of TFP between two adjacent subperiods) are quite sensitive to the particular way in which the entire sample period is divided into subperiods. The weighted (by value of shipments) averages of the industries' beginning-, middle-, and end-of-period TFP average annual growth rates shown in table 9.1 are 1.72, 0.86, and 0.10, respectively. If instead of measuring changes between the mean level of TFP over several years, we compute average annual TFP changes between single "peak" years in business activity (as measured by the Federal Reserve Board index of capacity utilization for total manufacturing), the beginning, middle, and end subperiod definitions are 1959–65, 1965–73, and 1973–76, and the corresponding weighted TFP growth rates are 1.67, 1.23, and −1.94; almost all of the apparent slowdown occurs at the end of the period.

Table 9.1   **Average Annual Rates of Total Factor Productivity Growth between Subperiod Averages: Industries in NSF Applied R&D by Product Field Classification, in Percent[a]**

Industry	1959–63 to 1964–68	1964–68 to 1969–73	1969–73 to 1974–76
Ordnance	3.9	−0.9	1.4
Guided missiles	3.3	1.2	1.3
Food	0.7	1.2	−0.3
Textiles	1.5	1.6	−0.5
Plastics	2.8	2.6	0.3
Agricultural chemicals	1.6	2.3	1.2
Other chemicals	1.6	1.5	−1.3
Drugs	4.9	3.6	2.4
Petroleum refining	3.5	1.4	−9.8
Rubber	1.8	1.5	−1.1
Stone, clay, and glass	1.8	0.4	0.2
Ferrous metals	1.6	−0.4	−0.2
Nonferrous metals	0.6	−0.6	−0.3
Fabricated metals	1.9	0.4	−0.9
Engines and turbines	2.0	0.8	−0.9
Farm machinery	1.9	0.2	2.3
Construction machinery	2.2	0.1	−1.0
Metalworking machinery	1.7	−0.3	0.3
Computers	1.9	1.3	3.8
Other machinery	2.1	0.3	−0.3
Electrical transportation equipment	2.7	1.9	−0.3
Electrical industry apparatus	3.4	−0.2	0.0
Other electrical equipment	2.7	1.2	0.0
Communications equipment	2.3	2.0	1.6
Motor vehicles	1.7	0.8	−1.1
Other transportation equipment	2.8	0.5	0.3
Aircraft	3.4	0.4	2.1
Instruments	2.1	1.5	1.5

[a]Based on Tornqvist-Divisia indexes constructed from the Penn-SRI data base.

merce's Bureau of Economic Analysis (BEA) to yield a set of deflators used in the detailed deflation of the GNP accounts. As is well known, the quality of these deflators is quite variable.[8] Moreover, there is some reason to suspect that it may deteriorate further in periods of rapid price change, such as 1974–75, where there may be a widening of the gap between quoted prices and the average realized prices by sellers, many of whose prices may have been actually set earlier or not changed as fast as some of the more standard and widely traded and hence also collected items.

We tried rather hard to pinpoint such a deterioration in the price data and to find ways of adjusting for it, but without much success. Looking at the detailed

8. E.g., consider the obvious ridiculously low estimate of TFP growth for the computer industry in table 9.1. It is caused by the absence of a decent price index.

Table 9.2   **Correlation Coefficients between Rates of Growth or Rates of Acceleration of Prices and of Total Factor Productivity in Four-Digit Industries within Two-Digit Industries 35, 36, and 37**

	SIC 35 Machinery except Electrical	SIC 36 Electrical and Communication Equipment	SIC 37 Transportation Equipment
Rates of growth by period:			
1959–65	−.505	−.701	−.212
1965–73	−.717	−.816	−.252
1973–76	−.821	−.747	−.633
Rates of acceleration, period to period:			
1959–65 to 1965–73	−.521	−.532	−.217
1965–73 to 1973–76	−.782	−.519	−.622
Number of four-digit industries	44	39	17

data (either the BLS I-O sectors set or the Penn-SRI one), it becomes quite clear that many of the large TFP declines that occurred in 1974 and 1975 are associated with above average increases in the output price indexes used to deflate the corresponding industry revenue data. Table 9.2 illustrates the negative relation between TFP and output price growth for selected industries (based on four-digit detail) and its growth over time. Some of the reported price movements are large and bizarre and raise the suspicion that they may be erroneous. But without some alternative direct price or output measurement, it is difficult to go beyond such suspicions since, given the accounting identities and the assumption of competitive behavior, declines in productivity would produce a rise in the associated output price indexes.[9] We can either not believe in the reality of some of the reported productivity declines, in which case we also cast doubt on the price indexes that "produced" such declines, or we can accept both of them as a fact. Both views are consistent with the data as we have them. It would take an independent source of price or output data to adjudicate between these two points of view.

Before we turn to the analysis of the relationship of TFP growth and R&D expenditures, which can be looked at only at the same level of industrial detail as is available for R&D data, we can use the available four-digit detail to look at a few additional aspects of these data. An analysis of variance of annual changes in TFP at the four-digit level during the 1959–73 period illustrates the rather high level of noise in these data. Even in this earlier, relatively calm period only 20 percent of the variance is common at the two-digit level. That

9. In fact, given these identities, if factor prices move similarly for different industries and if factor shares do not change much, the correlation between TFP changes and product price changes should be close to −1.

is, most of the variance in TFP changes as computed is within two-digit industries. Similarly, only 8 percent of the variance is accounted for by common movements over time. The vast majority of the computed TFP movements are not synchronized. If these numbers are to be interpreted on their face value, as reflecting changes in industrial efficiency, these changes are highly idiosyncratic. Alternatively, if one believed that substantive causal changes in technological levels occur together for subindustries within a two-digit classification and follow similar time patterns, then this lack of synchronization would indicate a rather high level of error in these data.

Another issue of potential interest is whether the observed retardation in TFP growth at the two-digit level is also apparent at the four-digit level and is not just an artifact of a faster growth of lower productivity industries. Computations for three two-digit industries (35, 36, and 37) presented in appendix C, table 9A.1 indicate that this is indeed the case. If one held the four-digit industrial mix constant at the beginning period levels, the recorded TFP growth would have been even lower. When one looks at the computed rates of retardation (in the second part of table 9A.1), the effects are reversed, but the differences are quite small. The observed retardation is not an artifact, a "mix" effect. It actually happened quite pervasively at the four-digit level of industrial detail.

9.4   Modeling the R&D to Productivity Relationship

Many of the theoretical issues that arise in the attempt to infer the contribution of R&D to productivity growth from usual types of data were discussed at some length in Griliches (1979) and will not be considered explicitly here. But we want to mention and try to deal with three specific topics: (1) TFP measures as indicators of growth in technological potential; (2) the lag structure of R&D effects; and (3) the functional form and the econometric model within which such effects are to be estimated.

We have already discussed briefly the possibility that the TFP measures as computed are subject both to significant measurement error (arising mainly from errors in the level and timing of the output price deflators) and to large, short-run, irrelevant fluctuations. Irrelevant in the sense that though they do indicate changes in the efficiency with which resources are used, these changes occur as the result of unanticipated fluctuations in demand and in relative prices, forcing firms to operate their plants and organizations in a suboptimal fashion (at least from the point of view of their original design). Whatever theory one has of such business cycle and capacity utilization fluctuations, observations that are not on the production possibilities frontier are unlikely to be informative about the factors that are intended to shift this frontier. By and large, R&D expenditures are spent on designing new products, which will provide more consumer or producer value per unit of resources used, or new processes, which would reduce the resource requirements of existing products.

TFP fluctuations obscure such effects because the observed efficiencies do not reflect the potential ones and because during business cycle downswings there is a significant slowdown in investment with an associated, slower than normal, introduction and diffusion of new products and processes.

Within the limits imposed by our data, we tried three different ways of coping with such problems. The first was to assume that "true" productivity can only improve (no forgetting) and hence allows the TFP series to only increase or stay constant, but not decline, by resetting every "lower" observation to the previously observed peak level. The second approach tried to rule out large downward shifts in TFP that appeared to be caused by large changes in the price deflator and seemed to be inconsistent with the observed variable input (labor and materials) data. For example, if sales went up by 10 percent, and variable inputs went up by 5 percent, while the output price index went up by 15 percent, we would assume that perhaps up to one-half of the price movement was in error. The actual formula used was more complicated than that (it is described in the notes to table 9.3). The gist of it is that in the four-digit industries whose output per unit of variable input declined by more than 3 percent, and whose output price increases exceeded their respective two-digit industry average price increases by more than 5 percent, output was redefined so as to make "variable input productivity" decline *exactly* 3 percent. This adjustment affected about 24 percent (119 out of 486) of our annual observations.

Because neither of these procedures had a noticeable effect on our final results, we ultimately turned to the third and simpler way of coping with some of these problems: averaging. We picked subperiods, averaged the total factor productivity within each of these subperiods, and then computed rates of growth between such subperiod averages. In particular, the growth rate of TFP at the beginning of the 1959–76 period was defined by the average annual change between the mean level of TFP during 1959–63 and its mean level during 1964–68; the growth rates at the middle and end of the period were defined in terms of the changes in the mean level of TFP from 1964–68 to 1969–73, and from 1969–73 to 1974–76, respectively. We hope, in this way, to mitigate, if not solve, some of the difficulties discussed above.

We have very little to contribute on the issue of R&D lag effects. In the earlier work, only some of which was reported in Griliches (1980), we experimented at length with various lag structures, but largely to no avail. The data did seem to prefer, weakly, the no depreciation to the any depreciation assumption, and there was also some evidence of the possibility of rather long lags. Unfortunately, given the shortness of the series and the overall level of noise in the data, we could not really distinguish between a small, slowly decaying effect of R&D long past and fixed industry differences in their average levels of TFP. Thus, in this paper, we do not focus on this issue, but we hope to come back to it some day with better methods and data.

The common approach to the estimation of such models is to use the generalized Cobb-Douglas function in which a term involving some measure of R&D "stock" is added on, paralleling the role of physical capital. There is a problem, however, in applying such a framework across industries, since it is unlikely that different industries have the same production function coefficients. The TFP approach goes some ways toward solving this problem, by assuming that conventional inputs are used at their competitive equilibrium levels and by using the observed factor shares as approximations to the relevant production function elasticities. This allows each industry to have its own (a priori imposed) labor, capital, and materials coefficients. One is left, then, only with the estimation of trend and R&D effects.

The usual procedure (e.g., Griliches 1980) still imposes a common trend rate and a common output-R&D elasticity on all the data. The common trend restriction can be lifted by shifting to an analysis of first differences—the acceleration (or deceleration) in TFP growth—at the cost of magnifying the role of errors and short-term fluctuations in both the dependent and independent variables. The assumption of a common elasticity of output with respect to R&D stock is bothersome when the relationship is estimated *across* industries with well-known and long-term differences in R&D intensity. Unless the difference between the observed R&D "shares" in sales and the estimated overall common R&D elasticity parameter is to be interpreted as reflecting exact differences between the level of social and private R&D returns (which is not very likely), the estimated model is not consistent with any reasonable optimal R&D choice behavior. An alternative approach, used earlier by Griliches (1973) and Terleckyj (1980), is to reparameterize the model in terms of a common *rate of return* (marginal product) of R&D across industries, rather than a common elasticity. Writing the contribution of the change in the stock of R&D to TFP growth as

$$\gamma \dot{K}/K = \frac{\partial Q}{\partial K}\frac{K}{Q}\frac{\dot{K}}{K} = \rho\frac{\dot{K}}{Q} = \rho\frac{R - \delta K}{Q} \simeq \rho\frac{R}{Q},$$

where γ is the elasticity of output (Q) with respect to changes in the stock of R&D capital (K); $\rho = \partial Q/\partial K$ is the rate of return or marginal product of R&D; R is investment in R&D; and δ is the average rate of depreciation of R&D capital, the TFP growth rate can be expressed as a function of the R&D *intensity* of an industry, provided that δ is zero or close to it. This is the form that we will use in much of what follows.

9.5   Models and Main Results

We postulate a Cobb-Douglas production function (which may be viewed as a local, first-order logarithmic approximation to any arbitrary production function) which includes the stock of R&D capital as a distinct factor of production:

(1) $$Q(t) = A \cdot K(t)^{\gamma} \cdot \prod_{i=1}^{4} X_i(t)^{\alpha^i} \cdot \exp(\beta t),$$

where $Q(t)$ = output; A = a constant; $K(t)$ = stock of R&D capital; $X_1(t)$ = labor input; $X_2(t)$ = stock of physical capital (structures and equipment); $X_3(t)$ = energy input; and $X_4(t)$ = nonenergy intermediate materials input. Define a conventional index of total factor productivity, $T(t)$, as

(2) $$T(t) = Q(t) \Big/ \prod_{i=1}^{4} X_i(t)^{\alpha^i},$$

normalized to 1 in 1972. By the first-order conditions for producer equilibrium, α_i—the elasticity of output with respect to the ith input ($i = 1, \ldots, 4$)—is equal to the share of the ith factor in total cost of production. Under the maintained hypothesis of constant returns to scale, $\Sigma \alpha_i = 1$.[10]

Combining (1) and (2),

(3) $$T(t) = A \cdot K(t)^{\gamma} \cdot \exp(\beta t),$$

(4) $$\log T(t) = \log A + \gamma \log K(t) + \beta t.$$

Differentiating (4) with respect to time and writing, for example, $[d\log T(t)]/dt = \dot{T}/T$,

(5) $$\frac{\dot{T}}{T} = \gamma \frac{\dot{K}}{K} + \beta.$$

It is apparent from (1) that γ is the elasticity of output with respect to the stock of R&D capital, that is,

$$\gamma = \frac{\partial \ln Q}{\partial \ln K} = \frac{\partial Q}{\partial K} \cdot \frac{K}{Q}.$$

Hence, one may rewrite (5) as

(6) $$\frac{\dot{T}}{T} = \frac{\partial Q}{\partial K} \cdot \frac{K}{Q} \cdot \frac{\dot{K}}{K} + \beta = \rho \frac{\dot{K}}{Q} + \beta,$$

where $\rho = \partial Q / \partial K$.

We estimated each of the three equations (4), (5), and (6) to measure the contribution of research and development expenditures to productivity. Although the deterministic versions of (4) and (5) are equivalent, they are not stochastically equivalent: in general, OLS estimation of (4) and (5) would yield different estimates of the parameter γ. In (4) and (5), the output elasticity of

---

10. There is a question about whether the coefficient of the R&D-stock variable should be included in the definition of constant returns to scale or not. Since the actual inputs purchased by the R&D expenditures are not segregated out of the conventional measures of labor and capital input, we avoid double counting by not including R&D in $\Sigma \alpha_i = 1$ and by interpreting its coefficient as representing both social and excess returns to this activity. See also note 13.

R&D capital is viewed as a parameter, that is, invariant across observations; in (6) the marginal productivity of R&D capital is a parameter. We argue below that ρ may be loosely interpreted as the social gross excess rate of return to investment in R&D. While there is no reason to expect the *social* rate of return to be equalized across industries, under the hypothesis that the discrepancy between social and private returns is distributed randomly across industries (or is at least uncorrelated with R&D intensity), an estimate of ρ obtained from (6) will be a consistent estimate of the *average* excess of social over private returns.

A variant of equation (4) was estimated on pooled time-series data (1959–76) for twenty-seven industries. Two modifications were made. First, each industry was specified to have its own intercept term, log A. Rather than including twenty-seven industry dummies in the estimating equation, log $T(t)$ and log $K(t)$ were measured as deviations from the respective industry means. Second, the time trend was generalized to a set of time dummies. These time dummies control for all "year effects" common to the included industries. The actual specification of the estimating equation is therefore

$$(4') \qquad \log \tilde{T}(t) = \gamma \log \tilde{K}(t) + \sum_{\tau=1}^{T} \beta_\tau D_\tau ,$$

where a tilde above a variable denotes the deviation of that variable from its industry mean, and $D_\tau(\tau = 1, \dots, T)$ is a set of time dummies.

It is well known that much of the year-to-year variation in total factor productivity is attributable to fluctuations in the level of capacity utilization. It is perhaps useful to view the TFP time series as the sum of a long-run trend and a serially correlated deviation from trend. We postulate that the level of the R&D stock is a determinant of the trend component of TFP, but not of its short-run deviations from trend; the latter are primarily the result of fluctuations in capacity utilization. A complete model of TFP should include variables accounting for both forces. Alternatively, if one is interested only in explaining the long-run behavior of TFP, one can attempt to remove some of the short-run variation from the observed series. We have tried both strategies in estimating equation (4'). In several equations we included a variable, average annual hours of work, postulated to be an indicator of the level of capacity utilization. In other equations we attempted to adjust TFP to its full-capacity level or to eliminate observations in which TFP was below capacity.

Table 9.3 presents regression results for variants of the model (4'). Line (1) includes no variable other than R&D stock and year dummies. Line (2) includes a measure of the age of the industry's plant ([gross plant − net plant]/gross plant), while line (3) also includes a utilization index, average annual hours of work per employee. In line (4), the dependent variable was defined as the minimum of the current level of TFP and the previous peak level of TFP. Observations in which TFP was below its previous peak were excluded in estimating the equation in line (5). The dependent variable in line (6) is "adjusted"

Table 9.3   **Summary of "Within" Industries' Total Factor Productivity Level on R&D Stock Regression Results: 27 Industries, 1959–76**

Dependent Variable	Coefficient (t-stat) on R&D Stock ($\delta = 0$)	Other Variables	R^2	Line Number
1	−.0014 (0.10)		.6317	(1)
1	−.0031 (0.22)	age	.6375	(2)
1	−.0048 (0.34)	age, hours	.6379	(3)
2	−.0387 (2.85)	age, hours	.7125	(4)
3	−.0014 (0.72)	age, hours	.7475	(5)
4	−.0012 (0.08)	age	.6589	(6)

Key to Dependent Variable (all variables defined as deviations from industry means):
1: Unadjusted TFP.
2: MIN (TFP, past peak TFP).
3: Excludes observations in which TFP < past peak TFP.
4: "Adjusted" TFP, based on the following rule for adjusting data at the four-digit level: If "variable input productivity" (output per unit of weighted index of labor, energy, and materials) declined by more than 3 percent, *and* the increase in the price of output exceeded the respective two-digit industry average price increase by more than 5 percent, redefine output so that variable input productivity declines exactly 3 percent.

TFP; the adjustment formula is described in the notes below the table. The coefficient on the R&D variable is negative in all cases and insignificantly different from zero in all but one case.

Before turning to a discussion of the results of estimating variants of the constant marginal productivity (or R&D intensity) model (6), we present in table 9.4 descriptive statistics on TFP and private R&D intensity (or R&D per unit of output) by subperiod for the twenty-seven industry sample.[11] Table 9.4 indicates that both the (unweighted) mean growth of TFP and the (unweighted) level of R&D declined throughout the period, and that the larger absolute decline in both variables occurred early. There is also a striking increase in the variability of TFP growth over time; the standard deviation rises by over 40 percent.

Plots of TFP growth against private R&D intensity by subperiod are shown in appendix C, figures 9A.1, 9A.2, and 9A.3. Note that the computer industry

11. We dropped petroleum refining (SIC 29) from our sample because of clearly erroneous TFP numbers for recent years. The unadjusted numbers show TFP declining at the rate of 10 percent per year during 1973–76, mainly because the material price deflators are for some reason not rising as fast as the output deflators.

Table 9.4   Descriptive Statistics: TFP Growth and Privately Financed R&D Investment per Unit of Output, by Subperiod, 1959–76

	Mean	Std. Dev.	Minimum	Maximum
Average annual percent change in TFP, between periods:				
1959–63 and 1964–68	2.25	0.93	0.64	4.85
1964–68 and 1969–73	0.92	1.05	−0.92	3.60
1969–73 and 1974–76	0.39	1.29	−1.33	3.77
Privately financed R&D investment as percentage of output, average during period:				
1959–63	3.53	4.10	0.10	14.70
1964–68	3.01	3.13	0.20	11.46
1969–73	2.71	2.50	0.20	10.54

Correlation coefficients:

	(1)	(2)	(3)	(4)	(5)	(6)
(1) TFP growth, 1959–63 to 1964–68	1.00	—	—	—	—	—
(2) TFP growth, 1964–68 to 1969–73	0.23	1.00	—	—	—	—
(3) TFP growth, 1969–73 to 1974–76	0.42	0.22	1.00	—	—	—
(4) R&D intensity, 1959–63	0.35	0.51	0.62	1.00	—	—
(5) R&D intensity, 1964–68	0.39	0.59	0.65	0.97	1.00	—
(6) R&D intensity, 1969–73	0.41	0.54	0.69	0.92	0.97	1.00

(R) is a consistent outlier in these charts. This is an industry whose productivity is clearly underestimated by the conventional measures.

At the bottom of table 9.4 we show correlation coefficients between TFP growth rates and R&D intensities. Note the extremely high, positive correlations between period-specific R&D intensities, indicating the stability of the industries' relative positions with respect to R&D performance. An alternative (nonparametric) way of analyzing the relationships between TFP growth and R&D intensity is to classify industries into groups, according to their rank in the R&D intensity distribution, and to compute the mean rate of TFP growth for each group. Mean TFP growth rates between adjacent subperiods by quartile of the R&D intensity distribution of the earlier period are reported in table 9.5. Industries were ranked according to both private R&D intensity and total R&D intensity. With a single exception, average TFP growth of industries in higher quartiles of the R&D intensity distribution is higher than average TFP growth of industries in lower quartiles, and this relationship appears to grow stronger over time.

We now turn to a discussion of estimates of the TFP growth, R&D intensity model. This model was estimated separately by subperiod under alternative assumptions about the rate of depreciation of R&D capital.[12] For each subperiod and depreciation rate assumption, two variants of the model were estimated: one in which R&D intensity is divided into privately financed and

12. Note that the R&D intensity is as of the beginning of the period. That is, the $\bar{R}$ associated with TFP growth between 1969–73 and 1974–76 is computed as $(K_{73} - K_{69})/5$, where K is the R&D capital stock constructed on the basis of the various depreciation assumptions.

Table 9.5   **Mean Rate of Total Factor Productivity Growth of Industries, by Quartile of (Private or Total) R&D Intensity Distribution**

Period and Source of R&D Financing	Industries Excluded from NSF R&D Classification[a]	Quartile of R&D Intensity Distribution			
		lowest 1	2	3	highest 4
1959–63 to 1964–68					
Private R&D	0.34	1.56	1.96	2.72	2.85
Total R&D		1.56	1.96	2.64	2.94
1964–68 to 1969–73					
Private R&D	0.13	0.43	0.39	1.08	1.92
Total R&D		0.43	0.55	0.99	1.84
1969–73 to 1974–76					
Private R&D	0.07	−0.24	−0.12	0.55	1.44
Total R&D		−0.15	−0.22	0.22	1.93

[a]These industries' investment in R&D is negligible.

government-financed components, and one in which only total R&D is included. The estimates, reported in table 9.6, indicate that substitution of the R&D measures classified by source of financing for the total R&D figure results uniformly in an improvement in the R^2; in the latter two periods this improvement is dramatic. This improvement arises from relaxing the a priori constraint that the coefficients on the two types of R&D be equal. Obviously, the unconstrained coefficients differ greatly in magnitude and even in sign in half of the regressions. Since we can reject the hypothesis of equality of coefficients for privately and government-financed R&D, we shall confine our attention to estimates with R&D disaggregated by source of financing.

The equation for each of the three TFP growth rates indicates that both the highest R^2 and the highest t-statistic on private R&D are obtained under the 0 percent depreciation rate assumption, and that both of these statistics decline monotonically as the assumed depreciation rises. In this sense, the data clearly favor the hypothesis of no depreciation of R&D capital in terms of its effects on physical productivity of resources at the industry level.[13]

Although the coefficient on private R&D is only marginally significant in the 1959–63 to 1964–68 equation, the corresponding coefficients in the two later equations are significantly different from zero at the 1 percent level. Both the coefficients and the associated t-statistics grow larger over the period. Recall that the coefficient on R&D intensity in the TFP growth equation may be interpreted loosely as the social gross excess rate of return to investment in R&D. It is a social rate of return because it is based on output in constant

13. Strictly speaking, the data favor the hypothesis of no depreciation, conditional on the maintained hypothesis of a constant geometric (declining balance) depreciation scheme. Earlier experimentation with other depreciation schemes and lag structures indicates that this conclusion is rather robust.

Table 9.6   **Estimates of the Relationship between Averaged Total Factor Productivity and R&D Intensity, under Alternative R&D Depreciation Assumptions, by Subperiod ($N = 27$)**

Period and Depreciation Rate	R^2	C	Total R&D	R^2	C	Private R&D	Federal R&D
1959–63 to 1964–68							
0%	.1461	2.06	2.69	.2138	1.89	9.15	1.51
		(10.7)	(2.07)		(8.4)	(1.96)	(1.00)
10%	.1088	2.11	3.84	.1516	1.98	12.90	2.20
		(10.9)	(1.75)		(9.0)	(1.52)	(0.83)
20%	.0906	2.13	4.88	.1261	2.03	17.07	2.76
		(11.1)	(1.58)		(9.3)	(1.34)	(0.73)
30%	.0793	2.15	5.86	.1109	2.05	21.46	3.23
		(11.3)	(1.47)		(9.5)	(1.24)	(0.66)
1964–68 to 1969–73							
0%	.0303	0.83	1.38	.3120	0.37	20.33	−1.35
		(3.7)	(0.88)		(1.5)	(3.28)	(0.84)
10%	.0295	0.84	3.00	.3044	0.41	42.84	−2.82
		(3.8)	(0.87)		(1.7)	(3.20)	(0.80)
20%	.0303	0.83	5.71	.2941	0.42	71.47	−4.50
		(3.7)	(0.88)		(1.8)	(3.15)	(0.68)
30%	.0325	0.82	10.40	.2785	0.41	102.01	−5.96
		(3.5)	(0.92)		(1.7)	(3.04)	(0.52)
1969–73 to 1974–76							
0%	.1538	0.11	5.19	.4574	−0.54	33.86	0.69
		(0.4)	(2.13)		(1.9)	(4.20)	(0.29)
10%	.1495	0.09	32.14	.2981	−0.18	74.63	−14.14
		(0.3)	(2.10)		(0.6)	(3.16)	(0.57)
20%	.0028	0.39	−2.13	.2196	−0.03	103.15	−22.47
		(1.5)	(0.27)		(0.1)	(2.49)	(2.10)
30%	.0110	0.38	−3.98	.1459	0.11	109.04	−22.18
		(1.5)	(0.53)		(0.4)	(1.86)	(1.88)

prices rather than profit calculations. It is gross because it also includes a possible allowance for depreciation. And it is excess because the conventional inputs of labor and capital already include most of the R&D expenditures once at "normal" factor prices.[14] The estimates imply an average 9.2 percent social excess rate of return to privately financed R&D investment undertaken during 1959–63, a 20.3 percent rate of return to 1964–68 R&D, and a 33.9 percent return to 1969–73 investments.

The coefficient on government-financed R&D is not significant in any of the three equations, and it has the wrong sign in the second one. In contrast to the private R&D coefficient, the government R&D coefficient is largest and most significant in the first period.

The regressions reported in table 9.6 are of the form

14. This is only approximately correct. See Schankerman (1981) for a more detailed discussion.

$$\log\left(\frac{Q(+1)}{Q}\right) - \log\left(\frac{IN(+1)}{IN}\right) = \alpha_0 + \alpha_1\frac{NRD}{Q},$$

where Q = output; IN = index of total input; and NRD = net investment in R&D. Note the presence of Q on both sides of the equation. This suggests the possibility that the observed positive correlation between R&D intensity and TFP growth may be partly spurious, arising, for example, from errors in measuring current output. One way of eliminating this potential source of spurious correlation is to estimate the equation using the *lagged* value of R&D intensity. Estimates of equations in which the lagged value of R&D intensity *replaced* the current value, and equations in which *both* lagged and current values were included are presented in table 9.7. For convenience, the zero-depreciation equations for the three subperiods from table 9.6 are reproduced in table 9.7. In view of our earlier results, the assumption of no depreciation of R&D capital was maintained throughout.

Substituting the lagged (i.e., 1959–63) value of total R&D investment per unit of output for the current (i.e., 1964–68) value in the 1964–68 to 1969–73 TFP growth rate equation slightly increases the R^2; when both variables are included, the lagged value dominates, although both are insignificant. When R&D intensity is disaggregated by source of financing, the R^2 of the current value equation is higher than that of the lagged value equation, although private R&D is significant in both cases. When both current and lagged intensity are included, current intensity dominates.

The current value of R&D intensity dominates the lagged value in all of the 1969–73 to 1974–76 TFP growth rate equations, although the lagged values are also generally significant, indicating that while perhaps slightly biased upward, the results reported earlier (in table 9.6) are not entirely spurious.

Although one's impressions about the timing and severity of the slowdown in TFP growth are sensitive to the periodization scheme adopted, that is, the particular way in which the entire sample period is divided into subperiods, some experimentation with alternative schemes indicated that the TFP growth/ R&D intensity estimation results reported in this paper are not substantially altered by changing the subperiod definitions. Indeed, the finding that the association between productivity growth and R&D activity became *increasingly strong* over the period is even more apparent in results not reported in the paper (i.e., those obtained using the "peak-to-peak" periodization scheme described in note 7) than it is in the evidence presented above.

To summarize the regression results reported above: variants of the constant elasticity version of the TFP/R&D model (equation [4']) estimated on pooled "within" annual data yielded estimates of the coefficient on R&D that were negative and insignificantly different from zero, whereas the constant marginal productivity version of the model (equation [6]) estimated on a cross section of subperiod averages yielded estimates of the R&D coefficient that were generally positive and significant, at least for private R&D when R&D expenditure was disaggregated by source of financing. In principle, this marked difference

Table 9.7   Total Factor Productivity Growth Related to "Current" and "Lagged" R&D Intensity

R^2	C	Current Total R&D	Lagged Total R&D	Current Private R&D	Lagged Private R&D	Current Federal R&D	Lagged Federal R&D
A. 1959–63 to 1964–68							
.1461	2.06 (10.1)	2.69 (2.07)					
.2138	1.89 (8.4)			9.15 (1.96)		1.51 (1.00)	
B. 1964–68 to 1969–73							
.0303	0.83 (3.7)	1.38 (0.88)					
.0333	0.82 (3.5)		1.45 (0.93)				
.0341	0.81 (3.3)	−1.23 (0.14)	2.65 (0.31)				
.3633	0.33 (1.4)			20.33 (3.28)		−1.35 (0.84)	
.2756	0.47 (2.0)				13.85 (3.02)		−0.97 (0.60)
.4283	0.28 (1.1)			49.99 (1.66)	−22.16 (0.94)	2.30 (0.13)	−4.30 (0.24)
C. 1969–73 to 1974–76							
.1538	0.11 (0.4)	5.19 (2.13)					
.1215	0.17 (0.7)		3.41 (1.86)				
.2777	−0.19 (0.7)	45.11 (2.28)	−29.67 (2.03)				
.4854	−0.58 (2.1)			33.86 (4.20)		0.69 (0.29)	
.4173	−0.41 (1.5)				26.22 (3.91)		0.35 (0.20)
.5263	−0.68 (2.4)			42.82 (1.24)	−7.19 (0.26)	33.89 (1.14)	−24.21 (1.09)

in results could be an artifact of either (a) difference in functional form; (b) difference in time period of observation (annual vs. subperiod average); or (c) both differences. To determine what the source of the difference in results was, we estimated the constant elasticity version of the model on subperiod averages, that is, we estimated equations of the form

$$\log \frac{TFP}{TFP(-1)} = \beta_0 + \beta_1 \log \frac{K}{K(-1)},$$

where $K =$ average net stock of R&D over the period. As before, the model was estimated under alternative assumptions about R&D capital depreciation. The R&D coefficients obtained from estimating these equations were never significantly different from zero and were negative in the first and third subperiods under all depreciation assumptions. We may conclude that the relatively good R&D intensity results (compared to the R&D stock results) are not due to the averaging of periods, but rather to the difference in functional form, that is, to the assumption of a constant marginal product rather than a constant elasticity across industries.

A different source of data allows us a more disaggregated glimpse at the same problem. Estimates of the fraction of all employees engaged in research and development by three-digit industry ($N = 139$) are available from the 1971 Survey of Occupational Employment and enable us to estimate the TFP growth/R&D intensity model on more detailed data.[15] Results based on these unpublished BLS data must be interpreted with caution, however, since their reliability is subject to question because of the underrepresentation of central office workers in the survey sample. To render the results of this analysis comparable to our earlier estimates, we multiplied the ratio of R&D employment to total employment by labor's share in total cost of production in 1971. Assuming real wages (adjusted for interindustry differences in labor quality) are equal across industries, the resulting figure is proportional to R&D employment expenditures per unit of output, a proxy for the desired measure—real net R&D investment per unit of output. Unfortunately, we have only a single cross section for the year 1971 and are therefore forced to assume stability with respect to relative R&D intensity (an assumption warranted by the evidence presented earlier).

Estimates of the TFP growth/R&D intensity equation based on the 139 industry sample for different periods of TFP growth are shown in table 9.8. The results indicate a positive and significant coefficient on R&D intensity in all subperiods. Given that the costs of R&D scientists account for about half of total R&D expenditures, the estimated R&D intensity coefficients should be divided by about half to make them roughly comparable to those reported in tables 9.6 and 9.7. The resulting numbers are significantly higher than those reported for total R&D there but lower than the comparable numbers for privately financed R&D alone. Since the employment numbers reflect both privately and federally financed R&D activities, this is approximately as it should be if the earlier results are attenuated because of aggregation. In any case, here too no evidence of a *decline* in the "potency" of R&D is found.

9.6   Tentative Conclusion

The relationship between the growth of total factor productivity and R&D did not disappear in recent years, though it was obscured by the overall decline in the average growth rate of TFP. While fine timing effects cannot be deduced

---

15. See Sveikauskas (1981) for details about these data. We are indebted to Leo Sveikauskas for making these data available to us.

Table 9.8   **Total Factor Productivity Growth Related to 1971 R&D Intensity, 139 Three-Digit Manufacturing Industries**[a]

	R^2	C	R&D Intensity
TFP growth, 1959–63 to 1964–68	.0323	1.572 (11.9)	48.361 (2.14)
TFP growth, 1964–68 to 1969–73	.0294	0.436 (3.4)	44.207 (2.04)
TFP growth, 1969–73 to 1974–76	.0672	−0.646 (3.2)	107.85 (3.14)

[a]R&D data derived from 1971 BLS Survey of Occupational Employment.

from the available data, when one does not impose a constant elasticity coefficient across different industries, there appears to be a rather strong relationship between the intensity of private (but not federal) R&D expenditures and subsequent growth in productivity.

Appendix A
Total Factor Productivity Data

The present investigation has the advantage of making use of consistent data on intermediate inputs as well as on gross output and primary inputs. The index of total factor productivity used in the empirical analysis is defined as the ratio of real gross output (shipments adjusted for inventory change) to a Tornqvist index (a discrete approximation to the Divisia index) of four inputs: capital, labor, energy, and materials.[16]

The Tornqvist index of total input is constructed as follows:

$$\ln\left(\frac{I_t}{I_{t-1}}\right) = \sum_i [.5^*(S_{it} + S_{i,t-1})] \ln\left(\frac{X_{it}}{X_{i,t-1}}\right),$$

where I_t = index of total input; S_{it} = share of factor i in total cost, $i = K, L, E, M$; X_{it} = quantity of factor i, $i = K, L, E, M$. This formula generates a sequence of growth rates of aggregate input; the *level* of the index in any given year is determined by an arbitrary normalization. The level of total factor productivity

---

16. Because expenditure on energy was included in materials expenditure in most years prior to 1971, the input index for the years 1959–71 is based on only three inputs: capital, labor, and the energy-materials aggregate. The input index for 1971–76 (the period during which the relative price of energy increased dramatically) treats energy and materials separately. Construction of the input index for the whole period consisted of defining a three-input index for 1959–71; defining a four-input index for 1971–76; normalizing both indexes to unity in 1971; and splicing the two indexes together in that year.

is defined as the ratio of output to aggregate input; the latter is normalized so that TFP equals unity in 1972.

The data base was developed jointly by the University of Pennsylvania, the U.S. Bureau of the Census, and SRI International as part of a project under the direction of Gary Fromm, Lawrence Klein, and Frank Ripley. It consists of annual time series (1959–76) on the value of output (shipments adjusted for inventory change), capital, labor, energy, and materials, in current and constant (1972) dollars, for 450 SIC four-digit industries in U.S. manufacturing. The source for most of these series is the Annual Survey and Census of Manufactures. Data for years prior to 1972 were reclassified to conform to the 1972 SIC scheme so that the industry classification is consistent throughout the period.

The following is a brief summary of salient characteristics of the data underlying the total factor productivity indexes. For a more detailed discussion of data sources and methodology, see the appendix to Fromm et al. (1979).

Output. Current dollar output is defined as value of industry shipments adjusted for changes in finished goods and work-in-process inventories. Constant dollar output is derived by deflating the current dollar series by deflators developed by the Industry Division of the Bureau of Economic Analysis. These deflators are constructed at the five-digit level and are generally weighted averages of BLS producer price indexes.

Capital. Consistent with the maintained hypothesis of constant returns to scale, the current dollar value of capital services is computed as the difference between the value of output and the sum of expenditures on labor, energy, and materials.[17] The real flow of capital services is assumed to be proportional to the real capital stock; the capital stock concept is the gross fixed reproducible stock of capital, that is, the stock of plant and equipment net of discards (land and working capital are excluded). The stocks are computed from a perpetual inventory algorithm, which takes account of the industry- and year-specific distribution of expenditures on investment goods across one plant and twenty-six equipment categories (based on a series of capital flow matrices extrapolated from a 1967 matrix by a biproportional matrix balancing procedure). This information on the composition of capital purchases enables development of industry- and year-specific weights for the construction of investment deflators and service lives (weighted averages, respectively, of the PPI's and the service life assumptions for the twenty-seven types of investments).

Labor. The current dollar value of labor services is measured as total expenditures by operating manufacturing establishments for employee compensation, including wages, salaries, and both legally required and voluntary supplements to wages and salaries. We adjusted for the compensation of employees in central administrative offices and auxiliaries. In the absence of data on hours of work of nonproduction workers, real labor input is defined as the ratio of

---

17. Because expenditures for business services such as advertising and legal services are not accounted for, the value of capital services and capital's share in total cost of production are probably slightly overstated.

total wages and salaries to average hourly earnings of production workers; under the assumption that the relative wages of production and nonproduction workers are equal to their relative marginal productivity, this ratio may be viewed as an index of "production worker equivalent" manhours. No adjustment was made for changes in labor quality from, for example, shifts in the age or sex distribution of employment.

Energy and other intermediate materials. Current dollar energy input is defined as the value of energy consumed in the production process; it includes energy produced and consumed within an establishment as well as purchases of energy from other establishments. Real energy input is obtained by deflating the current dollar series by a fixed-weighted index of three principal energy prices. Current dollar cost of materials is deflated by a fixed-weighted index of 450 four-digit manufacturing output price deflators and 7 one-digit nonmanufacturing price deflators. The weights for both energy and materials reflect the composition of the industry's purchases of intermediate inputs, as shown in the 1967 input-output table.

Appendix B
Smoothing the Applied R&D Series[18]

1972–75 Data Revision

The 1972–75 data were revised in 1976 because a new sample was drawn in 1976 and a response analysis study was conducted in 1975 which helped to improve respondents' interpretation of definitions of the survey. Consequently, the 1976 data may not be directly comparable to earlier ones. Among the twenty-seven product fields (excluding ordnance, guided missiles, and spacecraft) were three kinds of revision:

Revisions	No. of Product Fields
1. 1972–74 figures increased, 1975 figure decreased	17
2. 1972–74 figures unchanged, 1975 figure decreased	7
3. 1972–75 figures increased	3

Obviously, the first and second revisions result in sharp deceleration of the growth rates between 1974 and 1975, relative to the original series. The rationale behind this pattern of adjustment is unknown. As an alternative, the 1971–75 original annual growth rates were scaled by the 1975 adjustment factor,[19] thereby preserving the 1971–75 overall growth rates in smoothed series.

---

18. Prepared by Alan Siu.
19. Log (1975 revised/1975 original).

Stone, Clay, and Glass Products

The data for 1968–70 are given as 130, 157, and 128. The 1970 figure was originally reported as 159 and then revised to 128 in 1971, resulting in a big spike in 1969. The 1969 figure was set as 126 (157 × 128/159).

Fabricated Metal Products

Between 1967 and 1968 there is a 134 percent jump in the data. This break is the result of an abrupt increase of applied R&D done by the electrical equipment and communication industry in the fabricated metal product field, from $49 million to $224 million. To smooth out the series, the 1962–68 growth rate was used as a control total to adjust the annual growth rates within this period.

Electrical Equipment

The data for this product field are not broken down into four subfields between 1967 and 1970. The average shares in 1966–67 and 1971–72 were used to disaggregate the total figures.[20]

Appendix C

Table 9A.1   **Weighted Averages of Four-Digit Rates of Total Factor Productivity Growth and Acceleration, 1959–76, by Selected Two-Digit Industries**

	SIC 35	SIC 36	SIC 37
A. Weighted average of four-digit rate of TFP growth:			
1959 value of shipment weights	0.379	1.558	0.910
1976 value of shipment weights	0.421	1.821	0.925
Correlation coefficient between rate of TFP growth and change in share of two-digit industry value of shipments, 1959–76	.164	.304	.505
B. Weighted rates of acceleration of TFP between 1959–63 to 1964–68 and 1964–68 to 1969–73:			
1959 weights	.077	−1.81	−1.29
1967 weights	.022	−1.82	−1.31
C. Weighted rates of acceleration of TFP between 1964–68 to 1969–73 and 1969–73 to 1974–76:			
1967 weights	−3.52	−2.09	−2.35
1976 weights	−3.62	−2.39	−2.79
Number of industries	44	39	17

20. The 1967 data are available separately for the four subfields.

TFP Growth

SIC Code	TFP Growth			R&D Intensity			Federal Share in R&D	
	1959–63 to 1964–68	1964–68 to 1969–73	1969–73 to 1974–76	1959–63	1964–68	1969–73	1973	1977
348	3.9	−0.9	1.4	10.6	5.3	5.6	74.8	80.2
376	3.3	1.2	1.3	66.1	69.1	50.6	89.7	90.0
20	0.7	1.2	−0.3	0.2	0.2	0.2	0	0
22	1.5	1.6	−0.5	0.1	0.2	0.3	0	0
282	2.8	2.6	0.3	12.8	9.5	5.7	1.6	2.1
287	1.6	2.3	1.2	1.8	3.0	3.1	1.1	0.8
281, 284–286, 289	1.6	1.5	−1.3	3.5	3.1	2.4	1.1	2.1
283	4.9	3.6	2.4	8.5	8.3	7.0	1.6	1.3
30	1.8	1.5	−1.1	1.2	1.2	1.2	34.3	34.3
32	1.8	0.4	0.2	0.6	0.7	0.7	7.5	7.5
331, 332, 339	1.6	−0.4	−0.2	0.4	0.4	0.4	3.8	1.7
333–336	0.6	−0.6	−0.3	0.6	0.5	0.5	3.8	1.9
34	1.9	0.4	−0.9	0.6	0.7	1.4	44.0	52.5
351	2.0	−0.8	−0.9	6.1	5.9	5.0	7.6	9.6
352	1.9	0.2	2.3	3.1	2.5	1.9	7.6	0
353	2.2	0.1	−1.0	1.2	1.3	1.9	7.6	0
354	1.7	−0.3	0.3	1.3	1.1	1.1	7.6	0
357	1.9	1.3	3.8	15.9	12.4	11.4	13.7	7.5
355, 356, 358, 359	2.1	0.3	−0.3	1.7	1.2	1.0	12.3	7.4
361	2.7	1.9	−0.3	4.3	4.0	5.1	21.4	43.1
362	3.4	−0.2	0.0	3.5	3.0	3.7	21.4	13.1
363, 364, 369	2.7	1.2	0.0	2.4	2.1	2.1	21.4	28.8
365–367	2.3	2.0	1.6	25.0	14.7	11.6	55.0	48.7
371	1.7	0.8	−1.1	2.2	1.8	2.3	3.5	3.5
373–375, 379	2.8	0.5	0.3	0.8	0.9	1.5	55.2	55.2
372	3.4	0.4	2.1	14.9	12.5	14.2	67.8	68.8
38	2.1	1.5	1.5	4.5	5.6	5.6	27.6	21.7

Key to Symbols Used to Represent Industries in Appendix C Figures 9A.1, 9A.2, and 9A.3

Symbol	Industry	SIC Code
A	Ordnance and accessories, N.E.C.	348
B	Guided missiles and spacecraft	376
C	Food and kindred products	20
D	Textile mill products	22
E	Plastics materials and synthetic resins, rubbers and fibers	282
F	Agricultural chemicals	287
G	Other chemicals	281, 284–286, 289
H	Drugs and medicines	283
I	Rubber and miscellaneous plastics products	30
J	Stone, clay, and glass products	32
K	Ferrous metals and products	333, 332, 339
L	Nonferrous metals and products	333–336
M	Fabricated metal products	34
N	Engines and turbines	351
O	Farm machinery and equipment	352
P	Construction, mining, and materials-handling machinery and equipment	353
Q	Metalworking machinery and equipment	354
R	Office, computing, and accounting machines	357
S	Other machinery, except electrical	355, 356, 358, 359
T	Electric transmission and distribution equipment	361
U	Electrical industrial apparatus	362
V	Other electrical equipment and supplies	363, 364, 369
W	Communication equipment and electronic components	365–367
X	Motor vehicles and equipment	371
Y	Other transportation equipment	373–375, 379
Z	Aircraft and parts	372
7	Instruments	38

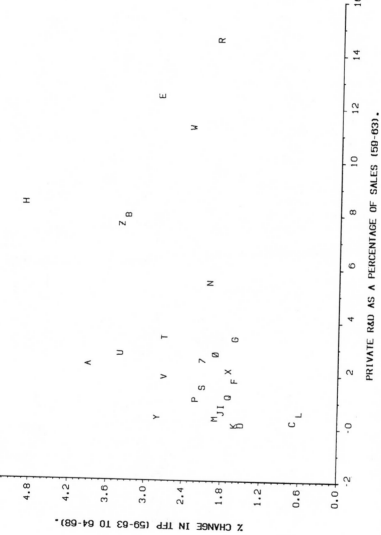

Fig. 9A.1 TFP growth versus private R&D intensity, 1959–63 to 1964–68

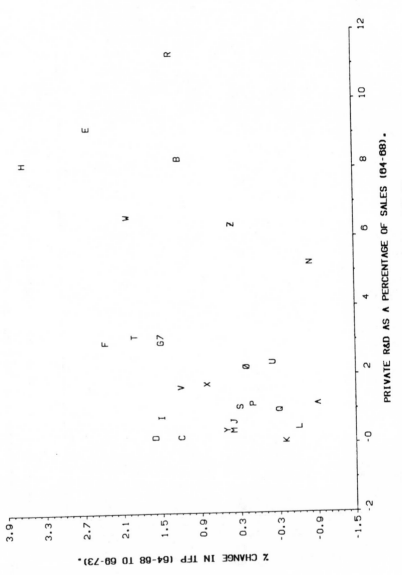

Fig. 9A.2 TFP growth versus private R&D intensity, 1964–68 to 1969–73

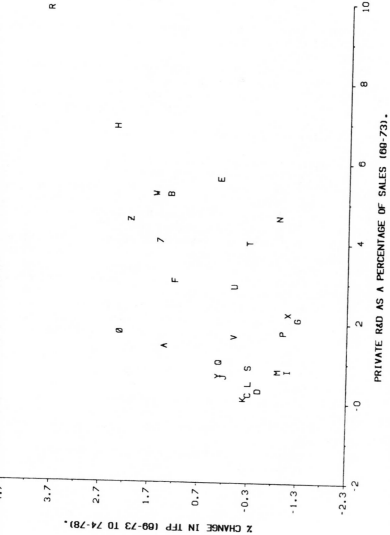

Fig. 9A.3 TFP growth versus private R&D intensity, 1969–73 to 1974–78

References

Agnew, C. E., and D. E. Wise. 1978. The impact of R&D on productivity: A preliminary report. Paper presented at the Southern Economic Association Meetings. Princeton, N.J.: Mathtech, Inc.

Fromm, G., L. R. Klein, F. C. Ripley, and D. Crawford. 1979. Production function estimation of capacity utilization. Manuscript, Univ. of Pennsylvania.

Gollop, F. M., and D. W. Jorgenson. 1980. U.S. productivity growth by industry, 1947–73. In *New developments in productivity measurement,* ed. J. W. Kendrick and B. Vaccara. NBER Conference on Research in Income and Wealth: Studies in Income and Wealth, vol. 44. Chicago: University of Chicago Press.

Griliches, Z. 1973. Research expenditures and growth accounting. In *Science and technology in economic growth,* ed. B. R. Williams, 59–95. London: Macmillan.

————. 1979. Issues in assessing the contribution of research and development to productivity growth. *Bell Journal of Economics* 10, no. 1:92–116. [Reprinted as chap. 2 in this volume.]

————. 1980. R&D and the productivity slowdown. *American Economic Review* 70, no. 2:343–48.

Kendrick, J. W., and E. Grossman. 1980. *Productivity in the United States: Trends and cycles.* Baltimore: The Johns Hopkins University Press.

National Science Foundation. 1977. *Research and development in industry,* serial 1957–77. Washington, D.C.: GPO.

Nordhaus, W. D. 1980. Policy responses to the productivity slowdown. In *The decline in productivity growth,* series no. 22. Federal Reserve Bank of Boston.

Schankerman, M. A. 1979. Essays on the economics of technical change: The determinants, rate of return, and productivity impact of research and development. Ph.D. diss., Harvard University.

————. 1981. The effects of double-counting and expensing on the measured returns to R&D. *Review of Economics and Statistics* 63, no. 3:454–58.

Scherer, F. M. 1981. Research and development, patenting, and the microstructure of productivity growth. Final report, National Science Foundation, no. PRA-786526.

Sveikauskas, L. 1981. Technological inputs and multifactor productivity growth. *Review of Economics and Statistics* 63, no. 2:275–82.

Terleckyj, N. E. 1974. Effects of R&D on the productivity growth of industries: An exploratory study. Washington, D.C.: National Planning Association.

————. 1980. R&D and U.S. industrial productivity in the 1970s. Paper given at the International Institute of Management Conference on Technology Transfer, Berlin.

U.S. Department of Labor. Bureau of Labor Statistics. 1979a. *Time series data for input-output industries: Output, prices, and employment.* Bulletin 2018. Washington, D.C.: GPO.

————. 1979b. *Capital stock estimates for input-output industries: Methods and data.* Bulletin 2034. Washington, D.C.: GPO.

10   Interindustry Technology Flows and Productivity Growth: A Reexamination

10.1

There is, by now, a substantial literature devoted to analyzing the effects of R&D investments by firms and industries on various measures of economic performance, especially profitability and productivity growth. Schmookler (1966) was among the first to articulate the view that improvements in performance associated with technological progress could result not only from R&D performed within an enterprise or sector, but also from R&D performed elsewhere and "embodied" in intermediate goods purchased by the sector. He proposed a method for measuring the transmission of R&D-generated knowledge from R&D-performing industries to industries purchasing their products. Scherer (1981) undertook the difficult task of constructing an "interindustry technology flows" matrix along the lines suggested by Schmookler, thus providing the basis for empirical investigation of the link between R&D "embodied" in purchased producers' goods and a sector's own economic performance. Scherer's (1982a) own analysis of productivity growth among U.S. manufacturing industries provides support for the view that "imported" or "embodied" R&D is an important determinant of productivity growth, contributing perhaps even more than some of the R&D performed *within* an industry.

The purpose of this note is to re-examine the role of interindustry technology flows in promoting productivity growth, in the light of more detailed and possibly better productivity data. Our analysis is also somewhat more general than Scherer's in the sense that we test a restriction on the equality of different R&D-coefficients which is imposed a priori in his study. Because an explicit theoretical foundation for the hypothesis of a productivity-accelerating effect

This chapter is coauthored with Frank Lichtenberg and is reprinted from the *Review of Economics and Statistics* 66, no. 2 (May 1984): 324–29. Published for Harvard University by the North-Holland Publishing Company. © 1984 by the President and Fellows of Harvard College.

of imported R&D has not, to our knowledge, been presented in the literature, we offer, in the next section, an interpretation of this effect in terms of errors in the measurement of intermediate input prices. In the third section we review Scherer's findings and present new evidence based on recently developed alternative productivity indices. A summary and conclusion follow.

10.2

The hypothesis that the productivity behavior of a given industry may be affected by the R&D performance of industries which supply it with intermediate inputs follows from the assumption that there are errors in the output deflators of supplying industries—and consequently in the intermediate input deflators of using industries—errors which are generated by and correlated with suppliers' R&D performance. By "errors" in the deflators we mean the failure of these deflators to reflect accurately changes in the user value, or marginal productivity, or quality, of the commodities whose prices they are supposed to index. As discussed in some detail in Griliches (1979, pp. 97–99) this failure may occur for at least two quite distinct reasons: (1) only a perfectly discriminating monopolist with a secure market position would be able to appropriate *all* of the (social) returns (or "quasi-rents") to his innovation; and (2) the U.S. Bureau of Labor Statistics (BLS), which constructs the official price indexes, generally does not adjust the indexes for "costless" quality improvements embedded in new products; instead, a new product is "linked in" at its introductory (or subsequent) price with the price index left unchanged. These considerations imply that, if a firm conducted R&D in order to build a better mousetrap (to choose a humble example), and subsequently succeeded in producing "twice as good" a mousetrap by virtue of its research efforts, the official mousetrap price index may not decline, even if the nominal price of the new mousetrap increased by less than 100%, due to competition in the mousetrap industry.

To formalize this argument, we begin by postulating the existence of errors in the measurement of the growth rate of materials deflators:

$$\dot{Pm}_j = \dot{Pm}_j^* + \varepsilon_j$$

where

Pm_j = actual deflator for jth intermediate input;
Pm_j^* = true deflator for jth intermediate input;
ε_j = measurement error, and dot superscripts indicate growth rates.

Assuming that the growth rate of the (current-dollar) value of intermediate transactions is measured without error, the accounting identity relating the value, quantity and price of intermediate input reveals a corresponding error in the growth rate of input quantity:

$$M_j = Vm_j/Pm_j$$

$$\dot{M}_j = \dot{Vm}_j - \dot{Pm}_j$$

$$\dot{M}_j^* = \dot{Vm}_j - \dot{Pm}_j^*$$

$$\dot{M}_j^* - \dot{M}_j = \dot{Pm}_j - \dot{Pm}_j^* = \varepsilon_j$$

where

M_j = measured quantity of jth intermediate input;
M_j^* = true quantity of jth intermediate input;
Vm_j = actual value of jth intermediate input.

Thus errors in the materials deflator result in errors in the measured rate of growth of total factor productivity of using industry i ($\dot{TFP}_i$):

$$\dot{TFP}_i = \dot{Q}_i - \sum_k S_{ik}\dot{X}_{ik} - \sum_j S_{ij}(\dot{M}_{ij}^* - \varepsilon_j)$$

$$\dot{TFP}_i^* = \dot{Q}_i - \sum_k S_{ik}\dot{X}_{ik} - \sum_j S_{ij}\dot{M}_{ij}^*$$

$$\dot{TFP}_i - \dot{TFP}_i^* = \sum_j S_{ij}\varepsilon_j$$

$$\dot{TFP}_j = \dot{TFP}_j^* + \sum_j S_{ij}\varepsilon_j$$

where

$\dot{Q}_i$ = output growth rate of industry i;
$\dot{X}_{ik}$ = growth rate of kth non-materials input to industry i;
S_{ik} = share of ith non-materials input in total cost of production of industry i;
S_{ij} = share of jth materials input in total cost of production of industry i.

Measured TFP growth of industry i thus deviates from its actual TFP growth by the weighted sum of errors in the various materials deflators, using respective cost shares as weights.

To this definitional relationship between *measured* productivity growth and errors in the deflators we add the assumption that the extent of mismeasurement of the growth in the jth intermediate-input deflator—in other words, in the output deflator of industry j—depends on the extent of *product-oriented* R&D activity in the supplying industry. Since *process-oriented* R&D does not alter the characteristics of products sold in interindustry transactions, it should not contribute to errors in the measurement of deflators corresponding to these transactions.

More specifically, we assume that the extent of measurement error in the rate of growth of the jth materials deflator is proportional to the R&D intensity (R&D expenditure per unit of output) of supplying industry j.[1] Then

$$\varepsilon_j = \gamma \frac{RD_j}{Vq_j},$$

where

RD_j = product-oriented R&D expenditures by industry j;
Vq_j = value of output produced by industry j.

Hence,

$$\dot{TFP}_i = \dot{TFP}_i^* + \sum_j S_{ij} \gamma \frac{RD_j}{Vq_j}$$

$$(1) \qquad = \dot{TFP}_i^* + \gamma \sum_j \frac{Vq_{ji}}{Vq_i} \cdot \frac{RD_j}{Vq_j}$$

$$= \dot{TFP}_i^* + \gamma \frac{1}{Vq_i} \sum_j \frac{Vq_{ji}}{Vq_j} RD_j .$$

Vq_{ji}/Vq_j is the share of the supplying industry j's output sold to using industry i. If the benefits of R&D enjoyed by one consumer (purchasing industry) are not available to other consumers, and the benefits of suppliers' R&D are distributed among purchasers in proportion to suppliers' sales to them, then $(Vq_{ji}/Vq_j) \cdot RD_j$ is an index of the benefits of industry j's R&D enjoyed by industry i. Summing over all supplying industries and dividing by the output of the ith industry yields a measure of the "embodied-R&D intensity" of the using industry, analogous to the "own" R&D-intensity variable often specified in previous investigations. The "true" own rate of industry i's TFP growth, $\dot{TFP}_i^*$, is, of course, unobservable but provided that this variable is uncorrelated with the R&D intensity embodied in its purchased inputs, estimation of (1) excluding $\dot{TFP}_i^*$ will yield an unbiased estimate of γ.[2]

10.3

The index of the quantity of R&D embodied in industry i's purchases of intermediate inputs in (1) is rather crude, in the sense that industry j's R&D activity is assumed to be homogeneous with respect to the interindustry distri-

---

1. We recognize that this is merely one—albeit a convenient one—of a class of "reasonable" possible assumptions about the effects of R&D on quality-adjusted output prices. For example, the measurement error might be postulated to depend on the *level* of R&D rather than R&D-intensity.
   2. A similar argument involving the direct contribution of process R&D to TFP growth in industry i, and its exclusion from the list of conventional inputs in the construction of the usual TFP measures, leads to a relationship between measured TFP and own R&D intensity. (See Griliches, 1979.)

bution of embodied benefits. In reality, some of industry j's R&D investments may benefit industry i more than others, and if it were possible to classify industry j's R&D expenditure by the extent of benefits (possibly zero) received by industry i, for all i and j, we could obtain a more precise measure of the technology flows embodied in interindustry transactions. Scherer attempts to do just this, using data on corporate patents, each of which was classified by "industry (or industries) of use" as well as by "industry of origin." The details of the rather complex procedure for developing estimates of embodied R&D, by origin and destination industry, are reported in Scherer (1981). It is these figures, aggregated over all supplying industries, that are used in order to estimate the contribution of embodied R&D to productivity growth; the index specified in (1) should be regarded as merely a rough approximation for heuristic purposes.

The productivity growth-rate equations estimated by Scherer on cross-sectional industry data included a measure of the industry's *own* or *performed* R&D intensity as well as of its embodied-R&D intensity. Scherer distinguished between product- and process-oriented R&D performed within an industry, and hypothesized that the intensity both of process R&D performed within the industry and of R&D embodied in purchased inputs should have stronger effects on measured productivity growth in the industry than the intensity of its "own" product R&D. He reports estimates of equations in which "own" process R&D and embodied R&D are added together to form a "used" R&D variable, and own product R&D is included as a separate regressor. Distinct versions of the model were estimated on productivity data derived from two different sources, both within the U.S. Bureau of Labor Statistics (BLS): the Office of Economic Growth's input-output industries' data (BLSIO) in which output is measured primarily as deflated shipments adjusted for inventory change, and physical-quantity-based output data published by the Industry Productivity Division (BLSPQ). In order to investigate whether the link between R&D intensity and productivity growth has exhibited structural change—in particular, secular weakening—the model was estimated separately for two definitions of the dependent variable, corresponding to two spans of years over which the growth rate of TFP was measured: 1964–69 and 1973–78.[3] Because the R&D data were available only for a single year, 1974, the same R&D-intensity measures are included in the regressions for both periods.

Scherer's estimates of the coefficients of the R&D-intensity variables and their associated t-statistics are reproduced in the first and third lines of table 10.1. The dependent variable in these regressions is the growth rate of labor productivity (output per man-hour); a measure of the growth rate of the capital-labor ratio was also included in these equations, but the corresponding coefficient estimates are not reproduced here. In the regressions in the first line, R&D intensity is defined as (own-product or user) R&D investment per unit

---

3. These spans of years were chosen because both of the beginning and end years were postulated to represent business cycle peaks.

Table 10.1   Comparison of Scherer and Griliches-Lichtenberg (G-L) Estimates of R&D-Intensity Coefficients

Investigator	Source of Productivity Data	Denominator of R&D-Intensity Variables	Number of Observations (industries)	Coefficients (*t*-statistics) on R&D-Intensity Variables			
				1964–1969		1973–1978	
				PROD	USER	PROD	USER
Scherer	BLSIO	Gross Output	87	0.133 (1.05)	0.643 (1.84)	0.289 (2.01)	0.742 (1.89)
G-L	Revised Census et al.	Gross Output	193	0.146 (1.78)	0.736 (3.97)	0.282 (2.58)	0.504 (2.03)
Scherer	BLSPQ	Value Added	37	0.051 (0.34)	0.401 (1.42)	0.089 (0.46)	0.711 (2.03)
G-L	Revised Census et al.	Value Added	193	0.083 (1.84)	0.404 (3.98)	0.160 (2.67)	0.255 (1.88)

of gross 1974 output; in the regressions in line 3 the denominator of the R&D-intensity variable is 1974 value added (gross output minus purchases of intermediate materials). In the second and fourth lines we present new, comparable estimates based on productivity indices derived from a more disaggregated and presumably superior data set, the revised Census-Penn-SRI 4-digit manufacturing data file. This data set, described in some detail in an appendix to Griliches and Lichtenberg (1982), consists essentially of time-series on gross output and four inputs—capital, labor, energy, and materials—in current and constant (1972) dollars, for the period 1958–1978. Productivity indices based on these data, unlike those used by Scherer, take account of the growth in energy and materials inputs, which is likely to be of particular importance in the 1970s due to the sharp increases then in the relative prices of these inputs. The BLSIO data appear to suffer from an additional defect, the "misalignment" of the output and labor input series,[4] which introduces unknown errors into the labor productivity indices. The discrepancies among data sets in the (unweighted) sample mean productivity growth rates, presented below, and in the implied deceleration of productivity result, in part, from these conceptual differences:

	1964–69	1973–78
Labor Productivity		
BLSIO	2.81	2.03
BLSPQ	2.99	2.54
TFP		
Revised Census	0.96	−1.16

Despite the differences in level of industry aggregation and in the sources and concept underlying the productivity indices, our new estimates in some respects closely replicate Scherer's earlier results. In all eight regressions, the coefficient on *USER* exceeds that on *PROD*, by a factor ranging from about 1½ to 8, although the difference in the two coefficients generally appears to be statistically insignificant. On the other hand, while the coefficient on *PROD* is insignificantly different from zero in 3 of the 4 reported Scherer equations, it is significant at the 10% level in all of the new regressions. Also, whereas Scherer's results indicate an increase in both the size and significance of the coefficient on *USER* between the first and second periods, our estimates point to a secular decline in the effect of "user" R&D on productivity growth.

A hypothesis maintained by the model, estimates of variants of which are presented in table 10.1, is that the coefficient on R&D embodied in purchased inputs is equal to the coefficient on process R&D performed within the industry. Our data permit us to test both this hypothesis and that of the equality of the coefficients on own-product and own-process R&D.

---

4. Industry output is defined as the total output of establishments classified in (i.e., whose primary product defines) the industry, *plus* the secondary production by establishments classified in other industries of products which are primary to this industry. Industry employment, on the other hand, is defined simply as persons employed in establishments classified in the industry.

Although we have annual data on industry productivity, allowing us to construct multiple (e.g., year-to-year) productivity growth observations for each industry, observations on the right-hand-side variables of our model are available only for a single year. One could estimate a pooled annual equation by imputing an industry's single (1974) values of the right-hand-side variables to that industry's productivity data for all years, but this procedure would produce a misleading impression of precision. In the absence of more complete data, we are forced to analyze the relationships between an industry's *average* rate of productivity growth and its (own- and embodied-) R&D intensity as of 1974 which we take as a good proxy of its *average* R&D intensity during the 1970s. (This is not too bad an assumption since such numbers change only very slowly over time. See the evidence presented in Griliches and Lichtenberg (1982).) Thus, we ran a set of cross-sectional regressions in which the dependent variable was defined as the growth rate in the average level of TFP between adjacent five-year periods. For example, the average level of TFP (indexed to 100.0 in 1972) during each of the five-year periods 1969–73 and 1974–78 was calculated, and then the five-year compound growth rate between these averages was computed. Differences between period averages, rather than differences between period endpoints, were used to reduce the transitory and cyclical components in measured TFP, but the actual results are not very sensitive to this treatment of the dependent variable.

A summary of regressions of this definition of the TFP growth rate, by subperiod, on selected R&D-intensity variables, is presented in table 10.2. Three models were estimated for each subperiod. In the first, or unrestricted, model, three "types" of R&D—"own" process R&D (i.e., process R&D performed by the using industry), "own" product R&D, and product R&D embodied in inputs purchased from other industries—are included as separate regressors in the equation. In the other two models, different pairs of the R&D variables are added together, in order to test the linear restriction of equality of the respective coefficients. Estimation of the second model provides a test of the hypothesis that the two types of "own" R&D have similar effects on productivity; similarity of the effects of "own" process and imported product R&D is considered in the third equation.

These results are consistent with the hypothesis that product-oriented R&D performed within an industry has less of an effect on that industry's measured TFP growth rate than either process R&D performed or R&D embodied in purchased inputs. The coefficient on own-product R&D is the smallest in both the unrestricted and restricted models for all three periods. For the first two periods we can reject the hypothesis at the 10% level that the two types of R&D performed within the industry have equal coefficients. In contrast, the hypothesis that own-process and imported R&D have equal coefficients cannot be rejected in any period, although this finding appears to be an artifact of the large standard errors associated with the imported-R&D coefficients. In this, it is similar to the results reported by Scherer (1982a, p. 633), except that we

from Scherer "Interindustry Technology Flows" Data Base

Dependent Variable	"Own" Process R&D	"Own" Product R&D	"Imported" Product R&D	"Own" Process + "Own" Product R&D	"Own" Process + "Imported" Product R&D	Constant	R^2	F-ratio (associated probability value) on Test of Equality of Coefficients	
								Process/Product	Process/Import
TFP Growth, 1959–63 to 1964–68	0.762 (2.82)	0.211 (2.45)	0.289 (0.60)			0.093 (4.51)	.1151		
			0.512 (1.09)	0.286 (3.73)		0.093 (4.45)	.0993	3.37 (0.07)	
		0.206 (2.40)			0.621 (3.19)	0.089 (4.51)	.1124		0.56 (0.15)
TFP Growth, 1964–68 to 1969–73	0.578 (2.84)	0.040 (0.61)	0.687 (1.89)			0.005 (0.34)	.1050		
			0.904 (2.54)	0.112 (1.94)		0.005 (0.29)	.0780	5.69 (0.02)	
		0.041 (0.63)			0.610 (4.17)	0.006 (0.43)	.1047		0.05 (0.82)
TFP Growth, 1969–73 to 1974–78	0.384 (1.37)	0.299 (3.35)	0.465 (0.93)			−0.100 (4.69)	.1078		
			0.499 (1.04)	0.310 (3.95)		−0.100 (4.71)	.1075	0.07 (0.78)	
		0.299 (3.38)			0.408 (2.03)	−0.099 (4.91)	.1078		0.02 (0.90)

Note: $N = 193$.

get statistically significant estimates for the coefficients of own-process R&D. Indeed, the significance of the composite *USER* R&D variable seems to be due primarily to the own-process component rather than to the embodied component.

10.4

The findings of our re-examination of the relationship between R&D embodied in purchased inputs and industrial productivity, while broadly consistent with Scherer's results, have somewhat different implications for the nature of this relationship. Both investigations yielded uniformly larger estimates of the coefficient of *USER* R&D than of the coefficient of own-product R&D. Scherer found also that the latter coefficients were generally insignificant and that the *USER* R&D coefficient was larger in the second than in the first period. In contrast, we find own-product R&D to be a generally significant determinant of measured TFP growth, and our evidence suggests a declining efficacy of *USER* R&D. Moreover, the explanatory power of the *USER* R&D variable appears to derive primarily from the own-process R&D component rather than the embodied component, whose influence on TFP is weak and unstable over time.[5]

References

Griliches, Zvi, "Issues in Assessing the Contribution of R&D to Productivity Growth," *The Bell Journal of Economics* 10 (Spring 1979), 92–116. [Reprinted as chap. 2 in this volume.]

Griliches, Zvi, and Frank Lichtenberg, "R&D and Productivity Growth at the Industry Level: Is There Still a Relationship?" (1984). In Zvi Griliches (ed.), *R&D, Patents, and Productivity* (Chicago: University of Chicago Press for NBER). [Reprinted as chap. 9 in this volume.]

Scherer, F. M., "Using Linked Patent and R&D Data to Measure Inter-industry Technology Flows" (1984). In Zvi Griliches (ed.), *R&D, Patents, and Productivity* (Chicago: University of Chicago Press for NBER).

———, "Inter-industry Technology Flows and Productivity Growth," *Review of Economics and Statistics* 64 (Nov. 1982a), 627–634.

———, "Demand-Pull and Technological Invention: Schmookler Revisited," *Journal of Industrial Economics* 30 (3) (1982b), 225–238.

Schmookler, Jacob, *Invention and Economic Growth* (Cambridge: Harvard University Press, 1966).

5. This finding may reflect both the fact that, relatively speaking, manufacturing industries do not "import" much R&D (though they "export" a lot to non-manufacturing industries) and that at the more disaggregated levels used by us Scherer's estimates are based on smaller samples and may be subject to more significant errors in variables problems. On the first point, see Scherer (1982b, p. 233).

11   The Search for R&D Spillovers

11.1

The recent reawakening of interest in increasing returns and R&D externalities, as in e.g. Benhabib and Jovanovic (1991), Romer (1990) and Sala-i-Martin (1990), provides the motivation for a review of the empirical literature on this topic to see what is known about the actual magnitude of such effects. The "New" growth economics has reemphasized two points: (i) technical change is the result of conscious economic investments and explicit decisions by many different economic units, and (ii) unless there are significant externalities, spillovers, or other sources of social increasing returns, it is unlikely that economic growth can proceed at a constant, undiminished rate into the future. The first observation is not new. It has been articulated by Griliches (1957, 1958 and 1964), Mansfield (1968), Schmookler (1966), Schultz (1954) and many others. The second point, the importance of externalities for growth theory and for the explanation of productivity growth, is the driving force behind the research effort to be surveyed here. Whether R&D spillovers will allow us to escape the fate of diminishing returns depends on their empirical magnitude, which is indeed the topic of this paper. Before we turn to it, however, we need to make a brief detour into taxonomy.

Both publicly supported and privately funded R&D produces ideas and information about new materials or compounds, about new ways of arranging or using them, and about new ways of designing new goods or services for the satisfaction of potential wants of consumers and producers. Often the idea or

Reprinted from the *Scandinavian Journal of Economics* 94, supplement (1992): S29–S47.

I have benefited (received spillovers?) from reading and re-reading other surveys on this topic, especially, Schankerman (1979, Chap. 5), Mohnen (1989), Huffman and Evenson (1991), Mairesse and Mohnen (1990) and Mairesse and Sassenou (1991). This work has been supported by grants from the Bradley and Guggenheim Foundations. An earlier version of this paper was presented at the NBER Conference on Economic Growth at Vail, Colorado, April 1990.

compound is embodied in a new product or range of products. In that case, the social returns to the particular stream of R&D expenditures can be measured by the sum of the producer and consumer surplus generated by it. Consider, for example, the development of hybrid corn seeds in the public agricultural research sector. If the seed is supplied to agriculture at marginal production cost and the official input price indexes do not adjust for such a "quality" change, then the product of this research will appear as part of the measured productivity growth in agriculture. If the seed is produced by a seed industry but still priced at marginal cost, because of competition there, and the pricing agency adjusts for this quality change, showing a decline in the "real" price of equivalent quality seed, then the product of this research will appear in the hybrid seed industry, rather than in agriculture per se. If the hybrid seed industry has some monopoly power which is competed away slowly and the price indexes do not register this as a quality change, the gain from this innovation will be divided, with shifting shares between both industries. To the extent that the new product is sold directly to consumers and the CPI components are not adjusted for the associate "quality" changes, as may be the case with certain drugs or personal computers bought by the household sector directly, the social "product" of the associated research may be missed entirely.

These examples are intended to illustrate that to the extent that a particular innovation is embodied in a product or service, its social product is computable in principle. How it actually will show up in our national product accounts will depend on the competitive structure of the industry and the ingenuity and energy of the "price" reporting agencies. In principle, a complete hedonic calculation would produce the right prices in the right industry and would allow us to attribute productivity growth where it actually occurred. Its influence in downstream industries could then be viewed as just another response to declining real factor prices, a "pecuniary" externality, one that is relatively familiar and easy to deal with.

The more difficult to measure and the possibly more interesting and pervasive aspect of R&D externalities is the impact of the discovered ideas or compounds on the productivity of the research endeavors of others.[1] This is a nonpecuniary externality which is not embodied in a particular service or product, though it might be conveyed by a printed article or a news release. It has the classic aspect of a nonrivalrous good and it is usually very hard to appropriate more than a tiny fraction of its social returns. Even if it were possible to establish some property rights in the idea (e.g. via patents), the resulting second-best prices would be nonlinear and would not provide us with appropriate measures of either marginal or total social returns. To measure them directly in some fashion, one has to assume either that their benefits are localized in a particular industry or range of products or that there are other ways of identi-

---

1. The distinction between the previous case and this one is related to Meade's (1952) distinction between "unpaid factors" and atmosphere.

fying the relevant channels of influence, that one can detect the path of the spillovers in the sands of the data.

There are other public goods which raise somewhat similar measurement problems: the provision of roads to the motor transport industry, of airports and flight controllers to the airlines, and of security services to private businesses. All of these have certain aspects of increasing returns to them but are also subject eventually to congestion in use and hence reasonable pricing schemes are feasible in principle. The education sector is possibly somewhere in between, providing both a private product which could be better priced and knowledge externalities, both in the small and in the large. Here I limit myself primarily to a discussion of the work on R&D spillovers though some of the issues discussed apply also to attempts to estimate other kinds of externalities.

11.2

There are basically two types of estimates to be found in the literature: estimates of social returns to a particular well-identified innovation or a class of innovations whose effects are limited to a particular industry or sector and can be measured there; and regression-based estimates of overall returns to a particular stream of "outside" R&D expenditures, outside the firm or sector in question. Most of the earlier work in either vein was devoted to measurement of social returns to public investments in agricultural research. This reflected, in part, the greater availability of agricultural data and, also, the more advanced state of applied econometric research in agricultural economics in the 1950s and early 1960s.[2]

Perhaps the earliest attempt to compute something like a social rate of return (actually a benefit-cost ratio) to public R&D appears in Schultz's (1954) book where, after having computed an index of total factor productivity growth for U.S. agriculture, he estimates the amount of resources saved by the technological change that occurred and compares it to the total public investments in agricultural research and finds it to have been a good investment.

This computation, I thought, could be improved by putting it explicitly within the consumer surplus framework. Using data collected for my Ph.D. thesis on the average yield improvement brought on by the use of hybrid seed, from a variety of experimental and observational data, detailed data on the cost of hybrid corn research collected from various agricultural experiment stations, and an estimate of the price elasticity of demand for corn from the existing agricultural economics literature, I computed current and future consumer surplus flows, discounted them back to the present, and compared them to the cumulated research cost; see Griliches (1958). The resulting benefit-cost ratio of about 7 was interpreted, wrongly, as implying a 700 percent rate of

---

2. See Griliches (1979), Norton and Davis (1981), Mairesse and Mohnen (1990) and Huffman and Evenson (1991) for reviews and additional references.

return to public investments in hybrid corn research. The associated internal rate of return was on the order of 40 percent, still very high, but it was the first number that got the most publicity and I did little to correct the record on this. In the same paper, similar computations were made using Schultz's numbers for total agricultural research and my own more sketchy numbers on the potential social returns to hybrid sorghum research.

In the work that followed, improvements were made in both the approximation formula for consumer surplus and the range of data used for the computation. Some major examples of subsequent work in agriculture were Peterson's (1967) estimate of returns to poultry breeding research, Barletta's (1971) estimate of the returns to corn breeding research in Mexico, and the Schmitz and Seckler (1970) estimate of returns to the tomato harvester. Weisbrod (1971) used a similar approach to estimate the social return to poliomyelitis research. Probably the most elaborate and impressive application of such ideas was in the work of Mansfield et al. (1977a). It is also the only set of case studies available for manufacturing innovations. In computing social returns, they tried to take into account also the research expenditures of related unsuccessful innovators and the losses in rents incurred by competitors. The median social rate of return for the 17 innovations they examined was 56 percent, somewhat more than double the comparable median private rate of return of 25 percent. Bresnahan's (1986) study of computer industry spillovers to the financial sector is also an extension of this general approach. He uses the estimated decline in "real" computer prices from earlier studies by Knight and Chow and an assumed elasticity of derived demand for computers by the financial services sector to compute the implied total welfare gains from such spillovers. Trajtenberg's (1990) estimates of welfare gains from CT scanners is based on a much more elaborate and estimated model, but could also be viewed as a descendent from this line of research.

11.3

Such case studies suffer from the objection that they are not "representative," that they have concentrated on the calculation of social rates of returns or spillovers only for "successful" inventions or fields. They are also much more difficult to do, requiring usually significant data collection, familiarity with the topic or event being analyzed and expose one, potentially, to criticism by those who actually know something about the subject. For these reasons, especially the desire to be more general and inclusive, and because of the growing availability of computer resources, much of the recent work has shifted to regression-based studies. Measures of output or TFP or of their rates of growth, across firms or industries, are related to measures of R&D "capital" or the intensity of R&D investment (R&D to sales or value-added ratios). A subset of such studies also includes measures of "outside" or "borrowable"

R&D capital in an attempt to estimate the contribution of spillovers to the growth in productivity.

Again, both the earliest and some of the most sophisticated studies of this topic have been done in agriculture. The first regression study, Griliches (1964), used the difference in agricultural outputs and inputs across states in the U.S. in three different time periods (1949, 1954 and 1959) and included in the "production function," among other variables, a measure of public expenditures on agricultural research, which differed from state to state and over time. The resulting elasticity estimate was on the order of 0.06, implying the rather high social rate of return of $13 per year (at the average farm level) for each dollar of public investments in research in agriculture. A number of other studies, e.g. Evenson (1968) and Huffman and Evenson (1991), improved on the original study in many respects, first by exploring more complicated lag functions in the construction of the public R&D variable, but second, and more importantly, by raising the question and facing up to the possibility of geographic spillovers, the fact that Iowa research may also have an effect on agricultural productivity in Nebraska.

Regression-based studies raise problems of their own. The main set of issues revolves around the question of how output is measured and whether the available measures actually capture the contribution of R&D (direct or spilled-over), and how R&D "capital" is to be constructed, deflated and depreciated. Since I have discussed these issues at some length in Griliches (1979 and 1988), I focus here only on issues raised by the attempt to measure spillovers.

11.4

The notion of externalities as a source of increasing returns and productivity growth has a long history in economics. Originally it was based on gains from specialization, from the development of "know-how," and on the interaction of craftsmen and engineers. The idea of reconciling competitive equilibrium with increasing returns by modeling the individual firm production (or cost) function as depending, parametrically, on industry aggregate activity variables (output or capital) goes back to Edgeworth and before; see Chipman (1965 and 1978) for surveys of the earlier literature. Explicit algebraic formulations appear in Simon (1947), Meade (1952), Chipman (1978), Arrow (1962) and Sheshinski (1967). In the latter papers the externality arises from "learning by doing" and is proxied by the size of the capital stock. I came across this kind of formulation first in an unpublished note by Grunfeld and Levhari (1962) and applied it to R&D in Griliches (1979).

In that version, the level of productivity achieved by one firm or industry depends not only on its own research efforts but also on the level of the pool of general knowledge accessible to it. Looking at a cross section of firms within a particular industry, such effects cannot be distinguished. If the pools of knowledge differ for different industries or areas, some of it could be deduced from interindustry comparisons over time and space. Moreover, the productivity of own research is affected by the size of the pool or pools it can draw upon. This leads to a formulation in which there is an interaction between the size of individual and aggregate research and development efforts.

A simple model of within-industry spillover effects is given by

$$Y_i = BX_i^{1-\gamma}K_i^{\gamma}K_a^{\mu},$$

where Y_i is the output of the ith firm which depends on the level of conventional inputs X_i, its specific knowledge capital K_i, and on the state of aggregate knowledge in this industry K_a. Note that constant returns are assumed in the firm's own inputs, X_i and K_i. This simplifies the example greatly. Assuming also that the aggregate level of knowledge capital $K_a = \Sigma_i K_i$ is simply the sum of all specific firm research and development capital levels and that own resources are allocated optimally and all firms in the industry face the same relative factor prices, then the individual K_i to X_i ratios will be given by

$$\frac{K_i}{X_i} = \frac{\gamma}{1-\gamma}\frac{P_x}{P_k} = r,$$

where P_x and P_k are the prices of X and K, respectively, and r, the K/X ratio, does not depend on i. The individual production functions can then be aggregated to yield:

$$\sum_i Y_i = \sum_i BX_i(K_i/X_i)^{\gamma}K_a^{\mu} = \sum_i BX_i r^{\gamma}K_a^{\mu} = Br^{\gamma}K_a^{\mu}\sum_i X_i.$$

Since the K_i/X_i ratios are all equal to r, so also is $\Sigma K_i/\Sigma X_i$, which we can substitute back into this equation, yielding:

$$\sum_i Y_i = B\left(\sum_i K_i \Big/ \sum_i X_i\right)^{\gamma} K^{\mu}\sum_i X_i = BX_a^{1-\gamma}K_a^{\mu+\gamma}.$$

Here, $X_a = \Sigma_i X_i$, $K_a = \Sigma_i K_i$, and the coefficient of aggregate knowledge capital is higher ($\gamma + \mu$) than at the micro level (γ only), reflecting at the aggregate level not only the private but also the social returns to research and development, thereby providing a framework for reconciling the results from micro and macro based R&D studies.

Of course, this formulation is rather simplistic and is based on a whole string of untenable assumptions, the major ones being: constant returns to scale with respect to X_i and K_i and common factor prices for all firms within an industry. These assumptions could be relaxed. This would add a number of "mix" terms to the equation, indicating how aggregate productivity would shift if the share of, say, the larger firms, were to increase (in the case of economies of scale). If the mix of firms and/or the firm specific prices stay stable then the above formula remains a reasonable approximation to a more complicated underlying reality.

The problem is much more complicated when we realize that we do not not deal with one closed industry, but with a whole array of firms and industries which "borrow" different amounts of knowledge from different sources according to their economic and technological distance from them; see Kislev and Evenson (1975, Chap. 4). The relevant concept of "distance" is very hard to define empirically. If we return to our previous example and now interpret the index i as referring to industries rather than firms, it makes little sense to define K_a as $\sum_i K_i$. Rather

$$K_{ai} = \sum w_{ij} K_j$$

is the amount of aggregate knowledge borrowed by the ith industry from all available sources. K_j measures the levels available in these sources, while w_{ij}, the "weighting" function, can be interpreted as the effective fraction of knowledge in j borrowed by industry i. Presumably w becomes smaller as the "distance," in some sense, between i and j increases. Thus we need an additional distributed (lag) over space function to construct a measure of the stock of borrowed knowledge.

What should such a weighting function be based on? Earlier suggestions were based on "vertical" borrowing; Brown and Conrad (1967) used the input-output table to measure the "closeness" of industries proportional to their purchases from each other, while Terleckyj (1974) used the capital and intermediate inputs purchases matrix weights, assuming that "borrowed" R&D is embodied in purchased inputs. Raines (1968) used the "horizontal" product field classification of NSF to include as inputs also the R&D expenditures of other industries which were reported as belonging to its product field. More recent examples of these approaches can be found in Terleckyj (1980), Wolf and Nadiri (1987) and partially in Sterlacchini (1989).

Actually, as noted in the introduction, there are two distinct notions of R&D "spillovers" here which are often confused in the literature. In the first, R&D intensive inputs are purchased from other industries at less than their full "quality" price. This is a problem of measuring capital equipment, materials and their prices correctly and not really a case of pure knowledge spillovers. If capital equipment purchase price indices reflected fully the improvements in their quality, i.e., were based on hedonic calculations, there would be no need to deal with it. As currently measured, however, total factor productivity in industry i is affected not only by its own R&D but also by productivity improvements in industry j to the extent of its purchases from that industry and to the extent that the improvements in j have not been appropriated by its producers and/or have not been incorporated in the official price indices of that (i) industry by the relevant statistical agencies. The use of purchase flow weighted R&D measures assumes that social returns in industry j are proportional to its R&D investment levels and that the amount of such returns transferred to industry i is proportional to its purchases from industry j.

A good example of such productivity transfers would be the computer industry. It has had a tremendous real productivity growth, though most of it, until recently, was unmeasured in the official indices, and unappropriated within the industry itself (because of rather intensive competitive pressures). Different industries have benefited differentially from it, depending on their rate of computer purchases. One way of accounting for it would be to adjust upward the relevant capital equipment figures by their computer content; see Berndt and Morrison (1991) and Siegel and Griliches (1992) for recent attempts along this line. The alternative is to "import" the computer industry's R&D in proportion to an industry's purchases from it.

But these are not real knowledge spillovers. They are just consequences of conventional measurement problems. True spillovers are ideas borrowed by research teams of industry i from the research results of industry j. It is not clear that this kind of borrowing is particularly related to input purchase flows. The photographic equipment industry and the scientific instruments industry may not buy much from each other but may be, in a sense, working on similar things and hence benefiting much from each other's research. One could argue that this is what the SIC classification is for. Presumably, the usefulness of somebody else's research to you is highest if he is in the same four-digit SIC classification as you are; it is still high if he is in the same three-digit industry group; and, while lower than before, the results of research by a firm in your own two-digit classification (but not three-digit) are more likely to be valuable to you than the average results of research outside of it. The problem arises when we want to extend this notion across other two-digit industries. Here there is no natural order of closeness (e.g. is "leather" closer to "food" or to "textiles"?). The situation is complicated further by the fact that micro R&D data are collected from firms rather than establishments and that major R&D performers are conglomerates, spanning several four-, three- and even two-digit SIC classifications. The NSF's applied R&D by product field data help a little, but not enough. Ideally, such data should be collected at the business-unit level. Unfortunately, the FTC stopped collecting within-firm product line R&D data in 1977.

There are two possible approaches to the construction of "spillover" stocks or "pools": (i) a symmetric approach, where every firm in a subindustry is treated equally, and all R&D within the industry or some alternative classification scheme is aggregated with equal weights, and (ii) where every possible pair of firms, industries, or countries is treated separately, and the relevant stock of spillovers for the "receiving" unit is constructed specifically for it, using its "distance" from the various spilling units as a weight.

The first type of construction corresponds to the first formula given above. At the two-digit level, total industry R&D was used as a measure of within-industry spillovers by Bernstein and Nadiri (1989) in analyzing individual firm cost functions. Rather than using the SIC classification as is, one could group three-digit SIC categories into clusters based on a priori notions about the extent of commonality in their technological and scientific base. This is similar to the use of crop-climatic regions by Evenson and Kislev (1973) with all units having equal access to all the research done by others in the same industry or region. In some models, e.g. Schankerman (1979, Chap. 5), the amount borrowed depends also on the level of own research expenditures, allowing thereby for an interaction and potential synergy between the two flows of research expenditures: "inside" and "outside." In the Huffman and Evenson (1991) work there is an effect not only from the research of others within the same climatic region but also an additional spillover, at a lower rate, from neighboring regions.

In the second type of construction, there is a wide choice of possible weights to model what is, essentially, an intellectual-scientific-technological "distance" between firms and industries. Among the various possibilities would be: (1) using the NSF's applied R&D product field by industry table to induce a distance metric, on the assumption that if an industry is doing R&D on some other industry's products, it is in some sense closer to it technologically than if it does not; cf. Raines (1968) and Schankerman (1979); (2) using company industrial diversification data from the Census of Enterprises or Compustat data to compute an alternative measures of closeness in the sales-demand space; see Jaffe (1986); (3) using information on rates of cross referencing of patents across product fields to infer the technological distance between them; (4) using a cross classification of patents, as in Scherer (1982) and Englander et al. (1988), or innovations, as in Robson et al. (1988) and Sterlacchini (1989), by industry of "production" and industry of use, to "flow-thru" R&D expenditures from performing to "using" industries; and (5) using the diversification of a firm's patenting activity across technologically determined patent classes to infer "overlap" and closeness measures for inventive activity, as in Jaffe (1988). In each of these cases one has to assume some simple weighting functions (e.g. influence declining exponentially with the particular concept of distance) or group the data into a few categories: immediate neighborhood, related fields and the rest. There are not enough degrees of freedom or independent variation in such productivity and R&D series to allow one to estimate very complex distributed lag schemes over both time and all the other firms and industries.

Much of the recent work has used patent data to develop measures of the "direction" of spillovers. A major data construction effort was pursued by Scherer (1982, 1984) who classified a large sample of patents by both the industry where the invention occurred and the industry (or industries) where it was expected to have its major impact. Having constructed such a "technology flows" table, Scherer used it to reweight the available R&D data by line of business into measures of both "origin" and "imported" (used) R&D from elsewhere, assuming that the flow of knowledge to industry i from industry j was proportional to the fraction of j's patents deemed to be "destined" for industry i. In explaining labor productivity growth at the two- and four-digit SIC level,

Scherer showed that the "transmitted" user R&D variable had a higher coefficient and was often more significant than the own "origin" or process R&D variables. His results are quite sensitive, however, both to the time period chosen for the analysis and the particular subset of industries included in it. Griliches and Lichtenberg (1984) used a more detailed set of data on TFP growth at the four-digit SIC level and found less of an effect for the "used" R&D component, in part because they concentrated on manufacturing industries only, excluding some of the more important spillover "using" industries outside of manufacturing. They also interpreted the equation as measuring improvements in materials and equipment bought from other industries, with the improvements being proportional to the R&D investments of the producing industries and the size of their flows being related to the allocation of R&D effort as measured by patents destined for the using industry. Englander et al. (1988) use Canadian patent data cross-classified by industry of origin and industry of potential use to construct similar measures of own R&D and a reweighted measure of the R&D from other industries and countries. Mohnen and Lepine (1988) use the same Canadian data to analyze cost reductions in 12 Canadian industries. In both studies the results differ by industry and time period and are sensitive to the exclusion of an overall measure of disembodied technical change, such as a time trend.

Jaffe (1986, 1988) comes closest in looking for the second type of spillovers, the disembodied kind. His distance measure is one of proximity in technological research space and does not imply flows in a particular direction. His measure of "closeness" between any two firms uses the overlap in the distribution of their patents by detailed patent class and indexes it by the uncentered correlation coefficients between them, their "angular separation." The assumption is made that two firms that are active in the same technological areas, as indicated by their taking out patents in the same patent classes, are more likely to benefit from each others research results. Jaffe constructs for each firm a measure of an available "pool" of outside R&D, with the R&D of other firms being weighted inversely to their estimated technological distance from the particular firm. Jaffe "validates" this measure by including it in the estimation of a production function and patent equation for these firms, finding a positive effect of the "pool" variable. He also estimates profit and Tobin's Q equations where the pool variable shows up with a negative coefficient. More recently, Jaffe (1989) has studied the effects of geographic proximity to university based research on the patenting of closely located firms with similar research objectives. Henderson, Jaffe and Trajtenberg (1990) are currently using patent citation frequencies to university based patents to assess the contribution of universities to industrial productivity in general.

The alternative to the search for a concept of technological closeness or distance is to use the research investments of different industries as separate variables. But that is not really feasible. At best we would have about 30 years of data for each of about 20 industries. Bernstein and Nadiri (1991) "solve" the problem by choosing only a few industries each, using "correct" sign restrictions for this purpose. But the multicollinearity between the various R&D series can easily produce "wrong" signs at some point in such a procedure. The alternative of using "significance tests" is also unattractive. Statistically insignificant spillovers may still be economically quite important. More generally, it is doubtful that such a discontinuous "in-or-out" modeling is really the right way to approach this problem. We need to weight and to aggregate somehow and that is what the idea of technological distance is for: to tell us how to weight the different research series and collapse them into one or a few variables so that the empirical importance of R&D spillovers can be estimated and assessed. With such estimates it would be possible to compute not only the return to a particular R&D expenditure in its "own" industry but also the total returns to R&D including the spillovers beyond its own industry's borders.

A number of studies have used the cost function framework to estimate the effect of spillovers; see Bernstein (1989), Bernstein and Nadiri (1988, 1989 and 1991) and Mohnen and Lepine (1988). The advantage of the cost function approach is that it is often more flexible in the functional form used and that it benefits from imposing more structure, considering the impact of R&D spillovers not only on total costs but also on the amount of labor and intermediate products demanded. The disadvantage is the required use of prices and the appearance of output on the right-hand-side of the equation. One is unlikely to have good input price data which differ significantly across firms and across time, especially R&D and physical capital prices. Moreover, both prices and output should be "expected" rather than actual values. The use of ex post output produces an unwarranted appearance of economies of scale and is likely to bias upward the own and outside R&D capital coefficients, especially in the absence of any other trend-like terms in the equations.

Another way of looking for R&D externalities is to look for measures of R&D output rather than input (expenditures). Schankerman (1979) uses a weighted measure of patents granted in other industries in explaining the productivity of R&D, in terms of patents granted, in a particular industry. He gets positive results for the variable, but their significance is suspect, since the underlying data, patents granted by SIC, were constructed by the Patent Office (OTAF) on the basis of a "concordance" which had a large amount of double counting of the same patents in different industries; see Griliches (1990). Wu (1990), following Caballero and Lyons (1989), uses total factor productivity growth in other industries (with an attempt to adjust for cyclicality) as her measure of potentially available externalities. This raises the more general question of what can be learned from looking at productivity residuals across and between industries.

The hypothesis of R&D spillovers does not really require the assumption that these effects are larger in the "home" industry and that they can be measured by the fraction of the total effect spilled out, using the own effect as a base of measurement. It is quite possible for an idea to have its entire effect elsewhere than where it was originated. Nevertheless, a common approach to the measurement of spillovers assumes that they are proportional to the "first order" effects within the "sending" industry. That is, an industry that has more productivity growth has also more to spill out. This view leads one to look for correlations, contemporaneous and lagged, among TFP or production function residuals across industries. Wu, for example, using 36 manufacturing industries tries to construct "spillover" measures weighting other industry residuals by various technological and input consumption distance measures. Her results are meager and difficult to interpret both because the mean effect of technological change across all industries, including the overall spillover effect, is already absorbed in the industry constants and cannot be distilled again from the residuals, and because current cross-correlations dominate the results. But it is unlikely that real technological spillovers are contemporaneous. One would expect them to be subject to quite long lags. Statistically, the procedure is equivalent to looking for particular patterns of "spatial" residual correlations in some technological space spanned by the various industries, both across and between industries and across time. While there is a literature on both spatial correlation and on dynamic factor models, it is doubtful that we can estimate today convincing models of overlapping, shifting relations of mutual causality, given the poorness of the underlying productivity measures. Moreover, such models are in general not identifiable in the context of a free contemporaneous cross-correlation of disturbances (errors) across industries. The prior information necessary to identify them consists exactly of the same kind of information on patterns of influence and their relative lag structures discussed earlier in the context of R&D spillovers. In econometrics there is also no free lunch.

The problem of the timing of such effects has yet to be given adequate attention. The usual procedure has been to construct some measure of R&D capital for each unit and then use it in the construction of the aggregated "pool" or available "spillover" measure. But this ignores the possibility that spillovers take more time than "own" effects, both because of secrecy and the time it may take for them to be expressed in new products and processes and diffused throughout the relevant industrial structure. Given the diffuse nature of such effects and the likely presence of long and variable lags, it is not surprising that "significant" findings are rare in this area. Moreover, it makes one somewhat skeptical about positive findings already reported even though one wants very much to believe in their reality.

The expectation of significant lags in such processes is also one reason why I do not put much trust in recent studies which find effects of "aggregate" externalities, either from aggregate activity, as in Caballero and Lyons (1989), or from investments in aggregate public capital, as in Aschauer (1989) and Munnell (1990). Besides partially adjusting for errors of measurement in the other variables and proxying for left out capacity utilization effects, the more or less contemporaneous timing of such effects is just not plausible. The apparent correlations are due more to common business cycle effects, partially induced by shifts in government expenditures, than to direct externalities. Not that I do not believe in the contribution of public capital to the functioning of our economy, only I doubt that it can be measured adequately in this fashion.

The major research questions in this area remain measurement questions. How much of the R&D in an area or industry is "spillable"? Who are the potential recipients? And is there an interaction between their own research endeavors and what they get out from the potentially available pool of the results of others? The first question is related to the level of aggregation in the data. This has been explored to some extent in the agricultural economics literature, especially by Evenson (1984 and 1988). The research done within a particular state experiment station is a mixture of a variety of research programs devoted to different sub-areas and sub-products. Only a part of it is relevant to the outside world. The larger the unit and the more variegated it is, the more likely it is that there will be less there to spill out than may be indicated by the aggregate numbers. Evenson, in his work, tries a number of "deflators" which are either proportional to the size of a state or unit, to the number of different climatic regions within a state, or to a variance like measure of the internal concentration of research within fields or subfields. The issue of the relevant size unit becomes very difficult but also crucial when we abandon the safe harbor of constant returns models and set sail looking for externalities. It is clear that a small specialized computer firm is likely to benefit from some of IBM's research results, but probably much less than would be implied by the total resources devoted by IBM to computer research. The small firm will have specialized in a much narrower niche than is described by the available SIC classification.

One other way of measuring externalities of R&D remains to be mentioned. If there are significant externalities to R&D within an industry, then the computed returns should be higher at the industry than the firm level. A comparison of firm-based R&D results with those found using various industry aggregates does not, however, indicate consistently higher R&D coefficients at the aggregate level; see Mairesse and Mohnen (1990, Tables 2 and 3). There may be two reasons for this negative finding. In the R&D "intensity" version of estimated productivity equations, the coefficient of the R&D variable can be interpreted as a gross rate of return, containing also a depreciation component. The relevant private rate of depreciation of R&D stock at the firm level is potentially much higher than what is likely to prevail at the overall industry level; see Pakes and Schankerman (1984). The latter contains a large component of social returns whose depreciation or obsolescence should be much less. Hence, without taking into account explicitly the difference between private and social obsolescence rates it may prove difficult to make much of such a comparison. Moreover, for the same reason, one should probably use different R&D capital concepts at different levels of aggregation, based on rather different depreciation assumptions.

In spite of all these difficulties, there has been a significant number of reasonably well done studies all pointing in the same direction: R&D spillovers are present, their magnitude may be quite large, and social rates of return remain significantly above private rates. A selective list of such findings is presented in Table 11.1. The estimated social rates of return look surprisingly uniform in their indication of the importance of such spillovers. While one must worry whether this is not just the result of self-imposed publication filters, my own involvement in this work and my acquaintance with many of the other researchers in this area leads me to believe in the overall reality of such findings.

Can R&D spillovers account for a significant proportion of the observed growth in per capita income and measured TFP? If we take the estimates in Table 11.1 seriously, they imply an estimate of μ, the elasticity of output with respect to aggregate "outside" R&D, between about half of and double the elasticity of output with respect to private R&D. Taking the upper range of these estimates, with $\gamma = 0.1$ (see Mairesse and Sassenou (1991) for a survey of estimates), and a set of "stylized" and optimistic facts about economic

Table 11.1   **Selected Estimates of Returns to R&D and R&D Spillovers**

I. *Agriculture*[a]	*Rates of Return to Public R&D*	
Griliches (1958) Hybrid corn	35–40	
Hybrid sorghum	20	
Peterson (1967) Poultry	21–25	
Schmitz-Seckler (1970) Tomato harvester	37–46	
Griliches (1964) Aggregate	35–40	
Evenson (1968) Aggregate	41–50	
Knutson-Tweeten (1979) Aggregate	28–47	
Huffman-Evenson (1991) Crops	45–62	
Livestock	11–83	
Aggregate	43–67	
II. *Industry*	*Rates of Return to R&D*	
Case Studies		
Mansfield et al. (1977a)	25	56
I-O Weighted	Within	From Outside
Terleckyj (1974) total	28	48
private	29	78
Sveikauskas (1981)	10 to 23	50
Goto-Suzuki (1989)	26	80
R&D Weighted (patent flows)		
Griliches-Lichtenberg (1984)	46 to 69	11 to 62
Mohnen-Lepine (1988)	56	28
Proximity (technological distance)		
Jaffe (1986)		30% of within
Cost functions		
Bernstein-Nadiri (1988, 1989)		20% of within
differs by industry	9 to 27	10 to 160
Bernstein-Nadiri (1991)	14 to 28	Median: 56% of within

[a]Adapted from Huffman-Evenson (1991, Table 14.2).

growth: y (growth in output per worker) = 0.03, c (growth in capital per worker) = 0.03, k (growth in R&D capital per worker) = 0.04, l (growth in number of workers) = 0.01, s (share of capital) = 0.3, which includes the assumption of rather rapid growth in knowledge capital (due, say, to a lower social depreciation rate), yields the following values for the growth equation

$$(y - 1) = 0.3(c - 1) + 0.1(k - 1) + 0.2k + t$$

$$0.03 = 0.3 \times 0.03 + 0.1 \times 0.04 + 0.2 \times 0.05 + t$$

$$= 0.009 = 0.004 + 0.010 + 0.007,$$

where R&D returns can account for up to half of the growth in output per worker and about three-quarters of the measured TFP growth, most of the explanatory effect coming from the spillover component, which is large, in part, because it is the source of increasing returns (the growth in l not being subtracted from it). A decline in overall R&D growth from about 5 percent per year to 2 percent (or less), such as happened between the early 1960s and middle 1970s, could, in this interpretation, have contributed significantly to the productivity slowdown, with the R&D contribution to growth dropping from 0.014 to 0.005, and accounting for about a half or more of the slowdown; see Griliches (1988).

This "back-of-the-envelope" calculation may exaggerate the potential magnitude and effect of such spillovers, both because of the upward selectivity bias in the results reported in Table 11.1, and because of a range of measurement issues discussed at greater length in Griliches (1979 and 1995). It does indicate, however, the importance of knowing the actual magnitude of such effects. But progress here awaits the appearance of better data and the development of better econometric techniques for tracing the interaction between firms and industries over time in an ill-defined and changing multi-dimensional space of technological opportunities.

References

Arrow, K. J.: The economic implications of learning by doing. *Review of Economic Studies 29* (3), 155–73, 1962.

Aschauer, D. A.: Is public expenditure productive? *Journal of Monetary Economics 23* (2), 177–200, 1989.

Barletta, N. A.: Costs and social benefits of agricultural research in Mexico. Unpublished Ph.D. thesis, University of Chicago, 1971.

Benhabib, J. & Jovanovic, B.: Externalities and growth accounting. *The American Economic Review 81* (1), 82–113, 1991.

Berndt, E. & Morrison, K.: Assessing the productivity of information technology equipment in U.S. manufacturing industries. NBER WP 3582, 1991.

Bernstein, J.: The structure of Canadian interindustry R&D spillovers, and the rates of return to R&D. *Journal of Industrial Economics 37* (3), 315–28, 1989.

Bernstein, J. I. & Nadiri, M. I.: Interindustry R&D spillovers, rates of return, and production in high-tech industries. *American Economic Review Papers and Proceedings 78* (2), 429–34, 1988.

Bernstein, J. I. & Nadiri, M. I.: Research and development and intra-industry spillovers: An empirical application of dynamic duality. *Review of Economic Studies 56*, 249–69, 1989.

Bernstein, J. I. & Nadiri, M. I.: Product demand, cost of production, spillovers, and the social rate of return to R&D. NBER WP 3625, 1991.

Bresnahan, T. F.: Measuring spillovers from "technical advance." *American Economic Review 76*, 741–55, 1986.

Brown, M. & Conrad, A.: The influence of research on CES production relations. In M. Brown (ed.), *The Theory and Empirical Analysis of Production*, Studies in Income and Wealth, Vol. 3, Columbia University Press for NBER, New York, 275–340, 1967.

Caballero, R. & Lyons, R. K.: The role of external economies in U.S. manufacturing. NBER WP 3033, July 1989.

Chipman, J.: A survey of the theory of international trade: Part 2, The neo-classical theory. *Econometrica 33* (4), 685–761, 1965.

Chipman, J.: External economics of scale and competitive equilibrium. *Quarterly Journal of Economics 84*, 347–85, 1978.

Englander, A. S., Evenson, R. & Hanazaki, M.: R&D innovation and the total factor productivity slowdown. *OECD Economic Studies*, No. 11, 1988.

Evenson, R.: The contribution of agricultural research and extension to agricultural production. Unpublished Ph.D. thesis, University of Chicago, 1968.

Evenson, R.: Technical change in U.S. agriculture. In R. Nelson (ed.), *Government and Technical Change: A Cross Industry Analysis*, Pergamon Press, New York, 1984.

Evenson, R.: Research, extension, and U.S. agricultural productivity: A statistical decomposition analysis. In S. M. Capalbo & J. M. Antle (eds.), *Agricultural Productivity: Measurement and Explanation*, Resources for the Future, Washington, DC, 1988.

Evenson, R. & Kislev, Y.: Research and productivity in wheat and maize. *Journal of Political Economy 81* (6), 1309–29, 1973.

Goto, A. & Suzuki, K.: R&D capital, rate of return on R&D investment and spillover of R&D in Japanese manufacturing industries. *Review of Economics and Statistics LXXI* (4), 555–64, 1989.

Griliches, Z.: Hybrid corn: An exploration in the economics of technological change. *Econometrica 25* (4), 501–22, 1957.

Griliches, Z.: Research cost and social returns: Hybrid corn and related innovations. *Journal of Political Economy LXVI*, 419–31, 1958.

Griliches, Z.: Research expenditures, education, and the aggregate agricultural production function. *American Economic Review LIV* (6), 961–74, 1964.

Griliches, Z.: Issues in assessing the contribution of research and development to productivity growth. *Bell Journal of Economics 10* (1), 92–116, 1979. [Reprinted as chap. 2 in this volume.]

Griliches, Z.: Productivity puzzles and R&D: Another nonexplanation. *Journal of Economic Perspectives 2* (4), 9–21, 1988.

Griliches, Z.: Patent statistics as economic indicators: A survey. *Journal of Economic Literature 28*, 1661–1707, 1990. [Reprinted as chap. 13 in this volume.]

Griliches, Z.: R&D and productivity: Econometric results and measurement issues. In P. Stoneman (ed.), *Handbook of the Economics of Innovation and Technological Change*, Basil Blackwell, Oxford, 1995.

Griliches, Z. & Lichtenberg, F.: Interindustry technology flows and productivity growth: A reexamination. *Review of Economics and Statistics LXVI* (2), 324–29, 1984. [Reprinted as chap. 10 in this volume.]

Grunfeld, Y. & Levhari, D.: A note on external economies. Mimeo, 1962.

Henderson, R., Jaffe, A. & Trajtenberg, M.: Telling trails out of schools: University patents and their citations. AEA Meeting, Washington, DC, 1990.

Huffman, W. E. & Evenson, R. E.: *Science for Agriculture,* Iowa State University Press, 1993.

Jaffe, A.: Technological opportunity and spillovers of R&D: Evidence from firms' patents profits and market value. *American Economic Review 76,* 984–1001, 1986.

Jaffe, A.: Demand and supply influences in R&D intensity and productivity growth. *Review of Economics and Statistics LXX* (3), 431–37, 1988.

Jaffe, A.: Real effects of academic research. *American Economic Review 79* (5), 957–70, 1989.

Kislev, Y. & Evenson, R.: *Agricultural Research and Productivity.* Yale University Press, New Haven, 1975.

Knutson, M. & Tweeten, L. G.: Toward an optimal rate of growth in agricultural production research and extension. *American Journal of Agricultural Economics 61,* 70–6, 1979.

Mairesse, J. & Mohnen, P.: Recherche-développement et productivité: Un sorvol de la littérature économétrique. *Economie et Statistique,* No. 237–8, 99–108, 1990.

Mairesse, J. & Sassenou, M.: R&D and productivity: A survey of econometric studies at the firm level. *STI Review,* No. 8, 9–43, OECD, Paris, 1991.

Mansfield, E.: *Industrial Research and Technical Innovation.* W. W. Norton & Co., New York, 1968.

Mansfield, E., Rapoport, J., Romeo, A., Wagner, S. & Beardsley, G.: Social and private rates of return from industrial innovations. *Quarterly Journal of Economics 77,* 221–40, 1977a.

Mansfield, E., Rapoport, J., Romeo, A., Villani, E., Wagner, S. & Husic, F.: *The Production and Application of New Industrial Technology,* W. W. Norton & Co., New York, 1977b.

Meade, J. E.: External economies and diseconomies in a competitive situation. *Economic Journal 62,* 54–67, 1952.

Mohnen, P.: New technologies and interindustry spillovers. OECD International Seminar on Science, Technology and Economic Growth, Paris, June, 1989.

Mohnen, P. & Lepine, N.: Payments for technology as a factor of production, University of Montreal, Department of Economics, Paper No. 8818, 1988.

Munnell, A. H.: Why has productivity growth declined: Productivity and public investment. *New England Economic Review,* Jan/Feb, 2–22, 1990.

Norton, G. W. & Davis, J. S.: Evaluating returns to agricultural research: A review. *American Journal of Agricultural Economics 63,* 685–99, 1981.

Pakes, A. & Schankerman, M.: The rate of obsolescence of patents, research gestation lags, and the private rate of return to research resources. In Z. Griliches (ed.), *R&D, Patents, and Productivity,* University of Chicago Press, Chicago, 73–88, 1984.

Peterson, W. L.: Return to poultry research in the United States. *Journal of Farm Economics 49,* 656–69, 1967.

Raines, F.: The impact of applied research and development on productivity. Washington University WP 6814, 1968.

Robson, M., Townsend, J. & Pavitt, K.: Sectoral patterns of production and use of innovations in the U.K.: 1945–83. *Research Policy 17* (1), 1–14, 1988.

Romer, P. M.: Endogenous technological change. *Journal of Political Economy 98* (5), S71–S102, 1990.

Sala-i-Martin, X.: Lecture notes on economic growth. NBER WP 3563, 1990.

Schankerman, M.: Essays on the economics of technical change: The determinants, rate of return and productivity impact of research and development. Ph.D. thesis, Harvard University, 1979.

Scherer, F. M.: Interindustry technology flows and productivity growth. *Review of Economics and Statistics LXIV,* 627–34, 1982.

Scherer, F. M.: Using linked patent and R&D data to measure interindustry technology flows. In Z. Griliches (ed.), *R&D, Patents, and Productivity,* University of Chicago Press, Chicago, 1984.

Schmitz, A. & Seckler, D.: Mechanized agriculture and social welfare: The case of the tomato harvester. *American Journal of Agricultural Economics 52,* 567–77, 1970.

Schmookler, J.: *Invention and Economic Growth.* Harvard University Press, Cambridge, MA, 1966.

Schultz, T. W.: *The Economic Organization of Agriculture.* McGraw-Hill, New York, 1954.

Sheshinski, E.: Optimal accumulation with learning by doing. In K. Shell (ed.), *Essays on the Theory of Optimal Economic Growth,* MIT Press, Cambridge, MA, 1967.

Siegel, D. & Griliches, Z.: Purchased services, outsourcing, computers, and productivity in manufacturing. In Z. Griliches (ed.), *Output Measurement in the Service Sectors,* University of Chicago Press, Chicago, 1992.

Simon, H.: Some models for the study of the economic effects of technological change. Cowles Commission DP213, University of Chicago, 1947.

Sterlacchini, A.: R&D innovations, and total factor productivity growth in British manufacturing. *Applied Economics 21,* 1549–62, 1989.

Sveikauskas, L.: Technological inputs and multifactor productivity growth. *Review of Economics and Statistics 63* (2), 275–82, 1981.

Terleckyj, N.: *Effects of R&D on the Productivity Growth of Industries: An Exploratory Study.* National Planning Association, Washington, DC, 1974.

Terleckyj, N.: Direct and indirect effects of industrial research and development on the productivity growth of industries. In J. N. Kendrick & B. N. Vaccara (eds.), *New Developments in Productivity Measurement and Analysis,* University of Chicago Press, Chicago, 1980.

Trajtenberg, M.: *Economic Analysis of Product Innovations.* Harvard University Press, Cambridge, MA, 1990.

Weisbrod, B. A.: Costs and benefits of medical research: A case study of poliomyelitis. *Journal of Political Economy 79* (3), 527–44, 1971.

Wolf, E. N. & Nadiri, M. I.: Spillover effects, linkage structure, technical progress, and R&D. C. V. Starr Center Research Report 87/43, New York University, 1987.

Wu, J. Y.: An empirical investigation into R&D externalities at the industry level. Honors thesis, Harvard College, 1990.

12   R&D and Productivity:
The Unfinished Business

Current work on the role of public and private research in productivity growth has deep roots in the early work of agricultural economists. The first micro production function estimates (Tintner 1944), the first detailed total factor productivity (TFP) calculations (Barton and Cooper 1948), the first estimates of returns to public R&D expenditures (Schultz 1953; Griliches 1958), and the first production function estimates with an added R&D variable (Griliches 1964) all originated in agricultural studies. Other original contributions to applied econometrics by agricultural economists include Waugh (1929) on hedonics, Nerlove (1958) on distributed lags, and Hoch (1955) and Mundlak (1961) on panel data econometrics.[1]

The specific subfield I want to discuss here, the impact of R&D on productivity, has expanded enormously from its modest beginnings. Given the large number of recent surveys of this field, I will not review it again, having just done it in Griliches (1995), except to note that one of the best surveys, Australian Industry Commission (1995, vol. 3, app. QA), lists 27 studies estimating the returns to R&D at the firm level, 28 at the industry level, 10 at the country level, and 20 studies for agriculture alone.[2]

A preliminary version of this paper appears in *Conference Proceedings on Global Agricultural Science Policy for the Twenty-First Century: Invited Papers*, pp. 1–20 (Melbourne, Australia: Conference Secretariat, Department of Natural Resources and Environment, August 1996), and is also forthcoming in the proceedings of the Conference on Economic Growth, Technology, and Human Capital, held 19–20 December 1996 in Tucuman, Argentina. The author is indebted to Jacques Mairesse for helpful comments on an earlier draft, to Steve Bond and Bronwyn Hall for providing him with the panel data update, to Chorching Goh and Aviv Nevo for able research assistance, and to the Mellon Foundation and the National Science Foundation for financial support.

1. See Heady and Dillon (1961); Berndt (1991, chap. 4); Griliches and Mairesse (1998); and Griliches (1996) for historical surveys of some of these topics.

2. Additional surveys can be found in Huffman and Evenson (1993, chap. 7); Mairesse and Sassenou (1991); Mairesse and Mohnen (1995); Nadiri (1993); Alston and Pardey (1996, chap. 6); and Hall (1996).

Major progress was made in the past thirty years in this field: new databases were developed at the firm, business-unit, and project levels, and other measures of innovation were added, especially observations on patents. Still I am not entirely happy. As progress was made, it became clearer how much we still don't know and how thin are our data.

I will divide my remarks into three parts: (1) puzzles about the current results in this field; (2) conceptual problems with the "central" R&D capital model; and (3) econometric problems: simultaneity, heterogeneity, and spillovers.

12.1   Recent Results and Puzzles

The major framework for the analysis of the relationship between R&D and productivity has been the "R&D capital in the production function" model (see Griliches 1973 for an early exposition): $Q = AX^{\beta}K^{\gamma}$, where Q is output, X is an index of conventional inputs including physical capital, K is the "stock of knowledge" (or R&D), A is the level of disembodied technology, and β and γ are the parameters of interest. The focus in such analysis is on estimating γ, the elasticity of output with respect to R&D capital. Recent studies using 1980s data have raised the possibility that γ may have declined over time. The issue is important substantively and needs further investigation. Is it a temporary phenomenon? Has it been reversed recently? Is it a drop in private rather than social returns (Hall 1993)? By the way, a change in γ is not the same as a change in the net rate of return to R&D: $\rho = \gamma \, (Q/K) - \delta$, where δ is the depreciation rate of such capital. The rate of return to R&D may decline if K grows faster than Q and/or if δ rises, without necessarily implying a change in γ.

There are three more bits of unfinished business in the "results" area: (1) Often the productivity growth equation is estimated with the R&D intensity rather than the growth in R&D capital as the relevant variable. Sometimes this version gives "better" results. An argument can be made for it (chap. 9 in this volume), but I have not seen a convincing reconciliation of the results of these two versions of the same model. An encompassing test is in order here. (2) There is a parallel literature on estimating the valuation of R&D capital (or investment) in the framework of market value equations (Griliches 1981; Pakes 1985; Hall and Hall 1993). It should be connected to the production function estimation literature. (3) Work has been done both at the firm and industry levels. One might expect higher estimates of the rate of return to R&D (ρ) at the industry level due to the internalization of spillover effects, but the bulk of the results does not go in this direction and no convincing exploration of the aggregation problem has been done yet, as far as I know, in this context. One possibility is a higher δ at the individual firm (private) level because of obsolescence and the "creative destruction" of rents as against a larger component of more slowly depreciating social returns at the more aggregate levels.

12.2 The "Central" Model and Its Discontents

The "central" model treats R&D as another investment stream, parallel to physical investment, and constructs an analogous "knowledge" capital stock using the perpetual inventory method and an assumed (fixed) depreciation rate δ. But knowledge is not like refrigerators, and each of the steps in the construction of such a "capital" concept is problematic.

The list of problems is long:

The standard approach aggregates R into a K concept linearly, ignoring the possibility that knowledge production depends nonlinearly not only on current R&D efforts but also on previously accumulated results. Moreover, R as a producer of additions to K may be subject to short-run decreasing returns to the intensity of research and to longer-run diminishing returns due to the depletion of technological opportunities, unless they are recharged by science or other sources of new discoveries. This is not a new concern. It is alluded to in chapter 2 in this volume, it was raised in a number of papers by Evenson (e.g., 1984), and it has been revived in a number of recent papers.

Formal properties of models where $\dot{K} = f(R, K)$ have been considered by Bachrach (1990), Hall and Hayashi (1989), Lach (1994), Jones (1995), and Klette (1994), among others. A reasonable version of such a model is:

$$\dot{K}_i = R^\gamma K_i^\phi K_A^h$$

where the ϕ parameter associated with the own stock of knowledge reflects the within-firm spillovers and time interdependencies in the research process, while the h parameter, associated with the aggregate state of knowledge, reflects both positive external spillovers and negative crowding-out effects. Having started with such a model, there is no clear role left for a separate depreciation effect, though some of the authors add a linear depreciation component to such models.

In estimation, such models lead to the solving out of the unobservable K stock and to the estimation of productivity growth as a function of R and lagged levels of output, TFP, or patent stocks. The current results along these lines are interesting but not fully convincing, both because of econometric problems associated with the use of lagged dependent variables, and because of the likely endogeneity of R, a topic to which I shall return below.

Other conceptual problems are associated with the whole notion of depreciation of knowledge and with the question of how knowledge should be incorporated into the production function. Much of what we think of as depreciation is not physical forgetting but rather the dissipation of rents as the result of obsolescence. It is a valid private cost component of innovation but not necessarily a social one. Its implications for measurement depend on the state of price index measurement technology and on the market structure of the relevant industries. In the computer industry, where the incumbents have little market power, prices and revenues fall, but quantities need not. If correctly "deflated," there is little depreciation to knowledge capital in a "true" quality-constant production function. In the pharmaceuticals industry, where incumbents choose to depreciate their patent monopolies optimally and the appearance of new substitutes does not cause incumbent prices to decline, deflated revenues will fall and we would interpret it as the depreciation of private R&D capital and a decline in productivity (since the same set of resources are still used in the industry producing essentially the same quantities as before). All that has happened is that the previously accumulated R&D capital is now available to others in the industry and hence cannot collect much rent. But it is still contributing to the productivity (technology) of the industry. From a social perspective the loss of patent protection does not result in a decline in such capital but rather a rise in its utilization! The fact that in most cases our micro production functions are closer to revenue functions than to true quantities makes the second case more prevalent than the first. But often the data are a mixture of the two, leading to great difficulties in the interpretation of the empirical results.

It is obvious that such capital does not depreciate just due to the efflux of time or to mechanical wear and tear. The obsolescence of privately generated R&D-based knowledge is clearly a function of the activity of others and is unlikely to occur at a constant rate. A major challenge before us is to model this process convincingly. A start has been made by Caballero and Jaffe (1993), but this has yet to be transferred to the work on micro production functions.

The above discussion does not imply that there is no obsolescence in social knowledge. There has surely been loss in the social value of the knowledge stocks associated with making carbon copies of documents and building ships, both in the sense that existing stocks are applied to much smaller industries and hence the implicit social returns, the consumer surpluses attributable to the original invention of these products, become smaller as demand falls, and in the sense that they become much harder to retrieve due to the lack of use, the retirement and death of associated human capital, and just plain forgetting. Such depreciation need not have the usual declining-balance (geometric) form, except possibly in the aggregate, where the population renewal theorem (Jorgenson 1973) comes into play.

The final set of problems is associated with the nonrivalrous nature of knowledge (Arrow 1962; Romer 1990). If $\dot{K}$ is to be measured by the outputs of the knowledge-producing processes, it becomes an index of the level of productivity along the lines of the quality ladders or variety models of Grossman and Helpman (1991) and not a parallel capital input within the list of standard inputs. If $\dot{K}$ is measured by R&D input rather than output, the question is still, should the resulting production function be interpreted as having constant returns including the R&D input? The usual solution to this internal versus external economies of scale question was to treat the own R&D effects as subject to decreasing returns and to include them in the standard list of inputs, while treating the spillovers from the R&D of others as externalities (see chaps.

2 and 11 in this volume), assuring perfect competition within the relevant sectors. But the nonrivalrous nature of R&D results makes perfect competition solutions unlikely, leading to the patent system and other appropriability mechanisms and a divergence between price and marginal costs of production. The recent revival of monopolistic competition theory and its application in this context make it clear that knowledge-producing firms will have nonnegligible markups whose magnitude will depend on the conditions of competition in their industries and the strengths of their appropriability positions. What we have then in our data are revenue functions with nonzero markups and downward sloping demand functions "solving" the increasing returns "problem" (it is only a problem for our models, not necessarily for the real world). In particular, as I will show below, if one assumes that R&D affects only demand, one would interpret estimates of γ as a measure of $-\phi/\eta$, where ϕ is the demand elasticity with respect to R&D and η is the price elasticity of demand. This is equivalent to the Dorfman and Steiner (1954) result for advertising. Even if only partially true this has serious implications for estimation, which is my next topic.

12.3 Econometric Issues

There are a number of sources of misspecification which afflict the "standard" production function estimates of the elasticity of output with respect to R&D capital (γ). The major ones are (1) the simultaneity of the R&D decision, (2) heterogeneity and endogeneity of individual product prices, (3) heterogeneity of the underlying production functions, and (4) the role of spillovers.

The more general topic of the simultaneity of input decisions was discussed recently in Griliches and Mairesse (1998). If R&D is chosen on the basis of economic incentives, it is unlikely to be fully independent of the shocks and errors which affect the production relations we are trying to estimate. This is the simultaneity problem. If all firms face the same production function and the same factor prices, it is not clear why different firms would choose different R&D levels. If they all do the same thing, we may not be able to estimate anything. If they do not, then we need to understand why not. That is the identification problem.

The simultaneity problem refers to the possible confusion in causality: future output and its profitability depend on past R&D, while R&D, in turn, depends on both past output and the expectation about its future. With long time series and detailed lag assumptions one might be able to analyze a recursive equations system with current output depending on past R&D, and past R&D depending on past rather than current output. In cross-sectional data with only a few observations per firm, it is much harder to make such distinctions, particularly since current expectations about the future are based on current and past data.

There are several "solutions" to the simultaneity problem. First, if one has good series on the real factor costs of the various inputs, one could use them as instrumental variables for the estimation of the production function. Unfortunately, in the R&D context one is unlikely to have good factor price series.[3] Even if one had the prices, they are likely to be highly collinear over time. There is one possible exception to this pessimistic view. With good data one could construct different "tax prices" of R&D facing different firms, which would provide us with some relevant cross-sectional variation. But, to my knowledge, that has not been implemented yet in this context.

Also, the implicit assumption of certainty about the future underlying such static models makes little sense in the R&D context. What is maximized here is the present value of all future profits, and the relevant output price concept is an expected one and not the current one, especially if current output (and demand) is subject to special and transitory circumstances.

Second, if both time series and cross-sectional data are available and one is willing to assume a simple permanent-transitory model: $u = \alpha + e$, where α is the permanent component which affects input demand choice while e, the transitory component, does not, then consistent parameter estimates can be had from the within-firm covariances. This is equivalent to allowing a separate constant term (dummy variable) for each firm, which would absorb the offending term in it. Unfortunately, such data sets are rare. Moreover, the covariance approach may exacerbate other problems, such as errors in the variables, which also afflict these kinds of data.

Third, one may be able to find other "indicator" variables of interest and they may help to solve the identification problem in such models. I shall discuss one such approach below.

The question whether the R&D stock measure is "contaminated" by simultaneity depends upon what is in the production function disturbance and to what extent it is anticipated by the decision makers. The usual construction of $K_\tau = \sum(1 - \delta)^j R_{t-1-j}$, with j going from zero to infinity, puts only lagged values of R&D into the equation. But to the extent that there are more or less permanent firm effects, reflecting market positions, differences in quality of the labor force, and other misspecifications, they would be correlated also with past R&D decisions. Going "within" or using growth rates eliminates such fixed effects but may still leave other specification errors, such as changing utilization rates and demand conditions. These may still influence current R&D decisions.

An example of current approaches to such problems can be seen in table 12.1, which is adapted from Griliches and Mairesse (1998). The first part, col-

---

3. First, there are no published R&D deflators at the detailed industry level; second, if they were available, they would still be very highly correlated with the cost of labor and cost of capital indexes, which are likely to be major ingredients of such indexes. What we will not have are changes in "real" R&D costs, in the productivity of such expenditures, in a field or industry, caused by various technological and scientific breakthroughs.

Table 12.1   **Alternative Estimates of Production Function Parameters:[a] U.S. R&D-Performing Firms, 1973, 1978, 1983, 1988 (standard errors in parentheses)**

	Balanced Panel		Full Sample[b]			
			Total OLS		Nonparametric F	
	Total	Within				
Variables[a]	(1)	(2)	(3)	(4)	(5)	(6)
Labor	.496	.685	.578	.551	.591	
	(.022)	(.030)	(.013)	(.013)	(.013)	
Physical capital	.460	.180	.372	.298	.321	.320
	(.014)	(.027)	(.009)	(.012)	(.016)	(.017)
R&D capital	.034	.099	.038	.027	.081	.077
	(.015)	(.027)	(.007)	(.007)	(.016)	(.019)
Investment	—	—	—	.110	—	
				(.011)		
Other variables[c]	—	—	—	—	Powers of h	Polynomial in P and h
N[d]		856		2,971		1,571

[a]The dependent variable in columns (1)–(4) is the log of sales, while in columns (5) and (6), the dependent variable is the log(value added) $- \hat{\beta} \times$ log(labor).

[b]Consult Griliches and Mairesse (1998) for details of the estimation algorithm leading up to columns (5) and (6).

[c]The other variables in the equations are Year and Year $\times$ Industry 357 (i.e., computers) dummy variables.

[d]The number of observations in the balanced panel for regressions in columns (1) and (2) are the observations for those firms that have continuous data over the period. Similarly, the 2,971 observations in columns (3) and (4) are all the observations in the full sample. (Only six observations had to be discarded because of zero investment.) The number of observations in the last two columns decreases to 1,571 because lagged values of some of the independent variables are needed in the estimation.

umns (1) and (2), presents standard OLS production function estimates for a heavily selected panel of 214 R&D firms in U.S. manufacturing. As usual, the capital coefficient declines as one moves to "within-firm" data, but the estimated R&D coefficient actually increases. Table 12.2, which is new, applies the more general Chamberlain (1984) Π-matrix approach to the estimation of such a model and asks whether the R&D coefficients have declined over time. As can be seen from comparing the estimated γ's in columns (3) and (5) or (4) and (6), they did not. The allowance for correlated effects hits the physical capital coefficient primarily, and the allowance for individual firm heteroskedasticity introduces an additional puzzling instability in the estimated coefficients (compare the estimates in the SUR versus MD columns) but leaves the R&D coefficients largely unchanged. Neither of these estimates, however, takes care of the simultaneity of the employment decision, if the latter is af-

Table 12.2   **Alternative Estimates of Production Function Parameters: U.S. R&D-Performing Firms, 1973, 1978, 1983, 1988, Balanced Panel**

Variables	Uncorrelated Random Effects		Correlated Effects			
	SUR (1)	MD (2)	SUR (3)	MD (4)	SUR (5)	MD (6)
Labor	.594	.686	.664	.805	.671	.818
	(.037)	(.020)	(.020)	(.029)	(.044)	(.030)
Physical capital	.334	.260	.163	.062	.164	.062
	(.031)	(.014)	(.033)	(.022)	(.033)	(.022)
R&D capital	.067	.065	.092	.080		
Combined	(.022)	(.015)	(.035)	(.022)		
1973					.086	.065
					(.036)	(.024)
1978					.087	.072
					(.035)	(.023)
1983					.073	.059
					(.036)	(.024)
1988					.094	.076
					(.035)	(.023)
Chi-square (degrees of freedom)		366 (45)		121 (33)		110 (30)

Notes: Number of observations = 214 firms × 4 = 856. SUR = seemingly unrelated (multivariate) regression estimates; MD = minimum distance (individual heteroskedasticity weighted). Dependent variable is log deflated sales. Other variables in the equation are year dummy variables, computer (357) industry dummy variable, and computer-year interaction variables.

fected by current shocks in production or correlated with unmeasured changes in capacity utilization.

An interesting new approach to the simultaneity problem is presented by Olley and Pakes (1996) in their paper "The Dynamics of Productivity in the Telecommunications Equipment Industry." This paper deals with two topics, selectivity and simultaneity, in an intertwined fashion. The sample selectivity problem may be quite serious for panel data. If observations (and data) are not missing at random, estimates that are based on "clean" and "balanced" subsamples could be badly biased. For example, a bad draw of u may force a firm or plant to exit from the industry. Such a negative correlation between estimated productivity shocks and future probabilities of exit was observed by Griliches and Regev (1995) in their analysis of Israeli industrial firms. They called it "the shadow of death." If the impact of negative u's on exit is stronger for smaller firms (the larger ones having more resources to survive them), then this will induce a negative correlation between u and the stock of capital among the surviving firms and bias the estimated capital coefficient downward in such samples. I will emphasize, however, their suggested solution to the simultaneity problem in this paper. (See Griliches and Mairesse 1998 for a more detailed exposition.)

The major innovation of Olley and Pakes is to bring in a new equation, the investment equation, as a proxy for α, the unobserved transmitted component of u.[4] Trying to proxy for the unobserved α (if it can be done right) has several advantages over the usual within estimators: it does not assume that α reduces to a "fixed" (over time) firm effect; it leaves more identifying variance in the "independent" variables and is therefore a less costly solution to the omitted variable and/or simultaneity problem; and it should also be substantively more informative.

Their argument goes roughly as follows: the investment demand of the firm at time t can be written as a function of the predetermined capital stock variables and that part of the shock in the production function u, the α, that is transmitted to both the employment and the investment decisions. Inverting this relationship and solving for α as a function of investment and capital stock, one can approximate it now semiparametrically and estimate the production function in two steps (three, if one also deals with selectivity at the same time): First one gets a consistent estimate of the coefficient of the labor variable, and then one retrieves the capital coefficient by using the estimated labor coefficient to move the endogenous labor variable to the left-hand side of the equation.

An application of their approach to our data is presented in columns (3)–(6) of table 12.1. Because exit is often a success for our R&D firms (being taken over) rather than a failure, the selection problem is not particularly severe in our data (compare the results in columns [1] and [3]). Once one shifts to the more complete unbalanced samples, the remaining selectivity (mainly attrition) does not appear to be too important (compare columns [5] and [6]).

As far as the simultaneity problem is concerned, either it is of no great import in these data or the introduction of investment and the associated Olley and Pakes procedure does not fully adjust for it. Investment is highly "significant" when added to the production function (see column [4]), but at the end of the procedure (having allowed for selectivity and unbalance), the coefficients change only a little (compare columns [1] and [3] with [6]) except that again we do get a higher R&D coefficient.

The Olley and Pakes solution to the simultaneity problem is a clever way to exploit the fact that the unobserved "productivity shocks" are transmitted to more than just one equation and should be estimated within a system of behavioral equations. It does rest, however, on two very strong assumptions: (1) that there is only *one* single-component unobservable in the system, the α_{it}, which follows a first-order Markov process and is fully transmitted to the investment equation, and (2) that no other variables or errors appear in it. Investment de-

---

4. In their notation α is ω and they refer to it simply as "productivity."

pends, however, also on other individual factors such as interest rate expectations, tax treatments, and changes in future demand prospects not yet fully captured in the initial state variables (the capital stocks). In principle, there may be additional instrumental variables and other indicators of α, such as R&D, which could help solve the errors in the investment equation problem, except for the extreme nonlinearities introduced by their semiparametric approach.[5]

Other approaches lean more heavily on assumptions about lags in the transmission of the disturbances to the other decision variables and use lagged values as instrumental variables in estimating such models (see Blundell and Bond 1995 and Mairesse and Hall 1996). One can write a simple model of the production function as

$$y_{it} = \beta x_{it} + \gamma k_{it} + \alpha_i + u_{it}, \qquad u_{it} = \rho u_{it-1} + e_{it},$$

where small letters represent the logarithms of the variables, x is a composite of conventional inputs including physical capital, k is a measure of the R&D stock, α_i is an unobserved permanent firm effect, while u is a randomly changing technical disturbance. The innovation in u, the e_{it}, is unpredictable, but whether x and k are independent of it depends on the assumed lag structure of the decisions affecting their evolution. (Of course, u could be modeled as a higher order autoregression.) In such a world, we could solve out u_{it} and rewrite the equation as

$$y = \beta(x - \rho x_{-1}) + \gamma(k - \rho k_{-1}) + \rho y_{-1} + e + (1 - \rho)\alpha_i,$$

and use past differences in x, k, and y, which should be independent of α_i and e_i, as instruments.[6]

In table 12.3, a larger sample (including non-R&D firms) is analyzed in this framework using the Generalized Method of Moments (GMM) approach (see Mairesse and Hall 1996 for a recent exposition in a similar context). Columns (1) and (6) present the OLS estimates for levels and first differences respectively. Column (2) allows for serial correlation and finds it very high (as could be expected). Columns (3) and (4) repeat these level computations allowing for the endogeneity of all the input (and lagged output) variables, using past differences in these variables as instrumental variables. Column (5) is similar, but only instruments the labor and lagged output variables, treating the two capital stocks as predetermined.[7] Columns (7) and (8) present the corresponding estimates of this equation in first differences, instrumented by past levels. The first differences transformation is optimal if $\rho = 1$, or if $\rho = 0$ and the "not-so-fixed effect" is a random walk, that is, $\alpha = \alpha_{-1} + e$. Column (7) uses

---

5. The current state of estimating nonlinear errors-in-variables models is not completely hopeless, but it is not easy either.
6. This assumption is right for "stationary" α's, where their effect on y is unchanged over time.
7. Using instruments from $t - 3$ rather than $t - 2$ increases the standard errors but has little effect on the reported results.

Table 12.3 **Alternative Estimates of Production Function Parameters: U.S. R&D and Non-R&D Manufacturing Firms, 1982–87, $N = 676$ (standard errors in parentheses)**

	Levels					First Differences		
	OLS		Instrumented by Differences			OLS	Instrumented by Levels	
Variable	(1)	(2)	(3)[a]	(4)[a]	(5)[b]	(6)	(7)[c]	(8)[d]
Labor	.567	.616	.665	.750	.652	.613	.705	.611
	(.008)	(.013)	(.048)	(.027)	(.046)	(.013)	(.024)	(.062)
Capital	.402	.122	.277	.289	.314	.114	.084	.110
	(.007)	(.012)	(.036)	(.027)	(.031)	(.012)	(.019)	(.037)
R&D stock	.016	.041	.033	.025	.030	.030	.046	.059
	(.004)	(.012)	(.017)	(.017)	(.010)	(.013)	(.017)	(.022)
Lagged output	0	.981	0	.573	.654	1	1	1
		(.004)		(.023)	(.031)			

Notes: Estimates in columns (2), (4), and (5) (equation 11) are constrained to the same ρ coefficient in $(x - \rho x_{-1})$ and ρy_{-1}. Additional variables included in the equations: no-R&D dummy variable, year dummies, computer industry dummy, and interaction with year.

[a]Instrument sets: all differences as of $t - 2$ and earlier, for l, c, k, and y_{-1}.

[b]Instrument sets: c and k treated as predetermined. Only l and y_{-1} instrumented.

[c]Instrument sets: levels of l, c, and k as of $t - 2$ and earlier.

[d]Instrument sets: only l instrumented.

past levels as instruments for all three variables, which is appropriate if there are random measurement errors in them or if there is some remaining contemporaneous simultaneity, while column (8) only instruments the labor variable.

The preferred specification, column (5), indicates a substantively and statistically significant R&D coefficient of about .03. It also finds that the individual firm effects are not entirely fixed but include a component which does depreciate, albeit slowly. If one approaches the limit of $\rho = 1$ (first differences), there is hardly any identifying variance left in the annual changes in our measures of physical and R&D capital. Measurement and timing errors now predominate, while the remaining information content in the instruments is too small to allow one to extract whatever signal is still left in these variables. In the end, what is clear is that there seems to be a significant R&D coefficient, but its magnitude is uncertain, varying from about .03 to .08 based on estimates from reasonably robust specifications (table 12.1 col. [6], table 12.2 col. [4], and table 12.3 col. [5]).

The GMM approach uses past values of the inputs and outputs as instruments. What is their identifying content? Inputs today depend on past demand and supply shocks because, presumably, there are lags in adjustment and also erroneous decisions. But without specifying nontrivial real factor demand and supply equations with measurable exogenous shifters of such functions, we have no interesting variables that could be used to interpret (identify) their behavior. There are no measures of shifts in the potential demands for a firm's products, or of changes in technological opportunities, market structure, or individual firm cost of capital. Without such shifters it is hard to tell whether such lagged values represent an interesting experiment which would allow us to identify something.

Another major specification problem revolves around the unlikely assumption that all firms within an industry charge the same price. If product prices are both different and endogenous, then what is estimated is a revenue function, not a production function, with left-out product prices in the residual. This problem is considered by Klette and Griliches (1996) who, reinventing an argument made by Marschak and Andrews (1944), start with a model of firms facing symmetric logarithmic market share (demand) functions

$$y_i - y_I = \eta(p_i - p_I) + e,$$

where y_i and y_I are respectively the real output of the firm and the industry, p_i is the firm's own price (or price index), η is demand elasticity with respect to the relative price of its own products, p_I is the aggregate industry price index (relative to the overall economy price level), and e are all other demand shifters for the products of this firm. If the variable that we observe is not real output y, but deflated revenue (sales)

$$r_i = (y_i + p_i) - p_I,$$

then the "revenue production" function is

$$r = \beta x + \gamma k + u + (p_i - p_I).$$

There would be no problem here if the p_i's were random and exogenous. But if firms have a modicum of market power, at least in the short run, p_i will be set by them and will be correlated with u, x, and k. Setting price equal to marginal revenue and solving out for p_i yields the pseudo–production function

$$r = [\beta x + \gamma k + u]/m - (y_I)/\eta - e/\eta,$$

where the markup coefficient $m = \eta/(1 + \eta)$ is likely to be larger than one. Since y_I and p_I are aggregates, they can be controlled for by the introduction of period dummy variables. It is clear now that the estimates of α and β will be biased *downward* on the order of $1/m$, implying diminishing returns to scale in contexts where there actually may be increasing returns.

This model can be extended by adding R&D capital to the demand function, with ϕ as its elasticity.[8] The coefficient of k in the deflated sales equation is then $(\gamma/m - \phi/\eta)$, a combination of its effects on both productivity and demand, attenuated by the price elasticity of demand. This coefficient can also

---

8. In this form, R&D capital is a separable demand shifter, leaving the price elasticity of demand unaffected. (See chap. 5 in this volume for an early formulation of this model.) A more complex model might also include an interaction term, making the price elasticity itself a function of K.

be rewritten as $\gamma + (\gamma - \phi)/\eta$, showing that the pure productivity effect of R&D will be underestimated as long as it is smaller than its demand effect (ϕ). Klette and Griliches show that if one has a measure of the demand shifter (they use aggregate industry sales y_I for that) one can identify η and β, but one cannot separate ϕ from γ, unless one assumes $\phi = 0$. Without actual individual firm prices, there may be little that we can do here except be more careful in our interpretation of such results.

All of this discussion has focused on estimating the effects of R&D, but what makes different firms choose to undertake different amounts of R&D? I have already noted the lack of good external causal variables. To the extent that differences in R&D reflect technological opportunities, they could be modeled as differences in γ, firms facing (or possessing) different knowledge-producing technologies (though keeping the conventional input component the same within an industry). But unless one brings in some substantive variables which would explain this heterogeneity, such generality adds very little content. (See Mairesse and Griliches 1990 for a parallel discussion of heterogeneity in the physical capital elasticity.) The open modeling question is how to use the observed differences in R&D intensity to infer something interesting about the underlying sources of the heterogeneity in γ.

The final estimation-specification problem I want to discuss is the estimation of spillover effects. The standard approach (for which I must take some responsibility, cf. chap. 2 in this volume) introduces a distance weighted measure of the research efforts of other firms within the same and/or neighboring industries or technological areas. It is clearly a first step in the right direction, but it is also subject to a serious identification problem: Does it work because a firm benefits from the efforts of others or is it just a reflection of spatially correlated technological opportunities? It could be a response to common differences across fishing grounds or, in more technical terms, the individual firm effects α_i may not be independent of each other but may be subject to some local clustering, which will be picked up by the spillover measures. This issue is discussed in a more general context by Manski (1991), under the title "the reflection problem." It would be nice if someone could come up with an approach that could distinguish between these two interpretations, but that is unlikely since the basic model is not identified without much more explicit parameter restrictions and priors on the possible channels of communication.

I have concentrated today on the unfinished business, not to emphasize the "glass-half-empty" aspect, but rather to indicate the rich research opportunities ahead. "Our song is not finished, it's only beginning!"

References

Alston, J. M., and P. G. Pardey. 1996. *Making science pay: The economics of agricultural R&D policy.* Washington, D.C.: AEI Press.

Arrow, K. J. 1962. Economic welfare and the allocation of resources for invention. In *The rate and direction of inventive activity: Economic and social factors,* 609–25. NBER Special Conference Series, vol. 13. Princeton, N.J.: Princeton University Press.

Australian Industry Commission. 1995. *Research and development.* Report no. 44. Canberra: Government Publishing Service, 15 May.

Bachrach, C. 1990. Essays on research and development and competitiveness. Ph.D. diss., Massachusetts Institute of Technology.

Barton, G. T., and M. R. Cooper. 1948. Relation of agricultural production to inputs. *Review of Economics and Statistics* 30 (2): 117–26.

Berndt, E. 1991. *The practice of econometrics: Classic and contemporary.* Reading, Mass.: Addison-Wesley.

Blundell, R. S., and S. Bond. 1995. Initial conditions and moment restrictions in dynamic panel data models. Working Paper W95/17, Institute of Fiscal Studies, London.

Caballero, R. J., and A. B. Jaffe. 1993. How high are the giants' shoulders? In *Macroeconomics Annual 1993,* ed. Oliver J. Blanchard and Stanley Fischer, 15–74. Cambridge, Mass.: MIT Press.

Chamberlain, G. 1984. Panel data. In *Handbook of econometrics,* ed. Z. Griliches and M. Intriligator, vol. 2, 1247–1318. Amsterdam: North-Holland.

Dorfman, R., and P. O. Steiner. 1954. Optimal advertising and optimal quality. *American Economic Review* 44 (December): 826–36.

Evenson, R. E. 1984. International invention: Implications for technology market analysis. In *R&D, patents, and productivity,* ed. Zvi Griliches, 89–123. Chicago: University of Chicago Press.

Griliches, Z. 1958. Research cost and social returns: Hybrid corn and related innovations. *Journal of Political Economy* 66 (5): 419–31.

———. 1964. Research expenditures, education and the aggregate agricultural production function. *American Economic Review* 54 (6): 961–74.

———. 1973. Research expenditures and growth accounting. In *Science and technology in economic growth,* ed. B. R. Williams, 59–95. London: Macmillan.

———. 1981. Market value, R&D, and patents. *Economics Letters* 7:183–87.

———. 1995. R&D and productivity: Econometric results and measurement issues. In *Handbook of the economics of innovation and technological change,* ed. P. Stoneman, 52–89. Oxford: Basil Blackwell.

———. 1996. The discovery of the residual: A historical note. *Journal of Economic Literature* 34 (September): 1324–30.

Griliches, Z., and J. Mairesse. 1998. Production functions: The search for identification. In *The Ragnar Frisch centennial symposium,* ed. S. Ström. Economic Society Monograph Series. Cambridge: Cambridge University Press, forthcoming.

Griliches, Z., and H. Regev. 1995. Firm productivity in Israeli industry, 1979–1988. *Journal of Econometrics* 65: 175–203.

Grossman, G. M., and E. Helpman. 1991. *Innovation and growth in the global economy.* Cambridge, Mass.: MIT Press.

Hall, B. H. 1993. Industrial research in the 1980s: Did the rate of return fall? *Brookings Papers on Economic Activity: Microeconomics* 2:289–331.

———. 1996. The private and social returns to research and development. In *Technology, R&D, and the economy,* ed. B. Smith and C. Barfield, 140–62. Washington, D.C.: Brookings Institution and AEI.

Hall, B. H., and R. E. Hall. 1993. The value and performance of U.S. corporations. *Brookings Papers on Economic Activity* 1–50.

Hall, B. H., and F. Hayashi. 1989. Research and development as an investment. NBER Working Paper no. 2973. Cambridge, Mass.: National Bureau of Economic Research, May.

Heady, E., and J. Dillon. 1961. *Agricultural production functions.* Ames: Iowa State University Press.

Hoch, I. 1955. Estimation of production function parameters and testing for efficiency. *Econometrica* 23 (3): 325–26.

Huffman, W. E., and R. E. Evenson. 1993. *Science for agriculture.* Ames: Iowa State University Press.

Jones, C. I. 1995. R&D-based models of economic growth. *Journal of Political Economy* 103 (4): 759–84.

Jorgenson, D. W. 1973. The economic theory of replacement and depreciation. In *Econometrics and economic theory,* ed. W. Sellekaerts, 189–221. New York: Macmillan.

Klette, T. J. 1994. R&D, scope economies and company structure: A "not so fixed effect" model of plant performance. Statistics Norway, Oslo. Mimeograph.

Klette, T. J., and Z. Griliches. 1996. The inconsistency of common scale estimators when output prices are unobserved and endogenous. *Journal of Applied Econometrics* 11:343–61.

Lach, S. 1994. Non-rivalry of knowledge and R&D's contribution to productivity. Working Paper no. 289, Hebrew University, Jerusalem, June.

Mairesse, J., and Z. Griliches. 1990. Heterogeneity in panel data: Are there stable production functions? In *Essays in honor of Edmond Malinvaud,* ed. P. Champsaur et al., vol. 3, 193–231. Cambridge, Mass.: MIT Press.

Mairesse, J., and B. H. Hall. 1996. Estimating the productivity of research and development in French and U.S. manufacturing firms: An exploration of simultaneity issues with GMM methods. In *International productivity differences and their explanations,* ed. K. Wagner and Bart Van Ark, 285–315. Amsterdam: Elsevier Science.

Mairesse, J., and P. Mohnen. 1995. R&D and productivity: A survey of the econometric literature. Institut National de la Statistique et des Études Économiques (INSEE), Paris. Mimeograph.

Mairesse, J., and M. Sassenou. 1991. R&D and productivity: A survey of econometric studies at the firm level. *STI Review* (Paris: OECD) 8:9–43.

Manski, C. 1991. Identification of endogenous social effects: The reflection problem. *Review of Economic Studies* 60 (3): 531–42.

Marschak, J., and W. Andrews. 1944. Random simultaneous equations and the theory of production. *Econometrica* 12:143–205.

Mundlak, Y. 1961. Empirical production function free of management bias. *Journal of Farm Economics* 43:44–56.

Nadiri, M. I. 1993. Innovations and technological spillovers. NBER Working Paper no. 4423. Cambridge, Mass.: National Bureau of Economic Research.

Nerlove, M. 1958. *Distributed lags and demand analysis.* USDA, Agriculture Handbook No. 141. Washington, D.C.: Government Printing Office.

Olley, S., and A. Pakes. 1996. The dynamics of productivity in the telecommunications equipment industry. *Econometrica* 64 (6): 1263–97.

Pakes, A. 1985. On patents, R&D and the stock market rate of return. *Journal of Political Economy* 93 (2): 390–409.

Romer, P. M. 1990. Endogenous technological change. *Journal of Political Economy* 98 (5): S71–S102.

Schultz, T. W. 1953. *The economic organization of agriculture.* New York: McGraw-Hill.

Tintner, G. 1944. A note on the derivation of production functions from farm records. *Econometrica* 12 (1): 26–34.

Waugh, F. V. 1929. *Quality as a determinant of vegetable prices.* New York: Columbia University Press.

IV   Patent Statistics

13   Patent Statistics as Economic Indicators: A Survey

Overheard at a Catskills Resort
(one guest to another):
—The food is so terrible here.
—Yes. And the portions are so small.

13.1 Introduction

Patents and patent statistics have fascinated economists for a long time. Questions about sources of economic growth, the rate of technological change, the competitive position of different firms and countries, the dynamism of alternative industrial structures and arrangements all tend to revolve around notions of differential inventiveness: What has happened to the "underlying" rate of technical and scientific progress? How has it changed over time and across industries and national boundaries? We have, in fact, almost no good measures on any of this and are thus reduced to pure speculation or to the use of various, only distantly related, "residual" measures and other proxies. In this desert of data, patent statistics loom up as a mirage of wonderful plentitude and objectivity. They are available; they are by definition related to inventiveness, and they are based on what appears to be an objective and only slowly changing standard. No wonder that the idea that something interesting might be learned from such data tends to be rediscovered in each generation.

I shall try, in this survey, to show why I think patent statistics are interesting in spite of all the difficulties that arise in their use and interpretation. To do so I shall first describe the nature of patents and the types of data generated by their issuance, their current availability, and some of the major problems that

Reprinted from the *Journal of Economic Literature* 28 (December 1990): 1661–1707.
I am indebted to my friends and collaborators for many ideas and comments. Parts of this survey borrow heavily (often verbatim) from our earlier work on this topic, especially from Griliches, Ariel Pakes, and Bronwyn Hall (1987), Griliches, Hall, and Pakes (1988), and Griliches (1989). I am indebted to the National Science Foundation (PRA85-12758 and SES 82-08006) and the National Bureau of Economic Research Productivity Program for financial support of this work and to B. Hall, A. Pakes, K. Pavitt, M. Schankerman, and F. M. Scherer for their comments on an earlier draft. The first draft of this survey was begun while I was a guest of the Rockefeller Foundation at the Bellagio Study and Conference Center in Italy. An earlier version of this paper was presented as the W. S. Woytinsky Lecture of 1989 at the University of Michigan.

arise when one tries to use them in economic analysis. I shall next review briefly some of the earlier work on this range of issues, focusing particularly on Jacob Schmookler's work and the questions raised by it. This will be followed by a review of the more modern, "computer age" work of the NBER group (Griliches, Hall, Hausman, Jaffe, Pakes, Schankerman and others), and I shall allude also to similar work of others, especially that of Scherer and the Yale group (Levin, Nelson, Klevorick, Winter, Reiss, Cohen, and others), and the SPRU group (Freeman, Pavitt, Soete, and others). I will not be able to do justice to all of this work (the work of others, of my collaborators, and even my own) but I hope to put up enough guideposts so that the interested reader can find his own way to and through this literature.[1]

Over all this work hovers the question, "What can one use patent statistics for?" Can one use them to interpret longer-term trends? If so, did inventiveness really decline in the 1930s and early 1940s, as indicated by such statistics, and again in the mid-1970s? Does the fact that large firms have a lower patents per R&D dollar ratio imply diminishing returns to such investments? Can one use such numbers to conclude that demand forces are stronger determining factors in the evolution of technological progress than supply factors, than the evolution of science, as Schmookler could be interpreted to say? These are the type of substantive questions that I will explore, though not necessarily answer, in this survey.

There is much that will not be covered in this survey. I will not discuss the literature that deals with the social value of the patent system and with alternative lengths of protection and licensing arrangements. Nor will I deal with the recent and rapidly growing theoretical literature on "patent races" and related game-theoretical topics. One has to draw the line somewhere and the task outlined above may be already too large for one article and one person to deal with. Nor will this be a fully "balanced" survey. I shall, perforce, concentrate more on topics that I and my research associates have found most interesting, slighting thereby, sometimes unwittingly, some of the work of others in this field.[2]

13.2   Patents and Patent Statistics

A patent is a document, issued by an authorized governmental agency, granting the right to exclude anyone else from the production or use of a specific new device, apparatus, or process for a stated number of years (17 in the U.S. currently). The grant is issued to the inventor of this device or process after an examination that focuses on both the novelty of the claimed item and its poten-

1. There are several other good surveys on this range of topics. See especially B. L. Basberg (1987), Keith Pavitt (1978, 1985), Pakes and M. Simpson (1989), Mark Schankerman (1989), and the earlier books by Jacob Schmookler (1966) and C. T. Taylor and Z. A. Silberston (1973).

2. This is especially true of some of the European work on related topics, because it often asks somewhat different questions in a different intellectual framework.

tial utility. The right embedded in the patent can be assigned by the inventor to somebody else, usually to his employer, a corporation, and/or sold to or licensed for use by somebody else. This right can be enforced only by the potential threat of or an actual suit in the courts for infringement damages. The stated purpose of the patent system is to encourage invention and technical progress both by providing a temporary monopoly for the inventor and by forcing the early disclosure of the information necessary for the production of this item or the operation of the new process.

The standard of novelty and utility imposed on the granting of such a right is not very high. (In this it probably does not differ greatly from the standards imposed in most fields on the publication of scientific journal articles.) In the U.S., for example, about 104,000 applications were filed in 1980 for ("utility") patents, of which about 65,000 were granted by the end of 1984; 1,400 more were granted by the end of 1988, with another 300 or so to follow over the next three to five years. These numbers are typical. In the U.S. the granting success rate fluctuated around 65 percent in the 1970s. Roughly speaking, two out of three applications are eventually granted. The granting rate, the stringency of examination, varies greatly across countries and also somewhat over time. It has been over 90 percent in France (until the mid-1970s), about 80 percent in the U.K., and only 35 percent in Germany (Schankerman and Pakes 1986, Table 1), and has varied in the U.S. from a low of 58 percent in 1965 to a high of 72 percent in 1967 (of domestic applications between 1965 and 1980). This variability is, as I will show later, largely associated with differences in the procedures and resources of the various patent offices, implying, therefore, also differences in the average "quality" of a granted patent across countries and periods.

Of the approximately 62,000 patents granted in 1980, 24,000 or 39 percent were granted to foreign inventors, a ratio that has been rising sharply over the last decades, from 19 percent in the early 1960s to 48 percent in 1988. U.S. corporations have accounted for about 73 percent of the total patents granted to U.S. inventors (in 1988), with 2 percent being granted to agencies of the U.S. government, and the rest, 25 percent, going to individual inventors. The fraction accounted for by foreign corporations of total foreign patenting in the U.S. has risen from 64 percent in the mid-1960s to 82 percent in 1988. The general trends in such numbers are depicted in Figures 13.1 and 13.2.

Even though grants can be thought of as a moving average of past applications, it can be seen in these figures that they tend to fluctuate as much or more than the number of patents applied for. It is also clear that economic conditions impinge on the rate of which patents are applied for. Applications were lower during the Great Depression and also during World War II, and their growth was retarded in the 1970s. Moreover, patents assigned to U.S. corporations have not grown at anywhere near the rate of growth of total R&D expenditures in industry (and hence even less than the rate of growth in company-financed R&D in industry). Because I will argue below that patents are a good index of

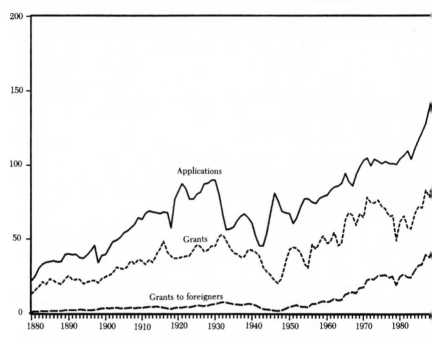

Fig. 13.1   U.S. patent applications and grants, 1880–1989, in thousands
Sources: National Science Board (1987); U.S. Patent and Trademark Office (1977, 1989 and subsequent releases).

inventive activity, a major aspect of which is also measured by R&D expenditures, this view will need reconciling with the aggregate facts depicted in Figure 13.2.

Data are also available at the firm level. In 1984 the largest patenters were General Electric, IBM, and Hitachi with 785, 608, and 596 patents granted respectively. Most of the major U.S. patenting firms experienced a declining trend in patents granted during the 1970s with some recovery in the 1980s, while there has been a rapid growth in U.S. patents granted to the major Japanese electronics and motor vehicles firms (see Griliches 1989, Figure 5).

What I have done in the preceding paragraphs is to discuss the information implicit in patent counts, in the number of patents issued at different times, in different countries, and to different types of inventors. This is the type of information that economists have largely focused on, also cross-classifying it by industry and firm, and it is the use of such numbers in economic analysis that will be the main topic of this survey. But a patent document, which is public after it has been granted, contains much more information than that. Besides information on the names of inventors and their addresses and the name of the organization to which the patent right may have been assigned, it also lists one or more patent classes to which it has been assigned by the exam-

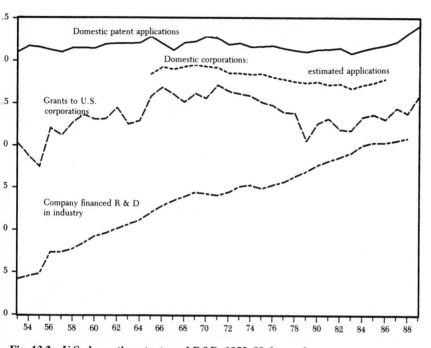

Fig. 13.2   U.S. domestic patents and R&D, 1953–89, log scale
Note: Domestic corporations: estimated applications—U.S. corporate grants by date applied for, inflated by 1/0.65, the average success rate.

iners, cites a number of previous patents and sometimes also scientific articles to which this particular invention may be related, and also finally, but from the social point of view most important, provides a reasonably complete description of the invention covered by this particular patent. Thus, there is much more information derivable from the patent documents than just simply their aggregated number in a particular year or for a particular firm. One can study the geographic distribution of particular inventions, one can investigate citation networks and patterns, and one can actually read the detailed text of a series of patents in a particular field as raw material for an economic-technological history of it. Also, in a number of foreign countries, and in the U.S. since 1982, a non-negligible renewal fee, which rises with the age of the patent, has to be paid. This results in a significant abandonment of patents before their statutory expiration date and generates, in passing, a set of potentially very interesting patent mortality statistics.

In the U.S., aggregate patent statistics classified in a variety of ways are released by the Office of Documentation (formerly the Office of Technology Assessment and Forecast) at the U.S. Patent Office. Major series are published in the National Science Foundation's biannual *Science Indicators* compendium. More detailed tabulations are available from or can be prepared by the

Patent Office and summary information on all recent patents is now also available on CD-ROM disks. The full text of the patents can be found in a number of depository libraries in the U.S. and now can also be accessed via several bibliographic computerized data base services, such as Dialog and BSR. Given the advanced search software available on these services it is possible to conduct a variety of specific searches of such data bases, looking for patents in a particular area or those mentioning a particular material, instrument, or a specific earlier patent, and tabulate the results at a reasonable cost. Patent data for other countries are being collected by the International Patent Documentation Center in Vienna, Austria, and published annually in *World Intellectual Property Annual*. Country summaries are published in OECD, *Main Science and Technology Indicators,* and by various country statistical offices, such as Statistics Canada. Current information on individual foreign patents is available on line from Dialog.

There are two major problems in using patents for economic analysis: classification and intrinsic variability. The first is primarily a technical problem. How does one allocate patent data organized by firms or by substantive patent classes into economically relevant industry or product groupings? I shall discuss this question shortly. The second problem is fundamentally much harder and will be discussed at some length below. It refers to the obvious fact that patents differ greatly in their technical and economic significance. Many of them reflect minor improvements of little economic value. Some of them, however, prove extremely valuable. Unfortunately, we rarely know which are which and do not yet have a good procedure for "weighting" them appropriately. I shall discuss the available scraps of evidence on this topic in Section 13.5 of this survey.

Patents are awarded for an invention of a chemical formula, a mechanical device, or a process (procedure), and now even a computer program. The Patent Office classifies patents into many classes (300+ in the mid-1950s) and even many more subclasses (over 50,000), based on its need to ease the search for prior art. The resulting classification system is based primarily on technological and functional principles and is only rarely related to economists' notions of products or well-defined industries (which may be a mirage anyway). A subclass dealing with the dispensing of liquids contains both a patent for a water pistol and one for a holy water dispenser. Another subclass relating to the dispensing of solids contains patents on both manure spreaders and toothpaste tubes (Schmookler 1966, p. 20). Nevertheless, with one notable exception (Scherer 1984a) and the more recent Canadian data-based studies, almost all attempts to relate patent numbers to industrial data use the subclass system as their basic unit of assignment.

Before any classification is attempted one has to face the inherent ambiguity of the task. Do we want to assign the invention to the industry in which it was made ("origin"), to the industry that is likely to produce it, or to the industry that will use the resulting product or process and whose productivity may benefit thereby (destination or industry of "use")? Consider, as an example, the case of a new plow invented in a chemical firm's research laboratory as part of its project on new combined fertilizer and tillage systems. It depends on what question is to be asked of the data. If we want to study the returns to R&D expenditures we may wish to count it in the chemical industry whence the money came to develop it. If we want to analyze the impact of technological change on the rate of investment, on the sale of new equipment, we may wish to count it in the farm equipment industry. If we are interested in its effects on measured productivity we are more likely to count it as being relevant to agriculture. This difference in questions reflects itself also in different classification strategies pursued by different researchers.

Schmookler, in his main work, chose to construct data on capital goods patents relevant to a particular industry by reviewing carefully a set of subclasses, sampling a number of patents in them, and deciding whether most of them were indeed likely to be used in the industry in question. He then aggregated the total number of patents in each of the accepted subclasses into an industrywide total. In this way he constructed time series for capital goods inventions of relevance for the railroad industry, the paper-making industry, petroleum refining, and building construction. By focusing on capital goods inventions only and on a few selected and better-defined industries, and by not insisting on completeness or inclusivity, he made life quite a bit easier for himself. This choice forced him, however, to forgo any serious analysis of the patenting of consumer goods or manufacturing processes. His industrial classification was based on the third type: the locus of potential use for the new or improved capital good.

In the mid-1970s the Patent Office established a research unit, the Office of Technology Assessment and Forecast (OTAF). One of its first jobs, on a contract from the Science Indicators Unit of the National Science Foundation (NSF), was to try to produce patent statistics at the three- and two-and-a-half-digit standard industrial classification (SIC) levels corresponding roughly to the NSF's classification of applied research and development by product field. This was done by developing a "concordance" between the patent class and subclass classification and the SIC. Where a subclass did not obviously belong in a single SIC industry, it was counted in all of the relevant ones, resulting in significant double counting. The industrial allocation was based primarily on the second notion of the relevant industrial classification: Patents were allocated to the industries that were expected to produce the products designed by them or to use the new processes in the manufacture of their products. The new plow patent, in the previous example, would be assigned by the OTAF concordance to the farm equipment manufacturing industry.

The OTAF concordance was criticized early on because of both the arbitrariness in the assignment of some of the subclasses and the misleading inferences that could arise from the pervasive double counting (F. M. Scherer 1982a; Luc Soete 1983).[3] One of the two most glaring examples of problems raised by such procedures was the appearance of significant and fast-growing patenting by the Japanese in the aircraft industry, a rather surprising and mysterious development given the rather rudimentary state of the Japanese aircraft industry at that time. It turned out to be the result of allocating the "engines" patents category to both motor vehicles and aircraft. Almost all of the Japanese engine patents were automobile engine patents and because patenting in the engine category was high relative to other kinds of aircraft patents, it came to dominate the aircraft patents category almost entirely. The other example was provided by the agricultural chemicals and drug industries where the assigned patents overlapped at the rate of 90 percent (!). That is, only 10 percent of the patents counted in those industries were unique to them. It is doubtful whether such heavily overlapping data can be used in economic analyses that try to learn something about sources of technical progress by examining the contrasting experiences of different industries. The OTAF "industry" data contains too little independent information on the patenting history of actual industries.

As a result of such criticisms, the 1985 version of this concordance has been improved by correcting some of the more obvious errors and by fractionalizing the allocation of dubious subclasses, reducing thereby their overall importance in the final totals. But most of the basic questions of classification still remain to be answered.

One way to get around some of these problems is to have the patent examiner assign the individual patent to one or several SIC industries, based on potential use. This is now being done in the Canadian patent system. One possibility, currently being pursued by Robert Evenson and his students, is to take a sample of U.S. patents also patented in Canada and to cross-tabulate the Canadian SIC assignments against the U.S. patent classification system, deriving thereby an empirically based and already naturally fractionalized alternative concordance (see annex A of A. S. Englander, R. Evenson, and M. Hanazaki 1988; Evenson, S. Kortum, and J. Putnam 1988; Kortum and Putnam 1989).

An alternative approach, first pursued by Scherer (1965a and 1965b) and more currently by the NBER group (see John Bound et al. 1984), starts from patent totals for particular firms and then groups them into industries according to the firm's primary activity. This is an "origin" classification. It may be useful for the analysis of firm level data, relating patents to R&D investments and the subsequent fortunes of the firms where they had been originally developed. But it is much less useful for the analysis of industrial data, both because of the conglomerateness of many of the large U.S. corporations and because particular patents may be having an impact far beyond the boundaries of their industry of "origin."

---

3. See OTAF 1985, the proceedings of the conference on the concordance, for a more detailed discussion of some of these issues.

The extensive diversification of many firms and also the various merger waves create severe technical problems in trying to use the patent data even at the individual corporation level. What is noted on the patent is the name of the organization to which it has been assigned. This organization can easily be a subsidiary or a separate division of a larger company. Moreover, a company may change its name and/or may merge. Because the patent office does not employ a consistent company code in its computer record, except for the "top patenting companies" where the list of subsidiaries is checked manually, the company patenting numbers produced by a simple aggregation of its computer records can be seriously incomplete (see B. H. Hall et al. 1988 for additional detail on this range of issues).

Because of such considerations and because he was interested in tracing through the spillover effects of R&D on productivity in industries that were most likely to benefit from them, Scherer (1982b, 1984a) undertook the large task of examining over 15,000 patents awarded from June 1976 through March 1977 to the 443 largest U.S. manufacturing corporations represented in the Federal Trade Commission Lines of Business survey in 1974. There are at least two unique aspects to this data construction effort: First, each patent was examined individually, classified as to product or process invention, and assigned to up to three potential industries of "use" or two possible general use categories. In addition, the patent was also assigned to an industry of "origin" on the basis of the information on the location of the inventors within the Lines of Business structure of the particular company. That is, and this is the second unique aspect of these data, the industry of origin was defined "below" the company level, at the more relevant "business" or divisional level, and the R&D expenditures of the companies were similarly subdivided and matched at this more appropriate industrial level. One of the final products of this work was a "technology flow" matrix, using the resulting cross-classification of patents by industry of origin and industry of use to "link" the industries in which R&D expenditures have been incurred to industries whose productivity growth may reflect the fruits of such expenditures. (Such a matrix was suggested by Schmookler 1966, p. 167.) Unfortunately, this large, one-time data construction effort does not really have a time-series dimension to it. Moreover, the FTC discontinued collecting data at the Lines of Business level in 1979, making it less likely that it could be replicated in the future.

A less ambitious but somewhat more extensive data construction effort was pursued by the NBER group (see Bound et al. 1984; Griliches, Pakes, and Hall 1987; and Hall et al. 1988), who tried to match the patent office data on patents issued to all organizations from 1969 through 1982 with income and balance sheet and stock market value data for all publicly traded manufacturing corporations, defined as of 1976, and also create a consistent historical record for them for the period 1959–81. The resulting data sets consisted of a cross-section of about 2,600 firms in 1976 (with over 1,700 firms receiving at least one patent between 1969 and 1979, about 1,000 firms applying for at least one, ultimately granted, patent in 1976, and about 1,500 firms reporting R&D expenditures in 1976) and a panel of about 1,000 to 1,800 firms with detailed data between 1963 and 1981, with a subset of about 700 firms reporting consistent R&D data between 1972 and 1980. These data sets formed the basis for a number of studies that will be discussed below.

13.3   Patents as Indicators of What?

There are two ways of asking this question: What aspects of economic activity do patent statistics actually capture? And, what would we like them to measure? Ultimately, only the first question is of relevance but it is useful to spend some time on the second, because it provides some understanding of the research in this field.

Roughly speaking, we would like to measure and understand better the economic processes that lead to the reduction in the cost of producing existing products and the development of new products and services. We would like to measure both the inputs and the outputs of such processes, to understand what determines the allocation of resources to such "technology changing" activities, and also what is happening and why to the efficiency with which they are pursued in different times and in different places. Assuming that different new products can be brought to a common denominator through the use of some meta-hedonic function, one can think of invention as shifting outward the production possibilities frontier for some generalized aggregate of potential human wants. Ideally, we might hope that patent statistics would provide a measure of the output of such an activity, a direct reading on the rate at which the potential production possibilities frontier is shifting outward. The reality, however, is very far from it.

The dream of getting hold of an output indicator of inventive activity is one of the strong motivating forces for economic research in this area. After all, a patent does represent a minimal quantum of invention that has passed both the scrutiny of the patent office as to its novelty and the test of the investment of effort and resources by the inventor and his organization into the development of this product or idea, indicating thereby the presence of a non-negligible expectation as to its ultimate utility and marketability. One recognizes, of course, the presence of a whole host of problems: Not all inventions are patentable, not all inventions are patented, and the inventions that are patented differ greatly in "quality," in the magnitude of inventive output associated with them. The first two problems, one thinks, can be taken care of by industry dummy variables, or by limiting the analysis to a particular sector or industry. For the third, one tries to invoke the help of the "law of large numbers": "The economic . . . significance of any sampled patent can also be interpreted as a random variable with some probability distribution" (Scherer 1965b, p. 1098). The question whether our samples are large enough, given the underlying heterogeneity in what is measured by a patent, is a topic to which I shall return below.

It is interesting to note that Schmookler started out thinking that he could use patent statistics as an index of inventive output and as an explanation of the growth in the aggregate efficiency of the U.S. economy. Schmookler was the first, as far as I can tell, to publish numbers on aggregate "total factor productivity growth" (Schmookler 1952) (though he never seemed to have claimed much originality for it), and to relate them to patent statistics (Schmookler 1951). Unfortunately, the relationship did not work. There seemed to be little correlation between aggregate total factor productivity and total patenting numbers. Schmookler did not give up on patent statistics but ultimately redefined what he thought they could do. In his hands patents became an index of inventive "activity," primarily an input rather than an output index.

He moved, essentially, in the direction of what patents can measure rather than what we would want them to measure. His interpretation of inventive activity became quite narrow. It excluded research, which he interpreted as a search for new knowledge, an attempt to discover new properties of classes of objects or processes, and it also excluded development, which is largely the development and refinement of already made inventions (even though quite a few patents are likely to be generated also during this phase). Inventive activity per se is "work specifically directed towards the formulation of the essential properties of a novel product or process" (Schmookler 1966, p. 8). This is an "input" definition, to be thought of as computable in man-hour equivalents, and corresponds to only a very thin slice, both quantitatively and in the time dimension, of what is usually covered by the notion of R&D and the associated R&D statistics.

One should keep in mind, however, the historical context of most of the earlier work on patents. There were no R&D expenditure statistics of any generality before the late 1950s and only scattered numbers on scientists employed in different industrial laboratories or on the distribution of the technically trained labor force (see David Mowery 1983). Thus, an indicator of input was also valuable. There was almost no substitute for it. Even today, with data much more plentiful, the available detail in the published R&D statistics is still quite limited. Thus, as I shall argue below, showing that patent statistics are a good indicator of inputs into inventive activity is a useful accomplishment on its own merit. It allows us an insight into what is going on in more areas and also in much more detail than is possible to glimpse from the available R&D statistics.

How does one come to know whether patent statistics measure anything interesting? Input or output? One way is to look for correlations between patent counts and other variables that are thought to matter: input measures such as R&D expenditures, and output measures such as productivity growth, profitability, or the stock market value of the firm. It is useful, therefore, to introduce here a figure (Figure 13.3) from Pakes and Griliches (1984) which essentially restates the previous sentence in graphic terms and allows a more detailed discussion of its underlying assumptions.

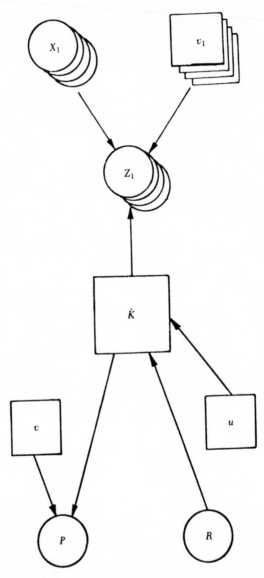

Fig. 13.3 Knowledge production function: a simplified path analysis diagram

Source: Pakes and Griliches (1984), figure 3.1.

Notes: R = research expenditures.

$\dot{K}$ = additions to economically valuable knowledge.

P = patents, a quantitative indicator of the number of inventions.

Z's = indicators of expected or realized benefits from invention.

X's = other observed variables influencing the *Z*'s.

u, v = other unobserved influences, assumed random and mutually uncorrelated.

In the center of Figure 13.3 is an unobservable variable, $\dot{K}$, the net accretion of economically valuable knowledge. This is the variable that we would like to measure. It is the measure of "inventive output" which one would hope that patents would be a good indicator of. The diagram indicates that and adds an error v to the determinants of patenting, making them an imperfect, fallible measure of $\dot{K}$. The causal part of this diagram starts in the lower right-hand corner with some observable measure of resources invested in inventive activity (R), usually R&D expenditures, or the number of research scientists, which are directed at the production of $\dot{K}$. Because knowledge production is stochastic, the u term is added to reflect its changing efficiency and the impact of other informal and unmeasured sources of $\dot{K}$. The variables that we are ultimately interested in explaining are represented by the Z's. These could be various measures of growth, productivity, profitability, or the stock market value of a firm or industry. They are all affected by the unobservable $\dot{K}$, by other measurable variables X, and by additional random components, the e's.

A number of extreme simplifications were made in drawing this figure and in defining the various terms. For example, the relationship between $\dot{K}$ and K should be defined explicitly to allow for the possibility of decay in the private value of knowledge. Also, R is taken as exogenous. If, as is likely, the u's are correlated over time, then one might expect them to feed back into R in subsequent periods. Nor do patents play an explicit economic role here. They are just an indicator of $\dot{K}$. The assumption being made is that some random fraction of $\dot{K}$ gets patented. It is a statistical descriptive model rather than a "theory" of patenting. A "theory" would have to be more explicit about the conditions (economic, technological, and legal) under which the benefits from applying for a patent outweigh the direct costs of application and the potential consequences of disclosing the technology. This would add more structure to the relationship between P and $\dot{K}$.

Such a theory would start with the underlying notion of a research project whose success depends stochastically on both the amount of resources devoted to it and the amount of time that such resources have been deployed. Each technical success is associated with an expectation of the ultimate economic value of a patent to the inventor or the employer. If this expectation exceeds a certain minimum, the cost of patenting, a patent will be applied for. That is, the number of patents applied for is a count of the number of successful projects (inventions) with the economic value of the patent right exceeding a minimal threshold level. If the distribution of the expected value of patenting successful projects remains stable, and if the level of current and past R&D expenditures shifts the probability that projects will be technically successful, an increase in the number of patents can be taken as an indicator of an upward shift in the distribution of $\dot{K}$. Whether the relationship is proportional will depend on the shape of the assumed distributions and the nature of the underlying shifts in them. What is depicted in Figure 13.3 is at best a very crude reduced-form-type relation whose theoretical underpinnings have still to be worked out. But one has to start someplace.[4]

There are also ambiguities in the definition of $\dot{K}$ and K. Are we talking about private or social returns to knowledge? That depends on the Z's available to us and the question we are particularly interested in answering. For an analysis of productivity movements at the level of industries, it is the social value that we care about. For an analysis of the stock market value of different firms, only the private value version makes any sense. One may also wish to distinguish between the value of patent *rights* and the economic value of a particular patent. It is the latter notion that we might be interested in, though it is the former that is likely to show up in survey responses of patentors or be implicit in the decision whether to pay a fee and renew a particular patent. Nevertheless, Figure 13.3 does provide a schema for discussing much of the research in this area and in particular the question of the "quality" of patent counts as indicators of economically valuable knowledge.

There are several different ways of rephrasing this question: (1) How good is P as an indicator of $\dot{K}$? (2) If P is an "output" measure and R is an "input" measure, are we better off in having one or the other if we had to, or could, make such a choice? (3) What is the value added of P, above and beyond R, to the explanation of the Z's? Because $\dot{K}$ is intrinsically unobservable, the first question cannot really be answered without embedding it in some model such as is sketched out in this figure. It may be helpful, at this point, to write down the simplest possible model that might correspond to this figure:

$$\dot{K} = R + u,$$

$$P = a\dot{K} + v = aR + au + v,$$

$$Z = b\dot{K} + e = bR + bu + e,$$

where the first equation is the "knowledge production function" with the unobservable $\dot{K}$ being measured in units of R; the second equation is the indicator function relating P to $\dot{K}$; and the third equation represents the influence of $\dot{K}$ on subsequent variables of interest. The important assumption that will be made here is that the various random components u, v, and e are independent of each other. I need not repeat the caveats about the simplicity of this model. It is adequate, however, for making the following points: (1) The "quality" of P as an indicator of $\dot{K}$ depends on the size of v, the error in the indicator relationship. If we take its variance as a measure of its error and we substitute R for $\dot{K}$ in this relationship, as in the right-hand part of the second equation above, we see that under the assumptions of the model the "quality" of the

---

4. Of course, one need not start here. It is a particularly American view, which finds thinking in terms of a "production function of knowledge" congenial and useful, and looks for patents to serve as a proxy for the "output" of this process. Less "neoclassically" oriented economists would deny the usefulness of this view or the uniform direction of causality that it implicitly espouses.

relationship between P and R provides a lower bound on the "quality" of P as an indicator of $\dot{K}$. That is, var($au + v$) > var(v). This argument suggests looking at the correlation between P and R and claiming that if $\dot{K}$ is the output of the R process and P is an indicator of its success then the correlation between P and $\dot{K}$ would have been even higher, if it could have been measured. This is the sense in which the correlation coefficient between P and R provides a downward biased measure of the quality of P as a indicator.[5] (2) The comparative qualities of P and R as proxies for $\dot{K}$ depend on the relative size of the variance of v and u. If the error of measurement in P is large relative to the stochastic fluctuation in $\dot{K}$, then R may be the better variable even if it does not reflect u. (3) If the stochastic component of $\dot{K}$ is important and if P actually captures any of it, there should be some value added in P above and beyond R. But if the error of measurement in P is large and the samples are small, we may not really see it in the regressions results when P is included as an additional variable.

13.4 Patents and R&D

In the attempt to "validate" patents as an economic indicator, investigators have repeatedly examined the relationship of patents to R&D activity. Schmookler (1966, ch. 2) and Scherer (1965a) are leading examples of earlier investigations. More recent results can be found in Bound et al. (1984), Hall, Griliches, and Hausman (1986), Pakes and Griliches (1984), Scherer (1983), and Acs and Audretsch (1989). Several conclusions as well as a number of unresolved questions emerge from this work.

A major conclusion, emphasized by Pakes and Griliches, is that there is quite a strong relationship between R&D and the number of patents received at the cross-sectional level, across firms and industries. The median R-square is on the order of 0.9, indicating that patents may indeed be a good indicator of unobserved inventive output, at least in this dimension. That this relationship is not just due to size differences can be seen in Figure 13.4 (taken from Bound et al. 1984), which plots both patents and R&D per unit of a firm's assets.

The same relationship, though still statistically significant, is much weaker in the within-firms time-series dimension. The median R-square here is on the order of 0.3 (in contrast to the 0.9 in the cross-sectional dimension). Nevertheless, the evidence is quite strong that when a firm changes its R&D expenditures, parallel changes occur also in its patent numbers. The relationship is

---

5. This conclusion depends on the additive nature of the error in the indicator function. If $\dot{K}$ were to be looked at just as an aggregation of inventive events, each with a potential value of its own, drawn independently from some value distribution, and P counted only some fraction of such events and was not related to their values (as in the calculations outlined in Section 13.6), then the above inequalities would not hold anymore. If, on the other hand, the patenting decision itself were a function of the size of the expected gain from the invention, as noted in the text, then the situation would be somewhere in between.

Log 10 of Patents/Assets

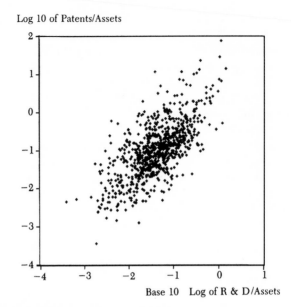

Base 10   Log of R & D/Assets

Fig. 13.4   Log of patents/assets versus log of R&D assets
Source: Bound et al. (1984), figure 2.4.

close to contemporaneous with some lag effects which are small and not well estimated (Hall, Griliches, and Hausman 1986). This is consistent with the observation that patents tend to be taken out relatively early in the life of a research project. Because the bulk of R&D expenditures are spent on development, most of the time-series variance in this variable must come from the differential success in the further development of existing projects rather than from the initiation of new ones.[6] The relatively low correlations in the time dimension should, therefore, not be all that surprising, but they imply that patent numbers are a much poorer indicator of short-term changes in the output of inventive activity or the "fecundity" of R&D.

The question "Are there diminishing returns to R&D?" hovers over much of this work. In the cross-sectional dimension it is related to the "Schumpeterian" question whether large firms and large R&D labs are more or less efficient as "engines of innovation" (see William Baldwin and John Scott 1987, ch. 3, and Cohen and Levin 1989 for more general reviews of this topic). In the time-series dimension one is faced with the declining ratio of patents received per R&D dollar spent and the worry that technological and inventive opportunities are being exhausted. There is also the question of how one reconciles the significantly larger estimates of the elasticity of patenting with respect to R&D in the cross-sectional versus the time-series dimension.

6. To the extent that some patents arise in the development stage, they would also be related to R&D with only a short lag.

At the cross-sectional level the story is relatively simple. Small firms appear to be more "efficient," receiving a larger number of patents per R&D dollar. This can be seen most easily in Figure 13.5 (from Bound et al. 1984), which plots the patents per R&D ratio as a function of the size of the R&D program. It shows both the much higher ratio for small firms and the fact that this relationship becomes effectively flat beyond some minimum size. At the larger firm level, where antitrust policy might be relevant, there is no strong evidence of diminishing returns to the size of the R&D effort. (This is also the conclusion reached by Scherer (1983) on the basis of a different and better set of data.) Given the nonlinearity and the noisiness in this relation, the finding of "diminishing returns" is quite sensitive to functional form, weighting schemes, and the particular point at which the elasticity is evaluated.

All of this can be seen in Figure 13.6, also taken from Bound et al., which plots the original data and the results of fitting various different models to the same data. Two of the estimation techniques, Poisson and nonlinear least squares (NLLS) indicate diminishing returns, while the other two techniques, ordinary least squares (OLS) and negative binomial (NB), imply increasing returns. A glance at the figure will make it clear how a differential emphasis on parts of the data (large versus small firms and the treatment of zeroes—not visible in the figure) could result in such conflicting estimates. Basically there is a sharp contrast between smaller and larger firms. For larger firms the relationship is close to linear while there is a reasonably large number of smaller firms that exhibit significant patenting while reporting very little R&D. When divided into two samples, small ($N = 1,015$) and large ($N = 483$), with \$2 million in R&D expenditures as the dividing line, the estimated average elasticities are 0.44 and 1.04 respectively. The latter number falls to 0.8 (0.1) if one allows separately for the zero patents observations. Though this estimate of the elasticity of patenting with respect to R&D for the larger firms is still "significantly" less than unity at conventional test levels, allowing for the possibility that the R&D numbers are themselves subject to error, one cannot really reject the hypothesis of constant returns in this size range, because the "reciprocal" regression of R&D on patents implies increasing returns to or decreasing costs of getting a patent. (The estimated elasticity of R&D with respect to patents is 0.76.)

The appearance of diminishing returns at the cross-sectional level is due, I think, primarily to two effects: selectivity and the differential role of formal R&D and patents for small and large firms. Most of the data sets available to us are not based on a random or carefully stratified sample from the relevant underlying population. Rather, they are "opportunity" samples, based on other criteria. For example, the 1976 cross-section of Bound et al. is based on all manufacturing firms listed on the New York and American stock exchanges and also on the over-the-counter market. But while almost all relevant large firms are so listed, only a relatively small number of the smaller firms trade in these markets. To be included in (listed on) the market, a small firm has to be

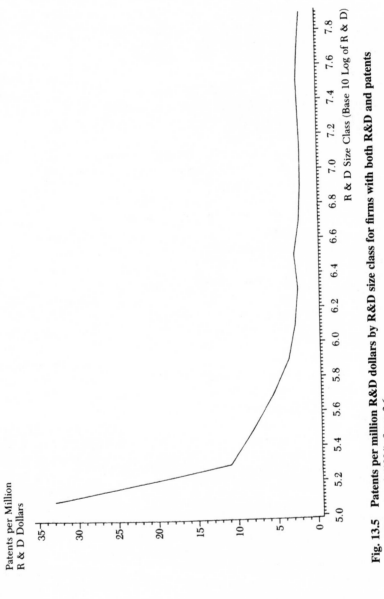

Fig. 13.5 Patents per million R&D dollars by R&D size class for firms with both R&D and patents
Source: Bound et al. (1984), figure 2.6.

Log of Patents

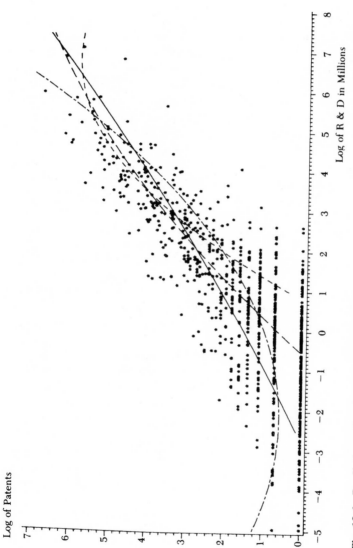

Fig. 13.6 Predictions of various patents models

Source: Bound et al. (1984), figure 2.5.

Note: *** = data; – – – = negative binomial; – – – = nonlinear least squares; –––––– = ordinary least squares; ––––– = Poisson.

Log of R & D in Millions

in some sense more "successful" than those that are not, more "interesting" to the traders. Thus, it is not surprising that it may also hold more patents than might be expected, given its size and R&D program. How atypical these small firms might be is suggested by the rarity of their selection. Table 13.1 shows the number of firms by size (employment) in this cross-section and the corresponding numbers in the relevant population. While about two-thirds of the large manufacturing firms are included, the smaller ones represent less than 1 percent of all small firms and are obviously a heavily selected lot. Unfortunately, we have no information on the firms not in the sample and hence cannot make an appropriate sample selectivity adjustment.

Another source of the difference between small and large firms is in the role of formal R&D in them and the differential importance of patents to them. A significant amount of patenting is not the result of formal R&D activities though the relative importance of organized R&D rises with the size of the company. Small firms are likely to be doing relatively more informal R&D, reporting less of it, and hence providing the appearance of more patents per reported R&D dollar.[7] Also, for such firms patents may represent their major hope for ultimate success and hence would lead them to pursue them with more vigor. A well-established major firm does not depend as much on current patenting for its viability or the survival of its market position. Thus, even at equal underlying true inventiveness rates, the propensity to patent may be lower for large firms, at least relative to the successful new entrants in their field. But in the major range of the data, from middle size to giant firms, there is little evidence for diminishing returns, at least in terms of patents per R&D dollar.[8] That is not surprising, after all. If there were such diminishing returns, firms could split themselves into divisions or separate enterprises and escape them.

The time-series dimension has been examined most extensively by Hall, Griliches, and Hausman (1986) (see also Pakes and Griliches 1984 and Jerry Hausman, Hall, and Griliches 1984). The estimated total elasticity of patents with respect to R&D expenditures is between 0.3 and 0.6, even after allowing for several lagged effects. This finding, in contrast to the cross-sectional results, is robust with respect to differential weighting and alternative estimation methods. It is tempting then to accept the diminishing returns result in the

7. Sirrilli (1987) shows that in small firms in Italy (fewer than 100 employees) over a third of the inventors (36 percent) come from production and quality and control activities, while in the large firms (more than 1,000 employees) only 11 percent of the inventors come from this category. The proportion of patents originating in formal R&D rises from 39 percent in small firms to 63 percent in the large ones with the rest (25 and 26 percent) being in the more ambiguous "design" category. Similar conclusions can also be inferred from A. Kleinknecht (1987), who reports a significant underestimate of R&D activities in small firms by the conventional data collection methodology.

8. See Jensen (1987) for similar results using new chemical entities rather than patents. For contradictory evidence, using other measures, see Scherer (1984b, ch. 11) and Acs and Audretsch (1989).

Table 13.1   **Selectivity of Firms in 1976 Cross-Section, by Size of Employment**

Employment	Number of Firms in Cross-Section[a]	Number of Firms in Census of Enterprises[b]	Ratio
<10	24	16,000	.0015
10–99	301	14,300	.021
100–999	952	9,000	.106
1,000+	1,267	1,900	.667
Total	2,541	41,200	.062

[a]With good employment data. Computed from the data used in Bound et al. (1984).
[b]In comparable manufacturing industries. From U.S. Bureau of the Census (1981), table 3, pp. 152–98.

within-time-series dimension and interpret it as reflecting real diminishing returns, in terms of patents received, to the expansion of existing research programs. But this conclusion is unnecessary. The relationship between annual changes in R&D and in patenting is very weak, although "statistically" significant, at the firm level. If one allows for the possibility that much of the annual fluctuations in R&D has little to do with that part of inventive activity that generates patents, being largely the result of fluctuations in and vagaries of the development portion of the various research projects, then the "relevant" R&D is measured with error and the estimated coefficients are downward biased. This is not a pure "measurement error" case, because reported R&D may be correctly reported as far as its own definition goes, but not exactly in the way we want (R&D directed at patentable inventions). This is parallel to the transitory-permanent distinction in consumption theory and is isomorphic to the "errors-in-variables" model. Invoking the latter, we may be able to "bracket" the true returns to scale coefficient by running the regression the other way, R&D on patents, and computing the reciprocal of the resulting coefficient. The low correlation between the two rates of change results also in a very low coefficient in this second dimension, on the order of 0.1–0.2, and an implication of *increasing* returns. The latter should not be taken seriously either, because it is the result of the great randomness in the patent series themselves. The point of this digression is, however, to remind one that the appearance of diminishing returns in such data could be an artifact of the incompleteness of the underlying data rather than a reflection of the characteristics of the invention process itself. As of the moment, the evidence is suggestive but not conclusive.

Besides differing by size of firm, the R&D to patents relationship differs also across industries. In absolute terms, the industries with the largest numbers of patents are drugs, plastics, other rubber products, and computers (in Scherer's line of business-based data) and instruments, communication equipment, and industrial chemicals (in the OTAF concordance–based data). In terms of the "propensity to patent" (patents per R&D dollar), the differences are less apparent and more difficult to interpret. One can look at the tables (5–9) in Griliches (1989) or the appendix to Iain Cockburn and Griliches (1988) and observe that industries with a "low" propensity to patent include obvious cases of large R&D industries with significant governmental research support, such as motor vehicles and aircraft, who patent very much less than would be predicted from their R&D numbers alone. Among the industries with a "high" propensity to patent, besides the expected presence of communication equipment, there are a number of industries (such as screws, nuts, and bolts) whose appearance is due to their doing very little R&D but still taking out occasional patents. An attempt to explain the dispersion in such numbers across industries using data from the Yale Survey (Levin et al. 1987) on the perceived differential effectiveness of patents as a method of appropriating the benefits from innovation was largely unsuccessful. The patent to R&D ratios appear to be dominated by what may be largely irrelevant fluctuations in the R&D numbers and the Yale Survey responses themselves appear to have little relevant cross-industry variability in them (see Griliches 1987; Cockburn and Griliches 1988; and Cockburn 1989). For example, while the drug industry has the highest rating on the "patents provide protection" scale, its patents per R&D ratio is much lower than that for firms in the paper industry, where the effectiveness of patents is rated to be somewhat below average (see Cockburn and Griliches 1988, appendix C). Because the effectiveness of patents as an appropriability mechanism will affect also the incentive to do R&D, the resulting impact on the ratio of the two is far from obvious. In drugs it clearly encourages research with the result that even with extensive patenting the observed ratio is not much above average. Thus, it is probably misleading to interpret such numbers as being direct indicators of either the effectiveness of patenting or the efficiency of the R&D processes.

13.5 Patent Rights and Patent Values

Because the economic significance of individual patents is so variable, there has been continued interest in trying to estimate the average value of patent rights, the average value of the invention represented by a particular patent, and the dispersion in both of these concepts. Looking at patents as indicators of success of the underlying inventive activity or R&D program, we are mainly interested in the second concept. The available data, however, are mostly informative only about the first: the value associated with the differential legal situation created by the possession of the patent.

There are basically three sources of data on this topic: (1) Results of direct surveys of patent owners or assignees about past returns and the potential market value of their rights. (2) The valuation implicit in the decision whether to pay a fee to renew the patent, a decision that had to be made by European patent holders in the past and is now also facing U.S. patent holders. (3) Econometric analyses of the relationship of some other value-denominated variable, such as profits or stock market value, to the number of patents. An example is the use of patent numbers as a proxy for "intangible" capital in stock market value of the firm regressions.

The most detailed and extensive survey of patent holders was conducted over 30 years ago by Barkev Sanders and associates at the Patent and Trademarks Foundation (see J. Rossman and B. S. Sanders 1957; Sanders, Rossman, and L. J. Harris 1958; and Sanders 1962, 1964, and the discussion of it in Schmookler's book, 1966, pp. 47–55). They conducted a mail survey in 1957 of the owners and assignees of a 2 percent random sample of all patents issued in 1938, 1948, and 1952. There were two major findings in this survey: (1) A surprisingly large fraction of all sampled patents was reported to have been "used" commercially, either currently or in the past. The actual fraction "used" is sensitive to the treatment of nonresponse: It is over 55 percent for those responding and about 41 percent if one assumes that nonresponse is equivalent to nonuse. The "use" percentage is higher for "small" companies, but so also is the nonresponse rate (71 percent used among respondents, 40 percent if adjusted for nonresponse). Thus, it is not true that most patents are never used and are hence not associated with a significant economic event. This finding is also consistent with the renewal information to be discussed below. In Europe, about 50 percent of all patents granted are still being renewed and a renewal fee is being paid ten years after they had been applied for. (2) The reported economic gain from the innovations associated with these patents was highly dispersed. Among the patents reported to be in current use and with relevant numerical responses and a positive gain (accounting for about 20 percent of all the relevant responses), the mean value was $577,000 per patent, but the median value was only about $25,000 (implying, under the assumption of log normality, 2.5 as the coefficient of variation and a standard deviation of about $1.5 million). If one includes all the no gain, loss, and not yet used patents, the mean gain falls to about $112,000, and the median is close to zero or below (computed from the tables in Sanders, Rossman, and Harris 1958, pp. 355 and 357). Even this lower mean number is quite impressive, roughly equivalent to $473,000 per average patent in 1988 prices (using the GNP deflator to convert it from 1957 prices), but so also is the associated dispersion. Scherer (1965b) reports that fitting a Pareto-Levy distribution to these data graphically yielded an estimate of the exponent (α) of about 0.5, implying a distribution with no finite mean or variance. If this were truly the case, then even in large samples the mean value of patents would not converge rapidly, if at all, to its underlying population average.

There have been only very few other attempts at such a survey and they all reach rather similar conclusions. Schmookler (1966, pp. 54–55) reports on a small mail sample with a mean value of $80,000 and a median of about zero. In 1982 the Chemistry Program of the NSF decided to evaluate the economic value of patents attributable to its grants (Cutler 1984). Of the 96 patents surveyed, 52 had been licensed or were deemed licensable with an average "economic value" of about $500,000 per patent. (The concept of "economic value" is unclear in this study. It appears to refer to total potential sales of the product rather than net returns to the owners of the patent.) A related study, done for the NSF by SRI International (1985), examined a sample of patents received by the grantees of the Engineering Program and estimated the royalty potential of each patent, which turned out to be about $73,000 on average, again with a very large dispersion. A more representative and large-scale survey of patent holders is both feasible and desirable but nothing has been done in this regard since 1957 and there does not seem to be anything like it in the works either in the U.S. or abroad.

In many countries and recently also in the U.S., holders of patents must pay an annual renewal fee in order to keep their patents in force. If the renewal fee is not paid in any single year the patent is permanently canceled. If we assume that renewal decisions are based on economic criteria, agents will renew their patents only if the value of holding them over an additional year exceeds the cost of such renewal. Observations on the proportion of patents that are renewed at alternative ages, together with the relevant renewal fee schedules, will then contain information on the distribution of the value of holding patents, and on the evolution of this distribution function over the lifespan of the patents. Because patent rights are seldom marketed, this is one of the few sources of information on their value. In a series of papers Pakes and Schankerman (1984), Pakes (1986), and Schankerman and Pakes (1986) present and estimate models that allow them to recover the distribution of returns from holding patents at each age over their lifespan. Because the renewal decision is based on the value of patent protection to the patentee, the procedure used in these articles directly estimates the private value of the benefits derived from the patent laws.

In Figure 13.7 typical European data on renewal fees and patent survival proportions are reproduced from Schankerman and Pakes (1986). They indicate several interesting facts that should be kept in mind. About half of all patents are renewed through age 10, indicating a significant expectation of some "usefulness" for the majority of patents for some non-negligible time period. On the other hand, the same data indicate that about half of all patents are not renewed within ten years, indicating that the expected value of the future income stream from these rights has fallen below the rather low renewal cost. This implies that the majority of patents are either of low value, or that their value depreciates (obsoletes) rapidly, or both. About 10 percent of all patents survive and pay the fees for the whole statutory period and obviously include a smaller number of very valuable patents. Pakes and Schankerman use these facts in their various papers to construct models of the renewal process and estimate both a distribution of the underlying patent right values and also their rate of depreciation. Given the existence of an open-ended class of patents in these data (those paying the renewal fees throughout the whole period) and the rather low and relatively stable renewal fee schedules, serious

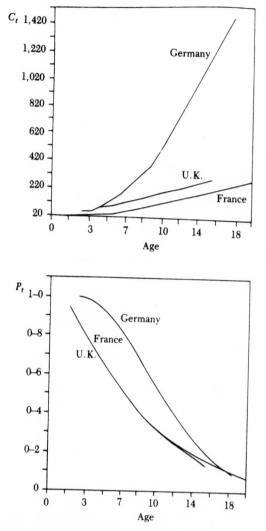

Fig. 13.7   Age paths of deflated renewal costs and renewal proportions

Source: Schankerman and Pakes (1986), figures 2 and 3.

Notes: Age = years since granting of patent.

C_t = deflated renewal costs.

P_t = proportion of patents renewed.

identification problems arise in such models. The estimates of the mean value of patent rights rest, therefore, on specific assumptions about the functional form of their distribution (how it looks in the unseen tail) and on assumptions about the form of the depreciation process. Some of these assumptions may be testable and some of the more interesting conclusions of their work do not depend on them, but ultimately we have to put some prior notions into such data to have them yield specific numerical answers. The issues of identification and estimation are discussed in much detail in the recent papers by Pakes and Simpson (1989) and Schankerman (1989), together with the presentation of interesting new results on additional countries and on industrial detail, and hence will not be pursued further here (see also J. O. Lanjouw 1989; Schankerman 1990; and Lanjouw and Schankerman 1989).

In the United States, patents that were applied for after 1980 have to pay renewal fees three and a half, seven and a half, and eleven and a half years after the granting date. These fees are currently $450, $890, and $1,340 respectively for corporations and somewhat less for individuals and "small entities." As of the end of 1988, 16 percent of the 1981–84 patents coming up to the payment of the first maintenance fee "expired," with a slightly higher expiration rate for the U.S. (17 percent) than for patents owned by foreign residents (15 percent) implying, possibly, a higher average value or "quality" for the latter.[9] An earlier study of a smaller sample of such data found that individually owned patents were expiring at a much higher rate than assigned patents (39 versus 13 percent for U.S. origin patents) and that "mechanical" patents had the highest and "chemical" patents the lowest rates of expiration (S. E. Manchuso, M. P. Masuck, and E. C. Woodrow 1987). The growing availability of such renewal data in the future will provide us with another very interesting window on the inventive process and its rewards in the U.S.

Returning to the specific results from the work on European patent renewals, using a learning model for the early years of a patent's life, Pakes (1986) finds that patents are applied for at an early stage in the inventive process, a stage in which there is still substantial uncertainty concerning both the returns that will be earned from holding the patents, and the returns that will accrue to the patented ideas. Gradually the patentors uncover more information about the actual value of their patents. Most turn out to be of little value, but the rare "winner" justifies the investments that were made in developing them. His estimates imply also that most of the uncertainty with respect to the value of a patent is resolved during the first three or four years of its life. Using this result, Schankerman and Pakes (1986) examine changes in the distribution of patent values over time and the correlates of these changes. The substantive results from these papers imply that the average value of a patent right is quite small, about $7,000 in the population of patent applications in France and the U.K. In Germany, where only about 35 percent of all patent applications are granted (about 93 percent and 83 percent were granted in France and the U.K. respectively), the average value of a patent right among grants was about $17,000. The distribution of these values, however, is very dispersed and skewed. One percent of patent applications in France and the U.K. had values in excess of

9. Based on unpublished tabulations of the Office of Documentation Information at the U.S. Patent Office.

$70,000 while in Germany 1 percent of patents granted had values in excess of $120,000. Moreover, half of all the estimated value of patent rights accrues to between 5 and 10 percent of all the patents. The annual returns to patent protection decay rather quickly over time, with rates of obsolescence on the order of 10 to 20 percent per year. Because about 35,000 patents were applied for per year in France and the U.K. and about 60,000 in Germany, these figures imply that though the aggregate value of patent rights is quite large, it is only on the order of 10 to 15 percent of the total national expenditures on R&D. Other means of appropriating the benefits of R&D must be, therefore, quite important.

Schankerman and Pakes used their results to adjust the aggregate patent time series for changes in their average "quality" (value). In their 1986 paper they find that even though the number of patents per scientist fell rather sharply between 1965 and 1975 in the three countries examined by them, the estimated "quality-adjusted" total value of patent rights per scientist and engineer was effectively stable in both Germany and the U.K., and dropped only slightly in France (Schankerman and Pakes 1986, table 6).[10]

13.6 Patents and Stock Market Value

Another line of work has used data on the stock market valuation of firms to investigate both the "value" of patents and the information content of the variability in their numbers. The use of stock market values as an "output" indicator of the research process has one major advantage. All other indicators of success, such as profits or productivity, are likely to reflect it only slowly and erratically. On the other hand, when an event occurs that causes the market to reevaluate the accumulated output of a firm's research endeavors, its full effect on the expected present value of a firm's future net cash flows should be recorded immediately. This, of course, need not equal what will eventually materialize. The downside of this type of measurement is the large volatility in stock market measures. The needle might be there but the haystack can be very large.

The simplest market value model starts from the market valuation identity, with the market value of the firm proportional to its physical ("tangible") and intangible capital, the latter being in part the product of its past R&D investments and possibly also reflected in its accumulated patent position (Griliches 1981; Uri Ben-Zion 1984; Hirschey 1982; Cockburn and Griliches 1988; among others). It can be written as follows:

$$V = q(A + gK) = qA(1 + gK/A),$$

where V is the market value of the firm, A is the current replacement cost of its tangible assets, K is its level of intangible ("knowledge") capital and g is its

---

10. See Pakes and Simpson (1989) and Schankerman (1989 and 1990) for an extension of these results and M. Trajtenberg (1990) for another approach to the same problem.

relative shadow price, and q is the current premium or discount of market value over the replacement cost of tangible assets.[11] Writing q as $\exp(a + u)$, where a represents individual firm differences in average valuation due to the exclusion of other unmeasured capital components or market position variables, taking logarithms, and approximating $\log(1 + x) = x$, we can rewrite the estimating equation as:

$$\ln Q = \ln(V/A) = a + gK/A + u,$$

where the dependent variable is the logarithm of what has come to be called *Tobin's Q*. Using different measures of current and past patents and current and past R&D expenditures as proxies for K, various researchers have estimated this kind of equation. Table 13.2 reproduces a number of results from the Cockburn and Griliches study. It shows that if we look at patents alone the estimated value of a recent patent is about $500,000. This estimate is halved when we put both past and current R&D expenditures in the equation. By and large, R&D is the "stronger" variable. The evidence for additional information in the patent variables varies from sample to sample (patents were stronger in the Griliches 1981 study, which was based on a much smaller sample of firms but also used the panel aspects of the data) and depends on which other variables are included in the equation (see the change in the coefficient from column 2 to 3 in this table).[12]

A more dynamic point of view is taken by Pakes (1985) in his analysis of the relationship between patents, R&D, and the stock market rate of return. Events occur that affect the market value of a firm's R&D program and what one estimates are the reduced-form relationships between the percentage increase in this value and current and subsequent changes in the firm's R&D expenditures, its patent applications, and the market rate of return on its stock. His empirical results indicate that about 5 percent of the variance in the stock market rate of return is caused by the events that change both R&D and patent applications. This leads to a significant correlation between movements in the stock market rate of return and unpredictable changes in both patents and R&D expenditures, changes that could not be predicted from past values of patents and R&D. On average, an "unexpected" increase in one patent is associated with an increase in the firm's market value of $810,000, while an unexpected increase of $100 of R&D expenditures is, on average, associated with a $1,870 increase in the value of the firm. Patents are estimated to contain a significant noise component (a component whose variance is not related to either the R&D or the stock market rate of return series). This noise component accounts for only a small fraction of the large differences in the number of patent applica-

11. This equation would hold exactly in a world in which all assets were fully traded in the same market. More generally, such an equation is valid in a multicapital setting only under very stringent conditions, such as the linear-homogeneity of the profit function. See Wildasin (1984) and Hayashi and Inoue (1990) for more discussion.

12. See Hall (1988), ch. 2, for similar results.

Table 13.2   **The Stock Market's Relative Valuation of R&D and Patents; Dependent Variable: Log (Q)**

SP/A	0.493	0.111	0.246
	(0.165)	(0.094)	(0.082)
K/A		1.374	0.741
		(0.182)	(0.152)
NR/A			11.99
			(1.556)
R^2	0.027	0.125	0.258

Source: Cockburn and Griliches (1987), table 3.
V = market value of the firm.
A = total net assets at replacement cost.
$Q = V/A$.
K = "stock" of R&D using 15 percent depreciation rate.
NR = "news in R&D": current R&D less depreciation of the R&D stock.
SP = "stock" of patents using 30 percent depreciation rate.
N = 722. Mean of the dependent variable = -0.272; standard deviation = 0.697.
Heteroscedasticitiy-consistent standard errors in parentheses.

All equations also contain an intercept term and the logarithm of assets, whose coefficient was small but consistently significant, on the order of -0.03 (0.01).

tions of different firms (about 25 percent), but plays a much larger role among the smaller fluctuations that occur in the patent applications of a given firm over time (about 95 percent). Similarly, the effect of unexpected increases in patents on market value is highly variable. Nevertheless, there is still some information in the time-series dimension. If we were to observe, for example, a sudden large burst in the patent applications of a given firm, we could be quite sure that events have occurred to cause a large change in the market value of its R&D program; but smaller changes in the patent applications of a given firm are not likely to be very informative.

The timing of the response of patents and R&D to events that change the value of a firm's R&D effort is quite similar. One gets the impression from the estimates that such events cause a chain reaction, inducing an increase in R&D expenditures far into the future, and that firms patent around the links of this chain almost as quickly as they are completed, resulting in a rather close relationship between R&D expenditures and the number of patents applied for. Perhaps surprisingly, Pakes finds no evidence that independent changes in the number of patents applied for (independent of current and earlier R&D expenditures) produce significant effects on the market's valuation of the firm. Hence it is not possible to distinguish between demand shocks, where demand shocks are loosely defined as events that cause increases in patenting only through the R&D expenditures they induce, and technological or supply shocks that may have a direct effect on patents as well as an indirect effect via induced R&D demand.

It is not obvious whether one can separate "demand" from "supply" factors in this area, even conceptually. One way of defining demand factors is to identify them with macro shifts in aggregate demand, population, exchange rates, and relative factor prices that make inventive activity more (or less) profitable at a given level of scientific information, a fixed "innovation possibilities frontier." Changes in technological "opportunity," on the other hand, are those scientific and technological breakthroughs that make additional innovation more profitable or less costly at a fixed aggregate or industry level demand. These distinctions are far from sharp, especially given our inability to measure the contributions of science and technology directly. Moreover, what is a technological opportunity in one industry may spill over as a derived demand effect to another. Nevertheless, there is something distinct in these factors, in their sources of change and dynamics.[13]

Patent data could help here if one were willing to assume that independent, "unanticipated" shifts in the level of patenting by firms represent shifts in technological opportunities and not responses to changes in economic conditions (demand forces). That is, the identifying assumption is that demand impinges on the level of patenting only through the level of R&D expenditures (and slowly changing trends) and that the "news" component in the patent statistics reflects technological "news," the information that a particular line of research has turned out to be more (or less) fruitful or easier (harder) than expected when the decision to invest in it was made originally. Changes in technological opportunity are thus identified with "abnormal," "unexpected," bursts (or declines) in the number of patents applied for.

Several implications of this formulation are immediate. If patent statistics contain additional information about shifts in technological opportunities, then they should be correlated with current changes in market value above and beyond their current relationship with R&D and they should affect R&D levels in the future, even in the presence of the change in market value variable because the latter variable is measured with much error. Patents should "cause" R&D in the sense of Granger (1969).

The available evidence on this point is not too encouraging: As noted above, Griliches (1981) found a significant independent effect of patents on the market values of firms, above and beyond their R&D expenditures, but Pakes did not detect a significant influence of lagged patents on R&D in the presence of lagged R&D and the stock market rate of return variables. Nor did Hall, Griliches, and Hausman (1986) find future R&D affecting current patenting as the "causality" argument might have implied. Griliches, Hall, and Pakes (1991) replicate some of Pakes's computations on a larger sample (340 firms) and expand his equation system to add equations for sales, employment, and invest-

---

13. This is, of course, related to Schmookler's distinction between patents classified by industry of origin versus industry of use. "Who does the invention" depends more on supply considerations. "For whom the invention is done" is more likely to be affected by demand shifts.

ment. Their results indicate that the addition of the latter variables is helpful, in the sense that fluctuations in their growth rates are related to fluctuations in both the growth rate of R&D and the stock market rate of return and hence should help in identifying the relationships we are interested in. But the expansion of the sample to include many small firms with low levels of patenting deteriorates significantly the informational content of this variable, raising its noise to signal ratio, and making it hard to discern a feedback from the independent variability in patenting to any of the other variables. Thus, at the moment, it does not look as if the data can sustain a model with two separate factors ("market" and "technological" innovations), even though in principle such a model is identifiable.

The difficulties in implementing such models arise to a large extent from the large "noise" component in patents as indicators of R&D output in the short-run within-firm dimension. While the problem may have been obvious from the beginning, it was the work of Pakes and Schankerman (1984) and their estimates of the dispersion and the skewness in patent value that alerted us to its actual magnitude.

To derive quantitative implications of such a skewed distribution of values for the quality of this indicator we can combine what we know about patent counts in both the time-series and cross-section dimension with estimates of the distribution of their values.

One can write the innovation in the value of the firm (net of its expected dividend and investment policy) as the sum of three components:

$$q_t V_t = w_t + \eta_t + u_t,$$

where q_t is the rate of return on stock holding, V_t is the total market value of the firm's assets, and the three components w_t, η_t, and u_t are defined to be orthogonal to each other; w_t corresponds to the change in the value of a firm's R&D "position" (program) arising from the "news" associated with current patent applications; η_t reflects revaluations of previous achievements associated with past patents (above and beyond their correlation with current patents); while u_t reflects all other sources of fluctuation in the value of the firm, including also possibly the contribution of not patented R&D. Looking first at w_t and the role of patent numbers as an indicator of it, we can ask about the possible magnitude of the variance of w_t (relative to the variance of $q_t V_t$). That is, how large could the contribution of current patents be to the explanation of fluctuations in market value, even if we had a perfect measure of these *values?*

To decompose the variance of the first component, we write it as

$$w = \sum_{i=1}^{p} y_i$$

and assume that (1) p, the number of patents applied for each year, is distributed as a Poisson random variable with a mean, λ, which is a distributed lag of past R&D expenditures (see Hausman, Hall, and Griliches 1984); and (2) y_i

is the underlying value of each patent and is distributed as a log-normal random variable with a mean and variance that will be derived from the earlier literature.

The first two moments of w (under independence) are

$$E(w) = E(py) = \lambda E(y) \quad \text{where} \quad \lambda = E(p)$$

$$V(w) = V\left(\sum_{i=1}^{n} y_i\right)\lambda V[y] + \lambda(Ey)^2.$$

The component of the variance of w that could be accounted for by patent *numbers* corresponds to the last term

$$\text{var}[p\bar{y}] = \lambda \bar{y}^2,$$

and its relative size is given by

$$\text{var}(py)/\text{var}(w) = 1/[1 + V(y)/E(y)^2]$$
$$= 1/(1 + \tau^2),$$

where τ is the coefficient of variation in the distribution of patent values.

Turning to the literature for some order of magnitude estimates of various parameters, we have estimates of the mean value of the news associated with patents in the U.S. of between \$200,000 (Griliches 1981) and \$800,000 (Pakes 1985) per patent. There is also some information on this point in Griliches, Hall, and Pakes (1991): an estimate of \$98,000 per unexpected patent at the geometric mean of their data (with a very large standard error). For the drug industry, where patents are more important, there is a larger and somewhat more precise estimate: an \$821,000 average increase in the value of the firm per unexpected patent. This, in fact, is very similar to the Pakes estimate which was based on a smaller sample of larger firms and is therefore more comparable to their drug firms' subset.

Taking the upper range of these numbers, \$800,000 per "unexpected" patent, and using $\lambda = 13$, the average (geometric) number of patents received in the Griliches, Hall, Pakes sample (per year, per firm), the expected contribution of the variance in patent *numbers* to the average variance in market value is $13(0.8)^2$ (mil\$)$^2 = \$8.3$ million squared. To get an estimate of var(y), I borrow the estimated coefficient of variation of the distribution of patent values from Pakes (1986) and Schankerman and Pakes (1986).[14] Both of these articles produced coefficients of variation on the order of 2 to 3.6. Because we are looking for upper-bound estimates, taking 3.6 and applying it to the "upper"-range estimate of $Ey = \$0.8$ million gives an estimate of the total variance of w as

---

14. Schankerman and Pakes estimate the value of the patent rights. I assume that the value of the underlying innovation is proportional to its patent right value and highly correlated to it.

$$13[(3.6 \times 0.8)^2 + (0.8)^2] = \$116 \text{ million sq.}$$

This is to be compared to the average variance of $q_t V_t$. The variance of q in the Griliches, Hall, and Pakes sample is 0.133 which, evaluated at the geometric average value of their firms (\$276 million), yields a variance of market value changes on the order of \$10,000 million squared. Comparing the two variances gives an estimate of the relative importance of fluctuations in the market value of new patented innovations as at about 1 percent of the total fluctuations in market value.[15] That is, even if one had good estimates of patent values, they would account for little of the fluctuations in market value. Having numbers instead of values makes matters much worse, reducing this fraction even further. The contribution of patent numbers to the variance in their values is only on the order of 7 percent $[1/(1 + (3.6)^2)]$, and their contribution to the explanation of the variance in the unexpected changes in the market values of individual firms is much smaller (less than 0.1 percent).[16] One should not, therefore, use data on stock market fluctuations in this fashion to test detailed hypotheses about the information content of patent statistics. On the other hand, while the estimated variance components are rather small, they should not be interpreted as implying that the returns to inventive activity are small or that the topic we have been pursuing is not interesting, only that we have been looking for our particular needle in a very large haystack.

13.7 Spillovers and Other Uses of Patent Data

A major unresolved issue in the area of economics of technology is the identification and measurement of R&D spillovers, the benefits that one company or industry receives from the R&D activity of another. It is difficult to trace such spillovers without having strong a priori notions about who are the potential beneficiaries of whose research (see Griliches 1979, pp. 102–5 for additional discussion of these issues). One way to approach this problem is to use

15. There are two major problems in using this procedure to estimate the variance of the news in the economic value of patents held by the firm: The first is that the distribution estimated by Schankerman and Pakes is a distribution of the value of patent rights, which may vary less than proportionally with the true economic value of the associated invention to the firm. The second problem probably goes in the other direction: Some of the change in the firm's patent value this year may not be news, and thus may have already been incorporated into the market value at the beginning of the year. Allowing for some predictability of patent numbers would only reduce such fractions further, multiplying them essentially by $1 - R^2$ of the prediction equation. (See Griliches, Hall, and Pakes 1991 for a more detailed discussion of this and related issues.)

16. An alternative approach to this question is developed in Griliches, Hall, and Pakes by modeling the components of variance in stock market value surprises explicitly as functions of current and past patenting and R&D activity, allowing one to estimate also the contribution of revisions in past patents' values to current changes in market value. Though the resulting estimates are rather imprecise, because they are based essentially on fourth moments of the data, they do imply that the variance in the news about the value of patents (current and past) could account for about 5 percent of the total variance in market value surprises, a number that may look low but is actually as high as any that have been found in other studies of market value revisions. Only about one-fifth of this, however, can be attributed to news associated with *current* patent applications.

the detailed information on patenting by type of patent (patent class) to cluster firms into common "technological activity" clusters and determine whether a firm's variables are related to the overall activity levels of its cluster.

In his thesis and several recent papers, Adam Jaffe (1983, 1985, 1986, 1988) has used firm level data on patenting by class of patent and on the distribution of sales by four-digit SIC to cluster firms into 21 distinct technological clusters and 20 industry (sales orientation) clusters. It turns out that these two criteria lead to different clusterings. Using the technological clusters, Jaffe constructed a measure of the total R&D "pool" available for spillovers (borrowing or stealing) in a cluster. He then looked at three "outcome" variables: R&D investment ratio for the firm (in 1976), patents received (average number applied for during 1975–77), and output growth, between 1972 and 1977. In each of these cases, his measure of the R&D pool contributed significantly and positively to the explanation of the firm level "outcome" variables even in the presence of industry dummies (based on sales clustering). Not surprisingly, perhaps, firms in technological clusters with large overall R&D "pools" invested more intensively in R&D than would be predicted just from their industrial (SIC) location. More interesting is the finding that firms received more patents per R&D dollar in clusters where more R&D was performed by others, again above and beyond any pure industry differences (based on a classification of their sales). Similarly, his analysis of firm productivity growth during the 1972–77 period showed that it was related positively to both the average R&D intensity of the individual firms and the change in the size of the R&D pool available to these firms. In terms of profits, or market value, there were, however, both positive and negative effects of neighboring firms' R&D. The net effect was positive for high R&D firms, but firms with R&D about one standard deviation below the mean were made worse off overall by the R&D of others. Here the idea of R&D spillovers is made operational by using the firm's patenting pattern to construct a measure of its location in "technological space" and showing that the R&D of others, weighted inversely to their distance from this location, has an observable impact on its own success. More recently, Jaffe (1989) has used regional data on patenting to investigate spillovers from academic research.

Patent documents also contain citations to other, previous patents. Following the growth of interest in citations in general and the development of computer software that allows the search for all subsequent citations of a particular patent (or article), there has been a growing interest in using citations counts as alternative "indexes" of differential quality. It should be noted here that patent citations differ from usual scientific citations to the work of others in that they are largely the contribution of patent examiners whose task is to delimit the reach of the new patent and note the context in which it is granted. In that sense, the "objectivity" of such citations is greater and may contribute to the validity of citation counts as indexes of relative importance. But in another sense, they are like citations added at the insistence of the editor; they may reflect the importance that is put in the field on particular papers but are not a valid indicator for channels of influence, for intellectual spillovers. On the other hand, they bring us closer to something that might be interpreted as measuring the social rather than just the private returns to these patents.

The use of patent citations as "indicators" is discussed, largely in a biblio-metric style, by R. S. Campbell and A. L. Nieves (1979), Carpenter, Narin, and Woolf (1981), Carpenter and F. Narin (1983), and Narin, E. Noma, and R. Perry (1987) (see also the more general discussion of bibliometric evidence in Office of Technology Assessment 1986, chap. 3). An interesting economic application is to be found in M. Trajtenberg (1990) who shows that citation-weighted patent numbers are more closely correlated with his "output" mea-sure, consumer surplus gains from the development and diffusion of CAT scan-ners (computed tomography), while unweighted patent counts are more closely related to "input," to R&D expenditures by the various firms in this field. (For another application of citation data see Lieberman 1987.) This way of using patent data is only in its beginnings and we are likely to see a much wider use of it in the future.

A number of studies have tried to "validate" patents as indicators of techni-cal change by connecting them to counts of innovations, new chemical entities, and subsequent measures of profits or growth. One of the earliest and best studies of this kind (William Comanor and Scherer 1969) related pharmaceuti-cal patents to the number of new chemical entities and all new products intro-duced by the different firms in subsequent years and found a closer relationship between patent applications (rather than grants) with all new products (rather than just the number of new chemical entities). I will not consider in detail a number of studies that found varying degrees of relationship between patents and "invention" or "innovation" counts, because the subjectivity and elasticity of such innovation count data make their results very difficult to interpret. For examples of such work see B. Achilladelis, A. Schwarzkopf, and M. Cines (1987), Basberg (1982), Kleinknecht (1982), and Walsh (1984). Scherer (1965a) shows a positive relationship between earlier patenting rates and sub-sequent profitability and sales growth differences in a cross-section of firms, but I know of no studies that relate "successfully" patenting rates or patenting stocks to subsequent *growth* of productivity at the firm level.

Patent data have been used by Pavitt and Soete and their associates to ana-lyze the relative "competitiveness" of various countries, to construct "revealed technology advantage" indexes for various countries, and to describe and con-trast the international location of inventive activity in different industries (Pav-itt and Soete 1980, 1981; Pavitt 1982; Pavitt and Patel 1988; Soete 1987). Patents have been used by economic historians to study regional patterns of economic growth and the externalities of population size and agglomeration (Allen Kelley 1972; K. L. Sokoloff 1988; Sokoloff and B. Z. Khan 1989, among others). There have been also many other attempts to use patent data in different areas of economic analysis. It is not possible, unfortunately, to do justice to all of them here.

13.8   Aggregate Trends in Patenting and the Bureaucratic Cycle

Among the various explanations of the worldwide productivity slowdown in the 1970s, the exhaustion of inventive and technological opportunities remains one of the major suspects in the case. This suspicion was fed by one of the more visible statistical facts: The total number of patents granted peaked in the U.S. around 1970 and then declined through most of the 1970s (see Figure 13.1). Similar trends could also be observed in patenting worldwide, except in Japan (see Robert Evenson 1984; Englander, Evenson, and Hanazaki 1988, and Soete et al. 1989). These same data also fed the idea that the United States had lost its competitive inventive edge. If one looks at the data on patents granted to U.S. corporations they peaked in the mid-1960s and have not really recovered since (see Figure 13.2). A related notion is diminishing returns to inventive activity, to investments in R&D. Looking at Figure 13.2 one notices the much more rapid rate of growth in national R&D expenditures than in total patenting and the implicit suggestion of diminishing returns.

Two important aspects of these data are visible in Figure 13.1: Trends in patent grants do not always follow those of patent applications and there have been cycles before. An application for a patent is filed when the expected value of receiving the patent exceeds the cost of applying for it. The expected value of a patent equals the probability that it will be granted, times the expected economic value of the rights associated with the particular patented item or idea, minus the potentially negative effects arising from its disclosure. A patent is granted if it passes certain minimal standards of novelty and potential utility. These standards can change over time, both as a result of changes in perception of what is an innovation and as the result of changing "applications" pressure on a relatively fixed number of patent office workers. Moreover, a change in the resources of the patent office or in its efficiency will introduce changes in the lag structure of grants behind applications, and may produce a rather misleading picture of the underlying trends. In particular, the decline in the number of patents granted in the 1970s is almost entirely an artifact, induced by fluctuations in the Patent Office, culminating in the sharp dip in 1979 due to the absence of budget for printing the approved patents.[17]

This can be seen most easily in Figure 13.8 which plots the number of grants that would be predicted by a "constant" Patent Office policy and performance, that is, a 65 percent approval rate and a constant lag structure. The graph of such a "prediction" is essentially flat throughout the 1970s, reflecting the rough constancy of total applications during this period and implying a marked change in the lag structure of the granting process during the last 20 years. In the late 1960s it took more than three years for half of the eventual grants to

17. The impact of changes in bureaucratic procedures on shorter-run aspects of these data is discussed in G. G. Brunk and G. Demack (1987), who point out that since 1968, the Patent Office has been issuing a fixed number of patents each week, with this number changing, from time to time, as the backlog varied.

Examiners

Patents

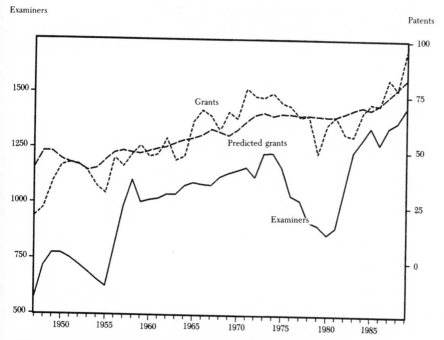

Fig. 13.8 **Actual versus predicted patent grants and the number of patent examiners, 1947–1989**

Source: Griliches (1989), figure 3, updated.

Note: Predicted grants (based on a "fixed" Patent Office policy) = .65(.1 $APPL_{-1}$ + .61 $APPL_{-2}$ + .25 $APPL_{-3}$ + .04 $APPL_{-4}$).

be issued. A campaign to reduce these lags and eliminate the accumulating backlog was begun in 1971 and brought down the fraction taking more than three years to about 10 percent by the late 1970s. But by the early 1980s the Patent Office ran into another budgetary crisis and the backlog began to grow again (see Griliches 1989, table 1).

Looking at shorter-run fluctuations in the total number of patents granted one can see that they are much more closely associated with the number of examiners than with the inflow of patent applications ("predicted grants" being just a scaled moving average of recent applications). It is obvious that the decline in patents granted in the 1970s came not from a decline in applications—they declined very little—but from the contraction in the resources of the Patent Office. This particular indicator of "technological decline" is, thus, nothing more than a bureaucratic mirage!

Another way of making this point is via the estimation of a Patent Office "production function," which looks at the number of patents granted as a function of two major "inputs": the internal resources available to it, the average number of patent examiners, and the "materials" it has to work with, lagged

Table 13.3   **The Patent Office "Production Function"**

	Coefficients (Standard Errors)				
	Log Total Grants		Log Domestic Grants		
Variables	1925–87	1945–87	1945–87		
Log average examiner	.916 (.145)	.879 (.129)	.938 (.153)	.957 (.146)	.899 (.130)
Log predicted grants	.479 (.188)	.419 (.129)			
Time	−.026 (.008)		−.010 (.003)		
Time squared	.00025 (.00010)				
Log domestic predicted grants			.625 (.325)	.400 (.301)	.333 (.311)
Log foreign predicted grants			−.195 (.071)		
Logit foreign applications ratio					−.102 (.031)
$\bar{R}^2$	.890	.950	.788	.796	.800
SEE	.107	.115	.119	.117	.116
AR(1)	.427 (.121)	.273 (.153)	.286 (.160)	.273 (.158)	.273 (.159)

Source: Griliches (1989), table 2.

Average examiner = [*examiners* (−1) + *examiners* (−2) + *examiners* (−3)]/3.

Predicted grants = .65[.1 *Appl* (−1) + .61 *Appl* (−2) + .25 *Appl* (−3) + .04 *Appl* (−4)].

Same formula for predicted domestic and foreign grants as a function of domestic and foreign applications.

AR(1) = first-order autoregressive serial correlation adjustment.

SEE = standard error of estimate (standard deviation of estimated residuals).

Logit foreign applications ratio: log[(*Fr Appl/Tot Appl*)]/[1 − (*Fr Appl/Tot Appl*)].

applications. Table 13.3 presents a number of such regressions for the 1925–87 and 1945–87 periods (examiner data are not available before 1920) and finds that the major determinant of the number of patents granted is the number of patent examiners employed by the Patent Office (averaged over the previous three years) with an estimated coefficient (elasticity) of approximately one. The supply of applications is important but it works largely through the examiner variable. Examiners are employed, in part, in response to application pressure and the state of the accumulating backlog. There is also a negative trend in the "efficiency" of patent examiners, perhaps as the result of the rising complexity of applications and the increasing size of the literature that needs to be searched.[18]

A parallel analysis of grants to domestic inventors yields similar results.

18. See Scherer et al. (1959, p. 134) for evidence of rising complexity.

Most of the variability in their numbers is again attributable to the number of examiners. But there is also evidence of a significant negative effect of the rising number of foreign applications, represented in Table 13.3 by the number of "predicted" grants to foreigners or the logit transformed ratio of foreign applications. Both versions of this variable indicate a "crowding out" of domestic patents by the rising tide of foreign applications and provide a substantive interpretation for the negative trend in this equation. This does not "solve," however, all of the mystery. In the case of domestic patents there has been also a decline in applications in the 1970s, which requires an interpretation of its own.

13.9   Aggregate Patenting and the Business Cycle

One explanation for the decline in the rate of domestic patent applications in the 1970s is the worldwide deterioration in economic conditions and expectations that occurred as the result of the two oil price shocks and the governmental efforts to contain the resulting inflationary forces (Griliches 1988). The notion that inventive activity is largely "demand" driven had its strongest proponent in Schmookler (1966), who showed that inventive activity (as measured by patents) was related to earlier movements in investment and output of the relevant industries. (See also the later summation of his position in Schmookler 1972, pp. 70–84.) His work can be, and has been, criticized on several levels. In the longer run, "supply" forces, in the form of new discoveries and the steady contribution of new scientific knowledge, surely have an important role to play (Nathan Rosenberg 1974). Moreover, by current econometric standards the evidence presented by Schmookler for his conclusions does not look all that strong (though it gains conviction by the cumulative force of the various bits and pieces examined, and by observing the working of a knowledgeable and first-rate mind grappling with the problem and coming to a considered judgment). Subsequent empirical work on this topic, by Scherer (1965a and 1982b), P. Stoneman (1979), Geoffrey Wyatt (1986), Derek Bosworth and Tony Westaway (1984), C. Papachristodoulou (1986), and Kleinknecht and B. Verspagen (1990), have either supported his original conclusions or weakened them, but no one has really overturned them.[19] In any case, at the level of annual fluctuations that we are looking at, demand forces are likely to be more important and easier to detect than the much slower "supply" forces whose effects take longer to accumulate.

Table 13.4 presents a number of different attempts to explain the total num-

---

19. A number of studies, following Stoneman, have regressed the log of patents on the log of R&D per patent, interpreting the latter variable as a measure of the "cost" of invention, and the resulting negative coefficient as an indication of the workings of "supply" forces. But the sign of this coefficient could reflect nothing more than the spuriousness of such a relationship, induced by the large transitory or measurement error component in patent numbers. On the latter possibility see Griliches, Hall, and Pakes (1991).

Table 13.4   **Determinants of Applications for U.S. Patents by U.S. Residents, 1953–87; Dependent Variable: Log of Domestic Patent Applications**

Variables	Regression Coefficients (Standard Errors) and Period					
	1953–87			1954–87		
Time	−.000 (.001)	−.017 (.005)	−.018 (.004)	−.013 (.003)	−.007 (.004)	−.007 (.001)
DLNTDF			−.279 (.097)	−.317 (.084)	−.314 (.074)	−.314 (.077)
DLNTDF(−1)			−.257 (.098)	−.203 (.081)	−.155 (.084)	−.155 (.076)
LCRD(−1)		.338 (.094)	.410 (.075)	.203 (.090)	.000 (.125)	
LRUNBR(−1)				.064 (.019)	.121 (.032)	.121 (.015)
LRRDDF					−.775 (.352)	−.776 (.233)
SEE	.0507	.0425	.0326	.0281	.0264	.0259
$\bar{R}^2$	−.029	.256	.561	.674	.713	.724
D-W	.72	1.21	1.74	2.00	2.04	2.02

Source: Griliches (1989), table 6.

SEE   = standard deviation of the estimated residuals.
D-W   = Durbin-Watson statistic.
DLNTDF   = the rate of growth in the national defense component of real GNP.
LCRD   = logarithm of company-financed R&D expenditures in industry, deflated.
LRUNBR   = logarithm of total "real" basic research expenditures in universities, deflated.
LRRDDF   = logarithm of the ratio of the R&D to the implicit GNP deflators.

ber of domestic patent applications in the U.S. during the last 30 years or so. Because reasonably consistent R&D data at the national level do not exist before 1953, most of the analyses are based on the 1954–87 period.[20] There are a number of interesting findings in this table. (1) For the period as a whole (1953 to 1987) there was no significant decline in the number of patent applica-

20. Taking the longer-run view and looking at periods with no R&D data, one can reproduce the main outlines of Schmookler's results. For example, for the whole 1880–1987 period (88 years), one gets (in first differences of logarithms format):

$$gda = -.006 + .110\ ggpdi + .299\ ggnp(-1)$$

$$(.009)\quad (.030)\qquad\qquad (.128)$$

$$R = 0.15,\ \text{SEE} = 0.075,\ \text{D-W} = 1.87,$$

where the rate of growth in domestic patent applications (*gda*) is related positively to the current rate of growth in gross private domestic investment (*ggpdi*) and the lagged rate of growth in real GNP (*ggnp*). Because the post–World War II period exhibits much less variance, the results are much weaker there, but not all that different. During this later period we have, however, actual direct "input" measures, such as R&D expenditures and the number of scientists and engineers engaged in R&D, and they dominate the aggregate economy indexes such as GNP or GPDI.

tions in the U.S. by U.S. residents. Because there was a positive rate of growth in real R&D over this period, at least if one uses the standard deflators, any attribution of a positive influence to them will imply the finding of a negative time trend in the patents "production function." (2) Fluctuations in R&D do affect the number of patents applied for, but less than proportionately. Among the various possible measures of R&D, company expenditures on R&D "work best," as long as only one measure of R&D is to be included in the equation. Findings (1) and (2) together imply a negative trend in the "propensity to patent" or in the "efficiency" of patent "production" of about −1 to −2 percent per year. The estimated coefficient of the company R&D variable is quite high and significant, between 0.2 and 0.4, and is consistent with earlier findings based on micro data (see Section 13.4). (3) Changes in the size of the defense establishment, in the form of current and lagged changes in real gross national product devoted to national defense, have a large and significantly negative effect on the number of domestic patents applied for and perhaps also on actual levels of inventive activity. The estimated effect is large, a decline of 5 percent in domestic patenting as the result of a 10 percent increase in defense GNP, and it is quite robust to the introduction or deletion of other variables. This finding is consistent with both the view that defense expenditures pull resources away from inventive activity and with the view that they channel inventive activity into areas where patenting is either more difficult or less important. (4) There is evidence in these data of a positive contribution of basic research in universities to the overall level of domestic inventive activity as measured by the total number of domestic patent applications. (5) There is also some evidence that the rising real cost of R&D, in the form of the ratio of the R&D to GNP price deflators, has had a negative impact on patenting, either because it reflects also the rising cost of patenting relative to other economic activities, or because it adjusts in part for the "underdeflation" of the R&D variables by the same set of deflators. All of these conclusions are tentative. They are based on highly aggregated data, a rather short time period, and a highly multicollinear set of examined variables.[21] Looking at industry (2.5 digit) level data does not help much, nor does it change the results significantly (see Griliches 1989).[22]

These macro results do not really help to explain the longer-run trends. For the period as a whole, 1954 through 1987, there is no actual decline in patenting to explain and also no substantive change in the rate of growth of defense expenditures. But unless the R&D deflators are all wrong, the data do indicate

21. The simple correlation of company R&D with time and real GNP is 0.99 and 0.98 respectively, and it is about 0.94 with either university basic research or total R&D in industry.

22. Attempts to extend these results by adding more "demand" side variables such as changes in real GNP, capacity utilization, or stock price indexes were not successful. Almost all of the systematic short-run variability in aggregate domestic patenting is picked up by fluctuations in the R&D and national defense variables. All of the other demand variables appear to be working via these variables.

a rather significant growth in both private company R&D expenditures in industry and basic R&D expenditures in universities at 5 and 8 percent per year respectively, which should have resulted in some increase in the observed rate of patenting. Thus, we are left more or less where we started, with a significant unexplained decline in U.S. patenting relative to the ongoing investment in R&D.

13.10   A Shrinking Yardstick?

Before we look at the longer-run trend in domestic patenting and discuss its interpretation as an indicator of inventive activity, it is worth stressing that from the point of view of the measurement of technical change in the U.S., using total factor productivity measures or related indexes, *domestic* patenting may not be the relevant magnitude. Total patents may be a better measure of shifts in "technology," in the "production possibilities frontier." Foreign inventions should have a similar impact on total factor productivity and therefore, from the point of view of measures of technological "opportunity" available to the U.S. economy, it may not matter whence the invention came. The level of domestic patenting may be more relevant, however, for studies of "competitiveness" and when thinking about rates of return to domestic R&D.

Figure 13.9 plots (on a common log scale) the long-term data on domestic patent applications, real GNP, and gross private domestic investment (in lieu of R&D data which are not really available before the 1950s).[23] Several interesting facts stand out in this chart: After growing at roughly the same rate as real GNP in the late nineteenth and early twentieth centuries, domestic patent applications peaked in the late 1920s and have not achieved such levels again. After a severe decline during the Great Depression and the early war years and a brief postwar recovery, they stayed essentially flat throughout the whole postwar period, while both GNP and total and corporate R&D expenditures were growing. These facts led Schmookler (1966, pp. 28–30) to declare such data not really comparable between the pre– and post–World War II periods. He gave three reasons for the "shortfall" in the more recent period: (1) the change in judicial and political climate in the late 1930s, which became much more hostile to corporate patenting and the enforcement of patent rights, reducing thereby the value of applying for one; (2) the growth in delays in processing patent applications at the Patent Office, which reduced the ultimate value of such protection; and (3) the rise of industries where there is less reliance on patents and more on secrecy and on first-mover advantage, and the realization by many corporations that they might be able to do without patenting. What Schmookler did not mention explicitly is the rise in the real wage

---

23. The domestic patent application numbers are extrapolated backward, before 1940, by the number of total patent applications, foreign applications constituting less than 10 percent of the total at that point.

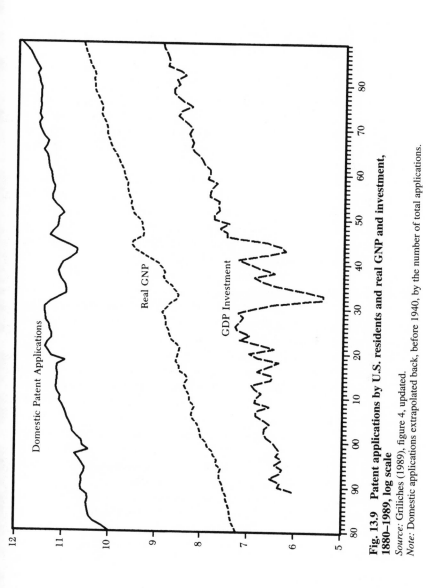

Fig. 13.9   Patent applications by U.S. residents and real GNP and investment, 1880–1989, log scale

Source: Griliches (1989), figure 4, updated.

Note: Domestic applications extrapolated back, before 1940, by the number of total applications.

and hence the rise in the opportunity cost of dealing with the patent system. This rise in real wages contributed to the significant decline in the number of patents issued to "independent" inventors and probably also to a higher threshold of potential value for corporations before they would file an application. If this is true, then the relative stagnation of domestic applications in the postwar period does not preclude the possibility that real inventive activity and its output were rising at the same time.

Schmookler's first two explanations appear less cogent today. (The judicial climate has actually reversed itself recently.) The third explanation, that the lack of growth in domestic patent applications is due to changes in the industrial mix, away from traditionally high patenting areas (such as chemicals) and toward the faster-growing, lower-patenting industries such as computers, has been disputed by Griliches (1989). He used "fixed" patent per R&D dollar intensities (from Bound et al. 1984 and Scherer 1984a) together with the industrial distribution of company R&D expenditures in 1957 and 1985 to compute a "predicted" average number of patents per R&D dollar, with a result that goes in the right direction but is rather small: a -3 percent adjustment for the whole 1957–76 period. It is small both because patenting intensities are not all that different across industries and because the industrial composition of R&D did not change drastically during this period.[24]

Another possible explanation is the overestimation of the growth in "real" R&D due to an underestimate by conventional R&D "deflators" of the growth in the real cost of doing science, in finding new drugs and new compounds, and in designing new chips. If the "real" cost of doing R&D has risen by about 3 to 4 percent more per year than is indicated by the conventional deflators, most of the observed decline in patenting per R&D dollar would be eliminated (Daniel Smith 1988).[25] It is rather difficult, however, to distinguish this from various other versions of the exhaustion of the scientific frontiers hypothesis. Why is the cost of real science rising faster than a reasonably weighted index of scientific salaries and a quality-adjusted price index of scientific instruments and equipment? Is it because the competition from other scientists within the country and abroad is driving up the resources necessary to produce a unit of visible advance in a field? Is this not just a reflection of diminishing returns to R&D investments when they are applied to a fixed or a slower-growing underlying scientific opportunities set, of crowding out and fishing out? (See also the discussion in Englander, Evenson, and Hanazaki 1988 on this.)

13.11   The Specter of Diminishing Returns

Aggregate patent numbers (applied and granted) have fluctuated greatly in the past. They have also grown more slowly in this century, much less so than

---

24. See Hall (1988) for similar results.
25. "For an institution viewed as a whole, with a constant complement of young scientists, typical weighted growth rates per scientist (in the 'sophistication factor') might be 2–5 percent in constant-value terms per annum . . ." A. V. Cohen and L. N. Ivins (1967, p. 28).

investments in R&D, which has led scholarly observers to wonder repeatedly about the implied slackening in the growth rate of technical progress. In 1935, Robert K. Merton wrote: "In the U.S., however, the number of patents has scarcely kept pace with the growth of population since 1885—a fact which may lead us to suspect the possibility of a slackening in the rate of technologic advance generally" (p. 454). At the same time, S. C. Gilfillan (1935) was blaming the decline in patenting on the decline in the native ability of the American people, due to immigration and dysgenics, because "the stupid have been breeding at a much higher rate" (pp. 218–19). In 1952, Alfred B. Stafford wondered "Is the Rate of Invention Declining?" as he observed a declining trend in patenting, from 1916 through 1947, in two-thirds of all the patent classes, and worried about diminishing returns on one hand and the increasing complexity of invention on the other[26] (see also Schmookler 1954). The same point was taken up by Scherer et al. in 1959: ". . . the sharp decline in patenting during the depressed 1930's can be attributed to unfavorable economic conditions, while the slump during World War II is explained by the historical tendency for patenting to decline during wartime. But no such ready explanation is available for the continued record of sluggishness during the booming postwar period" (p. 130). He then attributed some of this decline, as did also Schmookler (1966) later on, to a change in the judicial climate and especially to the increase in compulsory licensing decrees. But that does not seem to explain all of the decline, or its persistence into the 1970s. And this type of worry continues to this day, as can be seen in Baily and Chakrabarti (1988), Scherer (1986), and this paper itself. One can always worry that the world is coming to an end. Someday it undoubtedly will, but it does not look as if the end is already upon us, at least not yet.

What are the facts, so far as they can be discerned? There has been no absolute decline in the rate of patenting in the U.S. Total patent grants and applications are running about 30 percent above the early 1960s, and U.S. domestic patent applications have also recovered to the levels attained in the 1960s. The question then is, do we need a growing rate of invention (if patent numbers do indeed measure it) to sustain a steady positive rate of growth in total factor productivity? Does the faster growth in real R&D expenditures indicate diminishing returns to R&D or an improvement in the quality of patented inventions? And could the, we hope temporary, 11 percent decline in the average number of domestic patent applications, between its peak in 1968–71 and its trough in 1977–83, have been responsible for the productivity slowdown in the 1970s or have significant productivity growth implications for the future?

To the extent that an invention either reduces the cost of production or develops entirely new products, it has an aspect of increasing returns to it. The same invention could produce the same proportional effect, in different size markets

---

26. Stafford (1952) is a marvelous example of how easy it is to make wrong predictions about the future. See also the sharp and confused exchanges between Gilfillan, Schmookler, and Kunik in *Technology and Culture* (Gilfillan 1960).

or economies. The public good nature of most inventions and the "multiplicative" aspect of their impact do not require their number to grow just to sustain a positive rate of productivity growth. On the other hand, economies do not grow just by replication and expansion; they also get more complex, proliferate different products and activities, and develop in different geographical and economic environments. To that extent, the "reach" of any particular invention does not expand at the same rate as the growth of the overall economy, but only at the rate of growth of its "own" market. Therefore, I would expect that the "required" number of inventions for a steady positive rate of growth in productivity has also to grow, but at a rate that need not be as fast as that of the economy as a whole.

The preceding paragraph deals with the fundamentally unobservable quantum of invention or an advance in knowledge. It is clear, from the previous discussion and the earlier references, that its relationship to observed patent numbers is unlikely to have stayed constant over time. The important question, however, is what does an observed decline in patent numbers imply about the underlying stream of inventions and their ultimate effect on productivity. If the decline occurs because of a rise in the real cost of patenting, or even a decline in the expected value of the marginal patent, this may still have very little effect on the aggregate contribution of values of the inventions associated with these patents. The evidence discussed in Section 13.5 shows that the vast majority of patents are worth very little and that the bulk of the private and social total product of the inventive system is based on a relatively small number of very valuable patents. If the patent value were known to the inventor in advance then a rise in the cost of patenting or a decline in the return from inventing would only deter the marginal, low-value inventive activity, and would leave the total aggregate return effectively unchanged. Inventors are unlikely, however, to know the value of their inventions in advance. At the other extreme, one could assume that all of the estimated dispersion in patent values is "within," that all of it represents the uncertainty that faces each individual inventor. Then, a decline in patent numbers would imply a parallel decline in total inventive activity and results.[27] Inventors do, undoubtedly, face great uncertainty about the ultimate value of their inventions, as is emphasized and documented by Pakes (1986), but probably not as extensive as would be implied by the estimated cross-sectional dispersion in patent values. The truth, I believe, is somewhere in the middle, but closer to the first case, with some definite knowledge about the potential importance of the particular invention. In that case, and this is also what can be read into the numbers reported in Schankerman and Pakes (1986), a decline in patenting would be associated with an increase in the average "value" of a patent, and a much smaller impact, if any, on the aggregate social output of this activity.

Even if there were a real decline in inventive output associated with the

27. This is one way to read the evidence presented in Edwin Mansfield (1986) that major U.S. corporations have not reduced the fraction of their inventions that they patent.

observed decline in patent numbers, it is unlikely that we could discern its effects in the conventional productivity numbers. There are at least three reasons for this. First, not all of productivity growth is due to invention and only some fraction of the latter arises from patented inventions. If one takes 1.5 to 2.0 percent as the approximate growth rate per year in total factor productivity, at least half of it is likely to be due to the growth in the quality of the labor force, economies of scale, and various reallocations of capital between assets and industries. Moreover, it is unlikely that patented inventions could account for more than half of all the relevant advances in knowledge. This leaves us with at most a quarter of total productivity growth, and an unknown fraction of its fluctuations, to be attributed to patented invention.

Second, the effects of an invention on productivity appear with a long and variable lag and it is doubtful that the available data and current econometric techniques could identify them clearly. Moreover, the aggregation over many inventions and many lag structures is likely to smooth them out further, beyond recognition.

Third, the great variability in the magnitude and importance of the various inventions adds another source of variance here.[28] Given the great skewness in the value distributions one cannot take much comfort from the relatively large samples, or rather, population numbers (a point already noticed in the past by Nordhaus 1969 and others). To the extent that one does observe correlations between patent numbers and contemporaneous productivity numbers, the causality is most likely running the other way, from productivity as a measure of the economic environment to patents as a measure of inventive "effort" rather than from the impact of inventive "output" on subsequent productivity.

Thus, the question of diminishing returns to R&D and the implicit forecast of a declining productivity growth rate remains unresolved. If the relationship of patent numbers to inventive output has been changing then they cannot be used to make a judgment about this. The other evidence on this topic is also equivocal. A priori, one would expect to hit diminishing returns in any narrowly defined field, at least until the field or the product area is redefined anew by some other major breakthrough. Kuznets used detailed patent data to make this point already in 1930 (pp. 54–58). This also follows from the various theoretical models of the R&D process such as Evenson and Kislev (1975, ch. 8) and others. On the other hand, inventive effort moves from one "fishing" ground to another, and new fishing grounds open up as the result of basic R&D and other sources of discovery. Hence, in the longer run there is less evidence of exhaustion of opportunities, and studies that have tried to look for declines in the rates of return to R&D have found very little evidence of such a decline (see Griliches 1986 and Sveikauskas 1988, among others). The same conflict

---

28. See Griliches (1989, p. 316) for a "back of an envelope" calculation which concludes that if about one-third of the 10 percent decline in patent applications (between the late 1960s and 1970s) were to translate itself into a decline in real innovative output, it would take us over seven years, not counting any lags, to detect it with any statistical "confidence" even if there were no other sources of variation in productivity. And in the meantime, the trend might have reversed itself.

appears in the various estimates of the "patent production function" discussed in Section 13.4. Time-series estimates, which presumably measure returns to movements primarily along already established trajectories, all tend to come out with relatively low elasticities of patents received with respect to R&D invested, on the order of 0.2 to 0.45. On the other hand, cross-sectional studies, which presumably better represent the optimal migration of R&D resources across fields and the finding of new niches, yield elasticity estimates much closer to unity.

The assumption of diminishing returns is already contained in most R&D-based models of productivity and productivity growth. In such models, with the stock of knowledge capital proxied by a "stock" of accumulated past R&D expenditures, the estimated elasticities tend to be rather small, on the order of 0.06 to 0.2 (e.g., Mansfield 1984 and Griliches 1986). This, by the way, is not all that different from the time-series-based patent R&D coefficients estimates in Section 13.9. If productivity is a measure of knowledge accretion and patents are a proxy index for it, then there may be no paradox here, after all. This is what is also implied by Figure 13.10, which plots (on a common logarithmic scale) the index (level) of multifactor productivity in the private business sector of the U.S. economy (as computed by the BLS) together with a measure of the total "stock" of patent applications in the U.S. and the parallel concept of the stock of total R&D expenditures (both based on a 15 percent depreciation rate). Note the remarkably parallel behavior of the productivity series and the total patent stock series and the faster growth rate, at least during the earlier part of the period, of the total R&D stock series. The relationship would be poorer for the patent stock variable if only domestic patent applications were counted; it would have turned down significantly by the mid-1980s. This is a bit of evidence for my view that the relevant indicator for measures of technical change is total patents, not just domestic patents.

In the past I looked at such charts and thought that something was wrong with the productivity numbers. But if we are to believe the patent numbers, perhaps they are not so wrong after all. For reasons discussed above, I do think that over longer periods of time patent numbers are an imperfect index of inventive output whose relationship to the underlying "frontier shift" has been declining over time. More will have to be learned, however, before we can feel certain about such inferences. Thus, the patent numbers leave us where we began, with a suggestive, but possibly misleading puzzle.

13.12   Concluding Comments

In this survey I have described a number of recent studies, many of them spurred on by the growing availability of machine readable data files and on-line data bases, whose common denominator is the use of patent statistics to illuminate the process of innovation and technical change. A number of interesting and important findings have emerged from this work and also, as is

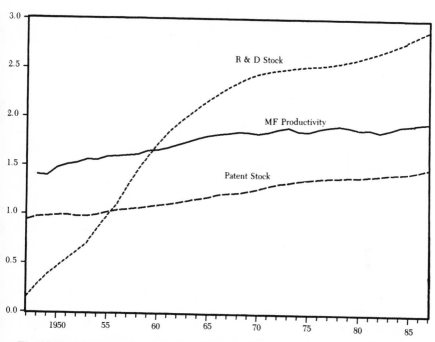

Fig. 13.10 **Multifactor productivity in the private business economy and patent and R&D capital "stocks," log scale**
Source: Griliches (1989), figure 6.
Note: R&D and patent stocks computed from aggregate data using a 15 percent declining balance depreciation formula and estimated initial conditions.

common in empirical work, quite a bit of frustration with our inability to really answer the "big" questions.

Among the major findings was the discovery of a strong relationship between patent numbers and R&D expenditures in the cross-sectional dimension, implying that patents are a good indicator of differences in inventive activity across different firms. While the propensity to patent differs significantly across industries, the relationship between R&D and patents is close to proportional, especially for firms above a minimal size. Small firms do receive a significantly higher number of patents per R&D dollar but this can be explained by their being a much more highly selected group. There is also a statistically significant relationship between R&D and patents in the within-firm time-series dimension, but it is weaker there. The bulk of the effect is contemporaneous, implying possibly also some reverse causality: successful research leading to both patents and to the commitment of additional funds for the further development of the resulting ideas.

The practical implication of these findings is that in the absence of detailed R&D data, the much more plentiful patent data can be used instead as an indicator of both inventive input and output. Care should be taken, however, not to overinterpret small and even sizable differences in patent numbers, especially in the time dimension. Analyses of survey responses by patent owners, the modeling of the renewal pattern of patents in Europe, and attempts to relate market values and changes in the stock market rates of return all conclude with very high estimates of both the variance and skewness in the distribution of patent values. These findings, especially the large amount of skewness in this distribution, lead to rather pessimistic implications for the use of patent counts as indicators of short-run changes in the output of R&D.

At the aggregate level the interesting finding is that the appearance of an absolute decline in inventive activity was largely a statistical mirage, caused by a bureaucratic rather than an economic or technological cycle. The question about the causes of the relative decline in patenting relative to the growth in R&D expenditures cannot be answered conclusively, though I remain rather sanguine on this matter. There is good reason to think that the relationship between inventive output and the number of patents has changed over time, that the yardstick shrank. Some evidence on this comes from patent renewals data pointing to a rising average "quality" of patents. Also, R&D numbers may be overestimating the real growth in inventive input. Moreover, it is not obvious that we need a growing number of inventions to sustain our current rates of growth, or that we should worry too much about the rising rate of foreign inventions. We are likely to be their ultimate beneficiaries.

In spite of all the difficulties, patent statistics remain a unique resource for the analysis of the process of technical change. Nothing else even comes close in the quantity of available data, accessibility, and the potential industrial, organizational, and technological detail. Moreover, there are other ways of using them besides simply counting them. It is possible to use a firm's distribution of patenting by field to infer its position in "technological space" and to use this information, in turn, to study how the results of R&D spill over from one firm to another, illuminating thereby also the process of strategic rivalry that the firm finds itself in. As U.S. patent renewal information becomes available at the individual patent and firm level, one will be able to use it together with data on patent citations to construct more relevant "quality-weighted" inventive "output" measures. Even without going that far, the currently available patent data can be used to study longer-run interfirm differences in levels of inventive activity and as a substitute for R&D data where they are not available in the desired detail. We should not be cursing the darkness, but rather, we should keep on lighting candles.

References

Note: A number of important references are included even if they are not cited in the text.

Achilladelis, B.; Schwarzkopf, A. and Cines, M. "A Study of Innovation in the Pesticide Industry: Analysis of the Innovation Record of an Industrial Sector," *Research Policy,* 1987, *16*(2–4), pp. 175–212.

————. "The Dynamics of Technological Trajectories: The Case of the Chemical Industry." Unpublished paper, Science and Public Policy Program, U. Oklahoma, June 1987.

Acs, Z. J. and Audretsch, D. B. "Innovation, Market Structure, and Firm Size," *Rev. Econ. Statist.,* 69(4), 1987, pp. 567–74.

————. "Patents as a Measure of Innovative Activity," *Kyklos,* 1989, 42(2), pp. 171–80.

Baily, Martin N. and Chakrabarti, A. K. *Innovation and the productivity crisis.* Washington, DC: Brookings Institution, 1988.

Baldwin, William and Scott, John T. *Market structure and technological change.* Chur and NY: Harwood Academic Publishers, 1987, ch. 1.

Basberg, B. L. "Technological Change in the Norwegian Whaling Industry: A Case Study of the Use of Patents Statistics as a Technology Indicator," *Research Policy,* 1982, 11(3), pp. 163–71.

————. "Patents and the Measurement of Technological Change: A Survey of the Literature," *Research Policy,* 1987, 16(2), 131–41.

Ben-Zion, Uri. "The R&D and Investment Decision and Its Relationship to the Firm's Market Value: Some Preliminary Results," in Griliches, ed., 1984, pp. 299–312.

Bosworth, Derek L. "The Rate of Obsolescence of Technical Knowledge—a Note," *J. Ind. Econ.,* Mar. 1978, 26(3), pp. 273–79.

————. *Intellectual property rights.* Vol. 19. *Reviews of U.K. Statistical Sources.* Oxford: Pergamon Press for the Royal Statistical Society, 1986.

Bosworth, Derek and Westaway, Tony. "The Influence of Demand and Supply Side Pressures on the Quantity and Quality of Inventive Activity," *Appl. Econ.,* Feb. 1984, 16(1), pp. 131–46.

Bound, John et al. "Who Does R&D and Who Patents?" in Griliches, ed., 1984, pp. 21–54.

Brunk, G. G. and Demack, G. "Short-run Trends in U.S. Patent Activity," *Scientometrics,* 1987, 12(1–2) pp. 111–33.

Campbell, R. S. and Nieves, A. L. "Technology Indicators Based on Patent Data: The Case of Catalytic Converters—Phase I Report: Design and Demonstration." Battelle, Pacific Northwest Laboratories, Sept. 1979.

Carpenter, M. P. and Narin, F. "Validation Study: Patent Citations as Indicators of Science and Foreign Dependence," *World Patent Information,* 1983, 5(3), pp. 180–85.

Carpenter, M. P.; Narin F. and Woolf, P. "Citation Rates to Technologically Important Patents," *World Patent Information,* 1981, 3(4), pp. 160–63.

Cockburn, Iain M. "Appropriability and the Propensity to Patent: Some Empirical Results." Paper presented at the NBER Productivity Program meeting, Dec. 1989.

————. "Essays on the Analysis of Technical Change." Unpublished PhD thesis, Harvard U., Dept. of Economics, 1990.

Cockburn, Iain and Griliches, Zvi. "Industry Effects and Appropriability Measures in the Stock Market's Valuation of R&D and Patents." NBER Working Paper No. 2465, Dec. 1987; Published in abridged form in *Amer. Econ. Rev.,* May 1988, 78(2), pp. 419–23.

Cohen, A. V. and Ivins, L. N. *The sophistication factor in science expenditure.* Dept. of Education and Science, Science Policy Studies 1. London: Her Majesty's Stationery Office 1967 pp. 1–53.

Cohen, W. M. and Levin, R. C. "Empirical Studies of Innovation and Market Structure," in *Handbook of industrial organization,* Vol. II. Eds.: Richard Schmalensee and Robert Willig, Amsterdam: North-Holland, 1989, pp. 1059–1107.

Comanor, William and Scherer, F. M. "Patent Statistics as a Measure of Technical Change," *J. Polit. Econ.,* May/June 1969, 77(3), pp. 329–98.

Cutler, R. S. "A Study of Patents Resulting from NSF Chemistry Program," *World Patent Information,* 1984, 6(4), pp. 165–69.

Englander, A. S.; Evenson, R. and Hanazaki, M. "R&D, Innovation and the Total Factor Productivity Slowdown," *OECD Econ. Stud.*, 1988, (11), pp. 8–42.

Evenson, Robert. "International Invention: Implications for Technology Market Analysis," in Griliches, ed., 1984, pp. 89–123.

———. "Patent Data: Evidence for Declining R&D Potency." Paper presented at the OECD International Seminar on Science, Technology and Economic Growth, Paris, 1989.

Evenson, Robert and Kislev, Yoav. *Agricultural research and productivity.* New Haven: Yale U. Press, 1975, ch. 8.

Evenson, R.; Kortum, S. and Putnam, J. "Estimating Patents by Industry Using the Yale-Canada Patent Concordance." Unpublished ms., Yale U., 1988.

Fagerberg, J. "A Technology Gap Approach to Why Growth Rates Differ," *Research Policy*, 1987, *16*(2–4), pp. 87–99.

———. "Innovation, Catching-Up and Productivity Growth." Paper presented at the OECD Seminar on Science, Technology, and Economic Growth, Paris, June 1989.

Faust, K. and Schedl, H. "International Patent Data: Their Utilization for the Analysis of Technological Developments," *World Patent Information*, 1983, *5*(3) pp. 144–57.

Freeman, Christopher. *The economics of industrial innovation*, 2nd ed., Cambridge: MIT Press, 1982.

———, ed. *Long waves in the world economy*. London: Frances Pinter, 1984.

Gilfillan, S. C. "The Decline of the Patenting Rate, and Recommendations," *J. Patent Office Society*, 1935, *17*, pp. 216–27.

———. "An Attempt to Measure the Rise of American Inventing and the Decline of Patenting," *Tech. Cul.*, Summer 1960, *7*(3), pp. 201–14.

Glismann, H. H. and Horn, E. J. "Comparative Invention Performance of Major Industrial Countries: Patterns and Explanations," *Management Science*, 1988, *34*(10), pp. 1169–87.

Grabowski, H. and Vernon, J. "Studies on Drug Substitution, Patent Policy and Innovation in the Pharmaceutical Industry." Final Report for NSF Grant, Duke U., 1983.

Granger, C. W. J. "Investigating Causal Relations by Econometric Models and Cross-Spectral Methods," *Econometrica*, July 1969, *37*(3), pp. 424–38.

Griliches, Zvi. "Issues in Assessing the Contribution of Research and Development to Productivity Growth," *Bell J. Econ.*, Spring 1979, *10*(1), pp. 92–116. [Reprinted as chap. 2 in this volume.]

———. "Market Value, R&D and Patents," *Econ. Letters*, 1981, *7*, pp. 183–87.

———, ed. *R&D, patents, and productivity*. Chicago: U. of Chicago Press, 1984.

———. "R&D and Innovation: Some Empirical Findings: Comment," in Griliches, ed., 1984, pp. 148–49.

———. "Productivity, R&D, and Basic Research at the Firm Level in the 1970s," *Amer. Econ. Rev.*, Mar. 1986, *76*(1), pp. 141–54. [Reprinted as chap. 4 in this volume.]

———. "Appropriating the Returns from Industrial Research and Development: Comments and Discussion," *Brookings Pap. Econ. Act.*, 1987, pp. 824–29.

———. "Productivity Puzzles and R&D, Another Nonexplanation," *J. Econ. Perspectives*, Fall 1988, *2*(4), pp. 9–21.

———. "Patents: Recent Trends and Puzzles," *Brookings Pap. Econ. Act., Microeconomics*, 1989, pp. 291–330.

Griliches, Z.; Hall, B. H. and Pakes, A. "R&D, Patents, and Market Value Revisited: Is There a Second (Technological Opportunity) Factor?" *Economics of Innovation and New Technology*, 1991, *1*, pp. 183–201.

Griliches, Z. and Lichtenberg, Frank. "R&D and Productivity Growth at the Industry Level: Is There Still a Relationship?" in Griliches, ed., 1984, pp. 465–96. [Reprinted as chap. 9 in this volume.]

Griliches, Z.; Pakes, Ariel and Hall, Bronwyn H. "The Value of Patents as Indicators of

Inventive Activity," in *Economic policy and technological performance.* Eds.: Partha Dasgupta and Paul Stoneman. Cambridge: Cambridge U. Press, 1987, pp. 97–124.

Hall, B. H. "Fishing Out or Crowding Out: An Analysis of the Recent Decline in U.S. Patenting." Unpublished ms., U. of California, Berkeley, 1988.

———. "Research and Development Investment and the Evolution of the U.S. Manufacturing Sector: Econometric Studies at the Firm Level." PhD thesis, Stanford U., 1988.

Hall, B. H. et al. "The R&D Master File," NBER Technical Paper No. 72, 1988.

Hall, B. H.; Griliches, Z. and Hausman, J. A. "Patents and R&D: Is There a Lag?" *Int. Econ. Rev.,* 1986, *27*(2), pp. 265–83.

Hausman, Jerry A.; Hall, Bronwyn and Griliches, Zvi. "Econometric Models for Count Data with an Application to the Patents-R&D Relationship," *Econometrica,* July 1984, *52*(4), pp. 909–38.

Hayashi, Fumio and Inoue, Tohru. "The Relation between Firm Growth and Q with Multiple Capital Goods: Theory and Evidence from Panel Data on Japanese Firms." NBER Working Paper 3326, Apr. 1990.

Hirschey, M. "Inventive Output, Profitability and Economic Performance," Wisconsin Working Paper, No. 5-82-28, Oct. 1982.

Huffman, W. E. and Evenson, R. "U.S. Agricultural Research and Education: An Economic Perspective After a Century." Unpublished ms., 1987, ch. 6–8.

Jaffe, Adam. "Using Patent Class Data to Measure Technological Proximity and Research Spillovers Among Firms." Unpublished ms., Harvard U., 1983.

———. "Quantifying the Effects of Technological Opportunity and Research Spillovers in Industrial Innovation." PhD thesis, Harvard U., Dept. of Economics, 1985.

———. "Technological Opportunity and Spillovers of R&D: Evidence from Firms' Patents, Profits, and Market Value," *Amer. Econ. Rev.,* Dec. 1986, *76*(5) pp. 984–1001.

———. "Demand and Supply Influences in R&D Intensity and Productivity Growth," *Rev. Econ. Statist.,* 1988, *70*(3), pp. 431–37.

———. "Real Effects of Academic Research," *Amer. Econ. Rev.,* Dec. 1989, *79*(5), pp. 957–70.

Jensen, E. "Research Expenditures and the Discovery of New Drugs," *J. Ind. Econ.,* 1987, *36*(1), pp. 83–95.

Johannisson, Bengt and Lindström, Christian. "Firm Size and Inventive Activity," *Swedish J. Econ.,* Dec. 1971, *73*(4), pp. 427–42.

Kelley, Allen C. "Scale Economies, Inventive Activity, and the Economics of American Population Growth," *Exploration Econ. Hist.,* Fall 1972, *10*(1), pp. 35–52.

Kitti, Carole. "Patent Invalidity Studies: A Survey," *IDEA, J. Law Tech.,* 1979, *20*(1), pp. 55–76.

Kleinknecht, A. "Patenting in the Netherlands: A Cross-Section Test of the Industry Life-Cycle." Unpub. paper, Paris: OECD/STIU, 1982.

———. "Measuring R&D in Small Firms: How Much Are We Missing?" *J. Ind. Econ.,* 1987, *36*(2), pp. 253–56.

Kleinknecht, A. and Verspagen, B. "Demand and Innovation: Schmookler Reexamined," *Research Policy,* 1990, *19*(4), pp. 387–94.

Kortum, S. and Putnam, J. "Estimating Patents by Industry: Parts I and II." Papers presented at the National Bureau of Economic Research Conference on Patent Count and Patent Renewal Data, Aug. 1989.

Kunik, S. J. "A Patent Attorney Takes Issue," *Tech. Cul.,* Summer 1960, *7*(3), pp. 221–27.

Kuznets, Simon. *Secular movements in production and prices.* Boston: Houghton Mifflin, 1930, pp. 54–58.

Lanjouw, J. O. "German Patent Renewal Data by Country/Industry Groups, 1953–1988: A First Look." Paper presented at the National Bureau of Economic Research Conference on Patent Count and Patent Renewal Data, Aug. 1989.

Lanjouw, J. O. and Schankerman, M. "Patent Renewal Data for Germany and the U.K., 1880–1980: A First Glimpse." Paper presented at the National Bureau of Economic Research Conference on Patent Count and Patent Renewal Data, Aug. 1989.

Levin, R. C. et al. "Appropriating the Returns from Industrial Research and Development," *Brookings Pap. Econ. Act.,* 1987, *3,* pp. 783–820.

Lieberman, M. B. "Patents, Learning by Doing, and Market Structure in the Chemical Processing Industries," *Int. J. Ind. Organ.,* 1987, *5*(3), pp. 257–350.

Manchuso, S. E.; Masuck, M. P. and Woodrow, E. C. "Analysis of Patent Expiration for Failure to Pay Maintenance Fees." Unpub. ms., Worcester Polytechnic Institute, Worcester, MA, 1987.

Mansfield, Edwin. "R&D and Innovation: Some Empirical Findings," in Griliches, ed., 1984, pp. 127–48.

————. "Patents and Innovation: An Empirical Study," *Management and Science,* 1986, *32*(2), pp. 173–81.

Merton, Robert K. "Fluctuations in the Rate of Industrial Invention," *Quart. J. Econ.* 1935, *49*(3), pp. 454–74.

Minne, B. and Noordman, H. G. A. "Technological Progress and Patent Applications in the Netherlands," *World Patent Information,* 1983, *5*(3), pp. 158–69.

Mowery, David C. "Industrial Research and Firm Size, Survival, and Growth in American Manufacturing, 1921–1946: An Assessment," *J. Econ. Hist.,* Dec. 1983, *43*(4), pp. 953–80.

Mueller, Dennis. "Patents, Research and Development, and the Measurement of Inventive Activity," *J. Ind. Econ.,* Nov. 1966, *15*(1), pp. 26–37.

Narin, F.; Noma, E. and Perry, R. "Patents as Indicators of Corporate Technological Strength," *Research Policy,* 1987, *16*(2), pp. 143–55.

Narin, F. and Olivastro, D. "Technology Indicators Based on Patents and Patent Citations," in *Handbook of quantitative studies of science and technology.* Ed.: A. F. J. van Raan. The Netherlands: Elsevier Science Pub. B.V., 1988, pp. 465–507.

National Science Board. *Science and engineering indicators, 1987.* NSB87-1. Washington, DC: U.S. GPO, 1987.

Nelson, R. R., ed. *The rate and direction of inventive activity.* Princeton, NJ: Princeton U. Press for the NBER, 1962.

Nordhaus, William. "An Economic Theory of Technological Change," *Amer. Econ. Rev.,* May 1969, *59*(2), pp. 18–28.

————. "The Recent Productivity Slowdown," *Brookings Pap. Econ. Act.,* 1972, *3,* pp. 493–536.

Office of Technology Assessment, U.S. Congress. *Research funding as an investment: Can we measure the returns?* 1986, Washington, DC: OTA-TM-SET-36.

OTAF (Office of Technology Assessment and Forecast). "Review and Assessment of the OTAF Concordance Between the U.S. Patent Classification and the Standard Industrial Classification Systems: Final Report." Unpublished ms., Patent and Trademark Office, U.S. Dept. of Commerce, Washington, DC, 1985.

Pakes, Ariel. "On Patents, R&D, and the Stock Market Rate of Return," *J. Polit. Econ.,* 1985, *93*(2), pp. 390–409.

————. "Patents as Options: Some Estimates of the Value of Holding European Patent Stocks," *Econometrica,* 1986, *54*(4), pp. 755–84.

Pakes, Ariel and Griliches, Zvi. "Patents and R&D at the Firm Level: A First Look," in Griliches, ed., 1984, pp. 55–72.

Pakes, Ariel and Schankerman, Mark. "The Rate of Obsolescence of Patents, Research Gestation Lags, and the Private Rate of Return to Research Resources," in Griliches, ed., 1984, pp. 73–88.

Pakes, Ariel and Simpson, M. "Patent Renewal Data," *Brookings Pap. Econ. Act.: Microeconomics,* 1989, pp. 331–410.

Papachristodoulou, C. "Inventions, Innovations and Economic Growth in Sweden: An Appraisal of the Schumpeterian Theory." PhD thesis, Uppsala U., 1986. Acta Universitatis Upsaliensis; Studia Oeconomica Upsaliensia, Stockholm, Sweden: Almqvist & Wiksell International, 1987. (Printed edition of doctoral dissertation.)

Pavitt, Keith. "Using Patent Statistics in Science Indicators: Possibilities and Problems," in NSF, *The meaning of patent statistics,* 1978, pp. 63–104.

———. "R&D, Patenting, and Innovative Activities: A Statistical Exploration," *Research Policy,* 1982, *11*(1), pp. 33–51.

———. "Patent Statistics as Indicators of Innovative Activities: Possibilities and Problems," *Scientometrics,* 1985, *7*(1–2), pp. 77–99.

Pavitt, K. and Patel, P. "The International Distribution of Determinants of Technological Activities," *Oxford Rev. Econ. Policy,* 1988, *4*(4), pp. 35–55.

Pavitt, K. and Soete, Luc. "Innovative Activities and Export Shares: Some Comparisons between Industries and Countries," in *Technical innovation and British economic performance.* Ed.: Keith Pavitt. London: Macmillan, 1980, pp. 38–66.

———. "International Differences in Economic Growth and the International Location of Innovation," in *Emerging technologies: Consequences for economic growth, structural change, and employment.* Ed.: Herbert Giersch. Institut für Weltwirtschaft an der Universität Kiel, Tubingen: J. C. B. Mohr, 1981, pp. 105–44.

Rosenberg, Nathan. "Science, Invention, and Economic Growth," *Econ. J.,* Mar. 1974, *84*(333), pp. 90–108.

Rossman, J. and Sanders, B. S. "The Patent Utilization Study," *Patent, Trademark, and Copyright J.,* June 1957, *1*(1), pp. 74–111.

Sanders, B. S. "Speedy Entry of Patented Inventions into Commercial Use," *Patent, Trademark, and Copyright J. of Research and Education,* 1962, *6*(1), pp. 87–116.

———. "Patterns of Commercial Exploitation of Patented Inventions by Large and Small Corporations," *Patent, Trademark and Copyright J. of Research and Education,* Spring 1964, *8,* pp. 51–92.

Sanders, B. S.; Rossman, J. and Harris, L. J. "The Economic Impact of Patents," *Patent, Trademark, and Copyright J.,* 1958, *2*(2) pp. 340–62.

Schankerman, Mark. "Measuring the Value of Patent Rights: Uses and Limitations." OECD International Seminar on Science, Technology, and Economic Growth, Paris, June 1989. (Forthcoming in OECD, *Science and Technology Indicators.*)

———. "The Private Value of Patent Rights in France 1969–87: An Empirical Study of Patent Renewal Data." Unpublished ms. Final Report to the NSF, Jan. 1990.

Schankerman, Mark and Pakes, Ariel. "The Rate of Obsolescence and the Distribution of Patent Values: Some Evidence from European Patent Renewals," *Revue Econ.,* 1985, *36*(5), pp. 917–41.

———. "Estimates of the Value of Patent Rights in European Countries During the Post-1950 Period," *Econ. J.,* Dec. 1986, *96*(384), pp. 1052–76.

Scherer, F. M. "Corporate Inventive Output, Profits, and Growth," *J. Polit. Econ.,* June 1965a, *73*(3), pp. 290–97.

———. "Firm Size, Market Structure, Opportunity, and the Output of Patented Inventions," *Amer. Econ. Rev.,* Dec. 1965b, *55,* pp. 1097–1125.

———. "The Office of Technology Assessment and Forecast Industry Concordance as a Means of Identifying Industry Technology Origins," *World Patent Information,* 1982a, *4*(1), pp. 12–17.

———. "Demand-Pull and Technological Invention: Schmookler Revisited," *J. Ind. Econ.,* Mar. 1982b, *30*(3), pp. 226–37.

———. "The Propensity to Patent," *Int. J. Ind. Organ.,* 1983, *1,* pp. 107–28.

———. "Using Linked Patent and R&D Data to Measure Interindustry Technology Flows," in Griliches, ed., 1984a, pp. 417–61.

―――. *Innovation and growth: Schumpeterian perspectives.* Cambridge: MIT Press, 1984b.

―――. "The World Productivity Growth Slump," in *Organizing industrial development.* Ed.: Rolf Wolff. Berlin: Walter de Gruyter, 1986, pp. 15–28.

Scherer, F. M. et al. *Patents and the corporation.* 2nd ed. Boston, James Galvin & Assoc., 1959.

Schmookler, Jacob. "Invention and Economic Development." Unpublished PhD dissertation, U. of Pennsylvania, 1951.

―――. "The Changing Efficiency of the American Economy: 1869–1938." *Rev. Econ. Statist.,* 1952, *34*(3), pp. 214–321.

―――. "The Level of Inventive Activity," *Rev. Econ. Statist.,* May 1954, *36*(2), pp. 183–90.

―――. "Inventors Past and Present," *Rev. Econ. Statist.,* Aug. 1957, *39*(3), pp. 321–33.

―――. "An Economist Takes Issue," *Tech. Cult.,* 1960, *1*(3), pp. 214–20.

―――. *Invention and economic growth.* Cambridge: Harvard U. Press, 1966.

―――. *Patents, invention, and economic change.* Eds.: Zvi Griliches and Leonid Hurwicz. Cambridge: Harvard U. Press, 1972.

Sirrilli, G. "Patents and Inventors: An Empirical Study," *Research Policy,* 1987, *16*(2–4), pp. 157–74.

Slama, Jiri. *One century of technical progress based on an analysis of German patent statistics.* Luxembourg: Commission of the European Communities, EUR 11044en, 1987.

Smith, Daniel W. "Will Producing More Scientists and Engineers Produce a More Innovative America?" Unpublished paper, Center for Technology and Policy, Boston U., 1988.

Soete, Luc. "Comments on the OTAF Concordance between the US SIC and the US Patent Classification." Mimeo, SPRU, U. of Sussex, Nov. 1983.

―――. "The Impact of Technological Innovation on International Trade Patterns: The Evidence Reconsidered," *Research Policy,* 1987, *16*(2–4), 101–30.

Soete, Luc et al. "Recent Comparative Trends in Technology Indicators on the OECD Area." Paper presented at the International Seminar on Science, Technology, and Economic Growth, OECD, Paris, June 1989.

Sokoloff, K. L. "Inventive Activity in Early Industrial America: Evidence from Patent Records, 1790–1846," *J. Econ. Hist.,* 1988, *48*(4), pp. 813–50.

Sokoloff, K. L. and Khan, B. Z. "The Democratization of Invention During Early Industrialization: Evidence from the U.S., 1790–1846." NBER HWP 10, 1989. Published in *J. Econ. Hist.,* June 1990, *50*(2), pp. 363–78.

SRI International. *NSF engineering program patent study.* Menlo Park, CA., Sept. 1985.

Stafford, A. B. "Is the Rate of Invention Declining?" *Amer. J. Soc.,* 1952, *57*(6), pp. 539–45.

Statistics Canada. "Canadian Patent Trends, 1984." Science, Technology, and Capital Stock Division Working Paper, Ottawa, 1986.

Stoneman, P. "Patenting Activity: A Re-evaluation of the Influence of Demand Pressures," *J. Ind. Econ.,* June 1979, *27*(4), pp. 385–401.

―――. "Comment on Hall et al.," in *Proceedings of the conference on quantitative studies of R&D in industry.* Ed.: J. Mairesse. Paris: ENSAE, 1987, Vol. 2, pp. 469–76.

Sveikauskas, L. "Productivity Growth and the Depletion of Technological Opportunities." Unpublished ms., 1988. [Forthcoming in *J. Productivity Analysis*]

Taylor, C. T. and Silberston, Z. A. *The economic impact of the patent system: A study of the British experience.* Monograph 23. Cambridge: Cambridge U. Press, 1973.

Trajtenberg, M. "A Penny for Your Quotes: Patent Citations and the Value of Innovations," *Rand J. Econ.,* Spring 1990, *21*(1).

Uno, Kimio. *Japanese industrial performance.* Amsterdam: North-Holland, 1987, ch. 17.

U.S. Bureau of the Census. *1977 enterprise statistics.* General Report on Industrial Organization, ES77-1, U.S. Govt. Printing Office, Washington, DC: U.S. GPO, 1981.

U.S. Patent and Trademark Office. *Technology assessment and forecast.* 7th Report, U.S. Dept. of Commerce, Washington, DC, Mar. 1977.

———. "All Technologies Report 1963–1988." Office of Document Information, Washington, DC, Apr. 1989 release.

Walsh, Vivien. "Invention and Innovation in the Chemical Industry: Demand Pull or Discovery Push?" *Research Policy,* 1984, *13*(4), pp. 211–34.

Wildasin, David E. "The *q* Theory of Investment with Many Capital Goods," *Amer. Econ. Rev.,* Dec. 1984, *74*(1) pp. 203–10.

Wyatt, Geoffrey. *The economics of inventions.* NY: St. Martin's Press, 1986.

V Interim Conclusions

14   Productivity, R&D, and the
        Data Constraint

Forty years ago economists discovered the "residual." The main message of this literature, that growth in conventional inputs explains little of the observed growth in output, was first articulated by Solomon Fabricant in 1954 and emphasized further by Moses Abramovitz (1956), John Kendrick (1956), and Robert Solow (1957).[1] The pioneers of this subject were quite clear that this finding of large residuals was an embarrassment, at best "a measure of our ignorance" (Abramovitz, 1956 p. 11). But by attributing it to technical change and other sources of improved efficiency they turned it, perhaps inadvertently, from a gap in our understanding into an intellectual asset, a method for measuring "technical change." Still, it was not a comfortable situation, and a subsequent literature developed trying to "explain" this residual, or more precisely, to attribute it to particular sources (Griliches, 1960, 1963a,b, 1964; Edward Denison, 1962; Dale Jorgenson and Griliches, 1967). The consensus of that literature was that, while measurement errors may play a significant role in such numbers, they could not really explain them away. The major sources of productivity growth were seen as coming from improvements in the quality of labor and capital and from other, not otherwise measured, sources of efficiency and technical change, the latter being in turn the product of formal and informal R&D investments by individuals, firms, and governments, and of the largely unmeasured contributions of science and other spillovers. The prescrip-

Reprinted from the *American Economic Review* 84, no. 1 (March 1994): 1–23.

Presidential address delivered at the one hundred sixth meeting of the American Economic Association, January 4, 1994, Boston, MA.

I am indebted to many friends for comments on an earlier draft, and to the Bradley, Sloan, and National Science Foundations for the support of my work.

1. The message itself was not exactly new. With hindsight, it is visible in the earlier work of Jan Tinbergen (1942), George Stigler (1947), Glen Barton and Martin Cooper (1948), Jacob Schmookler (1952), and Vernon Ruttan (1954, 1956). See Griliches (1996) for a more detailed account of these developments.

tion of additional investments in education, in science, and in industrial R&D followed from this reading of history as did also the hope and expectation that the recently observed rates of "technical change" would continue into the future.

This general view of the sources of growth was put into doubt by the events of the 1970s and 1980s. Beginning in 1974 (or perhaps already in 1968) productivity growth slowed down significantly in the United States and abroad, and it has not fully recovered yet, at least as far as national aggregates are concerned. The many explanations that were offered for these events were not very convincing (see e.g., Denison, 1979; Martin Baily and Robert Gordon, 1988; Griliches, 1988). As time went on and the direct effects of the energy-price shocks wore off but the expected recovery did not come or came only weakly, more voices were heard arguing that the slowdown might not be temporary; that the energy-price shocks just revealed what was already there—a decline in the underlying trend of technical change in the world economy; that the growth opportunities that had opened up in the late 1930s and had been interrupted by World War II have been exhausted, reflecting perhaps the completion of an even longer cycle, going back to the beginnings of this century (see e.g., Alfred Kleinknecht, 1987; Gordon, 1993a). Even more ominously, the slowdown was blamed on diminishing returns to science and technology in general and on the onset of widespread socioeconomic sclerosis (see e.g., William Nordhaus, 1972, 1989; Mancur Olson, 1982; F. M. Scherer, 1983, 1986; Robert Evenson, 1984; Baily and A. K. Chakrabarti, 1988).

This is a rather pessimistic view of our current situation, and I would like to argue that the observed facts do not really support it. But that will not be easy, both because some of the "facts" are contradictory and because our measurement and observational tools are becoming increasingly inadequate in the context of our changing economy. Nevertheless, I will review some of the evidence for such views and argue with their interpretation. There are several possibilities here: (i) this view is true and that is sad; (ii) it is not true and recovery is around the corner if not already underway; (iii) it may be true, but whatever is or is not happening has little to do with diminishing returns to science or industrial R&D. Or, (iv) it may be that we just do not know. As is the case with global warming, we may not have an adequate understanding of the mechanisms producing growth or adequate data to adjudicate whether there has or has not been an underlying trend shift. If that is true, as is most likely, the question arises as to why we don't know more after years of research done by so many good people. What is it about our data and data acquisition structure, and possibly also our intellectual framework, that prevents us from making more progress on this topic?

In discussing this range of topics, I will concentrate primarily on the R&D component of this story—not because it can explain much of the productivity slowdown (it cannot), and not just because this is where I have done most of my recent work, but because it illustrates rather well the major point I want to make here tonight: that our understanding of what is happening in our economy (and in the world economy) is constrained by the extent and quality of the available data. I will also allude briefly to similar issues which arise in interpreting the productivity contribution of computers in the economy. Parallel tales about data constraining our understanding could also be told about other potential productivity-slowdown villains: energy-price shocks, insufficient investment in physical capital, and possible declines in human-capital investments. Having reached the verdict of "not proven," largely on account of insufficient evidence, I shall make a number of more general remarks on the state of our data and the possible reasons for it. The major message that I will be trying to convey is that we often misinterpret the available data because of inadequate attention to how they are produced and that the same inattention by us to the sources of our data helps explain why progress is so slow. It is not just the measurement of productivity that is affected. Other fields of empirical economics are also struggling against the limitations imposed by the available data. Great advances have been made in theory and in econometric techniques, but these will be wasted unless they are applied to the right data.

14.1   The "Facts"

There are three sets of "facts" to look at: what has happened to productivity, what has happened to investment in R&D and science, and what has happened to the relationship between them. Sometime in the late 1960s measured productivity growth in the United States started to slow down. After a mild recovery in the early 1970s, the world economy was hit by two successive oil-price shocks which dropped economic growth rates in most of the developed economies to levels significantly below those experienced in the 1960s and early 1970s. While the effects of the oil-price shocks wore off and real energy prices declined to close to their earlier levels, productivity growth rates did not recover much. At this point, and also somewhat earlier, many observers started wondering whether something more fundamental than just an energy-price-shock-induced business cycle was afoot. Standing in the early 1980s and looking back at the recent past, one would have observed a decline in total patents granted in the United States beginning in the early 1970s and a decline in the share of GNP being devoted to industrial R&D starting in the mid-1960s, the timing looking suspiciously appropriate for declining productivity growth rates 5–10 years later. One could also see a continuous and worrisome decline in the number of patents received per corporate R&D dollar (see below). But there were also many other events clouding this picture, making one wonder whether faltering R&D and scientific efforts are really the culprits behind our current woes.

A number of discordant facts are important for an understanding of what happened. First, the productivity-growth decline in many other countries was larger, absolutely, than in the United States, and there it was not associated

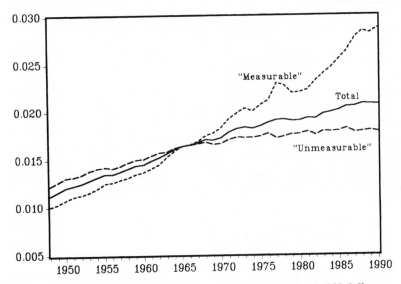

Fig. 14.1   Gross domestic product per man-hour (thousands of 1982 dollars, United States, 1948–1990)

Notes: Measurable sectors are agriculture, mining, manufacturing, transportation, communications, and public utilities; unmeasurable sectors are construction, trade, finance, other services, and government. Values for 1977–1987 are based on 1987 weights; values for 1948–1976 are based on 1982 weights (the series are linked at 1977).

with declines in R&D investment.[2] Second, as illustrated in Figure 14.1, the sectors where the productivity slowdown has persisted in the United States are largely outside of manufacturing, communications, and agriculture (see Gordon, 1987). Besides mining and public utilities, which were affected more specifically by the energy-price shocks, it has lingered particularly in construction, finance, and other services where output measurement is notoriously difficult. Third, the decline in patent grants in the 1970s was just a bureaucratic mirage, an example of fluctuations induced by changes in the data-generating process (a budgetary crisis in the Patent Office) rather than a reflection of the underlying activity itself.[3] The number of patent applications did not decline significantly during this period, but also it did not grow. The latter fact, coupled with a continuous upward growth in the absolute level of company-financed R&D, resulted in a persistent decline in the patents per R&D ratio in the United States (and also in most of the other countries for which we have data). This raised the specter of diminishing returns to R&D and offered the hypothe-

---

2. For example, the rate of growth in total factor productivity declined between the 1960s and the 1970s by 4.5 percent in Japan, 3.3 percent in France, and "only" 2 percent in the United States (see Organization for Economic Cooperation and Development, 1993).

3. See Griliches (1990) for more details on this story.

sis of "exhaustion of inventive opportunities" as a potential explanation for the productivity slowdown.

This hypothesis has been examined recently by various authors. There are basically two styles of analysis: one focuses directly on the link, if any, between R&D and productivity growth (see e.g., Griliches, 1986a; Bronwyn Hall, 1993; Scherer, 1993), while the other uses patents as indicators of the output of the R&D effort and looks at what has happened to the "knowledge-production function" (see e.g., Griliches, 1990; Ricardo Caballero and Adam Jaffe, 1993; Robert Evenson, 1993; Samuel Kortum, 1993). The bridge that is missing between these two approaches would examine the units in which patents affect productivity growth and ask whether they have stayed constant over time. Without such constancy, no clear interpretation is possible.

14.2   Productivity Growth and the Role of R&D

In parallel to the aggregate "residual" literature, a more micro-oriented approach had developed. It took the study of technical change, diffusion, and the role of formal R&D as its main challenge, with the hope of bringing more of it within the realm of economic analysis, helping thereby also to explain some of this residual away. Using modern language, one can interpret Edwin Mansfield's and my own early work on diffusion and on the role of R&D in agriculture and manufacturing as trying to endogenize as much of technical change as was possible (Griliches, 1957, 1958, 1964; Mansfield, 1961, 1965). Other important contributors to this literature were Richard Nelson, Scherer, Jacob Schmookler, and Nestor Terleckyj. By expanding the notion of capital to include also R&D capital and estimating its effects, this literature documented the contribution of public and private investments in R&D and their spillovers to the growth of productivity.[4] But the magnitude of the estimated effects was modest, not enough to account for the bulk of the observed residual or the fluctuations in it (Griliches, 1988). The experience here was similar to other attempts to account for the residual, such as using "embodiment" theories to magnify the potential effects of capital accumulation (Denison, 1962; Nelson, 1962) or looking for increasing returns to scale (Griliches and Vidar Ringstad, 1971). These various effects are real and nonnegligible, but not large enough.

There is one other way of trying to make something more out of the R&D story: the possibility that the productivity impact of R&D has declined over time—that the coefficients have changed. This hypothesis has been investigated repeatedly by a number of researchers with mixed results. Studies that used data through the 1970s and early 1980s found no decline in the relevant coefficients. More recent studies that analyze data through the late 1980s report more mixed results, varying strongly with how the computer industry and

4. This literature has been surveyed in Griliches (1979, 1991), Jacques Mairesse and Mohamed Sassenou (1991), Wallace Huffman and Evenson (1993), and M. I. Nadiri (1993).

Table 14.1   Industry TFP Growth Regressions: Coefficients of the R&D-Sales
Ratio by Period, Three-Digit SIC Level (N = 143 or 142)

Row	Period	With computers	Without computers
1	1958–1973	0.332 (0.066)	0.317 (0.066)
2	1973–1989	0.357 (0.072)	0.134 (0.059)
3a	1978–1989	0.300 (0.073)	0.115 (0.062)
3b	1978–1989 "revised"	0.461 (0.070)	0.348 (0.070)

Notes: The equations include also dlog(energy/capital) as an additional utilization variable. Standard errors are shown in parentheses. The ratio of company-financed R&D to total sales in 1974 is from Scherer (1984) for row 1; this ratio is updated for 1984 from National Science Foundation (1992) for rows 2 and 3. Row 3b shows total-factor-productivity growth revised downward for computers and upward for electronic components and drugs (computers = SIC 357).

its deflator are handled in the analysis.[5] At the same time, the stock market's valuation of R&D fell significantly, in terms of both ex post returns to R&D in the 1980s (Michael Jensen, 1993) and the market's view of current R&D investments (Bronwyn Hall and Robert Hall, 1993; B. Hall, 1993).

My own recent foray into this type of analysis of industry data at the three-digit SIC level is summarized in Table 14.1.[6] It reports estimates from regressions of growth rates in total factor productivity (TFP) on the rate of investment in R&D (the R&D-sales ratio), where the estimated coefficient can be interpreted as the excess gross rate of return to R&D (Griliches, 1979). The earlier 1958–1973 period yields an estimate on the order of 0.33, while the estimate for the later 1973–1989 period even rises a bit, to 0.36. So far, so good! But when one excludes the outlier computer industry (see Fig. 14.2) the estimated coefficient falls from 0.36 to 0.13 for 1973–1989 and even lower for 1978–1989. Only one observation out of 143 does this![7]

These results raise a major data conundrum: is it right to treat the computer industry as an outlier and exclude it from such calculations just because the

5. As reported in Griliches (1986a), I found no significant decline in the relevant coefficients through the mid-1970s. Frank Lichtenberg and Donald Siegel (1991) replicated and extended this work to the early 1980s and found *increases* in the relevant coefficients through 1985. B. Hall (1993) updated and extended the Griliches and Mairesse (1984) study of publicly traded U.S. manufacturing firms to the end of the 1980s and found that the R&D coefficients came close to disappearing in the 1970s and early 1980s but recovered in the late 1980s to about half or more of their original size. Her result is very sensitive, however, to the particular deflators used in constructing the output measure. When separate industry-level deflators are used, including the newly revised deflator for the output of the computer industry, there is no evidence of a decline in the "potency" of R&D at all; the estimated coefficients rise rather than fall. See also Englander et al. (1988), Pari Patel and Luc Soete (1988), Sveikauskas (1990), and Scherer (1993).

6. The total-factor-productivity numbers come from the National Bureau of Economic Research data base (Wayne Gray, 1992). The R&D numbers come from Scherer (1984), updated to 1984 using 2.5-digit-level information from National Science Foundation (1992).

7. Updating the Griliches and Lichtenberg (1984) results for 28 2.5-digit SIC industries and using a possibly more appropriate R&D-by-product-field measure yields essentially similar results, as does a parallel computation at the more aggregated two-digit SIC level using unpublished Bureau of Labor Statistics data on total (five-factor) productivity.

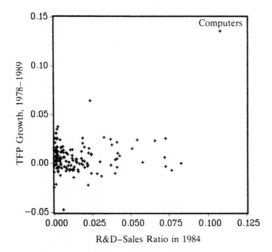

Fig. 14.2   Total-factor-productivity growth (per annum) and research intensity in U.S. manufacturing, three-digit SIC level, 1978–1989

productivity measure may be better there? It is quite possible that if other technologically advanced industries (such as instruments, communications equipment, and pharmaceuticals) had their price indexes adjusted in a similar fashion, Figure 14.2 would look much better, with the computer industry not being as much of an outlier and with the whole period showing much higher (social) returns to R&D. That this is indeed the case can be seen in Figure 14.3, where only three such adjustments are made, but before I discuss it, I need to digress briefly and remind you about the developments in computer price measurement.

Quality change is the bane of price and output measurement. Until 1986, computer prices were treated as unchanged in the national income accounts. It took 25 years for the recommendations of the Stigler committee (Griliches, 1961; National Bureau of Economic Research, 1961) to have a noticeable effect on official practice, but when they did, they did it with a bang! In 1986 the Bureau of Economic Analysis (BEA) introduced a new computer price index, based on hedonic regression methods, into the national accounts and revised them back to 1972 (Rosanne Cole et al., 1986).[8] This index was falling by about 15 percent per year or more (as compared to the assumed value of zero before), and that had several major implications, including the fact that it made the apparent recovery in manufacturing productivity in the 1980s much stronger, about one-third of the total coming from the introduction of this price index alone (Gordon, 1993b).

There was nothing wrong with the price index itself. It was, indeed, a major

---

8. For historical background on these developments see Jack Triplett (1989) and Ernst Berndt (1991 Ch. 4).

advance, and the BEA should be congratulated for making it, but the way it was introduced created some problems. First, it was a unique adjustment. No other high-tech product had received parallel treatment, and thus it stuck out like a sore thumb. This had the unfortunate consequence that the productivity growth in the computer industry itself was seriously overestimated, because some of its major inputs, such as semiconductors, were not similarly deflated. Second, it was introduced into a framework with fixed weights, wreaking havoc on it. Using fixed 1982 weights and a sharply falling price index implied the absence of a "real" computer industry in the early 1970s and a very rapid growth in its importance, leading to a more than doubling of the share of machinery in total manufacturing output by the late 1980s. This last problem has largely been solved recently with the introduction of "benchmark-weighted" estimates of gross domestic product (GDP) and the moving away from fixed-weights national income accounting (Allan Young, 1992). But the first problem, the uniqueness of this adjustment in the face of similar, though perhaps not as extreme, problems elsewhere remains to haunt us.

What I have done in Figure 14.3 (and in row 3b of Table 14.1) is to adjust the estimated TFP growth in the computer industry downward by deflating materials purchases in this industry, which to a significant extent consist of purchases of other computer components and semiconductors, by the same output price index. I have also substituted a similar price index in the semiconductors (electronic components) industry and also adjusted the growth of TFP in the pharmaceuticals industry upward to reflect the exclusion of price declines due to the introduction of generics in the current measurement procedures. (I shall come back to discuss this last adjustment later on.) So adjusted,

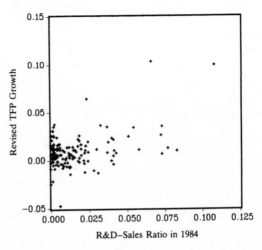

Fig. 14.3   Revised total-factor-productivity growth (per annum), U.S. three-digit manufacturing industries, 1978–1989

Note: Computers adjusted downward; electronic components and drugs adjusted upward.

Figure 14.3 does not look all that bad, and row 3b in Table 14.1 indicates no decline in the R&D coefficient even without the computer industry.

What is one to make of these conflicting stories? It seems that the observed decline in the R&D coefficients did not begin seriously until the latter half of the 1970s, with the second oil-price shock and the rise in the dollar exchange rate. The abruptness of the decline argues against a "supply-side" explanation in terms of exhaustion of inventive opportunities. It is more likely that the peculiar aggregate shocks of that time went against R&D-intensive industries: first, because they hit energy-intensive industries such as chemicals and petroleum refining more severely; and second, because the subsequent rise in value of the dollar and the expansion in imports that followed hit some of the more high-tech R&D-intensive industries even harder, leading to declines in "competitiveness," losses of rents, and the appearance of excess capacity. The subsequent rise in the R&D coefficients (if it did in fact occur), the rise in corporate R&D investments through most of the 1980s, and the rise in patenting in the late 1980s (as we shall see), all argue against interpreting these coefficient movements as reflecting "real" declines in the once and future "potency" of R&D. What did happen, though, was a sharp widening of the differential between social and private returns to R&D. The internationalization of R&D, the rise in the technical and entrepreneurial skills of our competitors, and the sharp rise in the dollar exchange rate in the mid-1980s, all combined to erode, rather rapidly, the rents accruing to the earlier accumulated R&D capital and to the technical-expertise positions of many of our enterprises. This rise in the rate of private obsolescence and the fall in the "appropriability" of R&D led to sharp declines in both profitability and real product prices. The latter, if they were actually reflected in the appropriate price indexes, would show up as an increase in productivity, rather than a decline.

Before accepting this inconclusive verdict, one still has to face the evidence of declining patent-to-R&D ratios. Figure 14.4 plots domestic patent applications divided by total company-financed R&D expenditures in U.S. industry (in 1972 dollars) and by the total number of scientists and engineers in industry. Looking at the right half of this plot (the last couple of decades) we see a more or less continuous decline with a small, but possibly significant, turnaround in the late 1980s. Similar trends can be seen also in other countries, even in Japan (Evenson, 1991). But before one takes this as an indicator of our recent problems, one should glance also at the left side of this figure, which goes back to the early 1920s. How long has this been going on? This ratio keeps falling, both through good times (while productivity growth rates were rising) and bad times. If this was not a cause for worry earlier, why should one worry about it now?[9]

---

9. Actually quite a few people worried about it then also: see Griliches (1990) for more detail and W. Fellner (1970), who worried about the rising real cost of R&D as an indicator of diminishing returns.

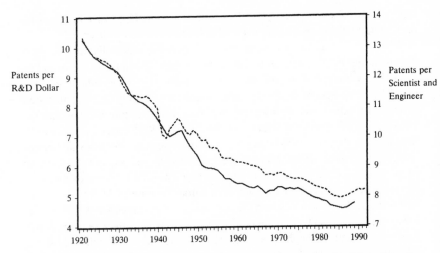

Fig. 14.4 Domestic patent applications per company-financed R&D in industry (dashed line; in 1972 dollars) and per scientist and engineer (solid line), log scale

14.3 Patents: A Shrinking Yardstick?

To decide whether we should be worried by what is happening with the patent numbers we need to know what they measure. Since I have discussed this at some length elsewhere (Griliches, 1990), I will make only two points here. First, the interpretation of Figure 14.4 need not be pessimistic. Its message may not be what meets the eye. And, second, the meaning of both the numerator and the denominators of the ratios plotted in Figure 14.4 may have changed significantly over time.

If patents can be taken as indicators of invention, and if the value of an invention is proportional to the size of its market (or economy), then the fact that their total numbers remained roughly constant over long time periods is consistent with nondeclining growth rates of output and overall productivity.[10] If inventions are "produced" by a combination of current R&D and the existing state of knowledge (incorporating the accumulated effects of science and spillovers from the previous research activities of others), and if R&D is invested approximately "optimally," then under reasonable assumptions, a rise (or fall) in the underlying knowledge stock will affect them both in parallel fashion and will leave their ratio unchanged.[11] There will be, therefore, no evidence in this

---

10. This follows from the nonrival nature of inventions (see Kenneth Arrow, 1962; Paul Romer, 1990).

11. Assume an aggregate inventions "production function" of the form $N = R^\gamma Z$, where R is a measure of current R&D inputs and Z represents all other shifters of this function: the accumulation of one's own past R&D successes and also spillovers from the research efforts of others. Then, $\gamma < 1$ implies short-run diminishing returns to current R&D, a "fishing-out" phenomenon given the current "state of the art" Z. To the extent that endogenous (and exogenous) forces "recharge"

ratio on the underlying state of the "stock of knowledge." Moreover, it will be declining with growth in the size of the market, since a rise in the value of inventions will push R&D up until present costs equal again the present value of future (private) returns.

The rate of growth of domestic patents was close to zero during the last three decades. That by itself should not be worrisome. If their average value had been growing at the same rate as the economy as a whole, there would be no reason for us to worry about it. But there were long periods when the actual numbers were worse than that. During 1965–1985 the number of domestic patent applications declined by −0.6 percent per year while company-financed R&D expenditures were growing by 4.8 percent per year, in constant prices. But a negative growth rate in the number of inventions and a positive one in R&D are inconsistent with an unchanging inventions production function, unless the overall pool of available knowledge is declining, or more likely, unless the relationship between inventions and the number of patents applied for has been changing.

The suspicion that the relationship between the number of patents and the number of inventions (weighted by their relative economic importance) has been changing is not new. Schmookler (1966) stops most of his analysis with pre–World War II data, believing that the meaning of the patent statistics changed at that time. What needs to be reconciled in the data is the sharp contrast between the rapidly growing R&D series during 1953–1968 (and earlier) and the essentially flat patent series. There are a number of not mutually exclusive possibilities here:

(i) The fast-growing R&D expenditures, fueled by the new global opportunities that opened up in the post–World War II period, were being invested in the face of rapidly diminishing returns.

(ii) Some of the observed growth in R&D could be spurious, the result of reclassification of informal technological activities into formal R&D under the pressure of tax accountants, public-relations experts, and R&D tax credits.

(iii) The rise of formal R&D-based invention crowded out smaller, less valuable individual-inventor-based patents, while the rise in the cost of patenting (in terms of the time costs of dealing with the patent system) and the more recent sharp rise in fees may have selected out a large number of

---

the pool (in Evenson's [1991] terminology) and change Z as the result of the direct and indirect additions to the overall stock of knowledge, there need not be diminishing returns to R in the long run. If R is chosen so as to equate the value of its marginal product, $V(\gamma N/R)$, to the marginal real cost of R, C, and if V is the expected present value of an invention, one can rewrite the first-order condition as $N/R = C/\gamma V$, which yields the major conclusion that the ratio of inventions per unit of R&D is independent of the state of general knowledge Z. Moreover, N/R will be declining in V, the size of the market. For a more detailed elaboration of such models see the "quality-ladders" approach of Gene Grossman and Elhanan Helpman (1991), Caballero and Jaffe (1993), and Kortum (1993).

potentially low-valued patents. Given the evidence that the value distribution of inventions and patents is extremely skewed, with only a small fraction having a high present value, such a crowding out could raise average values significantly, though the required rate is rather on the high side.[12]

It is also likely that the threshold for what is patentable has risen, given the large influx of foreign patent applications into the U.S. system all impinging on a relatively slow-growing and budget-constrained patent office.[13] On the other hand, the legal status of patents in the United States has improved significantly with the creation of a special patents court, driving up the expected private value of a patent. Given the presence of so many opposing forces, there is no compelling need to rely on the exhaustion-of-inventive-opportunities hypothesis, especially since patents-to-R&D ratios were falling much more drastically during the "good times" of the past than recently.[14] Moreover, if we do take these numbers seriously, then good news is just around the corner: domestic patent applications have risen sharply in the last five years (see Fig. 14.5), implying a potential resurgence in the rate of technological change. This leaves us, however, more or less where we started, with the productivity slowdown largely unexplained.

14.4   Why Is the Glass Half-Empty?

Economists have not been very successful in explaining what has happened to the economy during the last two decades, nor have they been able to agree on what should be done about it. I will argue that data and measurement difficulties may in fact be a major source of this failure. This point will be made not to provide us with an alibi, but rather to temper the pretentiousness of some of our pronouncements and to urge us toward the more mundane tasks of observation and measurement.

12. There is scattered evidence on the rising "quality" of patents from patent renewal data (see Mark Schankerman and Ariel Pakes, 1986; Pakes and Margaret Simpson, 1989) and from the rising number of claims per patent (see X. Tong and J. D. Frame, 1992). The latter, for example, rose at about 2.5 percent per year between 1970 and 1990. That is about right for this period but far too low for the 6+ percent earlier. On the other hand, Caballero and Jaffe (1993), using citation data, find that the average "size" of a patent did not grow during the last 20 years.

13. There is some evidence that such crowding-out may have occurred. Between 1966–1969 and 1981–1985 the "yield ratio" for domestic patent applications in terms of grants received fell by about 15 percent (from 0.68 to 0.58) before recovering somewhat in the late 1980s (to 0.62). See Griliches (1990) for a survey of these issues and citations of the relevant literature.

14. A similar story is also told by other scattered invention "output" indicators. In their study of innovations in the chemical, textile, and machinery-tools industries, Baily and Chakrabarti (1988) found a decline in the number of innovations in the 1970s in two out of these three industries, and some recovery thereafter. Similar patterns were observed in a study of British industrial innovations (see the figure in Gerhard Mensch et al. [1991]). In both cases the timing is not right for an explanation of the slowdown in the 1970s. The impact on productivity is too fast. Rather, it is likely to reflect the impact of the slowdown in the growth of aggregate demand and the recessions of the 1970s. In both cases there is an upturn in the 1980s.

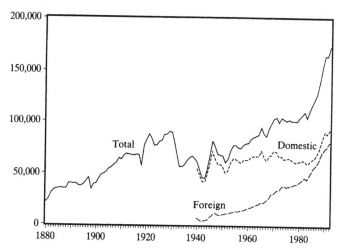

Fig. 14.5   Patent applications in the United States, 1880–1992

Why don't we know more after all these years? Our data have always been less than perfect. What is it about the recent situation that has made matters worse?

The brief answer is that the economy has changed and that our data-collection efforts have not kept pace with it. "Real" national income accounts were designed in an earlier era, when the economy was simpler and had a large agricultural sector and a growing manufacturing sector. Even then, a number of compromises had to be made to get measurement off the ground. In large sectors of the economy, such as construction and most of the services, government, and other public institutions, there were no real output measures or relevant price deflators. Imagine a "degrees of measurability" scale, with wheat production at one end and lawyer services at the other. One can draw a rough dividing line on this scale between what I shall call "reasonably measurable" sectors and the rest, where the situation is not much better today than it was at the beginning of the national income accounts. Table 14.2 shows the distribution of nominal GDP by major industrial sector. In the early post–World War II period, the situation was not all that bad: about half of the overall economy was "measurable" in this sense. By 1990, however, the fraction of the economy for which the productivity numbers are half reasonable had fallen to below one-third. Figure 14.6 tells the same story with employment numbers. Measurement problems have indeed become worse. Our ability to interpret changes in aggregate total factor productivity has declined, and major portions of actual technical change have eluded our measurement framework entirely.[15]

15. An argument could be made that this story would not be so bleak if we had focused on consumption expenditures instead, since many of the offending industries produce largely intermediate products and services. But personal consumption expenditures account only for about 68

Table 14.2   The Distribution of GNP by Major Industrial Sector, in Current Prices (Percentages)

Industry	1947	1959	1969	1977	1990
Agriculture	8.8	4.1	3.0	2.8	2.0
Mining	2.9	2.5	1.8	2.7	1.8
Construction	3.9	4.8	5.1	4.8	4.4
Manufacturing	28.1	28.6	26.9	23.6	18.4
Transportation and utilities	8.9	9.1	8.6	9.1	8.7
Wholesale trade	7.1	6.9	6.7	7.0	6.5
Retail trade	11.7	9.9	9.8	9.6	9.3
Finance, insurance, and real estate	10.1	13.8	14.2	14.4	17.7
Other services	8.6	9.7	11.5	13.0	18.9
Government	8.6	10.2	12.6	12.5	12.2
"Measurable" sectors[a]	48.7	44.3	40.3	38.2	30.9

Source: Tables 6.1 and 6.2 of the *National Income and Products Accounts* (1928–1982) and *Survey of Current Business* (May 1993).

Note: Numbers before 1977 are not strictly comparable, since the latest revision was carried back only to 1977.

[a]Agriculture, mining, manufacturing, and transportation and utilities.

An example of the consequences of this shift is what has come to be known as the "computer paradox." We have made major investments in computers and in other information-processing equipment. The share of "information" equipment in total producer investment in durable equipment, in current prices, has more than doubled, from about 17 percent in 1960 to 36 percent in 1992. Computers alone went up from less than 1 percent to 11 percent of the total; and that does not allow for improvements in the quality of this equipment, which has been happening at a very fast rate—on the order of 15–30 percent per year (see Jack Triplett, 1989; Berndt and Griliches, 1993). Why has this not translated itself into visible productivity gains? The major answer to this puzzle is very simple: over three-quarters of this investment has gone into our "unmeasurable" sectors (see Table 14.3), and thus its productivity effects, which are likely to be quite real, are largely invisible in the data.

That there were gains is not really in doubt. Just observing the changes in the way banks and airlines operate, and in the ways in which information is delivered to firms and consumers, would lead one to conclude that we are in the midst of a major technical revolution. Effective distances are declining rapidly in many parts of the world. The rise of ATM networks in banking has resulted in substantial though largely unmeasured time savings for consumers.

---

percent of GDP, while services represent 56 percent of personal consumption. Thus, it is unlikely that looking at consumption data in more detail would change the tenor of my remarks much. A cursory look at *Personal Consumption Expenditures* (Bureau of Economic Analysis, 1990) yields a rough estimate of 47 percent of total consumption expenditures not easily measurable in real terms. The two largest difficult items consist of hard-to-measure services in the medical, insurance, legal, entertainment, and education areas (23 percent) and housing-related services (21 percent).

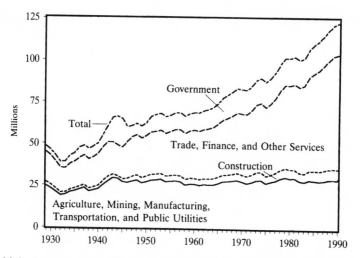

Fig. 14.6   Persons engaged in production by industry, United States, 1929–1990

Table 14.3   **Investment in Computers (OCAM) in the U.S. Economy (Percentage of Total)**

Industry	1979	1989	1992
Agriculture	0.1	0.1	0.1
Mining	2.4	1.1	0.9
Construction	0.1	0.3	0.2
Manufacturing	29.4	20.3	20.0
Transportation	1.3	2.0	1.0
Communication	1.5	1.4	1.5
Utilities	1.2	2.8	3.7
Trade	19.9	16.3	20.0
Finance, insurance, and real estate (F.I.R.E.)	32.5	38.7	37.8
Other services	11.6	17.0	13.9
"Unmeasurable" sectors[a]	64.1	72.3	71.9
Plus consumer and government purchases as percentage of all computer (OCAM) purchases	67.7	77.6	77.0

Source: Unpublished BEA tabulations.

Notes: OCAM = office, computing, and accounting machinery.

[a]Construction, trade, F.I.R.E., and other services.

It is less clear, however, whether the large expansion of the securities industry has been associated with a similar productivity increase or was primarily a response to a real decline in the cost of rent-seeking induced by the falling price of information processing (see Timothy Bresnahan et al., 1992).

There is also some scattered evidence for the positive contribution of computers in manufacturing, but given the needle-in-the haystack aspect of this problem, it is not particularly strong (see e.g., Alan Krueger, 1993; Donald

Siegel and Griliches, 1992; Erik Brynjolfsson and Lorin Hitt, 1993; Igal Hendel, 1993). Some of the gains from computers have been reflected in higher wages of their operators and in the more general rise in the returns to education and "skill" (Chinhui Juhn et al., 1993). More generally, we may be just at the beginning of the computer era, early in its diffusion and learning stages, with most of the productivity contributions still to come, as we learn how to use computers more effectively and integrate them more efficiently into the existing production structures (Paul David, 1991).

Similar arguments, can be (and have been) made about the difficulties in measuring the contribution of R&D to productivity growth (see Griliches, 1979). From one-third to over half of all industrial R&D is "sold" to the government, either in the form of research contracts and prototypes or indirectly in the form of weapons and space equipment, and its direct productivity effects do not show up in the data at all. Private R&D investment is also likely to have followed the economy and shifted its targets toward the faster-growing sectors, with more invention and technical change occurring exactly where we have more trouble in measuring them.

Not only has the economy shifted into uncharted waters, but even in the "measurable" sectors accelerating rates of change have destroyed the basis for some of the older compromises. Currently, new goods are introduced into the various official price indexes rather slowly. While attempts are being made to reduce the revision cycle in the producer price index from five to two years for some of the more high-tech goods, this may still not be fast enough. In the personal-computers market, for example, the life of a model has recently fallen to a year or less (Berndt et al., 1995).

Dealing with the quality-change problem by treating every version of a product sold to a different type of customer as a separate commodity, as is currently the predominant official practice, creates its own problems. By linking out the decline in prices experienced by consumers in their shift to supermarkets, discount stores, and mail-order purchases, it underestimates significantly not only the output of services, but also the output of some of the more "standard" manufacturing industries (Marshall Reinsdorf, 1993). A prime example of that is the treatment of generics in the pharmaceutical price indexes. The stylized facts are as follows:

(i) Generics are introduced at roughly half the price of the original brand.
(ii) The brand price, however, does not decline (it sometimes even goes up), with the ex-monopolist depreciating optimally her original position and with generics gaining between half and three-quarters of the market for the particular drug.
(iii) But because generic versions are treated as separate commodities, in spite of what the FDA says, the price index does not fall, and since the value of shipments declines as the market shifts to generics (and to hospital and

HMO formularies), so does measured "output" in this industry and the associated productivity measures (Griliches and Iain Cockburn, 1994).

This might explain the rather strange fact that during the last decade pharmaceuticals, an industry with one of the highest R&D-sales ratios, had a rather dismal productivity-growth performance. This was the period with an increasing penetration of generics, which should have reduced measured prices in this industry but did not.

The measurement environment has deteriorated also in other ways. There is less willingness on the part of firms and consumers to respond to detailed questions, and our government has done little to emphasize the importance of good economic data to its own functioning or to the overall understanding of our economy. The consequence of such deterioration can be illustrated by the uncertainty about the level of industrial investment in basic research, an investment which many think is crucial to our long-run economic performance (Griliches, 1986a). Because the question that asks about the allocation of total R&D expenditures by the "character of work" is not mandatory and is also not an easy one to answer, less than half of all the firms surveyed in 1988 answered it. As a result of such nonresponse, the best that can be done is to produce a "reasonable" range of estimates, based on alternative imputation algorithms, from $2.5 to $8.2 billion (and a "central" guess of $3.9 billion), which leaves us really in the dark as to what has happened to such investments recently (Eileen I. Collins, 1990).

14.5   Data Woes

Why are the data not better? The facts themselves are not in dispute. Every decade or so a prestigious commission or committee produces a report describing in detail various data difficulties and lacunae: the Stigler committee report on government price statistics (National Bureau of Economic Research, 1961) is still a living document, as are the related Ruggles report (Richard Ruggles, 1977), the Rees productivity report (National Academy of Sciences, 1979), the Bonnen report (J. T. Bonnen, 1981), the Creamer GNP improvement report (D. Creamer, 1977), the recent OTA report (Office of Technology Assessment, 1989), and many others. But life goes on, and change in this area is very slow. Why? I don't really have good answers to this question, and the topic itself is much larger than can be handled in this address, but at least three observations come to mind:

(i) The measurement problems are really hard.
(ii) Economists have little clout in Washington, especially as far as data-collection activities are concerned. Moreover, the governmental agencies in these areas are balkanized and underfunded.

(iii) We ourselves do not put enough emphasis on the value of data and data collection in our training of graduate students and in the reward structure of our profession. It is the preparation skill of the econometric chef that catches the professional eye, not the quality of the raw materials in the meal, or the effort that went into procuring them (Griliches, 1986b).

In many cases the desired data are unavailable because their measurement is really difficult. After decades of discussion we are not even close to a professional agreement on how to define and measure the output of banking, insurance, or the stock market (see Griliches, 1992). Similar difficulties arise in conceptualizing the output of health services, lawyers, and other consultants, or the capital stock of R&D. While the tasks are difficult, progress has been made on such topics. The work of Jorgenson and Barbara Fraumeni (1992) on the measurement of educational output is an example both of what can be done and of the difficulties that still remain. But it is not reasonable for us to expect the government to produce statistics in areas where the concepts are mushy and where there is little professional agreement on what is to be measured and how. Much more could be done, however, in an exploratory and research mode.[16] Unfortunately, the various statistical agencies have been both starved for funds and badly led, with the existing bureaucratic structure downplaying the research components of their enterprise when not being outright hostile to them, research being cut first when a budget crunch happens (Triplett, 1991).

Our current statistical structure is badly split, there is no central direction, and the funding is heavily politicized. How else can one explain that the national income accounts and the BEA as a whole receive only one-third, and health and education statistics each less than one-half of the funds allocated to agricultural statistics?[17] How does one explain the failure of the most recent attempt at getting more money for economic statistics, the late "Boskin initiative"? Central economic statistics do not have a clear constituency that lobbies on their behalf. Recent governments seem not to care enough, or to have enough energy to fight for something that has a more distant horizon than the next election. One hopes for some improvement in this situation from the current administration. It has people who know better in reasonably important positions. Still, with the main focus on the daily crisis and the continuing bud-

---

16. I refrain from offering a detailed list of my own favorite data improvements; but a census of real wealth (i.e., a survey of structure, equipment, and other resources and their utilization—not just what is on the books, but what is actually out there in the field) would be high on my list. I would also like to see a survey of patent owners on the use and potential value of their property rights.

17. I am not arguing that too much is currently being spent on agricultural statistics. That would require a substantive analysis, which has not been done. I am saying, however, that the other areas of federal statistics could use both more funding and a redirection of existing funding. We are also currently spending far more on *monthly* employment and average hourly earnings data than we spend to collect all of the other inputs and outputs *annually*. With Congressional prodding, we spend much more on local-markets data than on national-level data.

get battles with Congress, I am not all that optimistic. But if we want progress in this area, if we care, we need to make our opinions heard. We need to convince Congress (and ourselves) that the requests for additional funding of the statistical infrastructure are justified as investments in general knowledge and more informed policy formation; that they are not just self-serving, intended to allow us to publish more articles or run thousands more regressions; that it is indeed important to know what is happening and to understand where we might be going or drifting.[18]

We need also to make observation, data collection, and data analysis a more central component of our graduate teaching. How can we expect our community to fight for the budgets of the BEA, BLS, or Census, if the average student doesn't really know how the data that they use are manufactured or what the national accounts are made of?[19] We also need to teach them to go out and collect their own data on interesting aspects of the economy and to rely less on "given" data from distant agencies.[20] There are encouraging signs that some of this is happening, especially in the micro area. One is much more cheered by work such as that of Robert Fogel (1986) on heights and nutrition, Alan Krueger and Orley Ashenfelter (1994) on twins, Richard Levin et al. (1987) on the appropriability of technology, Rebecca Henderson and Cockburn on pharmaceutical R&D, Richard Freeman and Harry Holzer (1986) on inner-city youths, Schankerman and Pakes (1986) on patent renewal data, Manuel Trajtenberg (1990a) on CT scanners, and Trajtenberg (1990b) and Adam Jaffe et al. (1993) on patent citations, where researchers go out, collect, and create new data sets, than by the 20,000th regression on the Robert Summers and Alan Heston (1991) data set, illuminating as it may be. But unless we transmit this message to our students, we will not be able to convince others that this is a cause worth supporting.

14.6 Expanding the Framework

Is there something possibly wrong with the way we ask the productivity question, with the analytical framework into which we force the available data? I think so. I would focus on the treatment of disequilibria and the measurement of knowledge and other externalities. The current measurement framework

---

18. One should probably worry also about the overall level of support for economic research. As a percentage of total academic research funding, it fell from 1.5 percent in 1979 to 1.2 percent in 1990. While the number of economists doing academic research was rising at 5.5 percent per year, funds per researcher were falling in real terms at -2.3 percent per year, and the Federal share in these funds was also dropping from 48 percent to only 27 percent (in 1989). At the same time, real funds per researcher in the academy as a whole were rising at 0.4 percent per year (National Science Board, 1991). What is it that we have been doing wrong?

19. The recent shift toward a "three essays" Ph.D. thesis is also not conducive to a serious involvement with data creation.

20. Unfortunately, the usage is apt. Data already means "given" rather than collected or observed.

proceeds as if all investment and employment decisions are made at known and common factor and product prices, throwing all of the heterogeneity and uncertainty—the surprises and the disappointments—into the residual category. An alternative view would see measured productivity growth as a summation of above- (and below-) average returns to various current investment decisions and capital gains (or losses) on existing physical- and human-capital stocks.[21] The appearance of such investment opportunities is the essence of growth and change. They are largely disequilibrium phenomena, resulting in a lurching from one "steady state" to another rather than something smooth and exponential. The presence of locally increasing returns, network externalities, asymmetric information, and heterogeneous expectations, the appearance of new products and technologies, and the changes in the political and regulatory environments are all sources of such "excess" returns, while the ex post fixity of much of the investment in both physical and human capital causes capital gains and losses and unanticipated "obsolescence" in the various stocks. We will have to figure out how to take the residual apart along such lines to make more progress in understanding its proximate sources.

Our theories tend to assume that we are, indeed, at the frontier and that we can only either move along it or try to shift it, the latter being a difficult and chancy business. In fact we may be far from our existing "frontiers." Harvey Leibenstein's (1966) ideas about X-efficiency, or more correctly X-inefficiency, did not get much of a sympathetic ear from us. They were inconsistent with notions of equilibrium, the absence of unexploited profit opportunities, and the possibilities for economic arbitrage. But real economic growth is the consequence of both the appearance of such disequilibria and the devising of ways of closing them. How quickly they are eliminated depends on the strength of incentive systems within enterprises, and on their organizational quality. In spite of the large growth in the literature on organizations, we have not yet developed useful ways of quantifying their strengths and weaknesses. Nor are we close to having measures of such factors as the "work ethic" or aspects of the property-rights system which are likely to contribute much to the observed differences in productivity across nations.

The "new" growth theories have various externalities as their centerpiece (see Solow [1991] for a recent review). It is somewhat ironic that they have come to the fore just when growth started declining and notions of eternal exponential growth began to lose their luster. Knowledge externalities are obviously very important in the growth process, but they do not help us to explain what has happened in the last two decades. There is no reason to believe that they have declined over time. If anything, the communication and transportation advances should have expanded the availability of such externalities.[22] But we have no good models for the measurement of such processes.

21. This is not a new idea. Versions of it appear in Harry Johnson (1964), Arnold Harberger (1990), and Theodore Schultz (1990) and presumably also elsewhere.

22. The story is similar for externalities from human-capital investments, another linchpin of the new growth theories, but I will not pursue it here.

Knowledge is not like a stock of ore, sitting there waiting to be mined. It is an extremely heterogeneous assortment of information in continuous flux. Only a small part of it is of any use to someone at a particular point of time, and it takes effort and resources to access, retrieve, and adapt it to one's own use. Thus models of externalities must perforce be models of interaction between different actors in the economy. We have, however, very few convincing models of such interactions, and the identification problems are severe (see e.g., Charles Manski, 1993). Our measurement frameworks are not set up to record detailed origin and destination data for commodity flows, much less so for information flows. We do have now a new tool for studying some of this: citations to patents and the scientific literature (see e.g., Jaffe et al., 1993), but anyone currently active in the e-mail revolution and participating in the conferences and workshops circuit knows how small this tip is relative to the informal-communications iceberg itself.

14.7   The Glass Half-Full?

After a long detour I come back to the original question: why don't we know more about the sources of productivity growth and the causes for its recent slowdown? Why does it feel as if the glass is still half-empty? First note that in a trivial sense we are doing better: the residual is smaller. But that is the bad news, not the good. It is smaller not because we have succeeded in providing a substantively fuller explanation of output growth, but rather because measured output growth declined, leaving some of these explanations in the dust. But we are also doing better substantively. We know much more about the components of growth and where our measures are lacking. After decades of work and contributions by Denison, Jorgenson, Kendrick, and many others, the conceptual and measurement underpinnings of the growth accounts are in much better shape today. We now have extensive micro data on firms, their productivity, their R&D expenditures, and other variables. We have more data on individual investments in education and training, and we also have more asset detail on capital formation. More international data are now available, with the OECD both collecting R&D data and computing TFP numbers for many countries, and with Summers and Heston (1991) providing comparable real GNP numbers for many countries. Finally, we have much more computing power and better econometric techniques and frameworks for attacking many of the problems that arise in the analysis of such data. So what is still missing?

We are caught up in a mixture of unmeasurement, mismeasurement, and unrealistic expectations. The productivity situation is both better than we think and also worse. It is likely that there have been significant unmeasured productivity advances in many of the service sectors (Bresnahan, 1986; Baily and Gordon, 1988). Moreover, rising R&D investment rates in the mid-1980s and the recent rise in the number of patent applications augur well for the future. Also, productivity growth rates are probably underestimated even in the "measurable" sectors because they are based on "book value" estimates of physical-

and human-capital stocks and do not reflect the capital losses—the obsolescence that occurred, first as the result of the various energy-price shocks, and later as the result of increased international competition and the melting away of much of the previously existing monopoly rents to both types of capital. That is actually bad news. We are not as wealthy as we thought, but productivity growth, based on the lower remaining levels of input, is probably higher than we have measured it.

A cautionary remark needs to be added here: productivity growth contributes to the potential for welfare, but it is not the same thing. Welfare can move in the opposite direction if the resources released by productivity growth do not find adequate employment in other, economically valuable, activities (including leisure). Also the physical, economic, and political environments can change, both positively and negatively, overwhelming the productivity story.[23] So even though I have been focusing on it here tonight, it is not the be-all of economic welfare. But as George Bernard Shaw used to say when he was accused of money-grubbing: "Yes, I know that money is not happiness, but it is a pretty good substitute."

Nevertheless, the issues I have been discussing here tonight are important. Much depends on whether the "truth" is closer to the upper ("measurable") line in Figure 14.1, or the lower one. The country's mood is affected by bad data and incorrect perceptions. Are we really not much better off than we were in the 1960s? Would we really like to exchange the commodity assortment we have today for that of yesteryear? Our health system, warts and all? The air pollution? The civil-rights situation? The fear of nuclear war? These are not just idle intellectual curiosities. They affect what we feel about ourselves and the future.

Returning to the topic of technical change, our expectations of what economics can deliver here may also be excessive. It is unlikely that we can have a fully "endogenous" theory of technical change. Yes, both the rate and direction of inventive activity are subject to economic influences and analysis. So also is the diffusion of innovations. But the outcome of inventive activity is not really predictable. True "innovation" is an innovation. If it were knowable in advance it would not be one, and the innovators would not be able to collect any rents. In that sense it is futile to expect that we could control it fully or predict it well.[24] Given the fundamental uncertainties entailed in the creative act, in invention, and in innovation, there is no reason to expect the fit of our models to be high or for the true residual to disappear. We should, however, be able to "explain" it better ex post even if we cannot predict it.

23. Between 1970 and 1989, average hours of work per worker went down by 7 percent, air pollution went down significantly, and the crime rate came close to doubling (Baily et al., 1993). Of course, these data are also problematic (see Scott Boggess and John Bound, 1993).
24. "The set of opportunities for innovation at any moment are determined by what the physical laws of the world really are and how much has already been learned and is therefore 'accidental' from the viewpoint of economics" (Arrow, 1969 p. 35).

The metaphor of the glass half-empty is also misleading. As we fill it, the glass keeps growing. A major aspect of learning is that the unknown keeps expanding as we learn. This should be looked at positively. It is much better this way—especially for those of us who are engaged in research!

References

Abramovitz, Moses. "Resource and Output Trends in the U.S. since 1870." *American Economic Review,* May 1956 *(Papers and Proceedings), 46*(2), pp. 5–23.

Arrow, Kenneth J. "The Economic Implications of Learning by Doing." *Review of Economic Studies,* June 1962, *29*(3), pp. 155–73.

———. "Classificatory Notes on the Production and Transmission of Technological Knowledge." *American Economic Review,* May 1969 *(Papers and Proceedings), 59*(2), pp. 29–35.

Baily, Martin N.; Burtless, G. and Litan, R. E. *Growth with equity: Economic policymaking for the next century.* Washington, DC: Brookings Institution, 1993.

Baily, Martin N. and Chakrabarti, A. K. *Innovation and the productivity crisis.* Washington, DC: Brookings Institution, 1988.

Baily, Martin N. and Gordon, Robert J. "The Productivity Slowdown, Measurement Issues, and the Explosion of Computer Power." *Brookings Papers on Economic Activity,* 1988, (2), pp. 347–420.

Barton, Glen T. and Cooper, M. R. "Relation of Agricultural Production to Inputs." *Review of Economics and Statistics,* May 1948, *30*(2), pp. 117–26.

Berndt, Ernst R. *The practice of econometrics: Classic and contemporary.* Reading, MA: Addison-Wesley, 1991.

Berndt, Ernst R. and Griliches, Zvi. "Price Indexes for Microcomputers: An Exploratory Study," in M. F. Foss, M. E. Manser, and A. H. Young, eds., *Price measurements and their uses,* NBER Studies in Income and Wealth, Vol. 57. Chicago: University of Chicago Press, 1993, pp. 63–93.

Berndt, Ernst R.; Griliches, Zvi and Rappaport, Neal. "Econometric Estimates of Price Indexes for Personal Computers in the 1990's." *Journal of Econometrics,* 1995, *68,* pp. 243–68.

Boggess, Scott and Bound, John. "Did Criminal Activity Increase During the 1980s? Comparison Across Data Sources." National Bureau of Economic Research (Cambridge, MA), Working Paper No. 4431, 1993.

Bonnen, J. T. "Improving the Federal Statistical System: Issues and Options." *Statistical Reporter,* February 1981, pp. 133–221.

Bresnahan, Timothy F. "Measuring the Spillovers from Technical Advance." *American Economic Review,* September 1986, *76*(4), pp. 741–55.

Bresnahan, Timothy F.; Milgrom, P. and Paul, J. "The Real Output of the Stock Exchange," in Z. Griliches, ed., *Output measurement in the service sectors,* NBER Studies in Income and Wealth, Vol. 56. Chicago: University of Chicago Press, 1992, pp. 195–218.

Brynjolfsson, Erik and Hitt, Lorin. "Is Information Systems Spending Productive? New Evidence and New Results." Sloan School (Massachusetts Institutes of Technology) Working Paper No. 3571–93, 1993.

Bureau of Economic Analysis, U.S. Department of Commerce. *The national income and product accounts of the United States, 1929–82.* Washington, DC: U.S. Government Printing Office, 1986.

————. *Personal consumption expenditures,* Methodology Paper Series MP-6. Washington, DC: U.S. Government Printing Office, 1990.

Caballero, Ricardo J. and Jaffe, Adam B. "How High Are the Giants' Shoulders?" in Olivier J. Blanchard and Stanley Fischer, eds., *NBER macroeconomics annual,* Cambridge, MA: MIT Press, 1993, pp. 15–74.

Cole, Rosanne; Chen, Y. C.; Barquin-Stolleman, J. A.; Dulberger, E.; Helvecian, N. and Hodge, J. H. "Quality Adjusted Price Indexes for Computer Processors and Selected Peripheral Equipment." *Survey of Current Business,* January 1986, *66*(1), pp. 41–50.

Collins, Eileen I. "Estimating Basic and Applied Research and Development in Industry: A Preliminary Review of Survey Procedures," NSF 90–322. Washington, DC: National Science Foundation, 1990.

Creamer, D. *Gross national product improvement project report.* U.S. Department of Commerce, Office of Federal Statistical Policy and Standards. Washington, DC: U.S. Government Printing Office, 1977.

David, Paul A. "Computer and Dynamo: The Modern Productivity Paradox in a Not-Too-Distant Mirror," in *Technology and productivity.* Paris: Organization for Economic Cooperation and Development, 1991, pp. 315–48.

Denison, Edward F. *The sources of economic growth in the U.S. and the alternatives before us,* Supplementary Paper No. 13. New York: Committee for Economic Development, 1962.

————. *Accounting for slower economic growth.* Washington, DC: Brookings Institution, 1979.

Englander, A. S.; Evenson, R. E. and Hanazaki, M. "R&D, Innovation, and the Total Factor Productivity Slowdown." *OECD Economic Studies,* Autumn 1988, (11), pp. 7–42.

Evenson, Robert E. "Technical Change in U.S. Agriculture," in R. R. Nelson, ed., *Government and technical change: A cross industry analysis.* New York: Pergamon, 1984, pp. 233–82.

————. "Patent Data by Industry: Evidence for Invention Potential Exhaustion?" in *Technology and productivity: The challenge for economic policy.* Paris: Organization for Economic Cooperation and Development, 1991, pp. 233–48.

————. "Patents, R&D, and Invention Potential: International Evidence." *American Economic Review,* May 1993 *(Papers and Proceedings), 83*(2), pp. 463–68.

Fabricant, Solomon. *Economic progress and economic change.* New York: National Bureau of Economic Research, 1954.

Fellner, W. "Trends in Activities Generating Technological Progress." *American Economic Review,* March 1970, *60*(1), pp. 1–29.

Fogel, Robert. "Nutrition and the Decline in Mortality since 1700: Some Preliminary Findings," in Stanley Engerman and Robert Gallman, eds., *Long-term factors in American economic growth,* NBER Studies in Income and Wealth, Vol. 51. Chicago: University of Chicago Press, 1986, pp. 439–555.

Freeman, Richard and Holzer, Harry. *The black youth employment crisis.* Chicago: University of Chicago Press, 1986.

Gordon, Robert J. "Productivity, Wages, and Prices Inside and Outside of Manufacturing in the U.S., Japan, and Europe." *European Economic Review,* April 1987, *31*(3), pp. 685–739.

————. "Comment on Baily." *Brookings Papers on Economic Activity,* Microeconomics, 1993a, (2), pp. 131–52.

————. "American Economic Growth: One Big Wave." Unpublished manuscript, National Bureau of Economic Research, Cambridge, MA, 1993b.

Gray, Wayne. "Upgrading Productivity Data Through 1989." Mimeo, National Bureau of Economic Research, Cambridge, MA, 1992.

Griliches, Zvi. "Hybrid Corn: An Exploration in the Economics of Technological Change." *Econometrica,* October 1957, *25*(4), pp. 501–22.

———. "Research Cost and Social Returns: Hybrid Corn and Related Innovations." *Journal of Political Economy,* October 1958, *66*(5), pp. 419–31.

———. "Measuring Inputs in Agriculture: A Critical Survey." *Journal of Farm Economics,* December 1960, *42*(5), pp. 1411–33.

———. "Hedonic Price Indexes for Automobiles: An Econometric Analysis of Quality Change," in *The price statistics of the federal government.* Washington, DC: National Bureau of Research, 1961, pp. 173–96.

———. "The Sources of Measured Productivity Growth: U.S. Agriculture, 1940–1960." *Journal of Political Economy,* August 1963a, *81*(4), pp. 331–46.

———. "Production Functions, Technical Change, and All That." Netherlands School of Economics, Econometric Institute Report No. 6328, 1963b.

———. "Research Expenditures, Education and the Aggregate Agricultural Production Function." *American Economic Review,* December 1964, *54*(6), pp. 961–74.

———. "Issues in Assessing the Contribution of R&D to Productivity Growth." *Bell Journal of Economics,* Spring 1979, *10*(1), pp. 92–116. [Reprinted as chap. 2 in this volume.]

———. "Productivity, R&D and Basic Research at the Firm Level in the 1970s." *American Economic Review,* March 1986a, *76*(1), pp. 141–54. [Reprinted as chap. 4 in this volume.]

———. "Data Issues in Econometrics," in Z. Griliches and M. Intriligator, eds., *Handbook of econometrics.* Amsterdam: North-Holland, 1986b, pp. 1466–1514.

———. "Productivity Puzzles and R&D: Another Nonexplanation." *Journal of Economic Perspectives,* Fall 1988, *2*(4), pp. 9–21.

———. "Patent Statistics as Economic Indicators: A Survey." *Journal of Economic Literature,* December 1990, *18*(4), pp. 1661–1707. [Reprinted as chap. 13 in this volume.]

———. "The Search for R&D Spillovers." *Scandinavian Journal of Economics,* Supplement 1991, *94,* pp. 29–47. [Reprinted as chap. 11 in this volume.]

———. "Introduction," in Z. Griliches, ed., *Output measurement in the service sectors,* NBER Studies in Income and Wealth, Vol. 56. Chicago: University of Chicago Press, 1992, pp. 1–22.

———. "The Discovery of the Residual." *Journal of Economic Literature,* September 1996, *34,* pp. 1324–30.

Griliches, Zvi and Cockburn, Iain A. "Generics and New Goods in Pharmaceutical Price Indexes." *American Economic Review,* December 1994, *84*(5), pp. 1213–32.

Griliches, Zvi and Lichtenberg, Frank. "R&D and Productivity Growth at the Industry Level: Is There Still a Relationship?" in Zvi Griliches, ed., *R&D, patents, and productivity.* Chicago: University of Chicago Press, 1984, pp. 465–96. [Reprinted as chap. 9 in this volume.]

———. "Errors of Measurement in Output Deflators." *Journal of Business and Economic Statistics,* January 1989, *7*(1), pp. 1–9.

Griliches, Zvi and Mairesse, Jacques. "Productivity and R&D at the Firm Level," in Zvi Griliches, ed., *R&D, patents, and productivity.* Chicago: University of Chicago Press, 1984, pp. 339–74. [Reprinted as chap. 5 in this volume.]

Griliches, Zvi and Ringstad, Vidar. *Economies of scale and the form of the production function.* Amsterdam: North-Holland, 1971.

Grossman, Gene M. and Helpman, E. *Innovation and growth in the global economy.* Cambridge, MA: MIT Press, 1991.

Hall, Bronwyn H. "Industrial Research during the 1980s: Did the Rate of Return Fall?" *Brookings Papers on Economic Activity,* Microeconomics, 1993, (2), pp. 289–330.

Hall, Bronwyn H. and Hall, Robert E. "The Value and Performance of U.S. Corporations." *Brookings Papers on Economic Activity,* 1993, (1), pp. 1–50.

Harberger, Arnold C. "Reflections on the Growth Process." Unpublished manuscript, University of California, Los Angeles, 1990.

Hendel, Igal. "The Role of PC's in Manufacturing Industries." Unpublished manuscript, Harvard University, 1993.

Henderson, Rebecca and Cockburn, Iain. "Scale, Scope and Spillovers: The Determinants of Research Productivity in the Pharmaceutical Industry." National Bureau of Economic Research (Cambridge, MA) Working Paper No. 4466, 1993.

Huffman, Wallace E. and Evenson, Robert E. *Science for agriculture.* Ames, IA: Iowa State University Press, 1993.

Jaffe, Adam; Trajtenberg, Manuel and Henderson, Rebecca. "Geographic Localization of Knowledge Spillovers as Evidenced by Patent Citations." *Quarterly Journal of Economics,* August 1993, *108*(3), pp. 577–98.

Jensen, Michael C. "The Modern Industrial Revolution, Exit, and the Failure of Internal Control Systems." *Journal of Finance,* July 1993, *48*(3), pp. 831–80.

Johnson, Harry G. "Comment on Vaizey," in *The residual factor and economic growth.* Paris: Organization for Economic Cooperation and Development, 1964, pp. 219–27.

Jorgenson, Dale W. and Fraumeni, Barbara M. "The Output of the Education Sector," in Z. Griliches, ed., *Output measurement in the service sectors,* NBER Studies in Income and Wealth, Vol. 56. Chicago: University of Chicago Press, 1992, pp. 303–38.

Jorgenson, Dale W. and Griliches, Zvi. "The Explanation of Productivity Change." *Review of Economic Studies,* March 1967, *34*(3), pp. 249–83.

Juhn, Chinhui; Murphy, K. M. and Pierce, B. "Wage Inequality and the Rise in Returns to Skill." *Journal of Political Economy,* June 1993, *101*(3), pp. 410–42.

Kendrick, John W. *Productivity trends: Capital and labor.* New York: National Bureau of Economic Research, 1956.

Kleinknecht, Alfred. *Innovation patterns in crisis and prosperity.* New York: St. Martin's, 1987.

Kortum, Samuel. "Equilibrium R&D and the Patent-R&D Ratio: U.S. Evidence." *American Economic Review,* May 1993 *(Papers and Proceedings), 83*(2), pp. 450–57.

Krueger, Alan B. "How Computers Have Changed the Wage Structure: Evidence from Microdata, 1984–89." *Quarterly Journal of Economics,* February 1993, *108*(1), pp. 33–60.

Krueger, Alan and Ashenfelter, Orley. "Estimates of the Economic Return to Schooling from a New Sample of Twins." *American Economic Review,* December 1994, *84*(5), pp. 1157–73.

Leibenstein, Harvey. "Allocative Efficiency vs. 'X-Efficiency.'" *American Economic Review,* June 1966, *56*(3), pp. 392–415.

Levin, Richard; Klevorick, A.; Nelson, R. and Winter, S. "Appropriating the Returns from Industrial Research and Development." *Brookings Papers on Economic Activity,* Microeconomics 1987, (3), pp. 783–820.

Lichtenberg, Frank and Siegel, Donald. "The Impact of R&D Investment on Productivity: New Evidence Using Linked R&D-LRD Data." *Economic Inquiry,* April 1991, *29*(2), pp. 203–29.

Mairesse, Jacques and Sassenou, Mohamed. "R&D and Productivity: A Survey of Econometric Studies at the Firm Level." *STI Review* (OECD, Paris), 1991, *8,* pp. 9–43.

Mansfield, E. "Technical Change and the Rate of Imitation." *Econometrica,* October 1961, *29*(4), pp. 741–66.

――――. "Rates of Return from Industrial R&D." *American Economic Review,* May 1965 *(Papers and Proceedings), 55*(2), pp. 310–22.

Manski, Charles F. "Identification of Endogenous Social Effects: The Reflection Problem." *Review of Economic Studies,* July 1993, *60*(3), pp. 531–42.

Mensch, Gerhard; Haag, Gunter and Weidlich, Wolfgang. "The Schumpeter Clock," in *Technology and productivity.* Paris: Organization for Economic Cooperation and Development, 1991, pp. 523–44.

Nadiri, M. I. "Innovations and Technological Spillovers." National Bureau of Economic Research (Cambridge, MA) Working Paper No. 4423, August 1993.

National Academy of Sciences. *Measurement and interpretation of productivity.* Washington, DC: National Academy Press, 1979.

National Bureau of Economic Research. *The price statistics of the federal government,* General Series No. 73. New York: National Bureau of Economic Research, 1961.

National Science Board. *Science and engineering indicators—1991.* Washington, DC: U.S. Government Printing Office, 1991.

National Science Foundation. *Research and development in industry: 1989,* NSF 92-307. Washington, DC: National Science Foundation, 1992.

Nelson, Richard R. *The rate and direction of inventive activity.* Princeton, NJ: Princeton University Press, 1962.

Nordhaus, William D. "The Recent Productivity Slowdown." *Brookings Papers on Economic Activity,* 1972, (3), pp. 493–537.

――――. "Comment on Griliches." *Brookings Papers on Economic Activity,* Microeconomics 1989, pp. 320–25.

Office of Technology Assessment, U.S. Congress. *Statistical needs for a changing U.S. economy,* Background Paper OTA-BP-E-58. Washington, DC: U.S. Government Printing Office, 1989.

Olson, Mancur. *The rise and decline of nations.* New Haven, CT: Yale University Press, 1982.

Organization for Economic Cooperation and Development. *OECD Economic outlook,* No. 53. Paris: Organization for Economic Cooperation and Development, June 1993.

Pakes, Ariel and Simpson, Margaret. "Patent Renewal Data." *Brookings Papers on Economic Activity,* Microeconomics 1989, pp. 331–410.

Patel, Pari and Soete, Luc. "Measuring the Economic Effects of Technology." *STI Review* (OECD, Paris), 1988, *4,* pp. 121–66.

Reinsdorf, Marshall. "The Effect of Outlet Price Differentials on the U.S. Consumer Price Index," in M. F. Foss, M. E. Manser, and A. H. Young, eds., *Price measurements and their uses,* NBER Studies in Income and Wealth, Vol. 57. Chicago: University of Chicago Press, 1993, pp. 227–54.

Romer, Paul M. "Endogenous Technological Change." *Journal of Political Economy,* October 1990, *98*(5), pp. S71–S102.

Ruggles, Richard. *The wholesale price index.* Washington, DC: Council on Wage and Price Stability, 1977.

Ruttan, Vernon W. *Technological progress in the meat packing industry, 1910–47,* Marketing Research Report. Washington, DC: U.S. Department of Agriculture, 1954.

――――. "The Contribution of Technological Progress to Farm Output, 1950–1975." *Review of Economics and Statistics,* February 1956, *38*(1), pp. 61–69.

Schankerman, Mark and Pakes, Ariel. "Estimates of the Value of Patent Rights in European Countries During the Post-1950 Period." *Economic Journal,* December 1986, *96*(384), pp. 1052–76.

Scherer, F. M. "R&D and Declining Productivity Growth." *American Economic Review,* May 1983 *(Papers and Proceedings), 73*(2), pp. 215–18.

――――. "Using Linked Patent and R&D Data to Measure Interindustry Technology

Flows," in Z. Griliches, ed., *R&D, patents, and productivity.* Chicago: University of Chicago Press, 1984, pp. 417–64.

———. "The World Productivity Growth Slump," in R. Wolff, ed., *Organizing industrial development.* Berlin: de Gruyter, 1986, pp. 15–27.

———. "Lagging Productivity Growth: Measurement, Technology and Shock Effects." *Empirica,* 1993, *20*(1), pp. 5–24.

Schmookler, Jacob. "The Changing Efficiency of the American Economy 1869–1938." *Review of Economics and Statistics,* August 1952, *34*(3), pp. 214–31.

———. *Invention and economic growth.* Cambridge, MA: Harvard University Press, 1966.

Schultz, Theodore W. *Restoring economic equilibrium.* Oxford: Blackwell, 1990.

Siegel, Donald and Griliches, Zvi. "Purchased Services, Outsourcing, Computers, and Productivity in Manufacturing," in Z. Griliches, ed., *Output measurement in the service sectors,* NBER Studies in Income and Wealth, Vol. 56. Chicago: University of Chicago Press, 1992, pp. 429–60.

Solow, Robert M. "Technical Change and the Aggregate Production Function." *Review of Economics and Statistics,* August 1957, *39*(3), pp. 312–20.

———. "Growth Theory," in David Greenaway, Michael Bleaney, and Ian Stewart, eds., *Companion to contemporary economic thought.* London: Routledge, 1991, pp. 393–415.

Stigler, George J. *Trends in output and employment.* New York: National Bureau of Economic Research, 1947.

Summers, Robert and Heston, Alan. "The Penn World Table (Mark 5): An Expanded Set of International Comparisons, 1950–1988." *Quarterly Journal of Economics,* May 1991, *106*(2), pp. 327–68.

Sveikauskas, L. "Productivity Growth and the Depletion of Technological Opportunities." *Journal of Productivity Analysis,* June 1990, *1*(4), pp. 301–8.

Tinbergen, J. "Zur Theorie der Langfirstigen Wirtschaftsentwicklung," *Weltwirtschaftliches Archiv,* January 1942, *55*(1), pp. 511–49; reprinted in English translation in J. Tinbergen, *Selected papers.* Amsterdam: North-Holland, 1959.

Tong, X. and Frame, J. D. "Measuring National Technological Performance with Patent Claims Data." Unpublished manuscript, George Washington University, 1992.

Trajtenberg, Manuel. *Economic analysis of product innovation: The case of CT scanners.* Cambridge, MA: Harvard University Press, 1990a.

———. "A Penny for Your Quotes: Patent Citations and the Value of Innovations." *Rand Journal of Economics,* Spring 1990b, *21*(1) pp. 172–87.

Triplett, Jack E. "Price and Technological Change in a Capital Good: A Survey of Research and Computers," in D. W. Jorgenson and R. Landau, eds., *Technology and capital formation.* Cambridge, MA: MIT Press, 1989, pp. 127–213.

———. "The Federal Statistical System's Response to Emerging Data Needs." *Journal of Economic and Social Measurement,* 1991, *17*(3–4), pp. 155–201.

Young, Allan H. "Alternative Measures of Change in Real Output and Prices." *Survey of Current Business,* April 1992, *72*(4), pp. 32–48.

Author Index

Subject Index

Biases: caused by misspecification, 117–28; in cross-sectional level regressions, 91; in spillover analyses, 261

Bonnen report, 363

Capital, knowledge: 20, 25–27; effect of outside, 28–29

Capital, physical: biases in estimates of, 118–19; defining and measuring, 106

Capital, R&D: biases in estimates of, 118–19; defining and measuring, 9, 25–33, 106, 108, 270; depreciation of, 27–28, 53–54; elasticity of output with respect to, 270; model of in production function, 270–81; in relation of R&D to productivity growth, 142–54. *See also* Investment, R&D

Computer price index: with adjusted TFP growth, 354–55; based on hedonic regression methods, 353–54

Creamer GNP improvement report, 363

Data: availability of micro and international, 367; constrain understanding, 348–49; disaggregation of BLS-IO and NSF data, 213; firm-level, 188; on growth of R&D capital stock, 142; input price, 261; level of aggregation, 263; multicollinearity in data series, 33–36; on patent rights, 308; quality for observation and measurement, 358–65; simultaneity in data series, 33–36; smoothing R&D series, 233–34; stock market valuation to assess patent value, 313–19; TFP and R&D in manufacturing sector, 234–39

Data sources: aggregate patent data, 319–36; for analysis of returns to R&D, 20–21, 41–42; Census-Griliches-NSF Large-Company panel, 42, 49–51, 55–59, 77–80; for comparison of French-U.S. TFP growth, 179–85; for comparison of R&D and productivity growth in Japanese-U.S. manufacturing firms, 190, 192–95; firm R&D expenditures, 101–3; matching industry definitions across, 7; National Income and Product Accounts, 137, 140–41; National Science Foundation, 138–39; NEEDS *(Nihon Keizai Shimbun)* data base, 192–94, 207; NSF applied R&D data, 214–15, 233–36, 258; NSF R&D-Census match, 42, 82–86, 88–89; Office of Technology Assessment and Forecast, 293–94; patent data, 259–60, 291–92, 303, 306–7; Penn-SRI-Census data base, 7; PIMS data, 135–41; for productivity growth at firm level, 169–71, 179–83; R&D information at firm level in Japan, 207; for TFP, 215–19, 232, 235–36

Diffusion: curve or path of, 2; of innovations, 368; of new technology and knowledge, 1–2

Endogeneity: as source of misspecification, 273, 280–81; of technical change, 1–2, 8, 351, 368